57th Annual Meeting of the Association for Computational Linguistics (ACL 2019)

System Demonstrations

Florence, Italy
28 July – 2 August 2019

ISBN: 978-1-5108-9098-5

ACL 2019

The 57th Annual Meeting of the Association for Computational Linguistics

Proceedings of System Demonstrations

July 28 - August 2, 2019
Florence, Italy

Preface

Welcome to the proceedings of the system demonstrations session. This volume contains the papers of the system demonstrations presented at the 57th Annual Meeting of the Association for Computational Linguistics on July 28th - August 2nd, 2019 in Florence, Italy.

The ACL 2019 demonstrations track invites submissions ranging from early research prototypes to mature production-ready systems. We received 100 submissions this year, of which 34 were selected for inclusion in the program (acceptance rate of 34%) after review by three members of the program committee. We would like to thank the members of the program committee for their timely help in reviewing the submissions. The best demo paper was selected by the demo chairs based on the feedback received by reviewers. These are the papers nominated for the best demo paper:

- GLTR: Statistical Detection and Visualization of Generated Text by Sebastian Gehrmann, Hendrik Strobelt and Alexander Rush

- OpenKiwi: An Open Source Framework for Quality Estimation by Fabio Kepler, Jonay Trenous, Marcos Treviso, Miguel Vera and André F. T. Martins

- ConvLab: Multi-Domain End-to-End Dialog System Platform by Sungjin Lee, Qi Zhu, Ryuichi Takanobu, Zheng Zhang, Yaoqin Zhang, Xiang Li, Jinchao Li, Baolin Peng, Xiujun Li, Minlie Huang and Jianfeng Gao

- Texar: A Modularized, Versatile, and Extensible Toolkit for Text Generation by Zhiting Hu, Haoran Shi, Bowen Tan, Wentao Wang, Zichao Yang, Tiancheng Zhao, Junxian He, Lianhui Qin, Di Wang, Xuezhe Ma, Zhengzhong Liu, Xiaodan Liang, Wanrong Zhu, Devendra Sachan and Eric Xing

The winner of the best demo paper will be announced at ACL 2019. Lastly, we thank the many authors that submitted their work to the demonstrations track. Demonstrations papers will be presented during the three day conference along side the poster sessions.

Best,

Marta R. Costa-jussà and Enrique Alfonseca

ACL 2019 Demonstration Track Chairs

Demo Chairs:

Marta R. Costa-jussà, Technical University of Catalonia
Enrique Alfonseca, Google

Program Committee:

John Arevalo
Laurent Besacier
Eduardo Blanco
Vittorio Castelli
Angel Chang
Hai Leong Chieu
Christos Christodoulopoulos
Stephen Clark
Vincent Claveau
Bonaventura Coppola
Danilo Croce
Marina Danilevsky
Daniël de Kok
Jesse Dodge
Doug Downey
Dimitris Galanis
Marcos Garcia
Pawan Goyal
Dilek Hakkani-Tur
Xianpei Han
Ales Horak
Shajith Ikbal
Douwe Kiela
Mamoru Komachi
Valia Kordoni
Jayant Krishnamurthy
Carolin Lawrence
John Lee
Alessandro Lenci
Nikola Ljubešić
Wei Lu
Suraj Maharjan
Wolfgang Maier
Benjamin Marie
Stella Markantonatou
Pascual Martínez-Gómez
Ivan Vladimir Meza Ruiz
Makoto Miwa
Taesun Moon

Alessandro Moschitti
Philippe Muller
Preslav Nakov
Borja Navarro-Colorado
Pierre Nugues
Constantin Orasan
Yannick Parmentier
Stelios Piperidis
Maja Popović
Prokopis Prokopidis
Alessandro Raganato
German Rigau
Satoshi Sekine
Michel Simard
Sunayana Sitaram
Vivek Srikumar
Irina Temnikova
Juan-Manuel Torres-Moreno
Andrea Varga
Ivan Vulić
Huazheng Wang
Rui Wang
Qingyun Wu
Kun Xu
Tae Yano
Hai Zhao
Jun Zhao
Guangyou Zhou
Imed Zitouni

Table of Contents

Conference Program

Monday, July 29, 2019

13:50–15:30 Demo Poster Session 1

Sakura: Large-scale Incorrect Example Retrieval System for Learners of Japanese as a Second Language
Mio Arai, Tomonori Kodaira and Mamoru Komachi

SARAL: A Low-Resource Cross-Lingual Domain-Focused Information Retrieval System for Effective Rapid Document Triage
Elizabeth Boschee, Joel Barry, Jayadev Billa, Marjorie Freedman, Thamme Gowda, Constantine Lignos, Chester Palen-Michel, Michael Pust, Banriskhem Kayang Khonglah, Srikanth Madikeri, Jonathan May and Scott Miller

Rapid Customization for Event Extraction
Yee Seng Chan, Joshua Fasching, Haoling Qiu and Bonan Min

NeuralClassifier: An Open-source Neural Hierarchical Multi-label Text Classification Toolkit
Liqun Liu, Funan Mu, Pengyu Li, Xin Mu, Jing Tang, Xingsheng Ai, Ran Fu, Lifeng Wang and Xing Zhou

GLTR: Statistical Detection and Visualization of Generated Text
Sebastian Gehrmann, Hendrik Strobelt and Alexander Rush

ClaimPortal: Integrated Monitoring, Searching, Checking, and Analytics of Factual Claims on Twitter
Sarthak Majithia, Fatma Arslan, Sumeet Lubal, Damian Jimenez, Priyank Arora, Josue Caraballo and Chengkai Li

Texar: A Modularized, Versatile, and Extensible Toolkit for Text Generation
Zhiting Hu, Haoran Shi, Bowen Tan, Wentao Wang, Zichao Yang, Tiancheng Zhao, Junxian He, Lianhui Qin, Di Wang, Xuezhe Ma, Zhengzhong Liu, Xiaodan Liang, Wanrong Zhu, Devendra Sachan and Eric Xing

A Modular Tool for Automatic Summarization
Valentin Nyzam and Aurélien Bossard

TARGER: Neural Argument Mining at Your Fingertips
Artem Chernodub, Oleksiy Oliynyk, Philipp Heidenreich, Alexander Bondarenko, Matthias Hagen, Chris Biemann and Alexander Panchenko

13:30–15:10 Demo Poster Session 2

SLATE: A Super-Lightweight Annotation Tool for Experts
Jonathan K. Kummerfeld

lingvis.io - A Linguistic Visual Analytics Framework
Mennatallah El-Assady, Wolfgang Jentner, Fabian Sperrle, Rita Sevastjanova, Annette Hautli-Janisz, Miriam Butt and Daniel Keim

Jiuge: A Human-Machine Collaborative Chinese Classical Poetry Generation System
Guo Zhipeng, Xiaoyuan Yi, Maosong Sun, Wenhao Li, Cheng Yang, Jiannan Liang, Huimin Chen, Yuhui Zhang and Ruoyu Li

PostAc : A Visual Interactive Search, Exploration, and Analysis Platform for PhD Intensive Job Postings
Chenchen Xu, Inger Mewburn, Will J Grant and Hanna Suominen

AlpacaTag: An Active Learning-based Crowd Annotation Framework for Sequence Tagging
Bill Yuchen Lin, Dong-Ho Lee, Frank F. Xu, Ouyu Lan and Xiang Ren

KCAT: A Knowledge-Constraint Typing Annotation Tool
Sheng Lin, Luye Zheng, Bo Chen, Siliang Tang, Zhigang Chen, Guoping Hu, Yueting Zhuang, Fei Wu and Xiang Ren

An Environment for Relational Annotation of Political Debates
Andre Blessing, Nico Blokker, Sebastian Haunss, Jonas Kuhn, Gabriella Lapesa and Sebastian Padó

PerspectroScope: A Window to the World of Diverse Perspectives
Sihao Chen, Daniel Khashabi, Chris Callison-Burch and Dan Roth

HEIDL: Learning Linguistic Expressions with Deep Learning and Human-in-the-Loop
Prithviraj Sen, Yunyao Li, Eser Kandogan, Yiwei Yang and Walter Lasecki

My Turn To Read: An Interleaved E-book Reading Tool for Developing and Struggling Readers
Nitin Madnani, Beata Beigman Klebanov, Anastassia Loukina, Binod Gyawali, Patrick Lange, John Sabatini and Michael Flor

13:50–15:30 Demo Poster Session 3

A Multiscale Visualization of Attention in the Transformer Model
Jesse Vig

An Adaptable Task-oriented Dialog System for Stand-alone Embedded Devices
Long Duong, Vu Cong Duy Hoang, Tuyen Quang Pham, Yu-Heng Hong, Vladislavs
Dovgalecs, Guy Bashkansky, Jason Black, Andrew Bleeker, Serge Le Huitouze and
Mark Johnson

ConvLab: Multi-Domain End-to-End Dialog System Platform
Sungjin Lee, Qi Zhu, Ryuichi Takanobu, Zheng Zhang, Yaoqin Zhang, Xiang Li,
Jinchao Li, Baolin Peng, Xiujun Li, Minlie Huang and Jianfeng Gao

*Demonstration of a Neural Machine Translation System with Online Learning for
Translators*
Miguel Domingo, Mercedes García-Martínez, Amando Estela Pastor, Laurent Bié,
Alexander Helle, Álvaro Peris, Francisco Casacuberta and Manuel Herranz Pérez

*FASTDial: Abstracting Dialogue Policies for Fast Development of Task Oriented
Agents*
Serra Sinem Tekiroglu, Bernardo Magnini and Marco Guerini

A Neural, Interactive-predictive System for Multimodal Sequence to Sequence Tasks
Álvaro Peris and Francisco Casacuberta

ADVISER: A Dialog System Framework for Education & Research
Daniel Ortega, Dirk Väth, Gianna Weber, Lindsey Vanderlyn, Maximilian Schmidt,
Moritz Völkel, Zorica Karacevic and Ngoc Thang Vu

OpenKiwi: An Open Source Framework for Quality Estimation
Fabio Kepler, Jonay Trénous, Marcos Treviso, Miguel Vera and André F. T. Martins

Microsoft Icecaps: An Open-Source Toolkit for Conversation Modeling
Vighnesh Leonardo Shiv, Chris Quirk, Anshuman Suri, Xiang Gao, Khuram Shahid,
Nithya Govindarajan, Yizhe Zhang, Jianfeng Gao, Michel Galley, Chris Brockett,
Tulasi Menon and Bill Dolan

*Parallax: Visualizing and Understanding the Semantics of Embedding Spaces via
Algebraic Formulae*
Piero Molino, Yang Wang and Jiawei Zhang

MoNoise: A Multi-lingual and Easy-to-use Lexical Normalization Tool
Rob van der Goot

Flambé: A Customizable Framework for Machine Learning Experiments
Jeremy Wohlwend, Nicholas Matthews and Ivan Itzcovich

Sakura: Large-scale Incorrect Example Retrieval System for Learners of Japanese as a Second Language

Mio Arai   **Tomonori Kodaira**   **Mamoru Komachi**

Tokyo Metropolitan University

Hino City, Tokyo, Japan

`arai-mio@ed.tmu.ac.jp, kodaira.tomonori@gmail.com,`
`komachi@tmu.ac.jp`

Abstract

This study develops an incorrect example retrieval system, called Sakura, that uses a large-scale Lang-8 dataset for Japanese language learners. Existing example retrieval systems either exclude grammatically incorrect examples or present only a few examples. If a retrieval system has a wide coverage of incorrect examples along with their correct counterparts, learners can revise their composition themselves. Considering the usability of retrieving incorrect examples, our proposed system uses a large-scale corpus to expand the coverage of incorrect examples and present correct as well as incorrect expressions. Intrinsic and extrinsic evaluations indicate that our system is more useful than existing systems.

1 Introduction

A standard method that supports second language learning effort is the use of examples. Example retrieval systems such as Rakhilina et al. (2016) and Kilgarriff et al. (2004) particularly check for the appropriate use of words in the context in which they are written. However, in such a system, if the query word is incorrect, finding appropriate examples is impossible using ordinary search engines such as Google. Even if learners have access to an incorrect example retrieval system, such as Kamata and Yamauchi (1999) and Nishina et al. (2014), they are often unable to rewrite a composition without correct versions of the incorrect examples. Furthermore, existing example retrieval systems only provide a small number of examples; hence, learners cannot acquire sufficient information when they search. These systems are primarily developed for use by Japanese teachers; therefore, they are not as helpful for learners without a strong background in Japanese.

Another difficulty in learning Japanese as a second language is to learn the use of parti-

cles. Particles in Japanese indicate grammatical relations between verbs and nouns. For example, the sentence, "日本語を勉強する。", which means "I study Japanese." includes an accusative case marker "を", which introduces the direct object of the verb. However, in this case, Japanese learners often make mistakes, such as "日本語が勉強する。", which means "Japanese language studies." Thus, the appropriate use of particles is not obvious for non-native speakers of Japanese. Particle errors and word choice are the most common Japanese grammatical errors (Oyama et al., 2013), both of which require a sufficient number of correct and incorrect examples to understand the usage in context. Word n-gram search provides only few or no examples for a phrase because Japanese is a relatively free language in terms of word order, in which a syntactically dependent word may appear in a distant position.

Considering this, our study develops an incorrect example retrieval system, called Sakura[1], that uses the large-scale Lang-8[2] dataset for learners of Japanese as a second language (JSL) by focusing on the usability of incorrect example retrieval. The main contributions of this work are as follows:

- We use a large corpus; hence, the new system has far more examples than previous systems.

- Our system shows the incorrect sentences and the corresponding sentence as corrected by a native speaker. Thus, learners can rectify their mistakes during composition.

Figure 1 illustrates an example of the search result obtained using our system Sakura. Suppose a learner wants to view examples for the usage of "読みたり (*yomitari*, meaning "to read")",

---

[1] http://cl.sd.tmu.ac.jp/sakura/en

[2] Multi-lingual language learning and language exchange social networking service. http://lang-8.com/

Proceedings of the 57th Annual Meeting of the Association for Computational Linguistics-System Demonstrations, pages 1–6

Florence, Italy, July 28 - August 2, 2019. ©2019 Association for Computational Linguistics

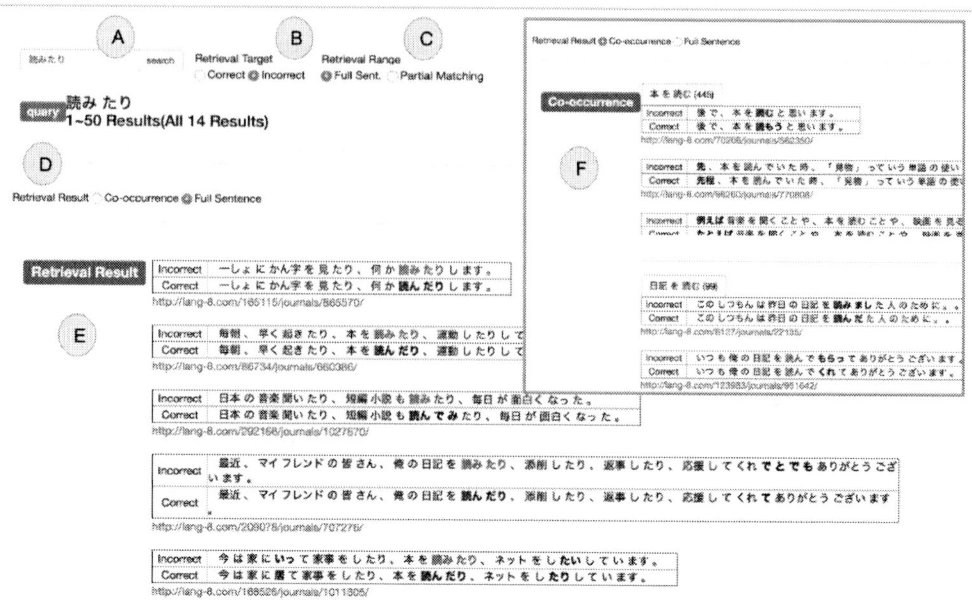

Figure 1: User interface of Sakura.

which is an incorrect or archaic expression. As shown in E of Figure 1, Sakura displays the incorrect examples with "読みたり" written in red and presents the correct examples using "読んだり (*yondari*, which is the correct euphonic form of "to read")". The learner can then identify that "読みたり" is the incorrect expression, and "読んだり" is the correct phrase. F in Figure 1 shows the collocation for "読む (*yomu*, which is the basic form of "読んだり")". The learner can grasp the common ways of using "読む", such as "本を読む (*hon wo yomu*, which means "I read a book.")".

2 Sakura: Large-scale Incorrect Example Retrieval System for JSL

This section describes the dataset and user interface of our proposed system, Sakura. Our system uses the data explained in Section 2.1 as the database for example retrieval. The user interface illustrated in Section 2.2 allows learners to search for incorrect examples.

2.1 Lang-8 Dataset

In this study, we used the Lang-8 Learner Corpora created by Mizumoto et al. (2011). The developers of the dataset used it for Japanese grammatical error correction, whereas we used it as an example retrieval database for JSL.

Each learner's sentence has at least one revised sentence. A learner's sentence is combined with a revised sentence to make a sentence pair. If a learner's sentence has more than one revised sentence, each of the revised sentences is paired with the learner's sentence as a separate sentence pair. Sentences with a length exceeding 100 words or with a Levenshtein distance of more than 7 are eliminated to remove the noise in the corpus.

We extracted 1.4 million pairs of the learner's sentences written by Japanese language learners and the revised sentences corrected by Japanese native speakers. The total number of included Japanese essays was 185,991.

The learner's sentences and the revised sentences are tokenized and POS-tagged by the morphological analyzer, MeCab (ver. 0.996)[3] with UniDic (ver. 2.2.0). Furthermore, we used the dependency parser CaboCha (ver. 0.69)[4] for the revised sentences to extract triples of a noun phrase, particle, and verb to be used as a co-occurrence.

2.2 User Interface

Figure 1 shows the user interface of Sakura. Its components are explained below.

A. Query Input the word to be searched for. The input query is assumed as a word or a phrase (se-

---

[3]https://github.com/taku910/mecab
[4]https://github.com/taku910/cabocha

quence of words).

B. Retrieval target Choose the target of retrieval as correct or incorrect usage. The default option is correct usage.

C. Retrieval range Choose the retrieval range from full sentence or partial matching with revised string. The system searches the entire sentence when a full sentence is selected. When partial matching with the revised string is selected, it searches the sentences where the query overlaps the revised string. The default option is full sentence. Learners can verify if their expressions are correct by selecting this option.

D. Retrieval result Choose the priority of displaying the retrieval result from the co-occurrence and the full sentence. The default option is co-occurrence.

E. Full Sentence The retrieval results that match the query are displayed when the user selects Full Sentence. The incorrect sentences written by learners are shown in the upper part, paired with the correct examples revised by native speakers. The query is represented in red, and the revised part is represented in bold.

F. Co-occurrence When the user searches for the query, including a noun or verb, Sakura displays up to 10 triplets of the noun, particle, and verb that co-occur with the query under the Co-occurrence tab. These triplets are shown with some example sentences, and the user can view up to 10 examples by scrolling. If the user searches for a POS other than a noun or a verb, Sakura shows the message "Not found" under the Co-occurrence tab, and retrieval results can be found under the Full Sentence tab.

3 Experiment

We compared Sakura with the search system for the "Tagged KY corpus" (hereafter, KYC) [5] in our evaluation experiment to confirm the effectiveness of presenting pairs of correct and incorrect examples. We evaluated our system in two parts, intrinsic and extrinsic evaluation.

3.1 Intrinsic Evaluation

We compared the accuracies of two systems, Sakura and KYC. We searched for the phrases in

each system (KYC and Sakura) and counted the number of matches for each system that led to correct expressions to ensure accuracy.

We randomly extracted 55 incorrect phrases from the learner's erroneous sentences with correct phrases from the Lang-8 dataset, which were not included in the corpus we used for our system. We classified the incorrect examples into seven types: alternating form (A), lexical choice (L), omission (O), misformation (M), redundant (R), pronunciation (P), and others (X). Table 1 lists examples of the test phrases.

Table 2 shows the frequency and accuracy of each type of error. Although KYC searches for incorrect and correct examples, it cannot find correct answers because it has very few examples. Even if it finds some examples that match the query, it cannot find the correct examples because it does not contain revised sentences corresponding to an incorrect sentence.

The accuracy was high for superficial errors, such as omission and redundant errors, because learners tend to make similar errors. For example, an incorrect word "ニュージランド" requires "ー" to make the correct phrase "ニュージーランド (New Zealand)." In contrast, the incorrect word "みんなさん" has an additional character "ん" when compared with the correct phrase "みなさん (everybody)." Such error patterns are common among learners of Japanese; therefore, our system can provide correct answers to JSL learners.

However, it is difficult for our system to find the correct answer for Types A (alternating form) and L (lexical choice) because they have too many error forms, which makes identifying the appropriate answer challenging. For instance, an incorrect phrase "本がもらえる (I can get a book)" is corrected to "本しかもらえない (I can only get a book)" in the test corpus, but "本がもらえる" can be paraphrased in many ways, such as "本をもらう (I get a book)." Thus, it is difficult for learners to determine the most appropriate phrase.

3.2 Extrinsic Evaluation

We recruited 10 Japanese non-native speakers majoring in computer science in a graduate school in Japan to solve 10 Japanese composition exercises. Participation was voluntary and unpaid. These prompts are shown in Table 3. We assigned

---

[5]http://jhlee.sakura.ne.jp/kyc/corpus/

incorrect phrase	pronunciation	correct phrase	pronunciation	Sakura	Error Type
おねさん	onesan	おねえさん (sister)	oneesan	×	O
ニュージランド	nyu-jirando	ニュージーランド (New Zealand)	nyu-ji-rando	✓	O
みんなさん	min'nasan	みなさん (everybody)	minasan	✓	R
大体に	daitaini	大体 (roughly)	daitai	×	R
疑問をして	gimonwoshite	疑問に思って (in doubt)	gimon'niomotte	×	M
驚い	odoroi	驚き (surprise)	odoroki	✓	M
がもらえる	gamoraeru	しかもらえない (only get this)	shikamoraenai	×	A
稼ぐ	kasegu	稼いだ (earned)	kaseida	✓	A
ちさい	chisai	少ない (few)	sukunai	✓	L
助けられる	tasukerareru	できる (can)	dekiru	×	L
しましだ	shimashida	いました (there was)	imashita	×	P
死んちゃう	shinchau	死んじゃう (will die)	shinjau	✓	P
ハウス	hausu	家 (house)	ie	✓	X

Table 1: Examples of test results. The column "Incorrect phrase" contains the phrases written by the learner. These are extracted from the Lang-8 test set. The column "Sakura" shows whether or not Sakura could identify the correct answer for that phrase.

system	type	frequency	accuracy
Sakura	ALL	55	0.44
	Alternating Form	19	0.37
	Lexical Choice	16	0.38
	Omission	8	0.75
	Misformation	6	0.40
	Redundant	3	0.67
	Pronunciation	2	0.50
	Others	1	1.00

Table 2: Frequency and accuracy of each type.

No.	Prompt
1	The event of your country.
2	The most impressive adventure in your life.
3	Your favorite feature about Japanese.
4	The most favorite movie or book.
5	The food of your country.
6	The pros and cons of English as a universal language.
7	Japanese supermarket.
8	Major incident in your country's history.
9	The place you'd like to visit.
10	Your favorite season and the reason.

Table 3: Prompts for extrinsic evaluation.

Learner	KYC	Sakura
A	22	**25**
B	25	**28**
C	26	**27**
D	21	**24**
E	27	27
F	21	**26**
G	20	20
H	**26**	24
I	21	**27**
J	7	**22**
ave.	21.6	**25.0**

Table 4: Extrinsic evaluation. The points assigned to the Japanese compositions of the participants. A higher point indicates a better score.

five learners to solve the odd-numbered exercises using KYC and the even-numbered exercises using Sakura. The other five learners solved the even-numbered exercises using KYC and the odd-numbered exercises using Sakura. The number of sentences in each exercise was three to ensure a fair comparison.

The results were evaluated using the following method. The composition exercise was scored by deducting points from an initial 30 points. One point was deducted per error. The total score of each system was summed up over five exercises.

Table 4 shows the score for each composition. The average writing score of the learners using Sakura was **25.0** and that with KYC was 21.6. In addition, 7 out of 10 learners received a higher score when using Sakura than when using KYC. These results indicate that Sakura is useful as a learner support system for writing a Japanese composition.

KYC had no revised sentences corresponding to the incorrect sentences; hence, the composition using KYC tended to include mistakes related to verb conjugation and lexical choice errors. In contrast, Sakura did not display the POS; thus, the composition using Sakura tended to contain particle errors.

4 Related Works

Web-based search engines are the most common search systems that can be used to search for example sentences. However, these search engines

Name	Correct Sent.	Incorrect Sent.	Revised Sent.	Co-occurrence
Learner's Error Corpora of Japanese Searching Platform	✓	✓	✓	✗
Tagged KY corpus	✓	✓	✗	✗
Natsume	✗	✗	✗	✓
Sakura	✓	✓	✓	✓

Table 5: Features of example retrieval systems for Japanese language learners. "Correct Sent." indicates whether the system can display the correct sentences or not; "Incorrect Sent." indicates whether the system can display the incorrect sentences or not; "Revised Sent." indicates whether the system can display the revised sentence corresponding to the incorrect sentence; and "Co-occurrence" denotes whether the system can provide co-occurrence examples.

are not intended to retrieve examples for language learners; therefore, the search engines show neither example sentences nor the correct version of a given incorrect sentence to aid learners.

Language learners can use several example retrieval systems. The following subsections present information on some of those systems for learners of English and Japanese as a second language.

4.1 Example Retrieval System for English as a Second Language

FLOW (Chen et al., 2012) is a system that shows some candidates for English words when learners of English as a Second Language (ESL) write a sentence in their native language by using paraphrase candidates with bilingual pivoting. In contrast, our system suggests incorrect examples and their counterparts based on corrections from the learner corpus.

Another system, called StringNet (Wible and Tsao, 2010), displays the patterns in which a query is used, together with their frequency. The noun and the preposition are substituted by their parts of speech, instead of the words themselves, to eliminate data sparseness. Our system shows collocation patterns for each query by using parts of speech information and dependency parsing; however, our system does not explicitly present the parts of speech because our dataset is sufficiently large and need not replace and display the part-of-speech tag.

The ESCORT (Matsubara et al., 2008) system shows example sentences to learners based on the grammatical relations of queries. The syntactic structure of the English sentences is stored in the database of a raw corpus. ESCORT analyzes the dependency relations of the input queries and only displays appropriate examples that match the relations. Our system does not parse the query; instead, it parses the learner corpus to present collocations and overcome data sparseness.

Furthermore, ESL learners can check examples while writing an English sentence by using WriteAhead (Yen et al., 2015). This system provides pattern suggestions based on collocation and syntax. For example, when the user writes "We discussed," the system displays the patterns for the use of the word "discussed." In our system, we also employ collocation patterns; however, we use a large-scale learner corpus to search for dependency structures.

Sketch Engine (Kilgarriff et al., 2004) displays grammar constructs associated with words along with thesaurus information. As previously mentioned, our system presents incorrect examples by using a learner corpus apart from the correct examples extracted from a raw corpus.

4.2 Example Retrieval System for Japanese as a Second Language

Recently, various Japanese example retrieval systems have been proposed. However, in practice, learners find them difficult to use. Herein, we explain why these systems are ineffective when used by JSL learners.

Table 5 lists the features of each system. Our proposed system, Sakura, employs a large-scale Japanese JSL corpus for correct and incorrect example sentences along with revisions for the incorrect example.

First, the "Learner's Error Corpora of Japanese Searching Platform"[6] was constructed by the Corpus-based Linguistics and Language Education at Tokyo University of Foreign Studies. This system displays sentences that includes incorrect sentences in the keyword in context (KWIC) format based on the learner's information, such as native language, age, and gender. Japanese language teachers can identify the features of the learner's mistakes by using this system. However, this sys-

---

[6]http://ngc2068.tufs.ac.jp/corpus_ja/

tem is primarily intended for educators rather than learners. As such, learners might find it confusing to use. In addition, this system has few examples; hence, learners cannot acquire sufficient information when they search.

Second, the "KY corpus" is a transcribed speech corpus for JSL learners. "Tagged KY corpus" (Kamata and Yamauchi, 1999) supersedes the "KY corpus" with a search engine using POS. It displays correct and incorrect examples for text written by learners. However, it oftentimes fails to provide results even for high-frequency words, because the number of incorrect examples is small; therefore, it is difficult for language learners to use the limited set of examples as a reference.

Third, a Japanese co-occurrence retrieval system, called "Natsume" (Nishina et al., 2014) [7], presents the words and particles that tend to co-occur with the searched word (e.g., verb and adjective for noun and noun for verb and adjective). However, this system only shows words, and it does not indicate concrete examples; therefore, using this system to write an actual composition is difficult. In addition, it does not include incorrect examples.

5   Conclusion

This study constructed an incorrect example retrieval system using the Lang-8 Learner Corpora. Our proposed system, Sakura, displays incorrect examples along with the revised sentences and example sentences. The results of our experiment indicated that Sakura was useful for JSL learners when writing Japanese compositions. Each example includes incorrect sentences; hence, language teachers can identify the difficulty faced by learners and use this information for language education.

Although this system was constructed for JSL learners, it can easily be customized for other languages. We plan to extend our system to support ESL learners (Tajiri et al., 2012).

Acknowledgements

We would like to thank the Lang-8 web organizer for providing the text data for our system.

References

Mei-Hua Chen, Shih-Ting Huang, Hung-Ting Hsieh, Ting-Hui Kao, and Jason S. Chang. 2012. FLOW: A first-language-oriented writing assistant system. In *Proceedings of the ACL 2012 System Demonstrations*, pages 157–162.

Osamu Kamata and Hiroyuki Yamauchi. 1999. KY corpus version 1.1. Report, Vocaburary Acquisition Study Group.

Adam Kilgarriff, Pavel Rychly, Pavel Smrž, and David Tugwell. 2004. The sketch engine. In *Proceedings of EURALEX*, pages 105–116.

Shigeki Matsubara, Yoshihide Kato, and Seiji Egawa. 2008. ESCORT: example sentence retrieval system as support tool for English writing. In *Journal of Information Processing and Management*, pages 251–259.

Tomoya Mizumoto, Mamoru Komachi, Masaaki Nagata, and Yuji Matsumoto. 2011. Mining revision log of language learning SNS for automated Japanese error correction of second language learners. In *Proceedings of IJCNLP*, pages 147–155.

Kikuko Nishina, Bor Hodošček, Yutaka Yagi, and Takeshi Abekawa. 2014. Construction of a learner corpus for Japanese language learners: Natane and Nutmeg. *Acta Linguistica Asiatica*, 4(2):37–51.

Hiromi Oyama, Mamoru Komachi, and Yuji Matsumoto. 2013. Towards automatic error type classification of Japanese language learners' writing. In *Proceedings of PACLIC*, pages 163–172.

Ekaterina Rakhilina, Anastasia Vyrenkova, and Elmira Mustakimova. 2016. Building a learner corpus for Russian. In *Proceedings of the Joint Workshop on NLP for Computer Assisted Language Learning and NLP for Language Acquisition*, pages 66–75.

Toshikazu Tajiri, Mamoru Komachi, and Yuji Matsumoto. 2012. Tense and aspect error correction for ESL learners using global context. In *Proceedings of ACL*, pages 198–202.

David Wible and Nai-Lung Tsao. 2010. StringNet as a computational resource for discovering and investigating linguistic constructions. In *Proceedings of the NAACL HLT Workshop on Extracting and Using Constructions in Computational Linguistics*, pages 25–31.

Tzu-Hsi Yen, Jian-Cheng Wu, Jim Chang, Joanne Boisson, and Jason Chang. 2015. WriteAhead: Mining grammar patterns in corpora for assisted writing. In *Proceedings of ACL-IJCNLP 2015 System Demonstrations*, pages 139–144.

---

[7]https://hinoki-project.org/natsume/

SLATE: A Super-Lightweight Annotation Tool for Experts

Jonathan K. Kummerfeld

Computer Science & Engineering
University of Michigan
Ann Arbor, MI, USA
`jkummerf@umich.edu`

Abstract

Many annotation tools have been developed, covering a wide variety of tasks and providing features like user management, preprocessing, and automatic labeling. However, all of these tools use Graphical User Interfaces, and often require substantial effort to install and configure. This paper presents a new annotation tool that is designed to fill the niche of a lightweight interface for users with a terminal-based workflow. SLATE supports annotation at different scales (spans of characters, tokens, and lines, or a document) and of different types (free text, labels, and links), with easily customisable keybindings, and unicode support. In a user study comparing with other tools it was consistently the easiest to install and use. SLATE fills a need not met by existing systems, and has already been used to annotate two corpora, one of which involved over 250 hours of annotation effort.

1 Introduction

Specialised text annotation software improves efficiency and consistency by constraining user actions and providing an effective interface. While current annotation tools vary in the types of annotation supported and other features, they are all built with direct manipulation via a Graphical User Interface (GUI). This approach has the advantage that it is easy for users who are not computer experts, but also shapes the design of tools to become large, complex pieces of software that are time-consuming to set up and difficult to modify.

We present a lightweight alternative that is not intended to cover all use-cases, but rather fills a specific niche: annotation in a terminal-based workflow. This goal guided the design to differ from prior systems in several ways. First, we use a text-based interface that uses almost the entire screen to display documents. This focuses attention on the data and means the interface can easily scale to assist vision-impaired annotators. Second, we minimise the time cost of installation by implementing the entire system in Python using built-in libraries. Third, we follow the Unix Tools Philosophy (Raymond, 2003) to write programs that do one thing well, with flat text formats. In our case, (1) the tool only does annotation, not tokenisation, automatic labeling, file management, etc, which are covered by other tools, and (2) data is stored in a format that both people and command line tools like `grep` can easily read.

SLATE supports annotation of items that are continuous spans of either characters, tokens, lines, or documents. For all item types there are three forms of annotation: labeling items with categories, writing free-text labels, or linking pairs of items. Category labels are easily customisable, with no limit on the total number and the option to display a legend for reference. All keybindings are customisable, and additional commands can be defined with relatively little code. There is also an adjudication mode in which disagreements are displayed and resolved.

To compare with other tools we conducted a user study in which participants installed tools and completed a verb tagging task in a 623 word document. When using SLATE, participants finished the task in 13 minutes on average, with more than half spending 3 minutes or less on setup.

Two research projects have used SLATE for annotation: token-level classification of 25,624 tokens of cybercriminal web forum data (Portnoff et al., 2017), and line-level linking of 77,563 messages of chat data (Kummerfeld et al., 2019).

2 System Description

Rather than specifying a task, such as named entity recognition, SLATE is designed to flexibly support any annotation that can be formulated as one of three annotation types: applying categorical labels, writing free text, or linking portions of text. These can be applied to items that are single docu-

Proceedings of the 57th Annual Meeting of the Association for Computational Linguistics-System Demonstrations, pages 7–12
Florence, Italy, July 28 - August 2, 2019. ©2019 Association for Computational Linguistics

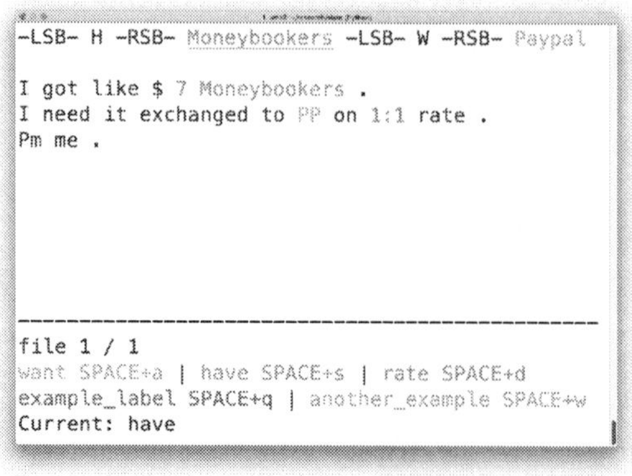

(a) Annotation of a cybercriminal forum post. The underlined token is the one currently selected. The mapping from colours to labels and the keys to apply them are indicated by the legend at the bottom. Two extra labels were added for this picture, to show how the legend will wrap as needed. The information about progress, the legend, and the current item can be hidden if desired.

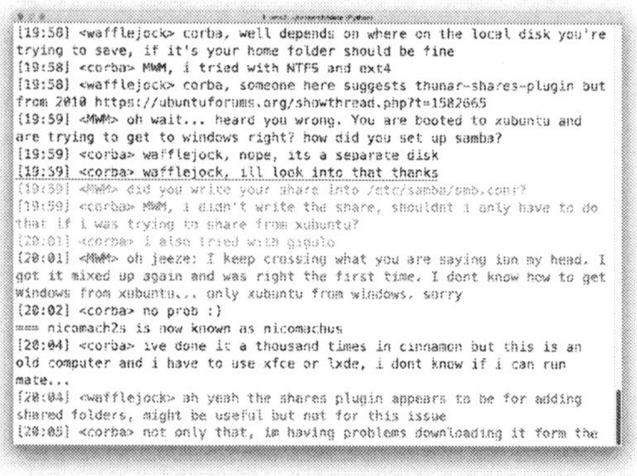

(b) Adjudication of a linking task annotating reply-to relations on IRC. The current message in green, an antecedent that is agreed on is dark blue, one that is not agreed on is light blue, other messages with disagreements are red, and the underline indicates a message that is being considered for linking to the green message (incorrectly in this case).

Figure 1: Screenshots of terminal windows with SLATE running. We have intentionally used two different font sizes to show how the user interface can scale, which is helpful for visually impaired users.

ments, lines, tokens, or characters, and continuous spans of lines, tokens, and characters. For example, from this perspective, NER is a task with categorical labels over continuous token spans.

The tool also supports adjudication of annotation disagreements. Multiple sets of annotations are read in and compared to determine disagreements to be displayed to the user, which can then be resolved, producing a new annotation file.

In the process of describing the tool, we will refer to two datasets that it was used to annotate:[1]

(1) Portnoff et al. (2017) studied cybercriminal web forums. Experts in computer security and NLP collaborated to label posts in which the user is trying to exchange money from one form into another. For each post, we labeled tokens that expressed what was being offered, what was being requested, and the rate. Three annotators labeled a set of 600 posts containing 25,624 tokens. 200 of the posts were triple annotated and disagreements were adjudicated using the tool.

(2) Kummerfeld et al. (2019) developed a new conversation disentanglement dataset an order of magnitude larger than all previously released datasets combined. 77,563 messages were annotated with links indicating the message(s) they were a response to. For 11,100 messages, multiple annotations were collected and adjudicated using the tool. Annotations took 7 to 11 seconds per

message depending on the complexity of the discussion, and adjudication took 5 seconds per message (lower because many messages did not have a disagreement, but not extremely low because those that did were the difficult cases). Overall, annotators spent approximately 240 hours on annotation and 15 hours on adjudication.

Display The interface is text-based and contained entirely within a terminal window. By default, the entire terminal area displays the text being annotated, as shown in Figure 1b. There are also options to use space to display information about current annotations, as shown in Figure 1a.

Colour is used to indicate annotations. For categorical labels a different colour is used for each label, and a special colour is used to indicate when multiple labels have been assigned to the same item. For linking, one colour is used to indicate the item being linked, another is used to indicate what items are currently linked to it, and a third is used to indicate any item that has a link.

The most frequently needed visual customisation is changing the colours used to indicate labels when assigning categories. These colours are specified in a simple text file. More substantial changes, such as a different colour to indicate disagreements, requires changing the code, but colours for each situation are defined in one place with intuitive names.

Input All interaction occurs via the keyboard. Commands are designed to be intuitive, e.g. arrow

---

[1] No formal user satisfaction surveys were conducted, but the tool received positive feedback on both projects.

System	Annotation Types	Adjud-ication	External Dependencies	Programming Language	User Interface
SLATE	Classify, Link	Yes	-	Python	Terminal
brat (Stenetorp et al., 2012)	Classify, Link	Yes	apache	Python, Javascript	GUI
GATE (Bontcheva et al., 2013)	Classify, Link	Yes	-	Java	GUI
YEDDA (Yang et al., 2018)	Classify	-	-	Python	GUI
ANALEC (Landragin et al., 2012)	Classify, Link	-	-	Java	GUI
Anafora (Chen and Styler, 2013)	Classify, Link	Yes	-	Python	GUI
CAT (Lenzi et al., 2012)	Classify	-	apache	Java	GUI
Chooser (Koeva et al., 2008)	Classify, Link	-	-	C++, Python, Perl	GUI
CorA (Bollmann et al., 2014)	Classify	-	-	PHP, JavaScript	GUI
Djangology (Apostolova et al., 2010)	Classify	Yes	Django	Python	GUI
eHost (South et al., 2012)	Classify, Link	Yes	-	Java	GUI
Glozz (Widlöcher and Mathet, 2012)	Classify, Link	Yes	-	Java	GUI
GraphAnno (Gast et al., 2015)	Classify, Link	-	-	Ruby	GUI
Inforex (Marcinczuk et al., 2012)	Classify, Link	-	-	JavaScript	GUI
Knowtator (Ogren, 2006)	Classify, Link	Yes	Protégé	Java	GUI
MAE and MAI (Stubbs, 2011)	Classify, Link	Yes	-	Java	GUI
MMAX2 (Müller and Strube, 2006)	Classify, Link	-	-	Java	GUI
PALinkA (Orasan, 2003)	Classify, Link	-	-	Java	GUI
SAWT (Samih et al., 2016)	Classify	-	-	Python, PHP	GUI
SYNC3 (Petasis, 2012)	Classify	Yes	Ellogon	C	GUI
Stanford (Lee, 2004)	Classify	-	-	Java	GUI
UAM (O'Donnell, 2008)	Classify	Yes	-	Java	GUI
WAT-SL (Kiesel et al., 2017)	Classify	Yes	apache	Java	GUI
WebAnno (Yimam et al., 2013)	Classify, Link	Yes	-	Java	GUI
WordFreak (Morton and LaCivita, 2003)	Classify, Link	Yes	-	Java	GUI

Table 1: A comparison of annotation tools in terms of properties of interest (in some cases tools support extra types of annotation, e.g. syntax, that we do not consider here).

keys change which item is selected. Keybindings can be modified to suit user preferences and multi-key commands can be defined, like the labels in Figure 1a (e.g. SPACE+a), providing flexibility and an unlimited set of combinations.

Basic commands cover selecting a span, assigning an annotation, and undoing annotations. Exact string search is included, which was used in the disentanglement project to search for previous messages by a given user. Typing a number before a command will apply the command that many times. A range of commands exist to toggle properties of the view, including line numbering, the legend, showing the label for the selected item, and progress through a set of files.

Data Items in annotations are represented by tuples of integers and labels are represented as strings. Tokens are defined by splitting on whitespace, and characters are counted with separate numbering for each token. This makes the annotations easy to read in and interpret.

Externally, annotations are saved in stand-off files, with one annotation per line. This makes them easy to process with command line tools, e.g. using wc to count the number of annotations.

Extension The system is written with a modular design intended to be easily modifiable. For exam-ple, at one point in the disentanglement project we wanted to go back and check messages that started conversations. This involved adding 21 lines of code, extending the existing search commands to jump to the next line that started a conversation.

Internal Architecture The system is written in 2,300 lines of Python, with extensive use of the standard built-in curses library for input and display handling. Setting up the tool involves down-loading and unzipping the code. The tool can then be run from anywhere, does not require adminis-trator privileges, and will only make modifications to the local directory it is being run from.

Dependencies On macOS and all Linux distribu-tions we are aware of, there is nothing else to in-stall: Python and the relevant libraries are already installed. On Windows, Python (either 2 or 3) and the curses library need to be installed.

3 Related Work

Table 1 presents a comparison of a range of an-notation tools.[2] Note that all prior work has fo-cused on graphical user interfaces. The top section shows the tools we consider in our user study, cho-

---

[2] Non-academic tools also focus on GUIs, including open source tools (e.g. DocAnno, Flat), and commercial tools (e.g. TagTog, Prodigy, MAT, LightTag, DataTurks).

sen because they are widely used (brat and GATE) or have a similar design motivation (YEDDA).

brat (Stenetorp et al., 2012), is a synchronous web-based system with a central server that users connect to using a web browser. The tool supports annotation of spans of text and relations between them, either binary relations, equivalence classes, or n-ary associations. It provides a search mechanism, automatic validation, tagging with external tools, multi-lingual processing, and a comparison mode that places two annotations side-by-side. The tool has been used to annotate a range of datasets, particularly for information extraction from biomedical documents.

GATE (Bontcheva et al., 2013), is both a desktop application and a web-based system. It is designed to support the entire lifecycle of a project, including data preparation, schema creation, annotation, adjudication, data storage and use. To achieve this, it contains a wide array of components, covering various annotation types and tools to define workflows that determine the stages of annotation of a document. The system has been used in a range of projects in both academic and commercial settings, including with users who did not have a computer science background.

YEDDA (Yang et al., 2018), is a desktop application that supports annotation of character spans with up to 8 categories using a GUI. It is designed to be lightweight, with no external dependencies, though it only supports Python 2. It has a built-in recommendation system that automatically proposes labels based on annotations so far, which Yang et al. (2018) found decreased named entity recognition annotation time by 16%. For input, the tool supports both selection with the mouse and specifying a sequence of character-level annotations with the keyboard, e.g. 2c3b to assign the label c to the next two characters and b to the three after that. The tool also has an analysis component that produces a LaTeX document comparing a pair of annotations of a document, or F-scores for all pairs of annotations. It does not support annotation of links or adjudication of disagreements.

4 User Study

We conducted a user study[3] to investigate the effort required to install and use four tools. For each tool, participants had 25 minutes to install the tool and use it to identify verbs in a 623 word news

Tool	Time (minutes)	
	Ubuntu	macOS
SLATE	10	16
YEDDA	14	14
GATE	21	22
brat	-	-

Table 2: Average time for users to set up the tool and identify verbs in a 623 word news article. Only one participant managed to install and use brat, taking 18 minutes on Ubuntu. The differences between GATE and either SLATE or YEDDA are significant at the 0.01 level according to a t-test.

article.[4] We measured how long they took to install the tool and to finish the task. After each tool, participants completed a survey asking about their experience installing and using the tool.

We set up the study to simulate a real usage scenario as closely as possible. Participants were computer science graduate students and all but one used their own computer. Four participants used macOS and four used Ubuntu. Every participant used all four tools. To reduce bias due to fatigue (which could make later tools appear slower) and familiarity with the news article (which could make later tools appear faster), the order of tools varied so that each one occurred 1st, 2nd, 3rd, and 4th once for each operating system.

Table 2 presents the time required to install each tool and complete the first annotation task. We combined these two because some participants read usage instructions while installing the tool, while others went back and forth during initial annotations. SLATE and YEDDA are comparable in effort, which fits with their common design as simple tools with minimal dependencies. Participants had great difficulty with brat, with only two managing to install it, one just as their time finished.

We also had an additional participant try using the tools in Windows. They were able to install and use SLATE and GATE, but did not complete the task on either. GATE had the easiest set up process, with a provided installer. SLATE required the curses package to be installed. They experienced difficulty with YEDDA because it is not Python 3 compatible, and rewriting the code to make it compatible led to other issues. brat only supports Windows via the use of a virtual machine.

---

[3] Approved by the Michigan IRB, ID: HUM00155689.

[4] We also considered having participants do a linking task, specifying the antecedents of pronouns, but found there was not enough time (also, linking is not supported by YEDDA).

4.1 Feedback Summary

brat Participants got stuck on various issues during installation and generally commented that they wanted more information in the documentation. The two most common issues were being unable to get the system to communicate with apache, and being unable to load files to annotate.

GATE Participants often had to try more than one installation method. Six participants commented on lag or missed clicks during annotation, and six commented that the documentation was not helpful for the process of installing the tool and understanding the user interface.

YEDDA All participants found installation easy, though three commented that it required familiarity with git, and one recommended adding it to the python package index. Every participant commented that the recommendation mode produced many false positives, making it inconvenient. Four commented that the way labels appear during annotation shifted the text in a way that made them lose their place or made it hard to read. All Ubuntu participants commented that the system scrolled to the top of the document after each annotation.

SLATE All participants found installation easy, though one recommended adding it to the python package index. One participant commented that they wished they could use their cursor as well, one suggested adding an explicit indication that saving was successful, one found the selected span hard to see, and one was surprised that pressing the down arrow selected the same position on the next line in terms of tokens, rather than visually.

Each of these tools has strengths and weaknesses, and this study was designed to test the specific gap our tool was designed to address. For projects with annotators who are not computer experts, we expect GUIs, and in particular web interfaces like the one provided by brat, will remain dominant. However, the results demonstrate that SLATE effectively fills the gap of an easy to use and efficient terminal-based tool.

5 Future Development

There are many directions in which we hope to develop SLATE further, by collaborating with other researchers and the open-source community. The system is designed to be simple to modify and extend, with some possible next steps including:

Multi-lingual Support The tool can already display a range of scripts given Python's unicode support, but to properly support annotation would require modifications. For example, changing the direction of script writing would involve adjusting the visual display module, while adding support for selecting parts of glyphs would require modifying the data representation.

Accessibility For users who require large fonts (or prefer small ones) the tool is extremely flexible and convenient. However, the extensive use of colour could be a problem for colour-blind users. The colours can be modified by editing a simple configuration file, or colour could be avoided entirely by modifying the display code to display inline labels.

Data Formats Support for additional data formats, such as CoNLL-U, and ISO 24612:2012.

Mouse Input While the motivation for this tool was to make a text-based interface controlled by the keyboard, the curses library does process mouse inputs, making it possible to add support for the mouse in the future.

6 Conclusion

A wide range of effective annotation tools already exist, but they all use a GUI and many involve substantial effort to set up. SLATE is designed for terminal-users who want a fast, easy to install, and flexible annotation tool. It supports a range of annotation types, and adjudication of disagreements in annotations. The code is publicly available[5] under a permissive open-source license. The tool has already been used in two research projects, including one that involved over 250 hours of annotation.

Acknowledgements

Thank you to Will Radford and the anonymous reviewers for helpful suggestions. Also thanks to the study participants, and to the annotators who have used the tool. This material is based in part on work supported by IBM as part of the Sapphire Project at the University of Michigan, and by ONR under MURI grant N000140911081. Any opinions, findings, conclusions or recommendations expressed above are those of the author and do not necessarily reflect the views of the sponsors.

---

[5]`http://jkk.name/slate/`

References

Emilia Apostolova, Sean Neilan, Gary An, Noriko To-muro, and Steven Lytinen. 2010. Djangology: A light-weight web-based tool for distributed collaborative text annotation. In *Proceedings of LREC*.

Marcel Bollmann, Florian Petran, Stefanie Dipper, and Julia Krasselt. 2014. Cora: A web-based annotation tool for historical and other non-standard language data. In *Proceedings of the LaTeCH Workshop*.

Kalina Bontcheva, Hamish Cunningham, Ian Roberts, Angus Roberts, Valentin Tablan, Niraj Aswani, and Genevieve Gorrell. 2013. Gate teamware: a web-based, collaborative text annotation framework. *Language Resources and Evaluation*, 47(4):1007–1029.

Wei-Te Chen and Will Styler. 2013. Anafora: A web-based general purpose annotation tool. In *Proceedings of NAACL, Demos*.

Volker Gast, Lennart Bierkandt, and Christoph Rzymski. 2015. Creating and retrieving tense and aspect annotations with graphanno, a lightweight tool for multi-level annotation. In *Proceedings of the ISA Workshop*.

ISO 24612:2012. 2012. Language resource management – Linguistic annotation framework (LAF). Standard, International Organization for Standardization.

Johannes Kiesel, Henning Wachsmuth, Khalid Al Khatib, and Benno Stein. 2017. Wat-sl: A customizable web annotation tool for segment labeling. In *Proceedings of EACL, Demos*.

Svetla Koeva, Borislav Rizov, and Svetlozara Leseva. 2008. Chooser: a multi-task annotation tool. In *Proceedings of LREC*.

Jonathan K. Kummerfeld, Sai R. Gouravajhala, Joseph Peper, Vignesh Athreya, Chulaka Gunasekara, Jatin Ganhotra, Siva Sankalp Patel, Lazaros Polymenakos, and Walter S. Lasecki. 2019. A large-scale corpus for conversation disentanglement. In *Proceedings of ACL*.

Frederic Landragin, Thierry Poibeau, and Bernard Victorri. 2012. Analec: a new tool for the dynamic annotation of textual data. In *Proceedings of LREC*.

Miler Lee. 2004. Annotator / stanford manual annotation tool. http://nlp.stanford.edu/software/stanford-manual-annotation-tool-2004-05-16.tar.gz. Stanford University.

Valentina Bartalesi Lenzi, Giovanni Moretti, and Rachele Sprugnoli. 2012. Cat: the celct annotation tool. In *Proceedings of LREC*.

Michal Marcinczuk, Jan Kocon, and Bartosz Broda. 2012. Inforex – a web-based tool for text corpus management and semantic annotation. In *Proceedings of LREC*.

Thomas Morton and Jeremy LaCivita. 2003. Wordfreak: An open tool for linguistic annotation. In *Proceedings of NAACL, Demos*.

Christoph Müller and Michael Strube. 2006. Multi-level annotation of linguistic data with MMAX2. In *Corpus Technology and Language Pedagogy: New Resources, New Tools, New Methods*. Peter Lang.

Mick O'Donnell. 2008. Demonstration of the UAM CorpusTool for text and image annotation. In *Proceedings of ACL, Demos*.

Philip V. Ogren. 2006. Knowtator: A protégé plug-in for annotated corpus construction. In *Proceedings of NAACL, Demos*.

Constantin Orasan. 2003. PALinkA: A highly customisable tool for discourse annotation. In *Proceedings of SIGdial*.

Georgios Petasis. 2012. The sync3 collaborative annotation tool. In *Proceedings of LREC*.

Rebecca S. Portnoff, Sadia Afroz, Greg Durrett, Jonathan K. Kummerfeld, Taylor Berg-Kirkpatrick, Damon McCoy, Kirill Levchenko, and Vern Paxson. 2017. Tools for automated analysis of cybercriminal markets. In *Proceedings of WWW*.

Eric S. Raymond. 2003. *Basics of the Unix Philosophy*. Addison-Wesley Professional.

Younes Samih, Wolfgang Maier, and Laura Kallmeyer. 2016. Sawt: Sequence annotation web tool. In *Proceedings of the Second Workshop on Computational Approaches to Code Switching*.

Brett South, Shuying Shen, Jianwei Leng, Tyler Forbush, Scott DuVall, and Wendy Chapman. 2012. A prototype tool set to support machine-assisted annotation. In *Proceedings of BioNLP*.

Pontus Stenetorp, Sampo Pyysalo, Goran Topić, Tomoko Ohta, Sophia Ananiadou, and Jun'ichi Tsujii. 2012. brat: a web-based tool for nlp-assisted text annotation. In *Proceedings of EACL, Demos*.

Amber Stubbs. 2011. Mae and mai: Lightweight annotation and adjudication tools. In *Proceedings of LAW*.

Antoine Widlöcher and Yann Mathet. 2012. The glozz platform: A corpus annotation and mining tool. In *Proceedings of the ACM Symposium on Document Engineering*.

Jie Yang, Yue Zhang, Linwei Li, and Xingxuan Li. 2018. Yedda: A lightweight collaborative text span annotation tool. In *Proceedings of ACL, Demos*.

Seid Muhie Yimam, Iryna Gurevych, Richard Eckart de Castilho, and Chris Biemann. 2013. Webanno: A flexible, web-based and visually supported system for distributed annotations. In *Proceedings of ACL, Demos*.

lingvis.io — A Linguistic Visual Analytics Framework

Mennatallah El-Assady[1], Wolfgang Jentner[1], Fabian Sperrle[1],
Rita Sevastjanova[1], Annette Hautli-Janisz[2], Miriam Butt[2], and Daniel Keim[1]
[1]Department of Computer Science, University of Konstanz, Germany
[2]Department of Linguistics, University of Konstanz, Germany

Abstract

We present a modular framework for the rapid-prototyping of linguistic, web-based, visual analytics applications. Our framework gives developers access to a rich set of machine learning and natural language processing steps, through encapsulating them into micro-services and combining them into a computational pipeline. This processing pipeline is auto-configured based on the requirements of the visualization front-end, making the linguistic processing and visualization design detached, independent development tasks. This paper describes the constellation and modality of our framework, which continues to support the efficient development of various human-in-the-loop, linguistic visual analytics research techniques and applications.

1 Introduction

Research at the intersection of computational linguistics, visual analytics, and explainable machine learning, is a vibrant, interesting field that broadens the horizons of all disciplines involved. Over the last years, a team of computer scientists, linguists, as well as social scientists from different areas, at the University of Konstanz, have come together to push their disciplinary boundaries through collaborative research. This collaboration resulted in the development of several mixed-initiative visual analyitcs approaches, ranging from generating high-level corpus overviews using *Lexical Episode Plots* (Gold et al., 2015) to sophisticated human-in-the-loop topic refinement techniques (El-Assady et al., 2018b, 2019).

This effort has helped establish the subarea of *Linguistic Visualization* (short: *LingVis*) research (Butt et al., 2019). Within this subarea, application topics we worked on include content analysis, e.g., *NEREx* (El-Assady et al., 2017b); discourse analysis, e.g., *ThreadReconstructor* (El-

Assady et al., 2018a); language change, e.g., *HistoBankVis* (Schätzle et al., 2017) or *COHA Vis* (Schneider et al., 2017); readability analysis, e.g., literature fingerprinting (Oelke et al., 2012); language modeling, e.g., *LTMA* (El-Assady et al., 2018c); argumentation analysis, e.g., *ConToVi* (El-Assady et al., 2016); explainable machine leraning, e.g., verbalization and active learning (Sevastjanova et al., 2018a,b); interactive model refinement, e.g., *SpecEx* (Sperrle et al., 2018); multi-corpora analysis, e.g., *Alignment Vis* (Jentner et al., 2017); modeling of speech features, e.g., *SOMFlow* (Sacha et al., 2018).

To make our linguistic visualization techniques accessible to a wider public, we strive to implement them as web-based applications. However, this is only possible on a larger scale using a framework architecture that accommodates the needs for rapid-prototyping, disguising the involved engineering complexity for application developers. Hence, we established the *lingvis.io* framework as a common platform, facilitating the share and reuse of implementation components. A prominent application powered by our framework is *VisArgue* (El-Assady et al., 2017a), an approach for multi-party discourse analysis.

In this paper, we report on our shared framework and infrastructure that drives a multitude of linguistic visualization projects, as depicted in Figure 1. The core of our framework is a flexible pipeline with automatic dependency resolution that enables application developers to request natural language processing (NLP) steps for their visualizations, which, in turn, are auto-configured based on user-defined parameters. These are chosen in a user interface that is designed to enable experts and non-experts, alike, to adapt the NLP processing to their tasks and data. The results of this processing are closely intertwined with the interactive visual analytics components, enabling,

13

Proceedings of the 57th Annual Meeting of the Association for Computational Linguistics-System Demonstrations, pages 13–18
Florence, Italy, July 28 - August 2, 2019. ©2019 Association for Computational Linguistics

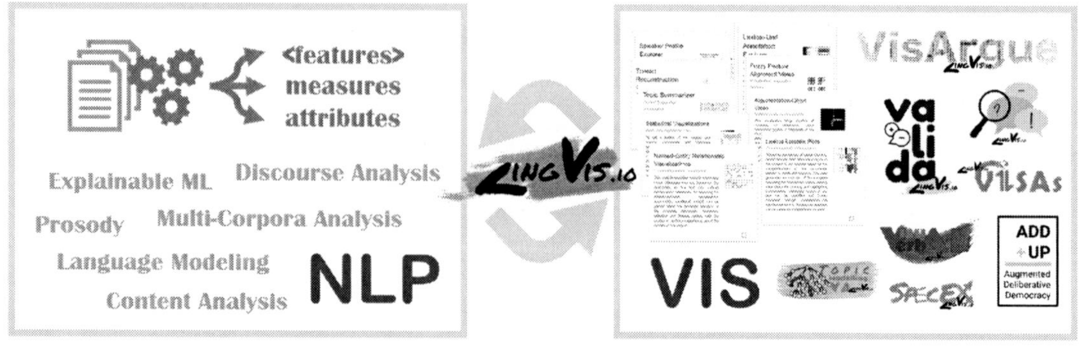

Figure 1: The lingvis.io framework driving various linguistic visualization projects based on rich NLP pipelines.

for instance, visual debugging for linguists, or insights for domain experts, such as writers, political scientists, etc. To address the trade-offs between tailored and expressive interface design, rapid-prototyping, and processing flexibility, our framework architecture strictly separates and modularizes tasks into atomic components that are compartmentalized in subdomains (i.e., auto-scaling cluster environments). Developers work on their designated feature branches and efficiently test their prototypes through continuous deployment.

Related Work – Other notable frameworks related to ours include Stanford CoreNLP[1], GATE[2] and Weblicht[3]. Facebook has recently released a deep-learning based framework for various NLP tasks, called pytext[4]. While they provide state-of-the-art models, they are code-only platforms that require developers to write processing pipelines from scratch every time. More general (deep learning) frameworks, including tensorflow[5] and pytorch[6] can also be used for text processing or to generate rich feature vectors like sentence- or word-embeddings. KNIME[7] and TABLEAU[8] are platforms for intuitively creating data science workflows with reusable components, but are not tailored to NLP tasks specifically. While we can communicate with those frameworks through APIs to enrich our own NLP pipeline, these toolkits are solely tailored to linguistic analysis and offer no, or very limited, visualizations possibilities.

---

[1] stanfordnlp.github.io/CoreNLP
[2] gate.ac.uk
[3] weblicht.sfs.uni-tuebingen.de
[4] github.com/facebookresearch/pytext
[5] tensorflow.org
[6] pytorch.org
[7] knime.com
[8] tableau.com

2 Auto-Configured Processing Pipeline

Our framework is based on the assumption that the individual processing steps can and should be atomic in their nature. Each step holds a well-defined list of dependencies which the respective step requires to execute its task successfully. This allows us to model a processing pipeline for a given type of data input as an *acyclic graph* which can be processed in parallel. For example, as shown in Figure 2, to retrieve the result of a topic model, the visualization requests one or more models. Based on their dependencies to other steps, a pipeline is generated (that takes into account all user-defined parameters). Here, the topic modeling is based on descriptor vectors extracted for each document in the corpus, as well as word embedding results.

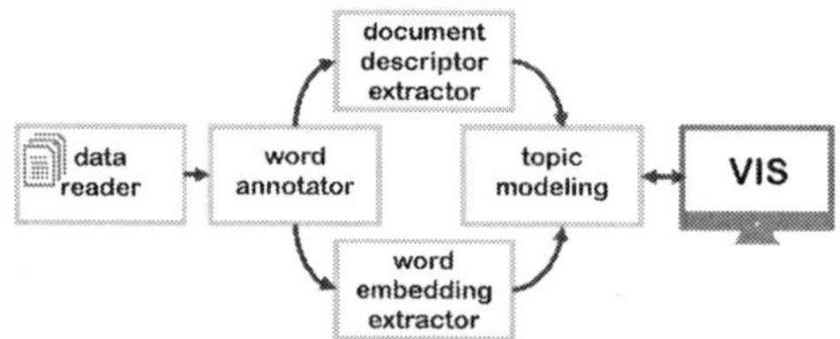

Figure 2: Dependency graph for topic model relations.

A successful implementation requires a consistent, flexible, and well-defined data model such that each step can use its transformation capabilities to semantically enrich the data. We therefore do not allow any step to modify or delete data but each step can further add metadata. This section describes the modeling of processing steps in our pipeline, as well as the underlying data structure.

2.1 Processing Steps

Our framework allows for *progressive* steps where intermediate results can be investigated and further steered by the user. As shown in Figure 3, in the user interface (UI), users first upload and select the data they want to process. Based on their intended tasks they then select suitable visualization components. Internally every visualization defines a list of *atomic* processing steps as *dependencies* that need to run in order to generate the desired information to visualize. In addition to a list of dependencies, visualizations define one or multiple controller endpoints. These serve as communication medium between the processing steps and the UI, and are characterized by the fact that they do not further enrich the data and cannot be defined as dependencies by any other processing step. This implies that visualization steps terminate the acyclic graph and, thus, the resulting processing pipeline.

For the initial processing, a controller in the streaming-control-layer handles the communication with every specific processing step and provides the parameter-configuration interface to the UI. This enables users to *parameterize* the processing for increasing flexibility. For example, a POS tagger step can be parameterized with different tagger models. Such a tagset does not need to be static but can depend on a language or be based on a user's selection. It is only constrained by the necessity of having a standardized tag set, as later steps use these tags to further process the data.

The endpoints in the two control layers separate *static* (default) from *streaming controllers*. In the default case, controllers are used to communicate the results of a completed processing step to the visualization. Streaming controllers, on the other hand, intercept a processing step while it is running to support direct user interactions. Here, progressive visualizations are shown while the respective processing step is running. The users can, therefore, directly observe, adapt, and refine the underlying machine learning models. This enables the design of tightly-coupled, human-in-the-loop interfaces for interactive model refinement and explainable machine learning.

2.2 Data Structure Modeling

We represent a corpus hierarchy as a recursively stacked data structure consisting of, so-called, *'document objects'*. These are a modular abstraction of all levels of the hierarchy, including corpora, documents, paragraphs, sentences, etc. The highest level of our data structure consists of a

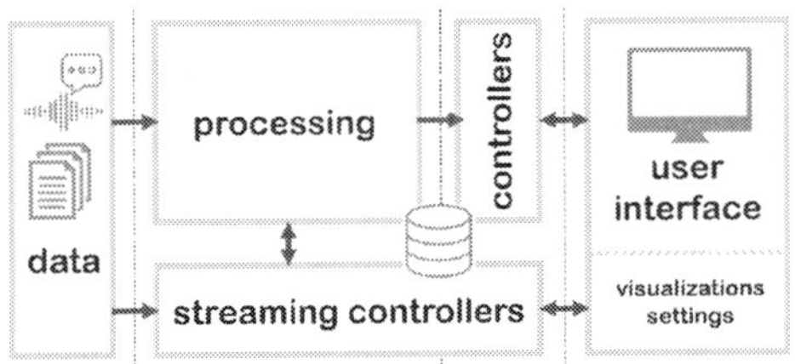

Figure 3: Schematic overview of the framework.

collection of document objects that typically represents all analyzed corpora, whereas the lowest level are single word tokens. Hence, from an ordered list of all corpora, we can descend the data structure to find a list of documents for each corpus, all the way to sub-sentence structures, multiword objects, and finally words consisting of an ordered list of tokens. This flexible data structure allows us to model arbitrary complex object hierarchies, with each object level containing an ordered list of the objects on the next level, while tokens define the terminal level.

Each processing step in the pipeline has access to the full data hierarchy. Throughout the processing, steps append additional data elements to the hierarchy objects to enrich them with computational results and metadata, making their processing results accessible to other steps downstream. Hence, through defining the pipeline dependencies, processing steps can request input data that is provided by its previous steps through defined formats, which ensures atomicity and encapsulation. This appended data is independent of a step's sophistication, which can range from simple wordlist lookups to complex deep neural network models. In the following, we describe the three data formats that can be appended to document objects.

(1) Weighted Feature Vectors (FV) – One of the key structures attached to document objects are feature vectors. These represent the transformation of text from a semi-structured data source to a high-dimensional feature space. Feature vectors represent the discretized elements of the text, often weighted descriptors extracted from the underlying text. These vectors are defined by a global signature vector that prescribes an ordered reference for the numerical weights contained in individual FVs for each document object. For example, to build a frequency-based bag-of-words model, we enable users to choose from a set of token-classes including POS-tags, named entities, lexical chains, n-grams, stop-words, etc. These are

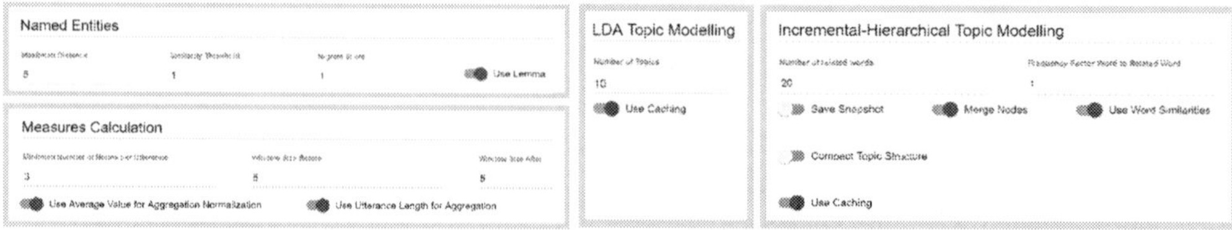

(a) Named Entity and Measure Settings UI   (b) Topic Modeling Settings UI

Figure 4: UI components for parameterizing processing steps. Available settings depend on the underlying models.

scored based on several weighting schemes, such as tf-idf, ttf-idf, log-likelihood ratio, and other metrics, as described by El-Assady et al. (2018b). Such weighted feature vectors can describe the importance of keywords on a global level (e.g., for all analyzed corpora) or on an individual object level (e.g., for a single document). Other types of feature vectors include ones extracted using word- or sentence-embeddings, as well as vectors based on linguistic annotation pipelines.

(2) Attributes (A) – As opposed to numeric feature vectors, attributes consist of labels or pointers attached during processing. Both of these attribute types can be used to aggregate feature vectors or measures in the data hierarchy. For example, for dynamically computing all measure values related to a particular speaker and topic in a conversation, these attributes are utilized.

Labels (L) can be single flags, such as POS tags, or could consist of n-tuples, for example, to inform the types of arguments contained in the underlying text. To accommodate for labels that describe only parts of a hierarchy, we also feature *window labels*. These are stored in the hierarchy level above the targeted level and contain a beginning and ending indices of the children. For example, the *sentence* hierarchy level may contain a label *consensus* with a beginning index of 0 and ending index of 6, pointing to a sub-sentence structure that encodes that the first six tokens of that sentence are indicating a consensus.

Pointers (P), on the other hand, are attributes that point to external structures, such as topics, speakers, or other entities. Such structures are usually modeled by specific processing steps and contain descriptive features of the elements they represent. For example, a topic might contain a list of descriptive keywords, whereas a speaker object would contain metadata and biography information on a speaker.

(3) Measures (M) – As a pendant to nominal attributes, measures are numeric or boolean values attached to the document objects. These are used to describe linguistic features of various types. As with the labels, a measure consists of a class name and a singular value. They are typically used to qualify properties of objects and, thus, can be aggregated through the data hierarchy. In addition, measures can be normalized, for example, based on the number of tokens in a document. We distinguish three types of measures: *Boolean*; *numeric continuous*; and *numeric bi-polar*. Such measures can be extracted through a variety of processing steps, ranging from simple word-list-based taggers, statistical analysis steps, rule-based annotators, through sophisticated machine learning based measure calculators. We use such measures to extract semantically relevant information or to monitor the quality of document objects with respect to selected criteria. Hence, such measures inform the visual analytics methods and expand the dimensionality of the underlying objects.

3 User Interface

"Simplicity comes at the cost of flexibility" (Jentner et al., 2018). The dependency-based processing model automatizes many decisions a user has to take in other frameworks. However, in order to allow domain-experts to use their knowledge and influence the underlying models, parameterization is necessary. We run a linearization of the *acyclic graph* prior to executing the pipeline. This allows us to display the steps and their parameters in the order of the processing-flow to support the users in their parameter estimation. To further support users we deploy guidance in the form of information pop-ups and built-in tutorials. This includes explaining how a respective processing step transforms the data and the value it adds to the task, but furthermore involves descriptions of the parameters and their estimated impact.

To exemplify this process, we describe a partial pipeline that is commonly used in our frame-

16

work to demonstrate its expressiveness and flexibility. Let this partial pipeline be: (1) *Named Entity Recognizer (A-L)* → (2) *Document Feature Extractor (FV)* → (3) *Topic Modeling (A-P)* → (4) *Measure Calculator (M)*. The (1) **NER** step *labels* (A-L) tokens with *Named Entities*. As shown in Figure 4a, the user can define parameters such as the *minimum distance* and *similarity score*. The (2) **DFE** creates *feature vectors* (FV) on all data hierarchies. Based on the data and task, the user selects and weights the features and selects an appropriate scoring scheme. In the (3) **TM** step, the user selects one or multiple of the available topic models (e.g., LDA, IHTM) and parameterizes them, for example, with the number of desired topics (Figure 4b). Note that this step uses only the feature vectors extracted in the previous step. It assigns additional *pointer attributes* (A-P) for each document reflecting their probability to belong to a certain topic. The (4) **MC** then uses, for example, the topic labels to calculate *measures* (M) such as *Topic Shift* where the topic of discussion is changed within a document, or *Topic Persistence* where a given topic continues to be pursued by the author or speaker.

Such a pipeline is part of multiple visualization creation cycles. For example, we utilize the results of topic modeling to analyze the dynamics of speakers in a conversation transcript in *ConToVi* (El-Assady et al., 2016). Hence, to build such visualization approaches, we rely on the auto-configuration of the processing pipeline, as well as the familiarity of users with their analyzed data and tasks, enabling application developers to focus on their encapsulated implementation environment without worrying about the complexity of the underlying linguisic processing.

4 Microservice Architecture

The modularity of our framework and atomicity of the steps is further emphasized by the use of microservices (Figure 5, *s1, s2, s3*). A microservice is a small, single-purpose service that exposes an API. Because our microservices are dockerized,[9] the microservice itself is independent of any programming language and environment which provides us with great flexibility. Additionally, individual microservices are easier to maintain than a large, monolithic framework. An example microservice from our framework returns POS tags

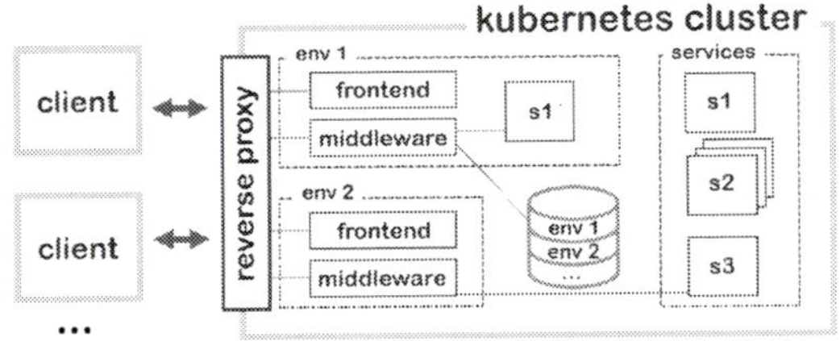

Figure 5: Multiple environments (*env1*, *env2*) of the *lingvis.io* framework are managed in a kubernetes cluster. Microservices (*s1*, *s2*, *s3*) are tailored to a specific task and resemble different steps of the pipeline. Any microservice can be redefined in a specific environment if variations of the functionality are needed.

for tokenized texts. Requests to that service contain a list of tokens, and are parametrized with the tagger model to use. The middleware handles the user authentication, the (processed) data, the pipeline steps, and the controllers (Figure 3). In addition, it coordinates the microservices and handles communication with their respective APIs to obtain results to add to the data.

Our framework lives in a kubernetes cluster[10] which effectively manages and orchestrates docker containers. This allows us to scale microservices, running multiple instances and balancing their load automatically—even across physical servers (Figure 5, see *s2*). We are further able to run multiple environments of the *lingvis.io* framework (middleware & frontend) in our cluster allowing our researchers to deploy a tailored version, for example, for a user evaluation. Kubernetes in combination with the reverse proxy *traefik*[11] automatically assigns a URL to the frontend and the middleware to make them accessible from anywhere in the world.

5 Conclusion

A demo of our framework is available under https://demo.lingvis.io/. Currently available visualizations with attendant NLP microservices are presented via the demo video or can be found under the "*Visualizations*" button. To the best of our knowledge, *lingvis.io* represents the first scaleable and modular web-based framework that combines NLP with visual analytics applications. Its unique contribution lies in combining these applications in a novel way on the one hand, but in separating NLP processing and visualizations on the operational level through an auto-configured pipeline on

---

[9] docker.com

[10] kubernetes.io

[11] traefik.io

the other hand. This enables developers to focus on the individual task at hand, rather than being distracted by needing to solve general NLP or visual analytics problems. As such, the framework is ideal for rapid prototyping and should serve as a productive base for more developments within LingVis, the interdisciplinary combination of, linguistics, NLP and visual analytics.

References

Miriam Butt, Annette Hautli-Janisz, and Verena Lyding. 2019. *LingVis: Visual Analytics for Linguistics*. CSLI lecture notes. CSLI Publications, to appear.

Mennatallah El-Assady, Valentin Gold, Carmela Acevedo, Christopher Collins, and Daniel Keim. 2016. ConToVi: Multi-Party Conversation Exploration using Topic-Space Views. *Computer Graphics Forum*, 35(3):431–440.

Mennatallah El-Assady, Annette Hautli-Janisz, Valentin Gold, Miriam Butt, Katharina Holzinger, and Daniel Keim. 2017a. Interactive Visual Analysis of Transcribed Multi-Party Discourse. In *Proceedings of ACL 2017, System Demonstrations*, pages 49–54, Stroudsburg, PA. ACL.

Mennatallah El-Assady, Rita Sevastjanova, Bela Gipp, Daniel Keim, and Christopher Collins. 2017b. NEREx: Named-Entity Relationship Exploration in Multi-Party Conversations. *Computer Graphics Forum*, 36(3):213–225.

Mennatallah El-Assady, Rita Sevastjanova, Daniel Keim, and Christopher Collins. 2018a. Thread-Reconstructor: Modeling Reply-Chains to Untangle Conversational Text through Visual Analytics. *Computer Graphics Forum*, 37(3):351–365.

Mennatallah El-Assady, Rita Sevastjanova, Fabian Sperrle, Daniel Keim, and Christopher Collins. 2018b. Progressive Learning of Topic Modeling Parameters: A Visual Analytics Framework. *IEEE Transactions on Visualization and Computer Graphics*, 24(1):382–391.

Mennatallah El-Assady, Fabian Sperrle, Oliver Deussen, Daniel Keim, and Christopher Collins. 2019. Visual Analytics for Topic Model Optimization based on User-Steerable Speculative Execution. *IEEE Trans. on Visualization and Computer Graphics*, 25(1):374–384.

Mennatallah El-Assady, Fabian Sperrle, Rita Sevastjanova, Michael Sedlmair, and Daniel Keim. 2018c. LTMA: Layered Topic Matching for the Comparative Exploration, Evaluation, and Refinement of Topic Modeling Results. In *International Symposium on Big Data Visual and Immersive Analytics (BDVA)*, pages 1–10.

Valentin Gold, Christian Rohrdantz, and Mennatallah El-Assady. 2015. Exploratory Text Analysis using Lexical Episode Plots. In *Proc. of EuroVis.*, pages 85–89. The Eurographics Association.

Wolfgang Jentner, Mennatallah El-Assady, Bela Gipp, and Daniel A Keim. 2017. Feature Alignment for the Analysis of Verbatim Text Transcripts. In *EuroVis Workshop on Visual Analytics, EuroVA 2017, Barcelona, Spain, 12-13 June 2017*, pages 13–17. Eurographics Association.

Wolfgang Jentner, Dominik Sacha, Florian Stoffel, Geoffrey P Ellis, Leishi Zhang, and Daniel A Keim. 2018. Making machine intelligence less scary for criminal analysts: reflections on designing a visual comparative case analysis tool. *The Visual Computer*, 34(9):1225–1241.

Daniela Oelke, David Spretke, Andreas Stoffel, and Daniel A. Keim. 2012. Visual readability analysis: How to make your writings easier to read. *IEEE Transactions on Visualization and Computer Graphics*, 18(5):662–674.

Dominik Sacha, Matthias Kraus, Jrgen Bernard, Michael Behrisch, Tobias Schreck, Yuki Asano, and Daniel A Keim. 2018. Somflow: Guided exploratory cluster analysis with self-organizing maps and analytic provenance. *IEEE transactions on visualization and computer graphics*, 24(1):120–130.

Christin Schätzle, Michael Hund, Frederik L Dennig, Miriam Butt, and Daniel A Keim. 2017. Histo-BankVis: Detecting Language Change via Data Visualization. In *Proceedings of the NoDaLiDa 2017 Workshop on Processing Historical Language*, 133, pages 32–39. University of Konstanz, Germany.

Gerold Schneider, Mennatallah El-Assady, and Hans Martin Lehmann. 2017. Tools and Methods for Processing and Visualizing Large Corpora. *Studies in Variation, Contacts and Change in English*, 19.

Rita Sevastjanova, Fabian Beck, Basil Ell, Cagatay Turkay, Rafael Henkin, Miriam Butt, Daniel Keim, and Mennatallah El-Assady. 2018a. Going beyond Visualization: Verbalization as Complementary Medium to Explain Machine Learning Models.

Rita Sevastjanova, Mennatallah El-Assady, Annette Hautli-Janisz, Aikaterini-Lida Kalouli, Rebecca Kehlbeck, Oliver Deussen, Daniel Keim, and Miriam Butt. 2018b. Mixed-initiative active learning for generating linguistic insights in question classification. In *Workshop on Data Systems for Interactive Analysis (DSIA) at IEEE VIS*.

Fabian Sperrle, Jürgen Bernard, Michael Sedlmair, Daniel Keim, and Mennatallah El-Assady. 2018. Speculative Execution for Guided Visual Analytics. In *Proc. of IEEE VIS Workshop on Machine Learning from User Interaction for Visualization and Analytics*.

SARAL: A Low-Resource Cross-Lingual Domain-Focused Information Retrieval System for Effective Rapid Document Triage

Elizabeth Boschee◇, Joel Barry◇, Jayadev Billa◇, Marjorie Freedman◇, Thamme Gowda◇,
Constantine Lignos◇, Chester Palen-Michel◇, Michael Pust◇, Banriskhem K. Khonglah♣,
Srikanth Madikeri♣, Jonathan May◇, Scott Miller◇

◇Information Sciences Institute, University of Southern California
♣Idiap Research Institute

```
{boschee,joelb,jbilla,mrf,tg,lignos,cpm,pust,
            jonmay,smiller}@isi.edu
{banriskhem.khonglah,srikanth.madikeri}@idiap.ch
```


Abstract

With the increasing democratization of electronic media, vast information resources are available in less-frequently-taught languages such as Swahili or Somali. That information, which may be crucially important and not available elsewhere, can be difficult for monolingual English speakers to effectively access. In this paper we present SARAL, an end-to-end cross-lingual information retrieval (CLIR) and summarization system for low-resource languages that 1) enables English speakers to search foreign language repositories of text and audio using English queries, 2) summarizes the retrieved documents in English with respect to a particular information need, and 3) provides complete transcriptions and translations as needed. The SARAL system achieved the top end-to-end performance in the most recent IARPA MATERIAL CLIR+summarization evaluations.

1 Introduction

The task of searching for a needle of relevant information in a haystack of documents is not as daunting as in previous eras, thanks to decades of information retrieval research progress. Most of us engage in this behavior daily when we search the web. Powerful IR algorithms choose the most likely matches for our queries, but humans also play a crucial role: we are typically presented with a list of ranked results, accompanied by small snippets of relevant content, and we make the final decision with this information in hand.

Unfortunately, when the information content is in a language the searcher does not understand, serious challenges can arise. This is the problem of cross-lingual information retrieval (CLIR), and there are several straightforward approaches to this problem, many of which have been well-studied.

One can translate queries into the language of the search corpus before matching, or conversely translate the documents into the language of the query. Both approaches naturally rely on the availability of good-quality translation, which improves as more parallel data is available. Thus, CLIR may be adequate when the languages are English, French, Spanish, etc., but will be less effective for lower-resourced languages such as Swahili or Somali.

Moreover, the crucial role played by humans in triaging results is complicated in a low-resource cross-lingual setting, since the system must somehow present the user with the context for its retrieval, e.g. an English speaker with the context for a Swahili document. But if the quality of the machine translation (MT) is too poor, just showing the surrounding text (à la Google) will be insufficiently helpful. This problem is exacerbated when the original source is audio transcribed by a low-resource automatic speech recognition (ASR) model, since ASR errors will propagate through MT.

In this paper we present SARAL (**S**ummarization and domain-**A**daptive **R**etrieval **A**cross **L**anguages[1]), an end-to-end system that addresses these challenges. SARAL operates over both text and audio input documents from a diverse set of genres (e.g. news, conversational speech, etc.), answering user queries by summarizing the retrieved documents *in English* with respect to a user's particular information need. Requests can be expressed as a combination of a query phrase (e.g. *foreign investments*) and a set of one or more desired document domains (e.g. *Health* or *Military*). The SARAL system achieved the top end-to-end performance in the most recent CLIR+summarization evaluations conducted by

---

[1]SARAL (सरल) is a Hindi word which can be translated as *ingenious* or *simple*, depending on the relevant context.

19

Proceedings of the 57th Annual Meeting of the Association for Computational Linguistics-System Demonstrations, pages 19–24
Florence, Italy, July 28 - August 2, 2019. ©2019 Association for Computational Linguistics

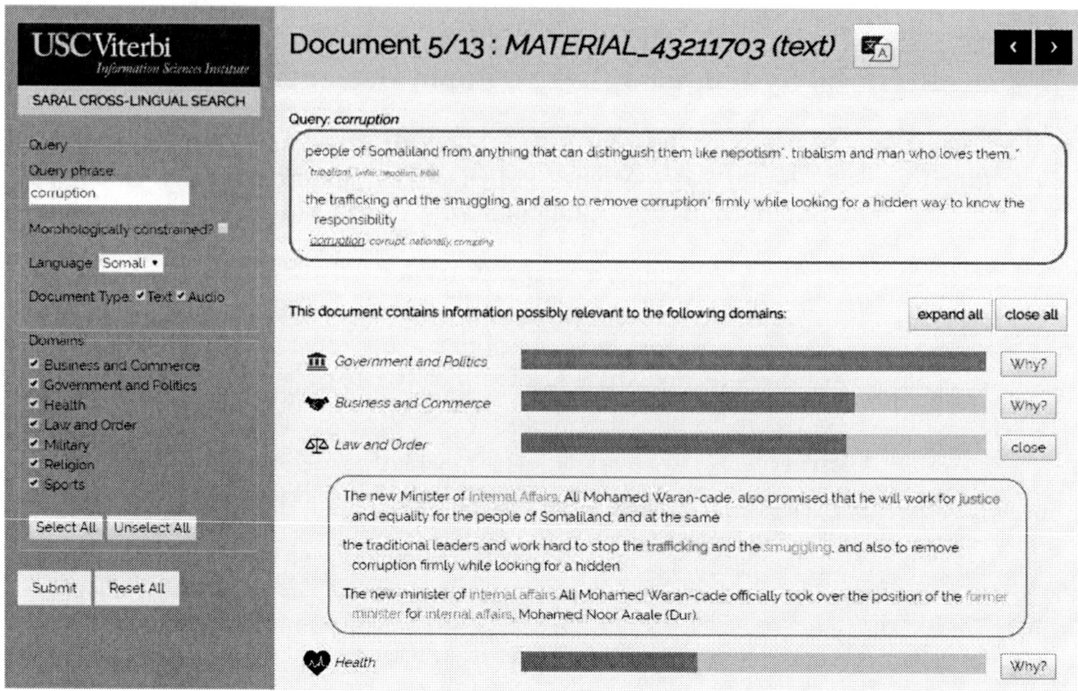

Figure 1: The SARAL cross-lingual search interface, which returns English query-focused snippets, domain relevance confidence backed up by domain snippets, and full-text transcription (where relevant) and translation.

the IARPA MATERIAL program.

The contributions of this paper are:

1. SEARCHER, a novel CLIR approach designed for low-resource conditions that relies on the construction of a shared semantic space learned from bitext and monolingual corpora
2. An intuitive snippet extraction and presentation design which has been shown in human studies to provide readers with sufficient evidence to filter out erroneous query matches and preserve good ones, even in low-resource conditions
3. The entire operable SARAL system itself, an end-to-end CLIR and summarization system that combines SEARCHER and traditional IR techniques and applies them to text and speech documents in low-resource languages

An example of the user interface is shown in Figure 1. An instance of the system with Swahili and Somali data may be queried at `https://material.isi.edu` (register with token *PpnOMgavHR3j*). A short demonstration video is also available.[2]

---

[2] `https://youtu.be/TslZiwPejcU`

2 SARAL System Overview

2.1 Automatic Speech Recognition

We transcribe audio data using two systems developed for SARAL by Idiap and ISI. The Idiap system trains 3 Kaldi-based LF-MMI models with a CNN-BLSTM architecture, with targets derived from alignments produced by HMM/GMM models. The first model is trained with standard data augmented by perturbing audio speeds, the second with data augmented by adding noise and then speed perturbation, and the third with bottleneck features extracted from a multilingual system (Tagalog, Swahili, Zulu, Turkish and Somali). The three systems are then fused by stacking lattices and minimum Bayes Risk (MBR) rescoring. The ISI system uses eight Kaldi-based end-to-end LF-MMI trained TDNN-F grapheme acoustic models. Audio data is decoded with each of the models with a trigram LM, followed by rescoring with an RNN-LM to generate lattices. Similar to the Idiap system, the final transcript is generated by stacking lattices from these models, followed by MBR rescoring on the composite lattice.

Based on performance on a development set, we use the Idiap system for conversational speech and the ISI system for topical and news broadcasts. All models are trained with 40 hours of the transcribed audio provided in the MATERIAL program, as well as ~500hrs of YouTube data used for unsupervised training. For Somali, language models use ~320M words, primarily composed of webcrawl data (~230M words) and the so16 Somali Web Corpus (~70M words); for Swahili, they use ~100M words of webcrawl data. For comparison, a high-resource language would typically be trained with thousands of hours of speech and a language model generated from more than a billion words of data.

2.2 Machine Translation

Our low-resource MT architecture is a system combination (Heafield and Lavie, 2010) of a Transformer-based neural model (Vaswani et al., 2017) and a statistical syntax-based model (Galley et al., 2006), which bring complementary strengths, particularly in low-resource conditions. All models are trained with fewer than 2M words of parallel data.[3] By contrast, in the WMT 2018 shared task (Bojar et al., 2018) most language pairs had 4M or more words, and many had more than 10M words. To further adapt to low-resource conditions, we augment our neural system with 14.5M words of crawled English region-relevant data with parallel Somali or Swahili obtained from backtranslation Transformer models (Sennrich et al., 2016a). Transformer model hyperparameters are "out-of-the-box" except that the shared Byte Pair Encoding (Sennrich et al., 2016b) vocabulary is set to approximately 8,000.

2.3 Cross-Lingual Information Retrieval

We employ a combination of two approaches to cross-lingual information retrieval. The first relies on term-level matching in both the original document and its machine translation(s). Source-language matching is mediated via translation tables derived from the word alignments used by our syntax-based MT system. Terms are expanded using transformations of varying expected accuracy, e.g. stemming, WordNet transformations (Fellbaum, 1998), paraphrases (Pavlick et al., 2015), semantic similarity (Huang et al., 2018), and combinations of the above. For multiword search strings, all terms must match in the same sentence, but not necessarily in the same translation or even the

same language. For instance, the Somali phrase *xilli roobaadka* could be translated *rainy season* or *rainy time*. An English-only search for *rainy season* might miss a translation that reported only *rainy time*. However, our hybrid search will match *rainy* in English and *xilli* in Somali, allowing for a match for the phrase across the two languages.

Our second approach, SEARCHER (**S**hared **E**mbedding **ARCH**itecture for **E**ffective **R**etrieval), maps both queries and documents into a shared embedding space and performs retrieval there, rather than relying on translation of either the document or the query terms. However, during development, we found that standard cross-lingual embeddings derived from monolingual corpora, even when aligned using sophisticated transformation techniques (e.g. Lample et al., 2018), did not provide the @1-precision necessary for the specific requirements of MATERIAL's "lexical" queries, where only documents containing precise translations of query terms are judged responsive.

To obtain sufficient precision, we train a proxy task based on sentence relevancy. Here, a sentence S is considered responsive to a query q if at least one plausible translation of S contains the term q. Training samples are derived from parallel corpora. Sample queries are drawn from the English side, with their corresponding foreign-language sentences as positive examples and other randomly-drawn foreign-language sentences as negative examples. The SEARCHER model consists of a convolutional encoder (similar to Gehring et al. 2017) for encoding foreign-language sentences, a query embedding matrix, an attention mechanism for aligning query terms with specific foreign-language terms, and a matching network to determine relevance. The model was optimized using a cross-entropy objective. In recent experiments, SEARCHER's performance exceeded that of the term-level matching approach, improving AQWV (see Section 3) from 23.1 to 25.2 on the Somali MATERIAL evaluation corpus, even when translation is performed by state-of-the-art MT systems.

2.4 Domain Identification

The New York Times Annotated corpus[4] provides ~2M articles with topic annotations from a closed topic set. For each domain of interest,[5] we manu-

---

[3]Data was provided by the IARPA MATERIAL program and by LDC as part of the DARPA LORELEI program (Somali: LDC2016E91; Swahili: LDC2017E64).

[4]https://catalog.ldc.upenn.edu/ LDC2008T19

[5]Business & Commerce, Government & Politics, Health, Law & Order, Military, Religion, Sports

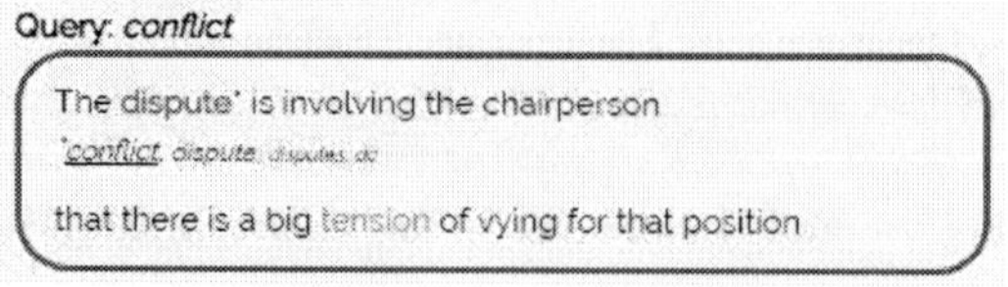

Figure 2: Example summary for the query *conflict*.

ally select the topics that best map to the domain, giving us a set of in-domain documents. We then calculate a score for each n-gram ($n \leq 3$) that represents how indicative it is of a particular domain, simply $count_{in\_domain} / count_{all}$. We discard all n-grams involving capitalized letters (mostly names) as likely irrelevant (or even misleading) to the target datasets (e.g. Somali news). Our binary domain classifier then has three parameters: a threshold for unigrams, a threshold for bi/trigrams, and the number of n-grams whose scores meet those thresholds that must be found for a document to be considered in-domain. We tune these parameters for each domain via grid search on the development corpus, optimizing for AQWV on the CLIR task.

2.5 Summary Generation

The goal of summarization is to concisely explain, in English, a particular document's relevance to a query. Our primary approach highlights in blue those terms ranked most highly by our CLIR and displays them in a fixed-context window. Semantically related words are colored in lighter blue, as with *tension* in Figure 2. When query terms are found in the source language or matched in the SEARCHER embedding space, we attempt to highlight aligned terms in one of our English machine translations, where possible. (In some cases, no translation of a particular foreign term might be found; in that case we simply present the whole sentence without highlighting.)

The primary barrier to providing accurate summaries is poor MT quality. Even if an exact match is highlighted, the context may be so garbled that a reader is unable to label it as a reliably relevant match. To mitigate this, we provide additional context for the MT system's decisions, specifically the set of options the system considers when producing word(s) matching the query. For instance, consider a summary for *back injuries*. If the word *back* was translated from the Swahili word *mgongo*, we might show alternate translations *spine*, *backbone*, and *spinal*, reassuring the reader that the translation of *back* is correct and of the appropriate word

sense. In contrast, if the word was originally translated from *kurejea*, we would present alternative translations *return*, *returning*, *referring*, leading the reader to correctly identify a false alarm.

For the purposes of summarization, we provide this kind of information via footnotes (see Figure 2), where the size of a word in the footnote reflects how likely the system thinks it is (in isolation) to be a translation of the original source term. We also underline the exact query term if it is present in that list, to help draw the user's attention to it.

We generate summaries for domains using the n-grams extracted for domain classification (Section 2.4). We identify these n-grams in an English machine translation of a document and create multiple candidate display windows of varying size for each. We then employ a greedy search to select and merge such windows to (a) include as much domain-relevant information as possible (a function of both the number of domain-relevant terms and their quality), (b) present exactly as much context as is necessary to make the terms understandable, and (c) avoid redundancy / prefer diversity. When presenting summaries to the user, we highlight domain-relevant terms in blue, with the shade intensity indicating the strength of its relevance to the domain. A sample summary for the Law and Order domain is shown in Figure 1.

2.6 User Interface Design

SARAL's user interface allows users to search for a single English query phrase. Following the most common practice of the MATERIAL program, we focus on direct cross-lingual search rather than conceptual expansion. So, for the query *vaccine*, synonyms (e.g. *immunization*) and morphological variations (e.g. *vaccinated*) would be considered responsive, but a sentence generically discussing *methods for the prevention of the flu* would not. (Users may also opt to exclude morphological variations.) Users also select the target language and optionally restrict to either text or audio documents.

In the MATERIAL program, queries typically require exactly one domain. However, a user's interests might extend to more than one domain at a time. We therefore allow the user to select multiple domains; any document that matches at least one domain of interest is allowed to be returned as relevant. To avoid crowding the screen when a document is relevant to multiple domains, we show instead, for each document, a bar graph displaying

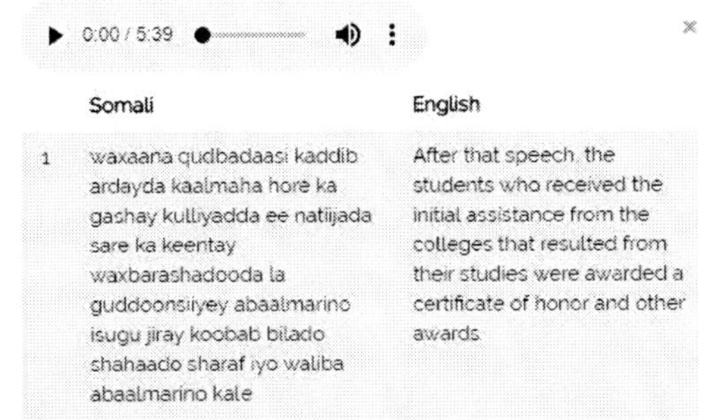

Figure 3: ASR & MT excerpt for an audio document.

the relative strength of each domain that the system identified as being potentially represented in a document. Clicking on the *Why?* button next to a domain displays the evidence that the system found for that domain, i.e. the domain-specific summary, as shown in Figure 1.

For the purposes of the demonstration, we restrict query summaries to 50 words, keeping them comfortably at the top of the page and quickly gistable. We allow 80 words for each domain summary, enough to provide convincing evidence without being too verbose to skim quickly.

Finally, we provide full access to each source document (original text or audio; if audio, we also provide the automatically-generated transcription) and an English machine translation, for the user who wants to dig deeper into the context of a response. A small excerpt is shown in Figure 3.

2.7 New Languages

It is simple to add a new language to the system. In a recent exercise, we brought up an end-to-end system in Lithuanian in three days using the speech and parallel text resources provided by the MATE-RIAL program; this required only a few hours of actual human effort. The two largest bottlenecks for improved performance over the three-day system are data collection (scraping monolingual data from the web to improve ASR language models) and ASR model training. With ten days, we were able to bring up a significantly improved ASR system in Lithuanian; with more efficient use of compute resources (e.g. parallelizing the web scraping), this time could be significantly reduced.

3   System Evaluation & Analysis

The Phase 1 MATERIAL evaluation was performed on a corpus of ~15K Somali documents annotated for relevance for 1,000 queries by native speakers. The official evaluation metric is AQWV (Average Query Weighted Value),[6] which uses a parameter β to balance missed detections and false alarms.

End-to-end AQWV was calculated after human readers triaged an initial set of system results, removing those documents they judged to be false alarms using *only* the English summaries generated by the system. Documents were sampled evenly across queries and across true positives and false alarms; system performance was then projected to any unassessed documents. For the SARAL system, ~15K query/document summaries were assessed, using Amazon Mechanical Turk. Overall, the SARAL system was the top-ranked end-to-end system in the evaluation.[7]

Projected across all responses, the SARAL summarization component results in the acceptance of 87% of true positives and the rejection of 45% of false negatives. Rates are essentially consistent across speech and text documents. Because the AQWV β for the evaluation penalizes misses much more than false alarms, these results are consistent with our goal of minimizing false rejections even if that means retaining more false positives.

The majority of errors on true positive documents come from insufficient summaries. For instance, a query about *deception* results in the summary text *Punamin was arrested for trafficking, but he made amazing* **cheating** *that he thought about the long arrest*. Two alternative translations provided for cheating are *deception* and *trick*. Still, the English context is difficult to understand. Thus although it is in reality a true positive, it is not unreasonable that a human rejected it.

Human acceptance of a false positive happens most frequently when readers accept an alternate translation as accurate when the context did not make sense. For instance, a query for *midwife* returns summary text *I would like to advise you to be united people who create their own* **skills** ... *you will be a company that will support themselves*. Our system indicates that an alternate translation for *skills* could be *midwife*, which is accepted by the reader even though clearly incorrect in context.

A so-called false positive found by the system—

---

[6]https://www.nist.gov/sites/default/files/documents/2019/04/02/openclir19_evalplan_v1.19.pdf

[7]Four end-to-end systems were evaluated from four separate teams. However, per program policy, only system rank may be publicly reported, so we cannot provide any further details on cross-system comparisons here.

and retained by human readers during triage—can actually be a true positive that was missed by the original foreign-language annotator. For instance, a query for *mockery* returns *will present a exhibition to show* **insults** *to our Prophet ... aimed at presenting images of* **insulting** *Prophet Muhammed.* It seems reasonable that *insults* here is a translation variant for *mockery*; both our system and a human reader think so. This shows the strength of the system; not only can it provide a monolingual speaker with access to content in low-resource foreign languages, but it can sometimes surpass search by native speakers.

4 Related Work

Recent research in CLIR and query-based summarization uses expansive, concept-based definitions of relevance. For example, given the query *agriculture*, documents are relevant if they describe fields, pastures, or crops, even if the word *agriculture* is not used, and the goal of summarization is to show that the document as a whole is relevant. In contrast, in this work we aim to retrieve documents that meet a more precise notion of relevance, similar to that used for keyword spotting. This goal influences our retrieval approach, which seeks to account for variation in translation but does not perform more expansive embedding-based query expansion, and the summarization approach, which presents in-context search term matches rather than a narrative summary of the document as a whole.

5 Conclusion

The SARAL system provides a monolingual user with effective access to multimodal information in lower-resourced languages through a user interface that enables rapid triage of system results. We look forward to future work improving the quality of the underlying components for low-resource settings as well as expanding the user interface to incorporate additional semantic constraints or requests.

Acknowledgments

Thanks to Heng Ji for fruitful discussions. This research is based upon work supported in part by the Office of the Director of National Intelligence (ODNI), Intelligence Advanced Research Projects Activity (IARPA), via contract # FA8650-17-C-9116. The views and conclusions contained herein are those of the authors and should not be interpreted as necessarily representing the official policies, either expressed or implied, of ODNI, IARPA, or the U.S. Government. The U.S. Government is authorized to reproduce and distribute reprints for governmental purposes notwithstanding any copyright annotation therein.

References

Ondřej Bojar, Christian Federmann, Mark Fishel, Yvette Graham, Barry Haddow, Matthias Huck, Philipp Koehn, and Christof Monz. 2018. Findings of the 2018 conference on machine translation (WMT18). In *Proc. WMT*, Belgium, Brussels.

Christiane Fellbaum. 1998. *WordNet: An Electronic Lexical Database*. Bradford Books.

Michel Galley, Jonathan Graehl, Kevin Knight, Daniel Marcu, Steve DeNeefe, Wei Wang, and Ignacio Thayer. 2006. Scalable inference and training of context-rich syntactic translation models. In *Proc. COLING/ACL*, Sydney, Australia.

Jonas Gehring, Michael Auli, David Grangier, Denis Yarats, and Yann N Dauphin. 2017. Convolutional sequence to sequence learning. In *Proc. ICML*, Sydney, Australia.

Kenneth Heafield and Alon Lavie. 2010. Voting on n-grams for machine translation system combination. In *Proc. AMTA*, Denver, Colorado, USA.

Lifu Huang, Kyunghyun Cho, Boliang Zhang, Heng Ji, and Kevin Knight. 2018. Multi-lingual common semantic space construction via cluster-consistent word embedding. In *Proc. EMNLP*, Brussels, Belgium.

Guillaume Lample, Alexis Conneau, Marc'Aurelio Ranzato, Ludovic Denoyer, and Hervé Jégou. 2018. Word translation without parallel data. In *Proc. ICLR*, Vancouver, Canada.

Ellie Pavlick, Pushpendre Rastogi, Juri Ganitkevich, Benjamin Van Durme, and Chris Callison-Burch. 2015. PPDB 2.0: Better paraphrase ranking, fine-grained entailment relations, word embeddings, and style classification. In *Proc. ACL*, Beijing, China.

Rico Sennrich, Barry Haddow, and Alexandra Birch. 2016a. Improving neural machine translation models with monolingual data. In *Proc. ACL*, Berlin, Germany.

Rico Sennrich, Barry Haddow, and Alexandra Birch. 2016b. Neural machine translation of rare words with subword units. In *Proc. ACL*, Berlin, Germany.

Ashish Vaswani, Noam Shazeer, Niki Parmar, Jakob Uszkoreit, Llion Jones, Aidan N Gomez, Łukasz Kaiser, and Illia Polosukhin. 2017. Attention is all you need. In *Proc. NeurIPS*.

Jiuge: A Human-Machine Collaborative Chinese Classical Poetry Generation System

Zhipeng Guo[1*], Xiaoyuan Yi[1*], Maosong Sun[1†],

Wenhao Li[1], Cheng Yang[1], Jiannan Liang[1], Huimin Chen[1], Yuhui Zhang[1], Ruoyu Li[2]

[1]Department of Computer Science and Technology, Tsinghua University, Beijing, China
Institute for Artificial Intelligence, Tsinghua University, Beijing, China
State Key Lab on Intelligent Technology and Systems, Tsinghua University, Beijing, China
[2]6ESTATES PTE LTD, Singapore

Abstract

Research on the automatic generation of poetry, the treasure of human culture, has lasted for decades. Most existing systems, however, are merely model-oriented, which input some user-specified keywords and directly complete the generation process in one pass, with little user participation. We believe that the machine, being a collaborator or an assistant, should not replace human beings in poetic creation. Therefore, we proposed *Jiuge*, a human-machine collaborative Chinese classical poetry generation system. Unlike previous systems, Jiuge allows users to revise the unsatisfied parts of a generated poem draft repeatedly. According to the revision, the poem will be dynamically updated and regenerated. After the revision and modification procedure, the user can write a satisfying poem together with Jiuge system collaboratively. Besides, Jiuge can accept multi-modal inputs, such as keywords, plain text or images. By exposing the options of poetry genres, styles and revision modes, Jiuge, acting as a professional assistant, allows constant and active participation of users in poetic creation.

1 Introduction

Language is one of the most important forms of human intelligence, among different genres, poetry is a beautiful, poetic and artistic genre which expresses one's emotions and ideas with relatively fewer words. Across various countries, nationalities, and cultures, poetry is always fascinating, impacting profoundly on the development of human civilization.

Recently, researchers have worked on automatic poetry generation. Meanwhile, neural networks have proven to be powerful on this task (Zhang and Lapata, 2014; Wang et al., 2016; Yan, 2016;

Zhang et al., 2017; Yi et al., 2017). Besides the research value of exploring human writing mechanism and computer creativity, these models and systems could also benefit electronic entertainment, advertisement, and poetry education.

However, the recently released Chinese poetry generation systems are mainly model-oriented, which take some user inputs and directly complete the generation in one pass, resulting in poor user participation. Moreover, these systems generate poetry in fewer styles and genres, and provide limited options for users. For example, the *Daoxiangju* system[1] requires the user to determine the rhyme, which creates a barrier for beginners. The *Oude* system[2] simplifies the user's choices and only allows the input of a few options and genres. The *Microsoft Quatrain*[3] provides limited candidates of a theme and each line, but it only supports the generation of quatrains.

Due to the lack of user participation, the above systems are mainly designed for entertainment. We argue that the leading role in literary creation should not be a machine, or at least not only a machine, because it is difficult for machines to handle the complex expressions of one's emotion and the use of images in poetic creation.

Rather than completely replace humans, a better way is to utilize the system to assist human creation. The human-machine collaboration mechanism in Jiuge system can not only improve the emotions and semantics of generated poems but also guide and teach beginners to understand poetic creation process.

In summary, the contributions of our Jiuge system are as follows:

- **Multi-modal input.** Jiuge can accept multi-

---

* indicates equal contribution
† Corresponding author: M.Sun(sms@tsinghua.edu.cn)

[1]http://www.poeming.com/web/
[2]https://crl.ptopenlab.com:8800/poem/index
[3]http://duilian.msra.cn/jueju/

Proceedings of the 57th Annual Meeting of the Association for Computational Linguistics-System Demonstrations, pages 25–30
Florence, Italy, July 28 - August 2, 2019. ©2019 Association for Computational Linguistics

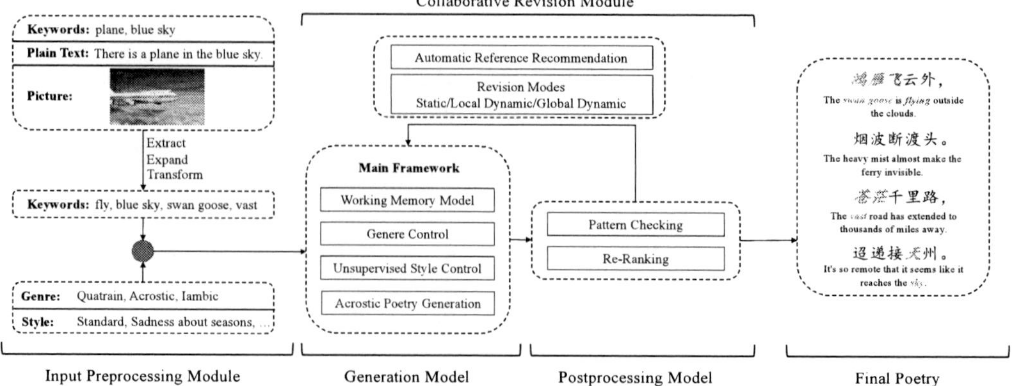

Figure 1: The architecture of Jiuge system.

modal input such as keywords, plain text, and even images. For modern concepts in the input, Jiuge utilizes a knowledge graph to map them into relevant keywords in classical Chinese poetry.

- **Various styles and genres**. Unlike previous systems, Jiuge provides more than twenty options of genre and ten options of style, and can generate more diverse poems.

- **Human-machine collaboration**. Jiuge supports human-machine collaborative and interactive generation. The user can revise the unsatisfied parts of a generated poem. In terms of the revision, Jiuge will dynamically update and re-generate the poem. During this process, Jiuge also offers candidate words and human-authored poetry as references for beginners.

2 Architecture

2.1 Overview

We show the overall architecture of Jiuge system in Fig. 1, which mainly consists of four modules: 1) *input preprocessing*, 2) *generation*, 3) *postprocessing* and 4) *collaborative revision*. Given the user-specified genre, style, and inputs (keywords, plain text or images), the preprocessing module extracts several keywords from the inputs and then conducts keyword expansion to introduce richer information. Jiuge also transforms the words in modern concepts, which are incompatible with classical Chinese poetry (written in ancient Chinese language), such as *refrigerator* and *airplane*, to appropriate relevant ones, e.g., *airplane → fly*. With these preprocessed keywords, the generation module generates a poem draft. The postprocessing module re-ranks the candidates of each line

and removes the ones that do not conform to structural and phonological requirements. At last, the collaborative revision module interacts with the user and dynamically updates the draft for several times according to the user's revision, to collaboratively create a satisfying poem.

We detail each module in the following parts.

2.2 Input Preprocessing Module

Keyword Extraction. Jiuge allows multi-modal input to meet the needs of generating poetry according to keywords, tweets or photos.

For plain text, we first use THULAC[4] (Li and Sun, 2009) to conduct Chinese word segmentation and compute the importance $r(w)$ of each word w:

$$r(w) = [\alpha * ti(w) + (1 - \alpha) * tr(w)], \quad (1)$$

where $ti(w)$ and $tr(w)$ are the TF-IDF (Term Frequency-Inverse Document Frequency) value and TextRank (Mihalcea and Tarau, 2004) score calculated with the whole poetry corpus respectively. α is a hyper-parameter to balance the weights of $ti(w)$ and $tr(w)$. Afterwards, we select top K words with the highest scores.

For each image, we use the Aliyun image recognition tool[5], which gives the names of five recognized objects with corresponding probability $s(w)$. Then we select top K words with the highest $s(w) \cdot r(w)$.

Keyword Mapping. The extracted or recognized keywords could be some modern concepts, such as *airplane* and *refrigerator*. Since these words never occur in the classical poetry corpus, the generation module will take them as a *UNK* symbol and generate totally irrelevant poems.

To address this problem, we build a Poetry Knowledge Graph (PKG) from Wikipedia data,

---

[4]http://thulac.thunlp.org/
[5]https://ai.aliyun.com/image

26

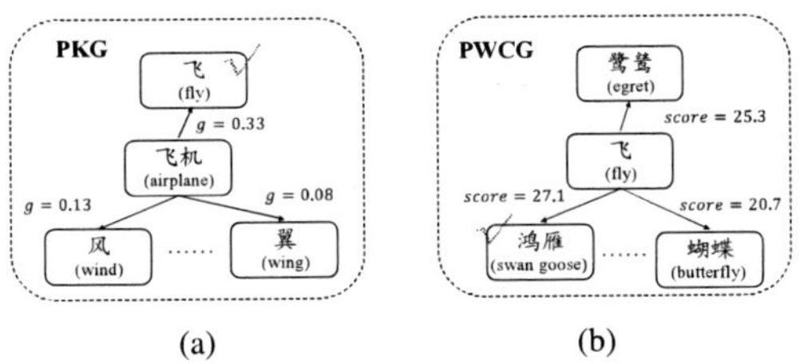

Figure 2: (a) A sampled subgraph of PKG. (b) A sampled subgraph of PWCG.

which contains $616,360$ entities and $5,102,192$ relations. $40,276$ of these entities occur in our poetry corpus. Before keywords extension and selection, we first use PKG to map the modern concepts to its most relevant entities in poetry, to guarantee both quality and relevance of generated poems.

For a modern concept word w_i, we score its each neighbor word w_j by:

$$g(w_j) = t f_{wiki}(w_j|w_i) \cdot \log(\frac{N}{1+df(w_j)}) \cdot \arctan(\frac{p(w_j)}{\tau}), \quad (2)$$

where $t f_{wiki}(w_j|w_i)$ is the term frequency of w_j in the Wikipedia article of w_i, $df(w_j)$ is the number of Wikipedia articles containing w_j, N is the number of Wikipedia articles, and $p(w_j)$ is the word frequency counted in all articles. We give an example of mapping the modern word "airplane" in Fig. 2(a).

Keyword Extension. The generation module can handle multi-keywords input. More keywords could lead to richer contents and emotions in generated poems. Therefore, if the number of extracted keywords is less than K, we further conduct keywords extension. To this end, we build a Poetry Word Co-occurrence Graph (PWCG) as shown in Fig. 2 (b). This graph indicates the co-occurrence of two words in the same poem. The weight of the edge between two words is calculated according to the Pointwise Mutual Information (PMI) as follows:

$$PMI(w_i, w_j) = \log \frac{p(w_i, w_j)}{p(w_i) * p(w_j)}, \quad (3)$$

where $p(w_i)$ and $p(w_i, w_j)$ are the word frequency and co-occurrence frequency in poetry corpus. For a given word w, we get all its adjacent words w_k in PWCG and select those with higher values of $\log p(w_k) * PMI(w, w_k) + \beta * r(w_k)$ where β is a hyperparameter.

2.3 Generation Module

As shown in Fig. 3, the core component of the generation module is our proposed working mem-

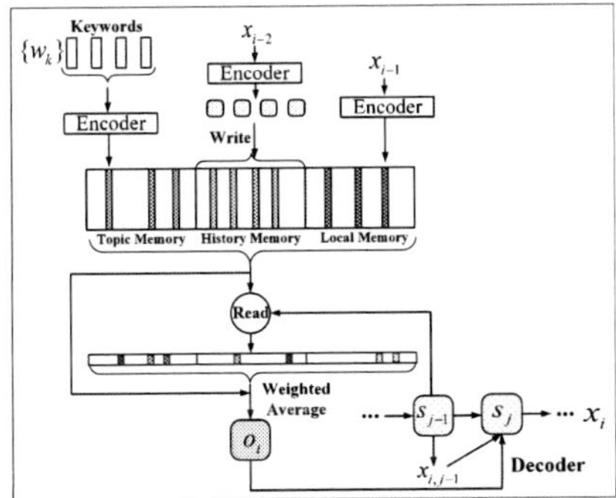

Figure 3: The simplified structure of the working memory model, which mainly comprise an encoder, a decoder and there memory components. x_i is the i-th line and $x_{i,j}$ is the j-word in the i-th line. Please refer to (Yi et al., 2018b) for more details.

ory model (Yi et al., 2018b), which takes at most K preprocessed keywords as input. The encoder maps each word or line into vector representations, and the decoder generates each line word-by-word. The topic memory stores keywords explicitly and independently, which can learn a flexible order and form of keywords expression. The history memory and local memory are dynamically read and written to improve the context coherence of generated poems.

Genere Control. Chinese classical poetry involves various genres, and each genre strictly defines the structural and phonological pattern of a poem, such as the length of each line, the tone of each word, and the number of lines. We use our designed genre embedding (Yi et al., 2018b) to disentangle the semantic content and the genre pattern. The genre embedding indicates the line length, word tone, and rhyme, which is fed to the decoder. By this way, we can train one model with all genres of poems and control the genre of generated poems by specifying a pattern.

Training patterns are automatically extracted from the corpus. For generating, we make the genre as a user option. However, the selection of rhyme may be difficult for users without relevant literature knowledge. Therefore, we train a classifier (implemented with a feedforward neural network) to predict an appropriate rhyme in terms of the keywords.

Unsupervised Style Control. Besides genres, there are also diverse styles in Chinese poetry such as *battlefield*, *romantic*, *pastoral*, etc. For certain contents or topics, creating different styles of poetry is one main user requirement. Since the labelled data is quite rare and expensive, we use our proposed style disentanglement model (Yang et al., 2018) to achieve unsupervised style control. This method disentangles the style space into M different sub-spaces by maximizing the mutual information between the style distribution and the generated poetry distribution.

It is noteworthy that this method is transparent to model structures which can be applied to any generation model. In this stage, we employ it for the generation of Chinese quatrain poetry (*Jueju*), which will be extended to more genres in the future. We set the number of styles $M = 10$. After training, we manually annotate each style with some descriptive phrases, such as *sorrow during drinking* and *rural scenes*, to indicate the theme of the corresponding style. The style selection is also set as a user option.

Acrostic Poetry Generation In Chinese poetry, there is another special genre called acrostic poetry. Given a sequence of words $seq = (x_{0,0}, x_{1,0}, \cdots, x_{n,0})$, which could be someone's name or a blessing sentence, the author is required to create a poem using each word $x_{i,0}$ as the first word of each line x_i and the created poem should also conform to the genre pattern and convey proper semantic meanings.

The input for this genre is the sequence seq. As our generation module takes keywords as input, we first use pre-trained word2vec embeddings (Mikolov et al., 2013) to get K keywords related to seq according to the cosine distance of each keyword and the words in seq. Then we directly feed each $x_{i,0}$ into the decoder at the first step.

To alleviate the disfluency caused by this constraint, we generate the second word with the conditional probability: $p_{gen}(x_{i,1}|x_{i,0}) = p_{dec}(x_{i,1}|x_{i,0}) + \delta * p_{lm}(x_{i,1}|x_{i,0})$, where p_{dec} and p_{lm} are probability distributions of the decoder and a neural language model respectively.

If the length of the input sequence is less than n (the number of lines in a poem), we also use the language model to extend it to n words.

2.4 Postprocessing Module

Jiuge takes a line-to-line generation schema and generates each line with beam search (beam size=B). As a result, we can get B candidates for each line. We design a postprocessing module to automatically check and re-rank these candidates, and then select the best one, which is used for the generation of subsequent lines in a poem.

Pattern Checking. The genre embedding introduced in Sec. 2.3 cannot guarantee that generated poems perfectly adhere to required patterns. Thus, we further remove the invalid candidates according to the specified length, rhythm, and rhyme.

Re-Ranking. Our preliminary experiments show that the best candidate may not be ranked as the top 1 because the training objective is Maximum Likelihood Estimation (MLE), which tends to give the generic and meaningless candidates lower costs (Yi et al., 2018a). To automatically select the best candidate, we adopt the automatic rewarders we proposed in (Yi et al., 2018a), including a fluency rewarder, a context coherence rewarder, and a meaningfulness rewarder. Then the candidate with the highest weighted-average rewards given by them will be selected.

2.5 Collaborative Revision Module

We call the poem generated by the generation module in one pass the draft, since the user may revise it for several times to collaboratively create a satisfying poem together with the machine. We implement such collaboration with a revision module.

Revision Modes. Define a n-line poem draft as $X = (x_1, x_2, \cdots, x_n)$, and each line containing l_i words as $x_i = (x_{i,1}, x_{i,2}, ..., x_{i,l_i})$. At every turn, the user can revise one word in the draft. Then the revision module returns the revision information to the generation module which updates the draft according to the revised word. We implement three revision modes in terms of the updating way: *static*, *local dynamic*, and *global dynamic*.

- **Static updating mode.** The revision is required to meet the phonological pattern of the draft and the draft will not be updated except the revised word. The rhythm and rhyme information is given to the user together with the generated draft and the invalid revision will be alerted. During the beam search process, we also store top 10 candidate words in each position as recommendations.

- **Local dynamic updating mode.** If the user revises word $x_{i,j}$, then Jiuge will re-generate the succeeding subsequence, $x_{i,j+1}, \cdots, x_{i,l_i}$, in the i-th line by feeding the revised word to the decoder for the revised position.

- **Global dynamic updating mode.**

If the user revises word $x_{i,j}$, Jiuge will re-generate all succeeding words, $x_{i,j+1}, \cdots, x_{i,l_i}, \cdots, x_{n,l_n}$. In terms of the revision position, e.g., the rhymed positions, a new phonological pattern may be adopted.

Thanks to this collaborative revision-updating process, the user can choose a mode and gradually revise the draft until she/he feels satisfied.

Automatic Reference Recommendation. For poetry writing beginners or these lacking professional knowledge, it is hard to revise the draft appropriately. To aid in the revision process, we implement an automatic recommendation component. This component searches several human-authored poems, which are semantically similar to the generated draft, for the user as references. Then the user could decide how to make revision with these references.

In detail, define a n-line human-created poem as $Y = (y_1, \cdots, y_n)$ and a relevance scoring function as $rel(x_i, y_i)$ to give the relevance of two lines. Then we return N poems with the highest relevance score $rs(X, Y)$, calculated as:

$$rs(X,Y) = \sum_{i=1}^{n} rel(x_i, y_i) + \gamma * I(Y \in D_{master}), \quad (4)$$

where D_{master} is a poetry set of masterpieces, I is the indicator function, and the hyper-parameter γ is specified to balance the quality and relevance of searched poems. For more details of the relevance scoring function, we refer the reader to our previous work (Liang et al., 2018).

3 Demonstration

We implement a webpage version of Jiuge[6] which allows users to create diverse poems and share with the others conveniently. The initial page provides some basic options: multi-modal input and the selection of genre and style, as shown in Fig. 4.

Jiuge is easy to use. After selecting the input mode and providing corresponding content, the user can further choose a favourite genre and style[7]. As shown in Fig. 5 (a), the user inputs two keywords, *desert* and *cavalry*, and chooses to generate a quatrain with the normal style. Then the user clicks the "Generate Poetry" button. After a few seconds, the system returns the processed keywords and a poem draft.

---

[6]Our system is available at https://jiuge.thunlp.cn/.

[7]Temporarily only the Jueju genre supports multiple styles.

Figure 4: The initial page of Jiuge System.

In order to help the user collaboratively revise the generated poem, Jiuge provides some high-quality human-authored poems which are semantically similar to the generated one, as the references. The user can click the button to change the references. At this time, the user can select an unsatisfying word to be revised in the draft and then Jiuge will give some recommended revision candidates. Besides these candidates, other choices are also allowed. After selecting the revision mode introduced in Sec. 2.5, Jiuge will update or re-generate the draft according to the revised word. Through several turns of collaborative revision, the user and Jiuge work together to create a satisfying poem, as in Fig. 5 (b)[8].

In addition, Jiuge also supports picture sharing. By clicking the "Share Poetry" button, Jiuge will print the created poem on a beautiful picture so that the user can share it with others.

4 Conclusion and Future Work

We demonstrate *Jiuge*, a human-machine collaborative Chinese classical poetry generation system. Our system accepts multi-modal input and allows deep user participation in the choice of various styles and genres, as well as in collaborative revision. With an easy-to-use web interface, the user can collaboratively create a satisfying poem together with the system. Instead of being a simple entertainment software, Jiuge takes a step towards professional AI assistant for poetic education.

We collect a large number of human usage records from the interface, laying the foundation for enhancing the collaborative creation method in the future. We will also continue to integrate

---

[8]The poems in Fig.5 are manually translated for better demonstration. In practice, we utilize a neural translation model to conduct automatic translation.

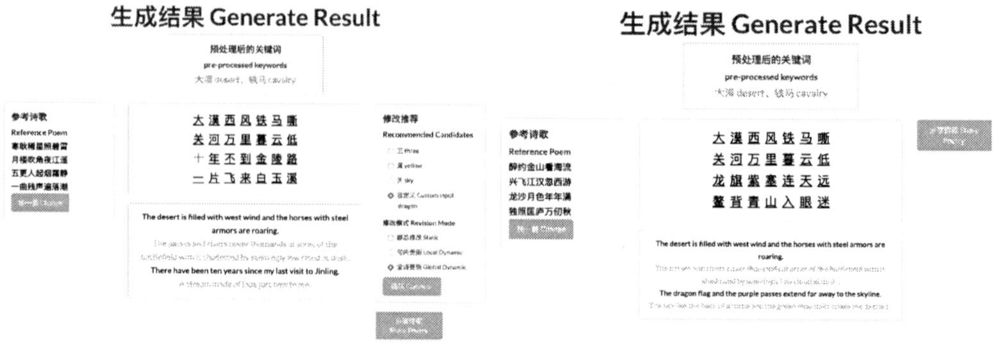

(a)　　　　(b)

Figure 5: The collaborative creation page: an example of revision. (a) The poem draft generated in one pass. (b) The poem after four turns of revision and updating.

more styles and extend the collaborative creation to more genres.

5 Acknowledgements

We would like to thank Cunchao Tu, Yunqiu Shao and anonymous reviewers for their insightful comments. It is supported by Natural Science Foundation of China (NSFC) Grant 61532001 and the NExT++ project, the National Research Foundation, Prime Ministers Office, Singapore under its IRC@Singapore Funding Initiative.

References

Zhongguo Li and Maosong Sun. 2009. Punctuation as implicit annotations for chinese word segmentation. computational linguistics. *Computational Linguistics*, 35(4):505–512,.

Jiannan Liang, Maosong Sun, Xiaoyuan Yi, Cheng Yang, Huimin Chen, and Zhenghao Liu. 2018. Neural network-based jiju poetry generation. In *Proceedings of the Seventeenth China National Conference on Computational Linguistics*, Changsha, China.

Rada Mihalcea and Paul Tarau. 2004. Textrank: Bringing order into text. In *Proceedings of the 2004 Conference on Empirical Methods in Natural Language Processing*.

Tomas Mikolov, Kai Chen, Greg Corrado, and Jeffrey Dean. 2013. Efficient estimation of word representations in vector space. *arXiv preprint arXiv:1301.3781*.

Zhe Wang, Wei He, Hua Wu nad Haiyang Wu, Wei Li, Haifeng Wang, and Enhong Chen. 2016. Chinese poetry generation with planning based neural network. In *Proceedings of COLING 2016, the 26th International Conference on Computational Linguistics:Technical Papers*, pages 1051–1060, Osaka, Japan.

Rui Yan. 2016. i,poet:automatic poetry composition through recurrent neural networks with iterative polishing schema. In *Proceedings of the Twenty-Fifth International Joint Conference on Artificial Intelligence*, pages 2238–2244, New York, USA.

Cheng Yang, Maosong Sun, Xiaoyuan Yi, and Wenhao Li. 2018. Stylistic chinese poetry generation via unsupervised style disentanglement. In *Proceedings of the 2018 Conference on Empirical Methods in Natural Language Processing*, pages 3960–3969, Brussels, Belgium.

Xiaoyuan Yi, Ruoyu Li, and Maosong Sun. 2017. Generating chinese plassical poems with rnn encoder-decoder. In *Proceedings of the Sixteenth Chinese Computational Linguistics*, pages 211–223, Nanjing, China.

Xiaoyuan Yi, Maosong Sun, Ruoyu Li, and Wenhao Li. 2018a. Automatic poetry generation with mutual reinforcement learning. In *Proceedings of the 2018 Conference on Empirical Methods in Natural Language Processing*, pages 3143–3153, Brussels, Belgium.

Xiaoyuan Yi, Maosong Sun, Ruoyu Li, and Zonghan Yang. 2018b. Chinese poetry generation with a working memory mode. In *Proceedings of the Twenty-Seventh International Joint Conference on Artificial Intelligence*, pages 4553–4559, Stockholm, Sweden.

Jiyuan Zhang, Yang Feng, Dong Wang, Yang Wang, Andrew Abel, Shiyue Zhang, and Andi Zhang. 2017. Flexible and creative chinese poetry generation using neural memory. In *Proceedings of the 55th Annual Meeting of the Association for Computational Linguistics*, pages 1364–1373. Association for Computational Linguistics.

Xingxing Zhang and Mirella Lapata. 2014. Chinese poetry generation with recurrent neural networks. In *Proceedings of the 2014 Conference on Empirical Methods in Natural Language Processing*, pages 670–680, Doha, Qatar.

Rapid Customization for Event Extraction

Yee Seng Chan, Joshua Fasching, Haoling Qiu, and **Bonan Min**
Raytheon BBN Technologies, Cambridge, Massachusetts
{yeeseng.chan, joshua.fasching}@raytheon.com
{haoling.qiu, bonan.min}@raytheon.com

Abstract

Extracting events in the form of *who* is involved in *what* at *when* and *where* from text, is one of the core information extraction tasks that has many applications such as web search and question answering. We present a system for rapidly customizing event extraction capability to find new event types (*what* happened) and their arguments (*who, when, and where*). To enable extracting events of new types, we develop a novel approach to allow a user to find, expand and filter event triggers by exploring an unannotated development corpus. The system will then generate mention-level event annotation automatically and train a neural network model for finding the corresponding events. To enable extracting arguments for new event types, the system makes novel use of the ACE annotation dataset to train a generic argument attachment model for extracting *Actor, Place,* and *Time*. We demonstrate that with less than 10 minutes of human effort per event type, the system achieves good performance for 67 novel event types. Experiments also show that the generic argument attachment model performs well on the novel event types. Our system (code, UI, documentation, demonstration video) is released as open source.[1]

1 Introduction

Event extraction is the task of identifying events of interest with associated participating arguments in text. For instance, given the following sentence:
S1: 21 people were wounded in Tuesday's southern Philippines airport blast.

Event extraction aims to recognize the two events (Injury and Attack), *triggered* by the words "wounded" and "blast" respectively. We also recognize that "21 people" and "airport" take on the event argument roles *Actor(s)* involved and *Place* respectively.

[1]github.com/BBN-E/Rapid-customization-events-acl19

For event trigger and argument extraction, state-of-the-art approaches employ supervised machine learning methods. These methods assume a predefined event ontology and learn from a corpus of manually labeled examples that are specific to that ontology. For instance, the popular Automatic Content Extraction (ACE) (Doddington et al., 2004) corpus contains 599 documents manually annotated with examples for 33 event types, such as *Attack* and *Justice* events.

However, producing such type-specific examples is labor intensive. To extract triggers and arguments of a new event type, one needs to annotate a large amount of training examples specific to that new event type. For instance, ACE provides event-type specific argument annotations, such as *Attacker* for *Attack* events. This prevents existing event argument examples from being useful towards extracting participants of new event types, as initially defined.

In this paper, we present a system that facilitates rapid extension of extraction capabilities to a large number of novel event types. We summarize the contributions of this paper as follows:

- We present an approach to rapidly gather event trigger examples for *new* event types, with minimal human effort.
- We develop a User Interface (UI) to further expedite and improve the time efficiency of our approach.
- For event arguments, we show how to leverage annotations of *existing* event types and argument roles, to train a classifier that extracts event arguments such as *Actor* (*who* is involved), *Place* (*where* it happened) and *Time* (*when* it happened) for the *new* event types.
- We demonstrate the practical utility of our approach by applying it on a set of 67 novel event types.

Proceedings of the 57th Annual Meeting of the Association for Computational Linguistics-System Demonstrations, pages 31–36
Florence, Italy, July 28 - August 2, 2019. ©2019 Association for Computational Linguistics

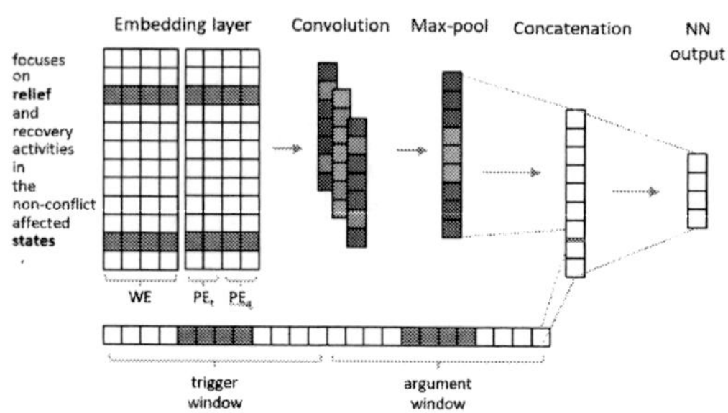

Figure 1: A user interface that allows a user to provide, expand, and filter event triggers for new types. A demonstration video is available on github.com/BBN-E/Rapid-customization-events-acl19.

We first describe the task of event extraction in the next section. In Section 3, we describe our extraction model, how we leverage our UI to rapidly gather event trigger examples for new event types, and how to extract event arguments for new event types. We present experiment results in Section 4. We discuss related work in Section 5 before concluding in Section 6.

2 Problem Definition

We focus on the problem of *rapid customization of event extractors* for new event types where we don't have a large amount of hand-labeled data available. Given an English sentence, we perform event extraction using a two-stage process:

- Trigger classification: Labeling words in the sentence with their predicted event type (if any). For instance, in sentence S1, the extraction system should label "wounded" as a trigger of an Injury event, and label "blast" as a trigger of an Attack event.
- Argument classification: If a sentence contains predicted event triggers $\{t_i\}$, we pair each t_i with each entity and time mention $\{m_j\}$ in the sentence to generate candidate event arguments. Given a candidate event argument (t_i, m_j), the system predicts its associated event role (if any). For instance, given ("wounded", "airport"), the system should predict the event role *Place*.

3 Approach

3.1 A Convolutional Neural Network Model for Event Extraction

We developed a convolution neural network (CNN) model to perform event trigger classification, and another CNN model for event argument classification used with our novel trigger and argument example collection approaches. Both CNN

Figure 2: A CNN based model for event argument classification. WE is word embeddings. PE_t and PE_a are position embeddings, capturing a token's distance to the candidate trigger and argument respectively. These position embeddings are randomly initialized and learnt during training.

models are very similar, with the argument model incorporating more features. Hence, we will describe the argument model in detail, then provide a summary of the trigger model.

As shown in Figure 2, the argument model consists of (1) an embedding layer to encode words and word positions in the sentence, (2) a convolution and max pooling layer to generate high-level features from the embedding representation of the sentence, (3) a layer which concatenates the max pool layer and local context window around the candidate trigger and argument, (4) followed by the softmax function for classifying the example into one of the target classes.

For argument classification, the input is a sentence in which a trigger word and a candidate event argument is identified, e.g. ("relief", "states") in Figure 2.

Embedding Layer encodes each word with:

- Word embeddings (WE): Given an input sentence $\mathbf{x}$ of length t, we first transform each word into a real-valued vector of dimension d_1 by looking up a word embedding matrix $W^1 \in R^{d_1 \times |V|}$, where V is the vocabulary. We use word embeddings trained by Baroni et al. (2014), which achieved state-of-the-art results in a variety of NLP tasks.

- Position embeddings (PE): PE_t encodes the relative distance of each word to the trigger word as a real-valued vector of dimension d_2 by a embedding matrix $W^2 \in R^{d_2 \times |D|}$, where D is the set of relative distances in a dataset. W^2 is randomly initialized and learnt during training. We similarly use PE_a to encode relative distances to the candidate argument, by defining $W^3 \in R^{d_3 \times |D|}$.

The final embedding dimension for each token is $n_1 = (d_1 + d_2 + d_3)$. This layer produces an embedding representation $\mathbf{x}^{(1)} \in R^{n_1 \times t}$ when fed with an input sentence $\mathbf{x}^{(0)} = \mathbf{x}$.

Convolution and Max Pooling Layer: We use a set of filters with different window sizes to capture important n-gram features from an input sentence. Due to space constraints, we omit the definitions of the convolution and max pool layers. We denote the max pool layer using a fixed-sized feature vector $\mathbf{x}^{(2)} \in R^{n_2}$, where n_2 is the total number of filters.

Concatenate Layer: We select the word embeddings of the trigger, the candidate argument, and their local windows. We define the window surrounding a word, as the $k=3$ tokens to the left and right of the word. We concatenate these embeddings to the max pool layer, to obtain a concatenated vector $\mathbf{x}^{(?)}$.

Event Argument Classification: We have $\mathbf{o} = W^{(3)}\mathbf{x}^{(3)} + \mathbf{b}^{(3)}$, where $W^{(3)}$ and $\mathbf{b}^{(3)}$ are parameters learnt in this layer. Here, $\mathbf{o} \in R^{n_3}$, where n_3 is equal to the number of event argument roles including the "NONE" label for candidate arguments which are not actual event arguments to the trigger. Given an input example $\mathbf{x}$, our network with parameters θ outputs the vector $\mathbf{o}$, where the i-th component contains the score for event role i. To obtain the conditional probability $p(i|\mathbf{x}, \theta)$, we apply softmax:

$$p(i|\mathbf{x}, \theta) = \frac{e^{o_i}}{\sum_j e^{o_j}} \qquad (1)$$

The CNN for trigger classification is largely the same as the above CNN for argument classification, omitting just the argument associated features, i.e. PE_a and the argument window shown at the bottom of Figure 2. The input is a sentence in which a word is the candidate trigger word, e.g. "relief" in Figure 2. The output is a softmax function predicting one of the event type or *NONE*, indicating the candidate word is not a valid trigger for any of the event types.

3.2 Rapid Customization for Event Trigger Extraction

Our system enables rapidly gathering of event trigger examples for new event types with minimal human effort, aided by the UI shown in Figure 1, using this work flow:

- Given a new target event type, the user first provides some initial keywords. The UI (backed by an unannotated text corpus) presents up to 3 text snippets (sentences) mentioning each trigger.
- The user can then easily gather additional discriminative keywords using the UI via interactive search. By clicking on the "Find similar" button in each pane, the system will suggest new event keywords that are similar to the current set of keywords, displaying these suggested keywords in the working pane on the left of the UI. Our system suggests new keywords using WordNet hyponyms and cosine similarity in a word embedding space.
- The user can then repeat this process for additional event types. This can be seen in Figure 1, where each pane (column) shows an event type name at the top, followed by event triggers (in red) and text snippets (clickable to expand to full sentence) mentioning these triggers.
- The user can edit between event types by drag and drop, moving a trigger or snippet from one event to another. The user can also click on "−" to remove an event, a trigger with its snippets, or just a snippet. The user can also click on the "More" button to the right of each trigger, to display additional text snippets containing the trigger.
- When the user is satisfied with the current set of keywords and associated text snippets, our system then performs distant supervision (Mintz et al., 2009) by using the occurrences of these keywords (their associated text snippets) as event trigger examples for the new event type.

In practice, over a set of 67 new event types described in Section 4.2, the user spent an average of 4.5 minutes to provide 8.6 initial triggers and associated text snippets. Then another 5 minutes interacting with the UI to expand and filter the triggers, for a total of less than 10 minutes per event type.

3.3 Argument Extraction for New Events

Current argument examples, such as those defined in ACE, are event type specific. For instance, the ACE corpus annotates Agent and Victim arguments for Injure events, Attacker and Target arguments for Attack events, etc. To decode event arguments for new event types, one need to annotate new event type specific argument examples as training data.

In this paper, we propose a simple approach to learn a *generic* event argument model to extract Actor, Place, and Time arguments for *any new* event types, without annotating new examples. We define Actor as a coarse-grained event argument role, encompassing Agent-like and Patient-like event roles. We map Actor-*like* argument roles in ACE to a common Actor role label, and use the Place and Time arguments in as they appear in ACE. The complete list of ACE event argument roles that we mapped to Actor are:

- Agent, Artifact, Adjudicator, Victim, Buyer, Seller, Giver, Recipient, Org, Attacker, Target, Entity, Defendant, Person, Plaintiff, Prosecutor

Using the above mapping approach, we train a *generic* event argument classifier that can extract Actor, Place, and Time arguments for any event type.

4 Experiments

4.1 Verifying Event Extraction Model

We first conduct experiments to verify that our CNN model implementation achieves comparable performance to state-of-the-art CNN-based event extraction systems (Chen et al., 2015; Boros, 2018) to ensure that it is suitable for use in our rapid event customization approach. Following these prior work, we use the ACE-2005 corpus, with the same sets of 529 training documents, 30 development documents, and 40 test documents. We use the same following criteria to judge the correctness of our event extractions: A trigger is correctly classified if its event subtype and offsets match those of a reference trigger; an argument is correct classified if its event subtype, event argument role, and offsets match any of the reference event arguments.

	$\mathcal{C}_{ds}$	$\mathcal{C}_{adj}$	$\mathcal{C}_{ds'}$	Dev	Test
#articles	818	618	618	274	273
#triggers	1674	1171	1258	643	752

Table 1: Counts of articles and trigger examples, in training corpora for distant supervision ($\mathcal{C}_{ds}$), distant supervision followed by human adjudication ($\mathcal{C}_{adj}$), and sampled distant supervision ($\mathcal{C}_{ds'}$), as well as corpora for development (Dev) and test (Test).

Since the ratio of positive (valid) vs negative examples is relatively skewed (for instance, most words in a sentence are not triggers), we tried different weights for the positive examples: 1, 3, 5, or 10. We tune this and other hyper-parameters (batch size, number of CNN filters, number of epochs) on the development documents. We also follow (Chen et al., 2015) by using the Adadelta update rule with parameters $\rho = 0.95$ and $\epsilon = 1e^{-6}$, and a dropout rate of 0.5. On the ACE test data, our trigger model achieves an F1 score of 0.65, close to the scores of 0.66 and 0.68 reported in (Chen et al., 2015) and (Boros, 2018) respectively. Our argument model using gold triggers[2] achieves an F1 score of 0.53, close to the score of 0.55 reported in (Boros, 2018).

4.2 Event Customization Evaluation

To evaluate the effectiveness of our event extraction system in customizing extractors for new event types, we present experiment results based on the Common Core Ontologies[3] (CCO). CCO comprises 11 ontologies and is aimed at representing semantics for many domains of interests. We sampled 67 event types that are not in existing event schemas (such as ACE and TAC-KBP[4]), to evaluate how well our system does on novel event types. As our experiment corpus $\mathcal{C}$, we use 6,000 allafrica.com news articles, published between 2016-2017.

4.2.1 Trigger Classification

Given the set of 67 new event types, we leverage our UI to obtain a set of keywords that are associated with about 3,000 trigger examples spanning 1,365 articles. We split these examples at the article level via a 60/20/20 train/development/test split. We show the statistics of our data in Table 1. We then trained the following models:

- We trained a trigger model T_{ds} using the 1,674 training examples $\mathcal{C}_{ds}$. Note that $\mathcal{C}_{ds}$

---

[2]Since comparisons using predicted triggers obfuscate event argument performance.

[3]https://github.com/CommonCoreOntology

[4]https://tac.nist.gov/2017/KBP/Event/index.html

Type	Triggers
Ceremony	celebration, ceremony, parade, commemoration, feast, ...
Criminal Act	abduction, assassin, assault, bandit, blackmail, bribery, ...
Cyber Attack	botnet, cyber attack, cyber war, cyber warfare, cybercrime, ...
Espionage	espionage, infiltrate, infiltrator, mole, saboteur, spy

Table 2: Sample triggers for some CCO event types.

	Precision	Recall	F1
T_{ds}	0.69	0.50	0.58
T_{adj}	0.69	0.46	0.55
$T_{ds'}$	0.62	0.40	0.48

Table 3: Event trigger results on new CCO event types.

Model	Overall			F1		
	P	R	F1	Actor	Place	Time
A_{gen}	0.65	0.41	0.50	0.49	0.37	0.61
A_{out}	0.41	0.62	0.49	0.49	0.45	0.62

Table 4: Event argument results using gold triggers.

consists of distant supervised (DS) trigger examples which are potentially noisy.

- We adjudicated $\mathcal{C}_{ds}$, obtaining a smaller set of 1,171 trigger examples $\mathcal{C}_{adj}$, which we used to train a trigger model T_{adj}.

Table 2 shows examples of triggers identified by our in-house developer for sampled CCO events. When evaluated on the test examples, T_{ds} and T_{adj} achieve F1 scores of 0.58 and 0.55 respectively (shown in Table 3).

The impact of corpora size Surprisingly, the DS model T_{ds} (trained on the noisy distance supervised $\mathcal{C}_{ds}$) performs better than the model T_{adj} (trained on the manually adjudicated $\mathcal{C}_{adj}$). One possible explanation is because $\mathcal{C}_{adj}$ is a subset of $\mathcal{C}_{ds}$ and contains significantly fewer examples, since only trigger examples that are judged to be correct for the event types are kept.

Table 1 shows that $\mathcal{C}_{adj}$ contains substantially fewer examples than $\mathcal{C}_{ds}$ (1,171 vs 1,674). To verify that the larger number of training examples is a reason for T_{ds}'s higher performance, we randomly down-sampled $\mathcal{C}_{ds}$ to have the same number of documents as $\mathcal{C}_{adj}$. Using the resulting $\mathcal{C}_{ds'}$, we trained the trigger model $T_{ds'}$. When evaluated on the test data, this obtains a F1 score of 0.48, which is indeed worse than T_{adj} as expected, thus confirming our hypothesized explanation. We show these results in Table 3.

4.2.2 Argument Extraction

We apply the mapping approach described in Section 3.3 on the ACE data. We learn a *generic* argument model A_{gen} on the mapped training data, obtaining a F1 score of 0.50 when evaluated on the mapped ACE test data (Table 4). For comparison, we also trained a model using the original ACE event roles in the standard way, but report results after mapping predicted and reference roles to a common Actor role. We obtained a similar test F1 score of 0.50.

We note that A_{gen} trains on the entire ACE training data. However, the motivation for the mapping is to learn an argument model for decoding on new event types not previously seen in its training data. Hence, we conduct an additional set of leave-1-out experiments A_{out}. ACE defines event types at a coarse-grained (8 types) and a fine-grained (33 types) level. Hence in each fold i, we omit argument examples associated with a coarse-grained ACE event type i from training, then proceed to calculate performance on just argument test examples associated with event type i. We aggregate the test results over all folds in row A_{out} of Table 4. We note that A_{out} achieves reasonable performance when compared against A_{gen}, demonstrating the viability of our approach towards extracting event arguments for previously unseen new event types.

Using T_{ds} and A_{gen} as the trigger and argument models, we decoded on our CCO test data. Of a set of randomly selected 78 Actor, 8 Place, and 14 Time arguments predicted by A_{gen}, we determine that 62 Actor, 7 Place, and 10 Time arguments are correctly predicted, for an overall precision of 0.79.

5 Related Work

Recent event extraction work usually employ neural network (NN) models, such as CNN-based models (Chen et al., 2015; Boros, 2018) and joint event extraction using recurrent neural networks (Nguyen et al., 2016a).

In event extraction using limited training data, Nguyen et al. (2016b) proposed a two-stage NN model for event type extension. Given a new event type with a small set of seed examples, they leverage examples from other event types. In another work, Peng et al. (2016) developed a minimally supervised approach to event trigger extraction by leveraging trigger examples gathered from the ACE annotation guidelines. Ferrero et al. (2017) presented InToEventS, an interactive tool for building event schemas. Their work differs from ours in several important aspects. Their tool produces schemas (triggers and role patterns) of events based on clusters, whereas our tool allows users to rapidly produce event trigger examples. Our tool also allows these examples to be adjudicated, allows multiple event types to be examined in parallel in the same UI, and triggers (or snippets) to be shifted across different event types. Finally, we demonstrate a viable approach for extracting Actor, Place, and Time arguments of new event types without any additional annotation effort.

A closely related direction is rapid customization of systems for other information extraction (IE) tasks. The ICE system (He and Grishman, 2015) allows a user to interactively create new classes of entities and relations. The main ideas are user-in-the-loop entity set expansion and boostrap learning for relation extraction. The WIZIE (Li et al., 2012) system guides users to write rules for IE. Finally, Michael and Akbik (2015) and Freedman et al. (2011) presented systems for interactively building relation extractors.

6 Conclusion and Future Work

We presented a system which allows a user to rapidly build event extractors to find new types of events and their arguments. We plan to use clustering techniques to automatically discover salient event trigger words in a new corpus, to further reduce human customization effort.

7 Acknowledgements

This work was supported by DARPA/I2O and U.S. Army Research Office Contract No. W911NF-18-C-0003 under the World Modelers program. The views, opinions, and/or findings contained in this article are those of the author and should not be interpreted as representing the official views or policies, either expressed or implied, of the Department of Defense or the U.S. Government. This document does not contain technology or technical data controlled under either the U.S. International Traffic in Arms Regulations or the U.S. Export Administration Regulations.

References

Marco Baroni, Georgiana Dinu, and German Kruszewski. 2014. Don't count, predict! a systematic comparison of context-counting vs. context-predicting semantic vectors. In *ACL-2014*, pages 238–247.

Emanuela Boros. 2018. *Neural Methods for Event Extraction*. Ph.D. thesis, Universite Paris-Saclay.

Yubo Chen, Liheng Xu, Kang Liu, Daojian Zeng, and Jun Zhao. 2015. Event extraction via dynamic multi-pooling convolutional neural networks. In *ACL-IJCNLP2-2015*, pages 167–176.

George R. Doddington, Alexis Mitchell, Mark A. Przybocki, Lance A. Ramshaw, Stephanie M. Strassel, and Ralph M. Weischedel. 2004. The automatic content extraction (ace) program - tasks, data, and evaluation. In *LREC*.

German Ferrero, Audi Primadhanty, and Ariadna Quattoni. 2017. InToEventS: an interactive toolkit for discovering and building event schemas. In *EACL Software Demonstrations*.

Marjorie Freedman, Lance Ramshaw, Elizabeth Boschee, Ryan Gabbard, Gary Kratkiewicz, Nicolas Ward, and Ralph Weishedel. 2011. Extreme extraction: machine reading in a week. In *EMNLP*.

Yifan He and Ralph Grishman. 2015. ICE: Rapid Information Extraction Customization for NLP Novices. In *NAACL-D-2015*, pages 31–35.

Yunyao Li, Laura Chiticariu, Huahai Yang, Frederick Reiss, and Arnaldo Carreno-fuentes. 2012. Wizie: A best practices guided development environment for information extraction. In *ACL-SD-2012*, pages 109–114.

Thilo Michael and Alan Akbik. 2015. A web toolkit for exploratory relation extraction. In *ACL-IJCNLP System Demonstration*.

Mike Mintz, Steven Bills, Rion Snow, and Daniel Jurafsky. 2009. Distant supervision for relation extraction without labeled data. In *ACL-IJCNLP*, pages 1003–1011.

Thien Huu Nguyen, Kyunghyun Cho, and Ralph Grishman. 2016a. Joint event extraction via recurrent neural networks. In *NAACL-HLT-2016*, pages 300–309.

Thien Huu Nguyen, Lisheng Fu, Kyunghyun Cho, and Ralph Grishman. 2016b. A two-stage approach for extending event detection to new types via neural networks. In *WRepL4NLP*, pages 158–165.

Haoruo Peng, Yangiu Song, and Dan Roth. 2016. Event detection and co-reference with minimal supervision. In *EMNLP-2016*.

A Multiscale Visualization of Attention in the Transformer Model

Jesse Vig
Palo Alto Research Center
3333 Coyote Hill Road
Palo Alto, CA 94304
`jesse.vig@parc.com`

Abstract

The Transformer is a sequence model that forgoes traditional recurrent architectures in favor of a fully attention-based approach. Besides improving performance, an advantage of using attention is that it can also help to interpret a model by showing how the model assigns weight to different input elements. However, the multi-layer, multi-head attention mechanism in the Transformer model can be difficult to decipher. To make the model more accessible, we introduce an open-source tool that visualizes attention at multiple scales, each of which provides a unique perspective on the attention mechanism. We demonstrate the tool on BERT and OpenAI GPT-2 and present three example use cases: detecting model bias, locating relevant attention heads, and linking neurons to model behavior.

1 Introduction

In 2018, the BERT (Bidirectional Encoder Representations from Transformers) language representation model achieved state-of-the-art performance across NLP tasks ranging from sentiment analysis to question answering (Devlin et al., 2018). Recently, the OpenAI GPT-2 (Generative Pretrained Transformer-2) model outperformed other models on several language modeling benchmarks in a zero-shot setting (Radford et al., 2019).

Underlying BERT and GPT-2 is the Transformer model, which uses a fully attention-based approach in contrast to traditional sequence models based on recurrent architectures (Vaswani et al., 2017). An advantage of using attention is that it can help interpret a model by showing how the model assigns weight to different input elements (Bahdanau et al., 2015; Belinkov and Glass, 2019), although its value in explaining individual predictions may be limited (Jain and Wallace, 2019). Various tools have been developed to visualize attention in NLP models, ranging from attention-matrix heatmaps (Bahdanau et al., 2015; Rush et al., 2015; Rocktäschel et al., 2016) to bipartite graph representations (Liu et al., 2018; Lee et al., 2017; Strobelt et al., 2018).

One challenge for visualizing attention in the Transformer is that it uses a multi-layer, multi-head attention mechanism, which produces different attention patterns for each layer and head. BERT-Large, for example, which has 24 layers and 16 heads, generates $24 \times 16 = 384$ unique attention structures for each input. Jones (2017) designed a visualization tool specifically for multi-head attention, which visualizes attention over multiple heads in a layer by superimposing their attention patterns (Vaswani et al., 2017, 2018).

In this paper, we extend the work of Jones (2017) by visualizing attention in the Transformer at multiple scales. We introduce a high-level *model view*, which visualizes all of the layers and attention heads in a single interface, and a low-level *neuron view*, which shows how individual neurons interact to produce attention. We also adapt the tool from the original encoder-decoder implementation to the decoder-only GPT-2 model and the encoder-only BERT model.

2 Visualization Tool

We now present a multiscale visualization tool for the Transformer model, available at `https://github.com/jessevig/bertviz`. The tool comprises three views: an attention-head view, a model view, and a neuron view. Below, we describe these views and demonstrate them on the GPT-2 and BERT models. We also present three use cases: detecting model bias, locating relevant attention heads, and linking neurons to model behavior. A video demonstration of the tool can be found at `https://vimeo.com/340841955`.

Proceedings of the 57th Annual Meeting of the Association for Computational Linguistics-System Demonstrations, pages 37–42
Florence, Italy, July 28 - August 2, 2019. ©2019 Association for Computational Linguistics

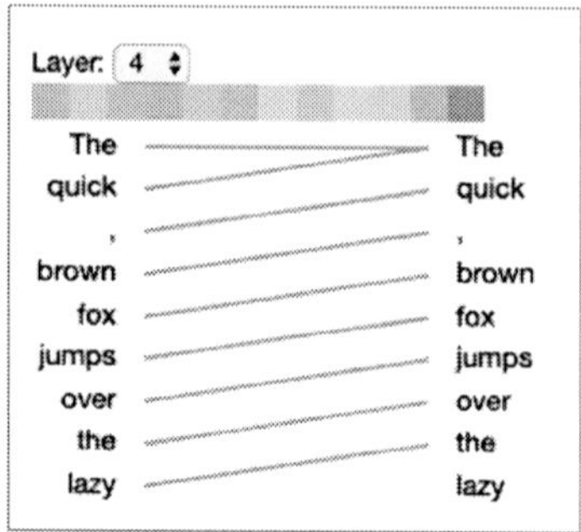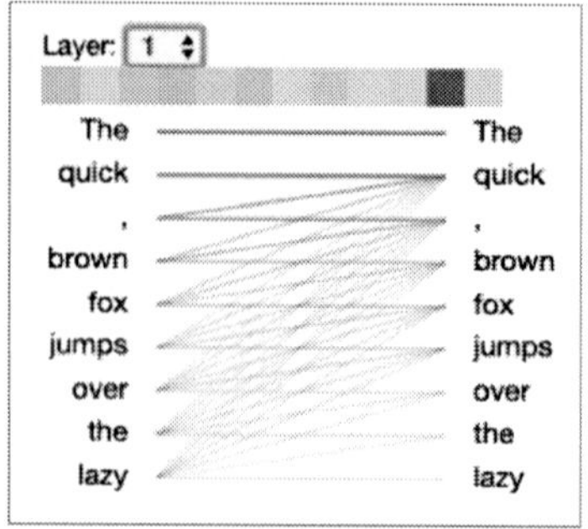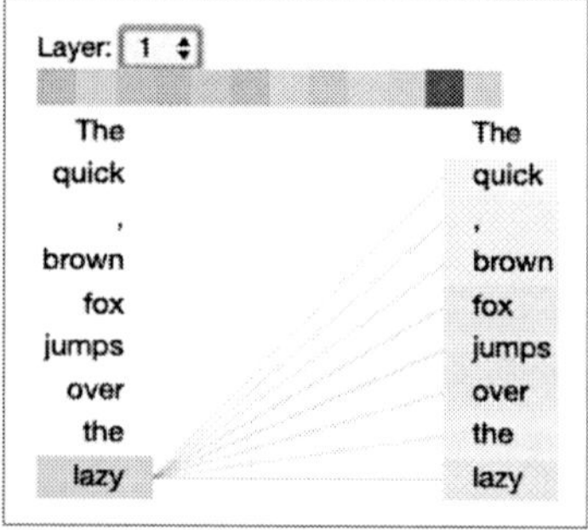

Figure 1: Attention-head view for GPT-2, for the input text *The quick, brown fox jumps over the lazy*. The left and center figures represent different layers / attention heads. The right figure depicts the same layer/head as the center figure, but with the token *lazy* selected.

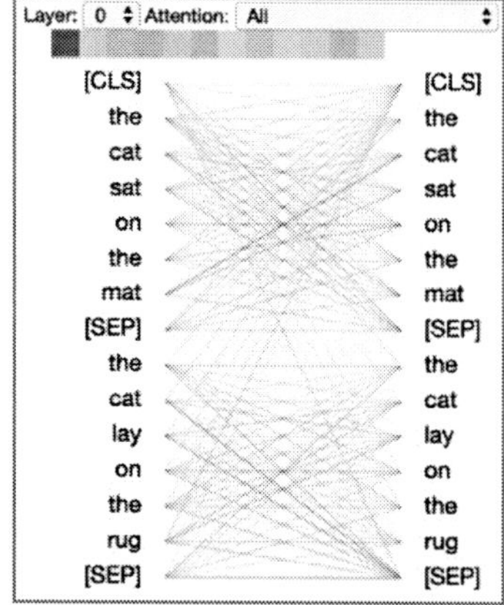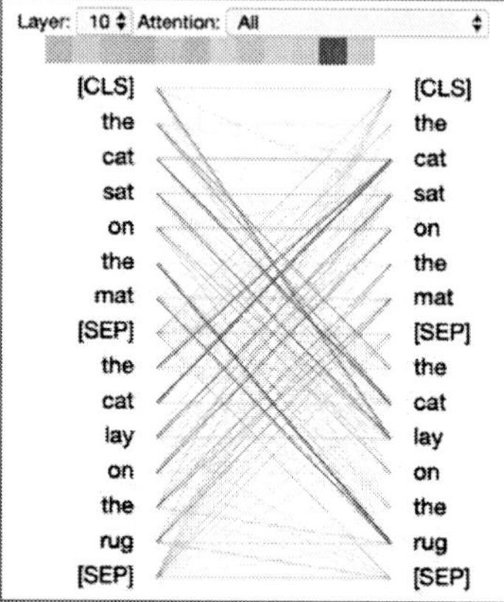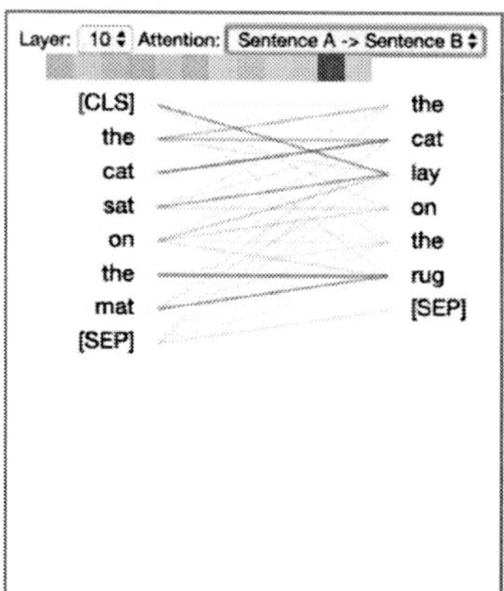

Figure 2: Attention-head view for BERT, for inputs *the cat sat on the mat* (Sentence A) and *the cat lay on the rug* (Sentence B). The left and center figures represent different layers / attention heads. The right figure depicts the same layer/head as the center figure, but with *Sentence A → Sentence B* filter selected.

2.1 Attention-head view

The *attention-head view* visualizes the attention patterns produced by one or more attention heads in a given layer, as shown in Figure 1 (GPT-2[1]) and Figure 2 (BERT[2]). This view closely follows the original implementation of Jones (2017), but has been adapted from the original encoder-decoder implementation to the encoder-only BERT and decoder-only GPT-2 models.

In this view, self-attention is represented as lines connecting the tokens that are attending (left) with the tokens being attended to (right). Colors identify the corresponding attention head(s), while line weight reflects the attention score. At the top of the screen, the user can select the layer and one or more attention heads (represented by the colored squares). Users may also filter attention by token, as shown in Figure 1 (right); in this case the target tokens are also highlighted and shaded based on attention weight. For BERT, which uses an explicit sentence-pair model, users may specify a sentence-level attention filter; for example, in Figure 2 (right), the user has selected the *Sentence A → Sentence B* filter, which only shows attention from tokens in Sentence *A* to tokens in Sentence *B*.

Since the attention heads do not share parameters, each head learns a unique attention mechanism. In the head shown in Figure 1 (left), for example, each word attends to the previous word in the sentence. The head in Figure 1 (center), in contrast, generates attention that is dispersed roughly evenly across previous words in the sentence (excluding the first word). Figure 2 shows attention heads for BERT that capture sentence-pair patterns, including a within-sentence pattern (left) and a between-sentence pattern (center).

---

[1] *GPT-2 small* pretrained model.

[2] *BERT-base, uncased* pretrained model.

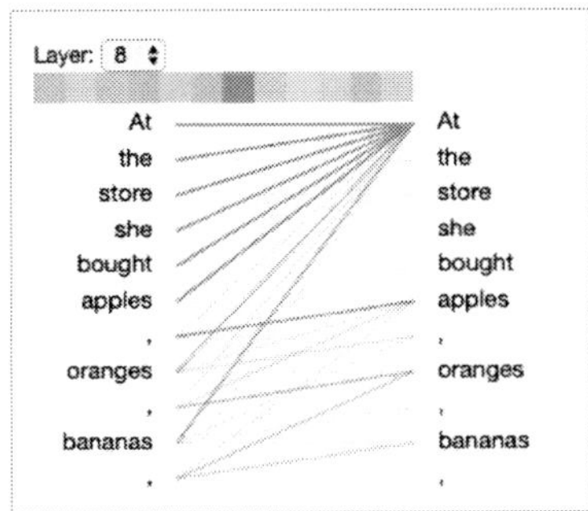
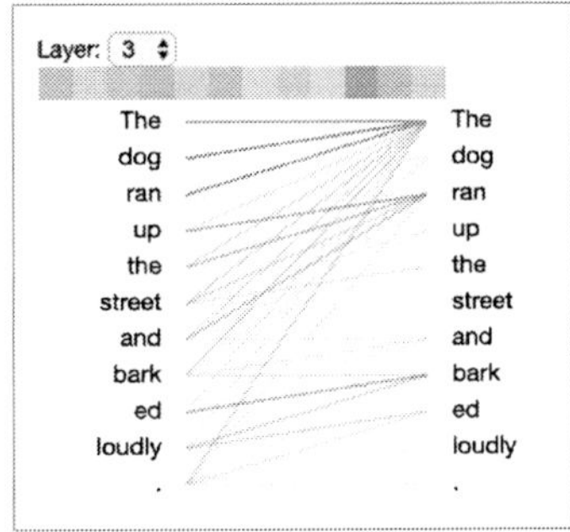
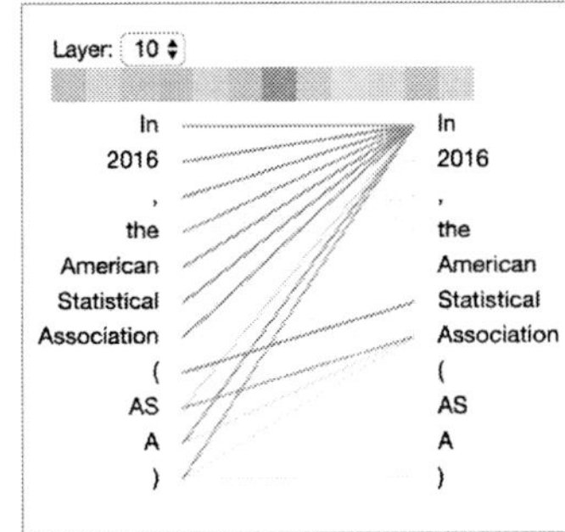

Figure 3: Examples of attention heads in GPT-2 that capture specific lexical patterns: list items (left); verbs (center); and acronyms (right). Similar patterns were observed in these attention heads for other inputs. Attention directed toward first token is likely null attention (Vig and Belinkov, 2019).

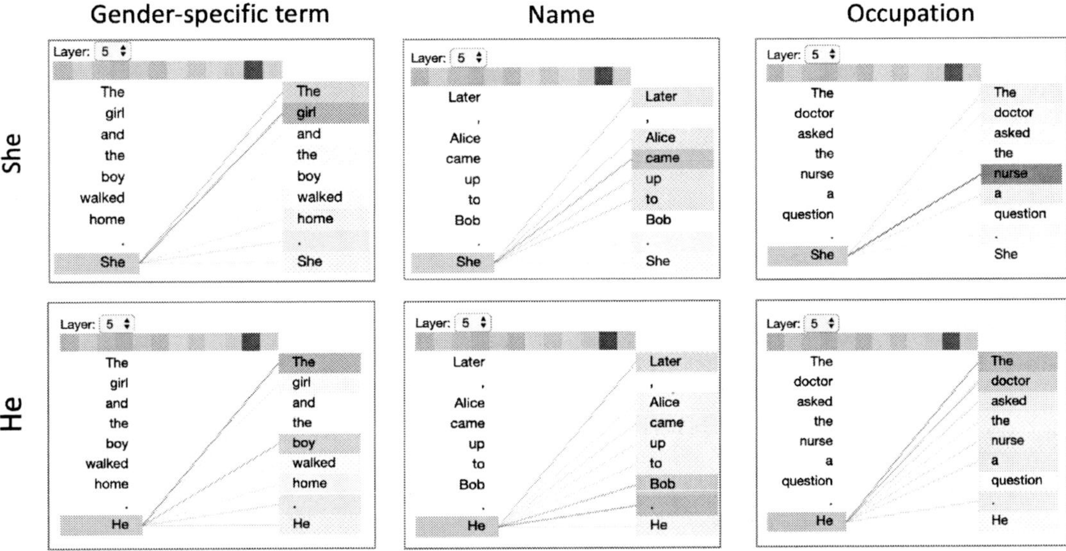

Figure 4: Attention pattern in GPT-2 related to coreference resolution suggests the model may encode gender bias.

Besides these coarse positional patterns, attention heads also capture specific lexical patterns, such as those as shown in Figure 3. Other attention heads detected named entities (people, places, companies), paired punctuation (quotes, brackets, parentheses), subject-verb pairs, and other syntactic and semantic relations. Recent work shows that attention in the Transformer correlates with syntactic constructs such as dependency relations and part-of-speech tags (Raganato and Tiedemann, 2018; Voita et al., 2019; Vig and Belinkov, 2019).

Use Case: Detecting Model Bias

One use case for the attention-head view is detecting bias in the model, which we illustrate for the case of conditional language generation using GPT-2. Consider the following continuations gen-

erated[3] from two input prompts that are identical except for the gender of the pronouns (generated text underlined):

- *The doctor asked the nurse a question. She said, "I'm not sure what you're talking about."*

- *The doctor asked the nurse a question. He asked her if she ever had a heart attack.*

In the first example, the model generates a continuation that implies *She* refers to *nurse*. In the second example, the model generates text that implies *He* refers to *doctor*. This suggests that the model's coreference mechanism may encode gender bias (Zhao et al., 2018; Lu et al., 2018). Figure 4 shows an attention head that appears to

---

[3]Using GPT-2 small model with greedy decoding.

perform coreference resolution based on the perceived gender of certain words. The two examples from above are shown in Figure 4 (right), which reveals that *She* strongly attends to *nurse*, while *He* attends more to *doctor*. By identifying a source of potential model bias, the tool could inform efforts to detect and control for this bias.

2.2 Model View

The *model view* (Figure 5) provides a birds-eye view of attention across all of the model's layers and heads for a particular input. Attention heads are presented in tabular form, with rows representing layers and columns representing heads. Each layer/head is visualized in a thumbnail form that conveys the coarse shape of the attention pattern, following the *small multiples* design pattern (Tufte, 1990). Users may also click on any head to enlarge it and see the tokens.

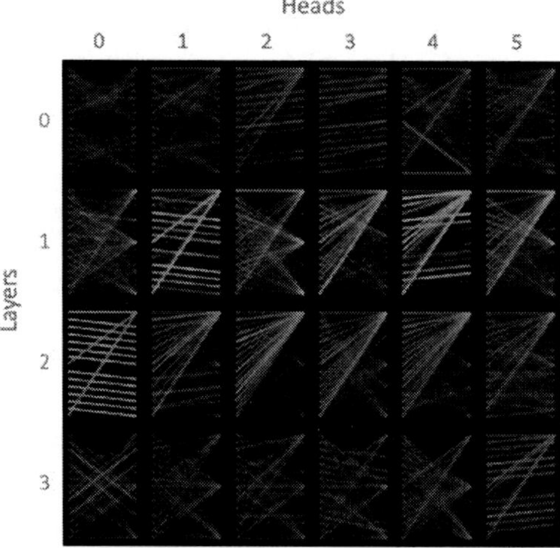

Figure 5: Model view of BERT, for same inputs as in Figure 2. Excludes layers 4–11 and heads 6–11.

The model view enables users to quickly browse the attention heads across all layers and to see how attention patterns evolve throughout the model.

Use Case: Locating Relevant Attention Heads
As discussed earlier, attention heads in BERT exhibit a broad range of behaviors, and some may be more relevant for model interpretation than others depending on the task. Consider the case of paraphrase detection, which seeks to determine if two input texts have the same meaning. For this task, it may be useful to know which words the model finds similar (or different) between the two sentences. Attention heads that draw connections

between input sentences would thus be highly relevant. The model view (Figure 5) makes it easy to find these inter-sentence patterns, which are recognizable by their cross-hatch shape (e.g., layer 3, head 0). These heads can be further explored by clicking on them or accessing the attention-head view, e.g., Figure 2 (center). This use case is described in greater detail in Vig (2019).

2.3 Neuron View

The *neuron view* (Figure 6) visualizes the individual neurons in the query and key vectors and shows how they interact to produce attention. Given a token selected by the user (left), this view traces the computation of attention from that token to the other tokens in the sequence (right).

Note that the Transformer uses scaled dot-product attention, where the attention distribution at position i in a sequence x is defined as follows:

$$\alpha_i = \text{softmax}\left(\frac{q_i \cdot k_1}{\sqrt{d}}, \frac{q_i \cdot k_2}{\sqrt{d}}, ..., \frac{q_i \cdot k_N}{\sqrt{d}}\right) \quad (1)$$

where q_i is the query vector at position i, k_j is the key vector at position j, and d is the dimension of k and q. $N=i$ for GPT-2 and $N=\text{len}(x)$ for BERT.[4] All values are specific to a particular layer / head.

The columns in the visualization are defined as follows:

- **Query q**: The query vector of the selected token that is paying attention.
- **Key k**: The key vector of each token receiving attention.
- **q×k (element-wise)**: The element-wise product of the query vector and each key vector. This shows how individual neurons contribute to the dot product (sum of element-wise product) and hence attention.
- **q · k**: The dot product of the selected token's query vector and each key vector.
- **Softmax**: The softmax of the scaled dot-product from previous column. This is the attention score.

Whereas the attention-head view and the model view show *what* attention patterns the model learns, the neuron view shows *how* the model forms these patterns. For example, it can help identify neurons responsible for specific attention patterns, as discussed in the following use case.

---

[4]GPT-2 only considers the context up to position i, while BERT considers the entire sequence.

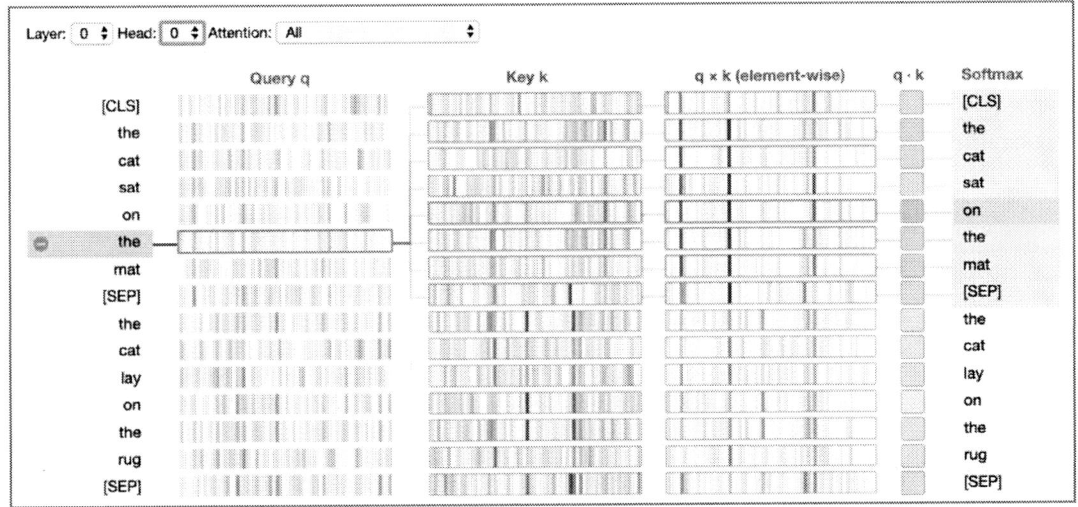

Figure 6: Neuron view of BERT for layer 0, head 0 (same one depicted in Figure 2, left). Positive and negative values are colored blue and orange, respectively, with color saturation based on magnitude of the value. As with the attention-head view, connecting lines are weighted based on attention between the words.

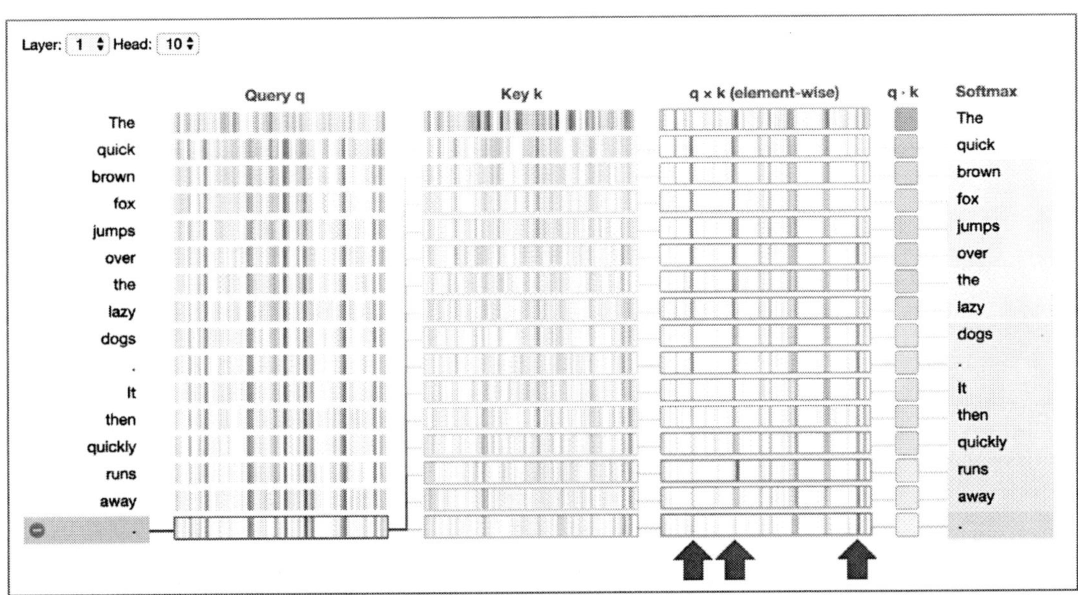

Figure 7: Neuron view of GPT-2 for layer 1, head 10 (same one depicted in Figure 1, center) with last token selected. Blue arrows mark positions in the element-wise products where values decrease with increasing distance from the source token (becoming darker orange or lighter blue).

Use Case: Linking Neurons to Model Behavior

To see how the neuron view might provide actionable insights, consider the attention head in Figure 7. For this head, the attention (rightmost column) decays with increasing distance from the source token. This pattern resembles a context window, but instead of having a fixed cutoff, the attention decays continuously with distance.

The neuron view provides two key insights about this attention head. First, the attention weights appear to be largely independent of the content of the input text, based on the fact that all the query vectors have very similar values (except for the first token). Second, a small number of neuron positions (highlighted with blue arrows) appear to be mostly responsible for this distance-decaying attention pattern. At these neuron positions, the element-wise product $q \times k$ decreases as the distance from the source token increases (either becoming darker orange or lighter blue).

41

When specific neurons are linked to a tangible outcome, it presents an opportunity to intervene in the model (Bau et al., 2019). By altering the relevant neurons—or by modifying the model weights that determine these neuron values—one could control the attention decay rate, which might be useful when generating texts of varying complexity. For example, one might prefer a slower decay rate (longer context window) for a scientific text compared to a children's story. Other heads may afford different types of interventions.

3 Conclusion

In this paper, we introduced a tool for visualizing attention in the Transformer at multiple scales. We demonstrated the tool on GPT-2 and BERT, and we presented three use cases. For future work, we would like to develop a unified interface to navigate all three views within the tool. We would also like to expose other components of the model, such as the value vectors and state activations. Finally, we would like to enable users to manipulate the model, either by modifying attention (Lee et al., 2017; Liu et al., 2018; Strobelt et al., 2018) or editing individual neurons (Bau et al., 2019).

References

Dzmitry Bahdanau, Kyunghyun Cho, and Yoshua Bengio. 2015. Neural machine translation by jointly learning to align and translate. In *Proc. ICLR*.

Anthony Bau, Yonatan Belinkov, Hassan Sajjad, Nadir Durrani, Fahim Dalvi, and James Glass. 2019. Identifying and controlling important neurons in neural machine translation. In *Proc. ICLR*.

Yonatan Belinkov and James Glass. 2019. Analysis methods in neural language processing: A survey. *TACL*.

Jacob Devlin, Ming-Wei Chang, Kenton Lee, and Kristina Toutanova. 2018. BERT: Pre-training of Deep Bidirectional Transformers for Language Understanding. *ArXiv Computation and Language*.

Sarthak Jain and Byron C. Wallace. 2019. Attention is not explanation. *CoRR*, abs/1902.10186.

Llion Jones. 2017. Tensor2tensor transformer visualization. https://github.com/tensorflow/tensor2tensor/tree/master/tensor2tensor/visualization.

Jaesong Lee, Joong-Hwi Shin, and Jun-Seok Kim. 2017. Interactive visualization and manipulation of attention-based neural machine translation. In *EMNLP: System Demonstrations*.

Shusen Liu, Tao Li, Zhimin Li, Vivek Srikumar, Valerio Pascucci, and Peer-Timo Bremer. 2018. Visual interrogation of attention-based models for natural language inference and machine comprehension. In *EMNLP: System Demonstrations*.

Kaiji Lu, Piotr Mardziel, Fangjing Wu, Preetam Amancharla, and Anupam Datta. 2018. Gender bias in neural natural language processing. *CoRR*, abs/1807.11714.

Alec Radford, Jeffrey Wu, Rewon Child, David Luan, Dario Amodei, and Ilya Sutskever. 2019. Language models are unsupervised multitask learners. Technical report.

Alessandro Raganato and Jörg Tiedemann. 2018. An analysis of encoder representations in transformer-based machine translation. In *EMNLP Workshop: BlackboxNLP*.

Tim Rocktäschel, Edward Grefenstette, Karl Moritz Hermann, Tomas Kocisky, and Phil Blunsom. 2016. Reasoning about entailment with neural attention. In *Proc. ICLR*.

Alexander M. Rush, Sumit Chopra, and Jason Weston. 2015. A neural attention model for abstractive sentence summarization. In *Proc. EMNLP*.

H. Strobelt, S. Gehrmann, M. Behrisch, A. Perer, H. Pfister, and A. M. Rush. 2018. Seq2Seq-Vis: A Visual Debugging Tool for Sequence-to-Sequence Models. *ArXiv e-prints*.

Edward Tufte. 1990. *Envisioning Information*. Graphics Press, Cheshire, CT, USA.

Ashish Vaswani, Samy Bengio, Eugene Brevdo, Francois Chollet, Aidan N. Gomez, Stephan Gouws, Llion Jones, Łukasz Kaiser, Nal Kalchbrenner, Niki Parmar, Ryan Sepassi, Noam Shazeer, and Jakob Uszkoreit. 2018. Tensor2tensor for neural machine translation. *CoRR*, abs/1803.07416.

Ashish Vaswani, Noam Shazeer, Niki Parmar, Jakob Uszkoreit, Llion Jones, Aidan N Gomez, Ł ukasz Kaiser, and Illia Polosukhin. 2017. Attention is all you need. *arXiv preprint arXiv:1706.03762*.

Jesse Vig. 2019. BertViz: A tool for visualizing multi-head self-attention in the BERT model. In *ICLR Workshop: Debugging Machine Learning Models*.

Jesse Vig and Yonatan Belinkov. 2019. Analyzing the structure of attention in a transformer language model. In *ACL Workshop: BlackboxNLP*.

Elena Voita, David Talbot, Fedor Moiseev, Rico Sennrich, and Ivan Titov. 2019. Analyzing multi-head self-attention: Specialized heads do the heavy lifting, the rest can be pruned. *arXiv preprint arXiv:1905.09418*.

Jieyu Zhao, Tianlu Wang, Mark Yatskar, Vicente Ordonez, and Kai-Wei Chang. 2018. Gender bias in coreference resolution: Evaluation and debiasing methods. In *NAACL-HLT*.

PostAc®: A Visual Interactive Search, Exploration, and Analysis Platform for PhD Intensive Job Postings

Chenchen Xu[1,2] **Inger Mewburn**[1] **Will J Grant**[1] **Hanna Suominen**[1−4]

1. The Australian National University (ANU) / Canberra, ACT, Australia
2. Data61, Commonwealth Scientific and Industrial Research Organization (CSIRO) / Canberra, ACT, Australia
3. University of Canberra / Canberra, ACT, Australia
4. University of Turku / Turku, Finland
`Firstname.Lastname@anu.edu.au`

Abstract

Over 60% of Australian PhD graduates land their first job after graduation outside academia, but this job market remains largely hidden to these job seekers. Employers' low awareness and interest in attracting PhD graduates means that the term "PhD" is rarely used as a keyword in job advertisements; 80% of companies looking to employ similar researchers do not specifically ask for a PhD qualification. As a result, typing in PhD to a job search engine tends to return mostly academic jobs. We set out to make the market for advanced research skills more visible to job seekers. In this paper, we present PostAc®, an online platform of authentic job postings that helps PhD graduates sharpen their career thinking. The platform is underpinned by research on the key factors that identify what an employer is looking for when they want to hire a highly skilled researcher. Its ranking model leverages the free-form text embedded in the job description to quantify the most sought-after PhD skills and educate information seekers about the Australian job-market appetite for PhD skills. The platform makes visible the geographic location, industry sector, job title, working hours, continuity, and wage of the research intensive jobs. This is the first data-driven exploration in this field. Both empirical results and online platform will be presented in this paper.

1 Introduction

The PhD was originally conceived - and is usually understood - to mark the commencement of an academic career. Yet the degree has never been entirely fit for purpose: as early as 90 years ago, Dale (1930) questioned the role of academic degree. But since then, both academic and industry needs have changed dramatically.

On the academic side, changing workforce structures over the last few decades have meant PhD graduates have faced ever greater difficulties landing academic employment (Bazeley et al., 1996). In Australia, recent research has revealed that up to 60% of students end up working outside of academia, making us ask whether their academic training is really fit for their final purpose (McGagh et al., 2016).

Outside academia, governments are starting to recognize the importance of highly trained graduates to innovation, and are thus putting pressure on universities to re-think PhD curricula so as to target both academic and wider industry needs (Mewburn et al., 2016). Yet limited data-driven research exists to explain how having a PhD actually impacts job seeking in non-academic sectors. Meanwhile, about 80% of the companies looking to employ highly skilled researchers do not specifically ask for PhD qualifications (Mewburn et al., 2018). In this paper, we demonstrate an online platform — PostAc® (short video) — that allows users to explore non-academic career options at scale and is able to accommodate a dynamic industry environment as the model evolves. This educational technology artefact builds on an exploratory study developed through multiple iterations of expert annotation, modelling, and empirical evaluation. The final fine-tuned model is able to correctly categorise jobs requiring PhD level skills at an accuracy of 88%.

We make the following three key contributions: First, we visualize probably the first job posting data set with labels from domain experts showing the intensity of PhD-level research skills. Second, we present a ranking-based model that has been successfully applied to predicting PhD skills intensity from job postings, with empirical performance evaluation. Third, we design and construct a real-world online platform that offers PhD graduates a dedicated job search functionality, as well as helps governments, universities, and employers

Proceedings of the 57th Annual Meeting of the Association for Computational Linguistics-System Demonstrations, pages 43–48
Florence, Italy, July 28 - August 2, 2019. ©2019 Association for Computational Linguistics

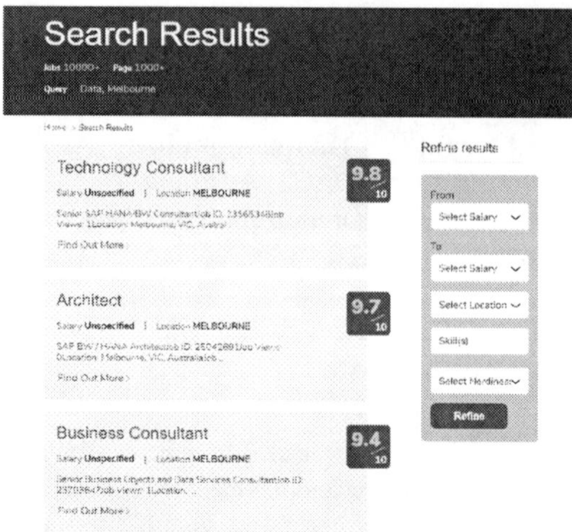

Figure 1: Search Results in the Exploration View

in increasing the understanding of different industries' absorption of PhD graduates.

Since its launch in late 2018, PostAc® has been sharpening the research career thinking of over $1,300$ participating PhD students. Its analysis scales out for over 1.2 million job advertisements to quantify the most sought-after PhD skills and educates information seekers about the Australian job-market appetite for PhD skills in terms of geographic location, industry sector, job title, working hours, continuity, and wage. Its 2017 pilot (Mewburn et al., 2018) revealed the hidden job market for research talents to the government.

2   Data Set

To the best of our knowledge, no empirical studies on big data have previously been conducted in this field, so we commenced the work by preparing our own data set. Over 1.2 million jobs postings published during 2015 were collected from Burning Glass International Inc. as the seeding data set. Each posting came with the original job title and job description, as well as 41 unique attributes, including the employer, salary, and discipline codes. As in this study we sought to understand and support PhD graduates finding careers outside academic institutions, academic jobs (university lecturers, fellows, professors, etc.) were removed (approximately 1%).

To facilitate the study of PhD-shaped jobs and the training of our ranking model, human experts manually annotated $1,315$ job postings based on an agreed schema (details can be found in (Mew-

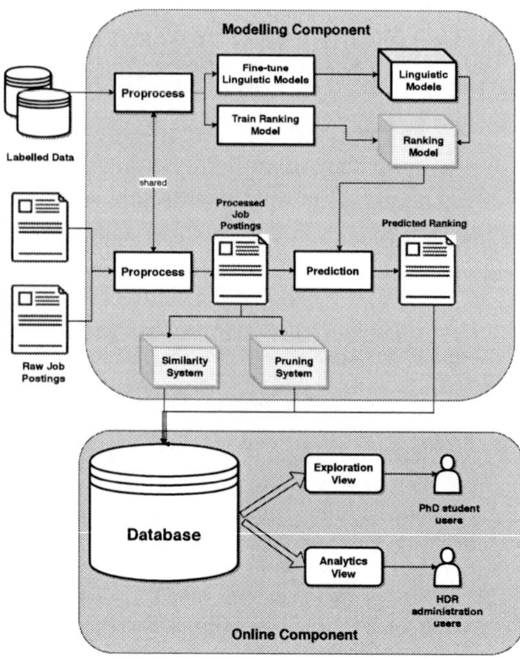

Figure 2: System Architecture

burn et al., 2018)) so that each job is associated with a 'PhDness score (Figure 1) that took values from 1 (least PhD-shaped) to 10 (most PhD-shaped). As expected (not that many jobs require PhD skills), the highly ranked jobs comprised only a small proportion of the entire set. We alleviated this imbalance in the generation of the annotated data set by adding a simple rule-based filter after the random sampling process, resulting in jobs fairly unlikely to require a PhD (e.g., a job paid by the hour) being removed.

3   System Overview

The PostAc® platform is structured into two major components based on the consideration of progressive enhancement of analytic models and platform scalability (Figure 2). More specifically, the model fine-tuning component has been separated out and thus can run in parallel with the continuous integration of data for the online platform component. The general data processing pipeline is shared between the two components to guarantee a consistent process can be applied to data from different sources. After this, the fine-tuning process is invoked on the data set to re-train the ranking model. This process is also responsible for preparing models to handle the extraction of important linguistic attributes, which will later be used in the construction of the database (e.g., tokenization for full-text searching and semantic embedding for similarity measurement) and fine-tuning of word embeddings. The online component leverages the models from the modelling component to digest the incoming job data set, which is mostly unlabelled. Along with the ranking results, the jobs are enriched with the aforementioned linguistic attributes before finally being saved to the database. Regarded as important principles in the design of any system, the scalability and modularity are examined upon each component to be integrated.

The modelling component is built with Tensorflow, where a scheduling system arranges the fine-tuning work in a distributed manner. Meanwhile, the storage engine is built on top of ElasticSearch, making it possible to handle the digestion of approximately $100,000$ job postings coming monthly, as well as to support future extension.

Since the database is prepared in the backend engine, PostAc® provides two dedicated view flows for the needs of both PhD students and staff members (e.g., careers advisors and curriculum designers). PhD students can use the Exploration view flow to search, compare, and investigate the millions of jobs available on the system. Their behaviors can be analyzed as implicit feedback to further enhance the training data set, and thus contribute to optimization of the modelling component. Staff members from universities and academic institutions will be given access to the Analytics view, allowing them to improve their understanding of the potential job market for PhD graduates, and high degree education policy making.

4 System Features

In addition to our major objective of revealing those jobs most likely to require PhD skills, in practice we needed to provide users with similar job postings to assist them in comparing how the recommended ones can fit better. These two targets lead to the two main modules in our system, namely PhDness **ranking model** and job **similarity system**. Acknowledging the nature that jobs of high requirements are hard to satisfy and likely to be reposted, we also elaborate in building a pruning system to cope with it.

4.1 Ranking Model

The ranking model predicts the PhDness for given job postings (Figure 3). This problem can be

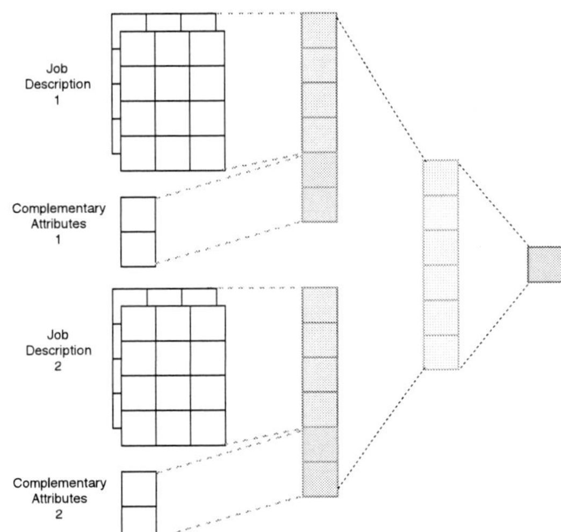

Figure 3: Ranking Model Architecture

treated as a regression task, where each job is evaluated with a numeric PhDness score. Instead, as one of targets in this project is to study what requirements make a job more PhD related, we compose the problem as a ranking task. That is, given any two job postings, the model will learn to judge the one with higher PhDness.

The backbone network for learning the representation of a job posting is modified from the FastText model (Joulin et al., 2017). We incorporate the following input features:

The job description provides key knowledge to PhDness, and we process it the same as the FastText model. Given the input description text of W words, $w = [w_1, w_2, \ldots, w_W]$, a weight matrix $\mathbf{A}$ is a lookup table over the whole vocabulary that maps the individual word tokens to their latent space representation (see Mikolov et al. (2013)). During the seeding phase, we use a pretrained word embedding fine-tuned from Glove (Pennington et al., 2014) to populate $\mathbf{A}$ and then do not change it during the training of the ranking model.[1]

The word representations are then averaged to form the text-level representation:

$$E^w(x_i) = \frac{\mathbf{A} x_i}{W} \qquad (1)$$

where x_i refers to the job posting x_i, $i \in \{1, 2, \ldots, I\}$.

---

[1]The job description can contain many rare or domain-specific words. Even though we have a very large volume of job postings as the training corpus, it may still be insufficient to learn the representation of those words.

We also add the bag of N-grams as additional features to capture some single word-group level knowledge, as this aspect might be blurred in the text-level representation. First, let the bag of N-grams be $N_k = \{w_k, w_{k+1}, \ldots, w_{k+N-1}\}$. Then, similar to word representations (1), the N-gram representations are also averaged:

$$E^{N_k} = \frac{\sum \mathbf{A}\{N_k\}}{N}.$$

The job posting comes with other complementary job attributes, denoted as $a_1, a_2, \ldots, a_A$, also providing useful knowledge to the job's PhD-ness (e.g., MinimumSalary or Employer), although they are not always presented as the job description. The one-hot encoding f_e is applied and the transformed attributes are normalized and appended to the text representation to form the final input feature, using the concatenation function f_c:

$$E(x) = f_c(E^w, \{E^{N_k}\}, f_e(a_1, a_2, \ldots, a_A)). \tag{2}$$

Now with the input features, the ranking task is defined similarly to the ordinal regression setting (Joachims, 2006). Given any two input job postings x_i and x_j that are comparable, $i \neq j$, i and $j \in \{1, 2, \ldots, I\}$, $y_i \neq y_j$, the target value (i.e., PhDness ranking) is $y_i = \text{sign}(y_i - y_j)$. We apply the hinge loss here as our focus is to learn the comparative rank, and the model then is to minimize, using the final input feature (2):

$$\ell = \sum_{i,j,y_i \neq y_j} \max(0, 1 - y_i f_2(E(x_i) - E(x_j) + b))$$

where b is the bias term and f_2 is a two-layer neural network. The second layer has a linear activation function as the sign is for the hinge loss to learn.

We evaluate the ranking model by using the **K-fold** cross validation ($K = 5$ specifically) on the human annotated training data. Two evaluation measures are used to justify the performance from different perspectives: First, the normalized discounted cumulative gain (NDCG) at t (Järvelin and Kekäläinen, 2002) is a widely used measurement for ranking quality in information retrieval measures the usefulness of the top t rated items. We adopt it with t to be 15% of the total number of testing examples. Second, the normalized

Kendall's τ distance (Kendall, 1938) is calculated to measure the overall ranking quality by looking at the number of discordant pairs.

Our fine-tuned model is able to achieve **0.89** for the NDCG at t score and **0.13** for the normalized Kendall's τ distance, showing evidence that the model can both find the most PhD intensive job postings overall and also perform well enough in comparing the PhDness among any randomly chosen pair of job postings.

As for the inference stage, first the model is used to predict a grid of comparative scores for all pairs of candidate job postings. The final prediction of the PhDness score for a given posting is the average of its relative scores against the other postings.

4.2 Similarity System

In addition to the PhDness score prediction from the ranking model, the platform also recognizes similar job postings to help users to perform comparisons. Analogously to the ranking model discussed above, we also incorporate both the text features and complementary attribute features here. However, an unsupervised approach is adopted due to the following considerations: first, the similarity system should not be bounded by the annotation set and thus generalize easily to all job postings; and second, the speed.

Specifically, the term frequency $\times$ inverse document frequency (TF$\times$IDF) features are extracted from the job description text and other textual attributes (e.g., Employer). Numerical attributes (e.g., Salary) are categorized and attached to the feature list with a small normalization factor. The final similarity scoring is calculated using the Euclidean distance.

4.3 Pruning System

The preliminary research reveals a problem that some jobs are re-posted for a few times during the period until being fulfilled. One of the key modules in PostAc$^\circledR$ is its pruning system that removes those duplicated postings. The module adopts a heuristic approach to avoid laborious annotation by hand.

For any two job postings from the same employer published within 4 to 16 weeks, a duplication score is calculated for checking. Here we first have the difference in the publish date d as one input. A similarity score s is also evaluated based on the aforementioned similarity system. Similarly to

Xia et al. (2010), the duplication score d' is defined as

$$d' = \frac{s}{\alpha d}.$$

The publish date difference in the denominator (with the normalizer α) acts as a factor that penalizes when two job postings are too far away from each other. Later, the postings whose duplication score is larger than a given threshold are filtered out.

5 Implementation

The PostAc® platform is implemented as a web tool, with the back-end natural language processing systems responsible for ranking, similarity measurement, and pruning built on Python. The front-end website for storing and managing data and users is built using the PHP programming language. This separation enables the interface to be usable from lightweight environment and also support large amount of users. At the back-end side, two major optimizations are applied:

Ranking Model: Although by the nature of a pairwise ranking model the prediction takes $O(I^2)$ time complexity, it is worth noting that the prediction of each individual posting is performed independently of other postings. The fine-tuned ranking model is serialized and replicated for a few copies. The platform now runs a few prediction process in parallel and this can also easily scale up to future extensions.

Similarity System: The output TF×IDF feature matrix can still have a fair number of dimensions even with a pruned vocabulary. Finding the nearest neighbors in this big set can be time-consuming. We saved the extracted feature matrix on a KD-tree data structure (Bentley, 1975) and this is progressively maintained as new data comes into the system. Once the KD-tree is up to date, the nearest neighbor search is performed right after with the results being saved. This incurs a reasonably large cost up front but once made available, it greatly reduces the processing time for the front-end service. The separation of two components makes it possible to perform the process at the back-end side and push the results to the front-end, without interfering it in most of the time.

With regard to the front-end side, as aforementioned, the PostAc® platform contains two major usage ows: Exploration View for PhD graduates to look at individual job advertisements and Analytics View for policy makers and supervisors who are interested in demand for graduates in different industry sectors.

5.1 Exploration View

Individual users seeking PhD-shaped jobs can access the exploration view flow via a search box. The users can enter a few keywords related to the fields of research they are interested in, or words that relate to their existing skill set. The system ranks all jobs based on the combined score from both the keyword matching and the PhDness score predicted by the ranking model.

The search results (Figure 1) are displayed as a list of job titles that can be further refined by adding more filters. A user can click on a job posting to navigate to the page with more detailed information. In this page, complementary job attributes are provided along with top-ranked similar jobs from the similarity system. Users' navigation and click-through behaviors are recorded as feedback to complement the seeding training data and fine-tune the ranking system in the future.

5.2 Analytics View

One of the main aims of the PostAc® platform is to improve PhD graduate awareness of the demand for their research skills. Aggregated data can also help universities and policy makers to target policy interventions and education efforts appropriately. The Analytics View is designed to help users by showing a range of visualisations of the data set characteristics as well as the key factors our ranking system has been able to discover from the data.

The **Time Series Graph** visualizes the seasonal changes in the demand for jobs in various industries, reflecting the industry and market level changes, month by month, over a year.

The **Distribution Graph** (Figure 4) visualizes how the PhD-shaped jobs are distributed among different areas. Users from government agencies can use these graphs to support regional policy making.

The **Skill Set Graph** visualizes the commonly requested skill sets and abilities for jobs requiring PhD level skills.

6 Conclusion

In this paper, we have presented PostAc®, an evolving platform that makes high level research jobs in the Australian economy more visible. The platform is based on evaluating a human experts'

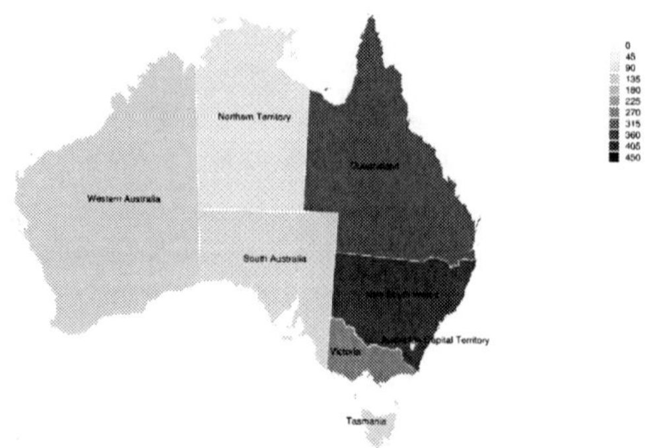

Figure 4: Distribution of PhD Jobs in the Healthcare Sector by a Region: urban Australian areas tend to call for more PhD graduates for healthcare jobs.

hand-annotated data set and its results give empirical evidence of the underlying ranking model being scalable and effective. Currently, the online platform enables a visual-interactive search, exploration, and visualisation of the findings from our machine learning model. This platform will help boost the awareness of the value of PhD level skills and better match PhD graduates to great jobs outside academia.

Acknowledgments

This research partnership of the ANU and Data61/CSIRO was supported by the ANU Discovery Translation Fund 2.0, Australian Government Department of Industry, Innovation and Science (DIIS), On Prime program, and data provided by Burning Glass International Inc. We gratefully acknowledge the funding from the Data61/CSIRO for the first author's PhD studies.

References

Pat Bazeley, Lynn Kemp, Kate Stevens, Christine Asmar, Carol Grbich, Herb Marsh, and Ragbir Bhathal. 1996. *Waiting in the Wings: A Study of Early Career Academic Researchers in Australia*. Canberra, Australia: Australian Government Publishing Service.

Jon Louis Bentley. 1975. Multidimensional binary search trees used for associative searching. *Communications of the ACM*, 18(9):509–517.

Edgar Dale. 1930. The training of Ph.D.'s. *The Journal of Higher Education*, 1(4):198–202.

Kalervo Järvelin and Jaana Kekäläinen. 2002. Cumulated gain-based evaluation of IR techniques. *ACM Transactions on Information Systems*, 20(4):422–446.

Thorsten Joachims. 2006. Training linear SVMs in linear time. In *Proceedings of the 12th ACM SIGKDD International Conference on Knowledge Discovery and Data Mining*, KDD '06, pages 217–226. New York, NY, USA: Association for Computing Machinery.

Armand Joulin, Edouard Grave, Piotr Bojanowski, and Tomas Mikolov. 2017. Bag of tricks for efficient text classification. In *Proceedings of the 15th Conference of the European Chapter of the Association for Computational Linguistics: Volume 2, Short Papers*, pages 427–431. Valencia, Spain: Association for Computational Linguistics.

Maurice G. Kendall. 1938. A new measure of rank correlation. *Biometrika*, 30(1/2):81–93.

John McGagh, Helene Marsh, Mark Western, Peter Thomas, Andrew Hastings, Milla Mihailova, and Matt Wenham. 2016. *Securing Australias Future: Review of Australia's Research Training System*. Melbourne, Australia: Australian Council of Learned Academies.

Inger Mewburn, Will J. Grant, Hanna Suominen, and Stephanie Kizimchuk. 2018. A machine learning analysis of the non-academic employment opportunities for Ph.D. graduates in Australia. *Higher Education Policy*, pages 1–15.

Inger Mewburn, William Grant, Hanna Suominen, and Stephanie Kizimchuk. 2016. What do non academic employers want? A critical examination of 'PhD shaped' job advertisements for doctoral employability. *Society for Research into Higher Education (SRHE) Annual International Conference 2016*, pages 1–3.

Tomas Mikolov, Ilya Sutskever, Kai Chen, Greg Corrado, and Jeffrey Dean. 2013. Distributed representations of words and phrases and their compositionality. In *Proceedings of the 26th International Conference on Neural Information Processing Systems — Volume 2*, NIPS'13, pages 3111–3119. Lake Tahoe, NV, USA: Curran Associates Inc.

Jeffrey Pennington, Richard Socher, and Christopher Manning. 2014. Glove: Global vectors for word representation. In *Proceedings of the 2014 Conference on Empirical Methods in Natural Language Processing (EMNLP)*, pages 1532–1543. Doha, Qatar: Association for Computational Linguistics.

Chaolun Xia, Xiaohong Jiang, Sen Liu, Zhaobo Luo, and Zhang Yu. 2010. Dynamic item-based recommendation algorithm with time decay. In *2010 Sixth International Conference on Natural Computation*, volume 1, pages 242–247. Piscataway, NJ, USA: Institute of Electrical and Electronics Engineers.

An adaptable task-oriented dialog system for stand-alone embedded devices

**Long Duong, Vu Cong Duy Hoang, Tuyen Quang Pham, Yu-Heng Hong,
Vladislavs Dovgalecs, Guy Bashkansky, Jason Black,
Andrew Bleeker, Serge Le Huitouze, Mark Johnson**
Oracle Digital Assistant
`first.last@oracle.com`

Abstract

This paper describes a spoken-language end-to-end task-oriented dialogue system for small embedded devices such as home appliances. While the current system implements a smart alarm clock with advanced calendar scheduling functionality, the system is designed to make it easy to port to other application domains (e.g., the dialogue component factors out domain-specific execution from domain-general actions such as requesting and updating slot values). The system does not require internet connectivity because all components, including speech recognition, natural language understanding, dialogue management, execution and text-to-speech, run locally on the embedded device (our demo uses a Raspberry Pi). This simplifies deployment, minimizes server costs and most importantly, eliminates user privacy risks. The demo video in alarm domain is here youtu.be/N3IBMGocvHU.

1 Introduction

Communicating directly using voice is a more natural way to interact with computer and household appliances. People already interact with smart appliances such as microwaves and alarm clocks using voice control. However, these devices need to connect to cloud services to process user requests. We focus on building entire task-oriented dialog applications on cheap edge devices such as the Raspberry Pi [1] which operate independently of any internet connection. This approach: **a)** ensures user privacy, **b)** abolishes server costs, and **c)** eliminates network connection latency. Specialized neural network chips and generic embedded CPU devices are becoming significantly cheaper, making voice interfaces price-competitive with display-based controllers. Our vision is that in the next few years, AI-powered devices will be in ap-

pliances throughout everyone's home. This paper describes an end-to-end smart alarm clock demo run offline on a small device as a proof of concept for our vision. The approach proposed in this paper is general and easily adapted to different languages and domains.

We describe how we meet the challenges of implementing a complete speech-based task-oriented dialogue system on a small embedded device with low memory and computational power. Our design makes no assumption on the availability of peripherals such as a display screen or buttons for user responses. Just as in many cloud-based dialogue systems, our system is a pipeline of standard components, including a wake word detector, automatic speech recognition (ASR), natural language understanding (NLU), dialogue manager (includes dialogue state tracker and dialogue policy, and execution), natural language generator (NLG) and text-to-speech (TTS). Figure 1 shows the overall organisation of these components. ASR converts spoken user requests to text, which is then fed to NLU components consisting of a Named Entity Recogniser (NER) and a Semantic Parser. The NLU output is a *logical form* (LF1) which encodes the current user request. The Dialogue State Tracker (DST) integrates LF1 with the previous dialogue states and dialog acts to produce an updated dialogue state (LF2). While LF1 only represents a single dialogue turn, LF2 represents the entire dialogue prior to this point in time. The domain-specific Execution component executes LF2, and the results of Execution are returned to Dialog Policy component and also saved to Context Stack which contains all intermediate results. The Dialogue Policy uses the execution results and LF2 to produce a dialogue act response (LF3), which is also recorded in the Context Stack. LF3 is used to generate output to the user which is converted to speech using a Text-To-

---

[1] https://www.raspberrypi.org/

49

Proceedings of the 57th Annual Meeting of the Association for Computational Linguistics-System Demonstrations, pages 49–57
Florence, Italy, July 28 - August 2, 2019. ©2019 Association for Computational Linguistics

Speech (TTS).

Given the hardware constraints of embedded devices, we decided to use rule-based approaches where possible, and to reserve classifier-based and deep learning approaches for components such as the NER and the Semantic Parser, where linguistic variation and construction would be difficult to capture with hand-written rules. We use a rule-based Dialogue Manager and a template-based NLG for this reason. To make it easier to adapt the system to new domains and languages, the domain-specific code is concentrated in the ASR, NER, Semantic Parser, Execution and NLG components. The system is implemented in C++11 to simplify deployment on embedded devices.

2 Logical Forms Design

Information is exchanged between components using representations that we call Logical Forms (LFs). A variety of logical forms have been proposed in the literature, such as lambda.DCS and the lambda calculus (Zettlemoyer and Collins, 2005). Intent plus slots representations are standard in many dialog systems, but they cannot express complicated scenarios involving conditionals, nested structures, multi-intents and quantifier scope.

Our LFs are JSON objects[2] that we call Topic-Action Attribute-Value Logical Forms (TAVLFs). These are attribute-value structures (Johnson, 1988) whose organisation is inspired motivated by CUED standard dialog acts (Young, 2007).

At the top level, TAVLFs have a bipartite structure consisting of topic and action attributes. The topic identifies the primary entities under discussion, while the action specifies what the user requests the system to do with these entities. For example, the request *Move my work out alarm tomorrow 1 hour earlier* is translated to TAVLF:

```
1  {"topic": { "name": "work out"},
2   "action": { "edit": '
3       {"offset_direction": "
            earlier",
4          "offset_time": "1 hour"}}}
```

Here the topic attribute selects calendar entries that satisfy "name":"workout". The action attribute specifies what the system should do to the Topic entities; in this case apply the edit action with arguments offset_time and offset_direction.

<hr>

[2]www.json.org

TAVLFs can express complicated use cases such as multi-intent requests, nested finds, conditional requests, as well as quantifiers and superlatives. The bipartite separation into Topic and Action makes it easier to handle follow-up requests, since it is likely that the next utterance will involve the previous topic. We explain how we handle follow-up utterances in more detail in Section 5. Thus we demonstrate that embedded systems, despite limitations in both memory and computational power, can handle complicated utterances.

3 Wake Word Detection and Automatic Speech Recognition

We use similar technology for both Wake Word detection and ASR. After a wake word is detected, the ASR is activated to convert the following speech into text. The user needs to wake the system for each utterance, except for cases where the system requests a response from user; e.g., no wake work is required when system asks for additional information. Porting an ASR system to a small embedded device is challenging. After evaluating a variety of approaches we decided to use a DNN-based acoustic model together with a fast HMM-based language model decoder. This permits us to easily customise the ASR vocabulary for a new domain. We developed a customised version of Kaldi (Povey et al., 2011) which achieves real time factor of 0.23 even on a small embedded device. The ASR also provides a confidence score based on the HMM posterior probability, which the Dialog Manager uses to detect likely cases of ASR failure.

4 Natural Language Understanding

The Natural Language Understanding (NLU) component translates each utterance into its corresponding logical form (LF1). There are two steps to this process: Named Entity Recognition (NER) and seq2seq based Semantic Parsing. First, the user utterance is NER-tagged and delexicalised (i.e., named entities are replaced with their named entity types). The delexicalized utterance forms the input to the seq2seq semantic parser, which produces delexicalized logical form. This logical form is relexicalized (i.e., the named entity types are replaced with the original named entities) to produce the output logical form (LF1). Figure 2 shows the NLU pipeline. We use a CRF tagger based on CRFSuite (Okazaki, 2007) for NER, and

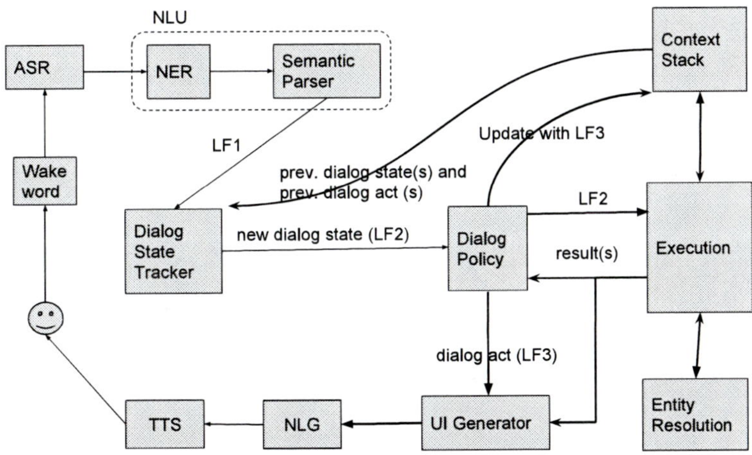

Figure 1: End-to-end embedded dialogue system architecture.

User	make my work out alarm 1 hour earlier
NER	make my <NAME>work out</NAME>alarm <TIME_SPAN>1 hour</TIME_SPAN>earlier
Delex	make my <NAME>#0 alarm <TIME_SPAN>#0 earlier
Seq2seq	{"action":{"edit":{"offset_direction":"earlier","offset_time":"<TIME_SPAN>#0"}}, "topic":{"name":"<NAME>#0"}}
Relex (LF1)	{"action":{"edit":{"offset_direction":"earlier","offset_time":"1hour"}}, "topic":{"name":"work out"}}

Figure 2: The NLU pipeline that maps utterances to Logical Forms (LF1).

employ a deep learning seq2seq model for Semantic Parsing.

4.1 Semantic Parser

Our Semantic Parser is based on the dual-RNN sequence-to-sequence architecture with attention originally proposed for neural machine translation (Bahdanau et al., 2014). We use it to generate Logical Forms as in Dong and Lapata (2016). The seq2seq model also generates a log loss confidence score, which the Dialog Policy Manager uses to detect likely Semantic Parser errors (see section 5).

It is challenging to fit a seq2seq model into a small embedded device. We solve this problem by extensive hyper-parameter tuning using the successive halving process proposed in Hyperband (Li et al., 2016). This approach enables us to explore a large number of hyper-parameter configurations quickly. We randomly generate around a thousand different configurations, which vary the source and target cell architectures (e.g. LSTM, GRU), number of layers, learning rates, drop out rate and mini batch size. We measure memory usage and latency as well as accuracy on the development set. We select the hyper-parameter con-figuration with the highest dev set accuracy that satisfies our memory constraints and has the acceptable latency (usually 100 ms/utterance). Models are trained using Tensorflow on a GPU cluster. Trained models are quantized and exported to our C++ runtime.

One of the challenges in building a semantic parser is obtaining suitable training data. We adapt and extend the crowd-based "overnight" approach of Wang et al. (2015) by adding an additional *validation task*, where other crowd workers validate the paraphrases from the *paraphrase task*. We run the validation task in real-time so we can provide on-line bonuses or penalties, which dramatically reduces spam and improves paraphrasing quality.

5 Dialogue Management

Dialogue management is central to any task-oriented dialog system. It is responsible for Dialogue State Tracking, executing the task (Execution), and determining how to interact with the user (Dialogue Policy).

5.1 Dialogue State Tracking

The Dialogue State Tracking (DST) component combines LF1 with information from the dialogue

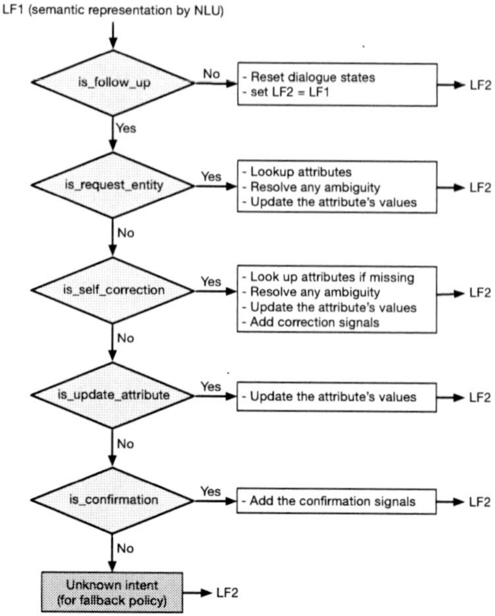

Figure 3: Logics for rule-based DST.

context (previous dialogue states and acts) to compute a Logical Form representation LF2 of the entire dialogue so far. We adopted a rule-based approach for the DST component because it: **a)** is easy to implement, **b)** requires no data, **c)** is extremely fast at run time, and **d)** provides an easy way to incorporate domain-specific information.

The high-level organisation of our rule-based DST is shown in Figure 3 (Appendix A.1). First, the DST distinguishes between follow-up and root (or non-follow-up) utterances by inspecting the Semantic Parser output LF1. If the utterance is a root utterance, the DST sets LF2 to be LF1 and resets the current dialogue state context to start a new conversation. The DST distinguishes four different kinds of follow-up utterances by inspecting LF1: *is_request_entity*, *is_self_correction*, *is_update_attributes*, and *is_confirmation*. Section A.1 presents an example of how the DST functions in alarm clock domain.

5.2 Execution and Dialogue Policy

In our system, execution and dialogue policy work closely together. The Dialogue Policy component takes LF2 as input and passes it to the Execution component. The Execution component is responsible for actually executing user requests; in our system it translates them into SQL queries and executes against a database, producing a set of execution results. The Execution component inter-

acts with Named Entity Resolution if any named entity string in LF2 is not exactly matched in the database for retrieval. For example, the named entity "7 pm" must match the time 19:00 in the database.

Our system consists of a largely application-independent Dialogue Policy component and an application-specific Execution component. Execution is typically domain specific because it requires specific knowledge about the application. The Dialogue Policy component uses the execution results to generate the system response, which is encoded as a LF3. The Dialogue Policy component is associated with a set of types that encode the different kinds of information that the Execution component can return. For instance, if the execution is successful, the Dialog Policy needs to inform the user of the Execution results. But if there are execution errors (e.g., because the request is lacking essential information) the Dialogue Policy component may request additional information or clarification. Our Dialog Policy component uses 8 domain-independent execution return types (see our table 1 in Appendix A for more detail). For each type, the dialogue act (LF3) is constructed accordingly. By separating the Dialogue Policy and Execution components we make it easier to port our system to new applications.

We use the NLU and ASR confidence scores to trigger fall-back dialog policies that vary based on the kind of error we believe has occurred. For example, the system might ask user to speak more clearly if ASR confidence score is low, or to express the request differently if NLU score is low. We set the thresholds for each component using development data. The Dialog Policy component is also update the Context Stack, which stores all the information from LF2, the execution results, and the dialog act for current dialog turn.

6 Other components

6.1 UI Generator

Our modular design includes a User Interface (UI) component, which is responsible for the user interface. The UI depends on the device hardware, e.g., touch screen, buttons etc. Because our current system uses speech input and output, the UI component directly passes the dialog act (LF3) to the NLG component.

Dialog Act	Template 1	Template 2 ...
{inform:{count:0,when_date:X}}	There aren't any alarm for {X}	no alarm for X
{inform:{count:C,when_date:X}}	There are {C} alarms for {X}	...
{request:{confirm:{}}}	Are you sure?	Can you confirm?

Figure 4: Example NLG templates for alarm clock domain. Our templates are delexicalized; C, X, Y are variables which will be replaced with real values. Multiple variants are provided for each schematic LF to increase the diversity of the generated output.

6.2 Natural Language Generator

We use a template-based NLG, which translates dialog acts (LF3) produced by the Dialog Policy component into text that the TTS system can pronounce. Figure 4 shows some example templates. We use a hash function for efficient template retrieval. If multiple templates are found, we prefer the best match. For example, the dialog act *inform:{count:0,when_date:tomorrow}* matches the first two templates in Figure 4, so the first one is selected because the value of *count* attribute matches exactly.

6.3 Text to Speech

We need a TTS engine that is lightweight and fast enough to run on embedded devices. Open source TTS systems based on deep learning technology, such as Tacotron2 (Shen et al., 2017) and Deep-Voice3 (Ping et al., 2017), produce high quality output but very slow on embedded devices. Other open source TTS that use HMM-based synthetic voices, such as MaryTTS (Charfuelan and Steiner, 2013) or Mimic [3], are fast but either of low quality or are difficult to port to embedded devices. We decided to use a commercial embedded TTS solution targeted at embedded devices.

7 Case Study: Alarm Clock Showcase

We built an alarm clock application to showcase our system. The application supports features such as create, delete, cancel, edit and snooze alarm, with attributes such as date, time, day and name. It also provides more advanced features such as conditionals, negation and multi-intent requests. It handles a variety of dialog use cases, such as request for confirmation, request for additional information, provide suggestions and inform about invalid values.

The alarm bot is deployed on a Raspberry Pi 3+ with Cortex-A53 CPU at 1.4GHz clock rate

and 1GB Ram, which currently costs $35 not including microphone and speaker. The NER and Semantic Parser is trained on ≈11k paraphrases of more than 1k Logical Forms, which we collected using our extension of the "overnight" process. The exact match accuracy on development set which is randomly sampled from training set is 85%. Hyper-parameter tuning using HyperBand searched 400 configurations to find the highest accuracy model with a maximum latency of 100ms on the target device. The Semantic Parser model size is 2.5 MB, while the NER model size is 0.4 MB; these consume 15.6 MB and 0.4 MB RAM at run time respectively. The ASR acoustic model size is 7.9 MB and SLM takes 47MB on disk. End to end examples with intermediate results can be found in Appendix A.3

8 Conclusion and Future Work

We presented a full end-to-end task-oriented dialog system that can be deployed on a cheap embedded device. The proposed framework is sufficiently general for rapid adaptation to new domains and languages. We demonstrate the capabilities of our system with an alarm clock application that can understand complicated user requests and handle complex dialog use cases. In future work we plan to improve the robustness of the whole pipeline by using pretrained embeddings for semantic parser, and investigate combining the NER, Semantic Parser and DST into a single deep learning model.

References

Dzmitry Bahdanau, Kyunghyun Cho, and Yoshua Bengio. 2014. Neural machine translation by jointly learning to align and translate. *CoRR*.

Marcela Charfuelan and Ingmar Steiner. 2013. Expressive speech synthesis in MARY TTS using audiobook data and EmotionML. In *Interspeech*, pages 1564–1568, Lyon, France.

³https://mimic.mycroft.ai/

Li Dong and Mirella Lapata. 2016. Language to logical form with neural attention. In *ACL*, pages 33–43.

Mark Johnson. 1988. *Attribute Value Logic and The Theory of Grammar*. Number 16 in CSLI Lecture Notes Series. Chicago University Press, Chicago.

Lisha Li, Kevin G. Jamieson, Giulia DeSalvo, Afshin Rostamizadeh, and Ameet Talwalkar. 2016. Efficient hyperparameter optimization and infinitely many armed bandits. *CoRR*.

Naoaki Okazaki. 2007. Crfsuite: a fast implementation of conditional random fields (crfs).

Wei Ping, Kainan Peng, Andrew Gibiansky, et al. 2017. Deep voice 3: 2000-speaker neural text-to-speech. *CoRR*.

Daniel Povey, Arnab Ghoshal, Gilles Boulianne, et al. 2011. The kaldi speech recognition toolkit. In *IEEE 2011 Workshop on Automatic Speech Recognition and Understanding*.

Jonathan Shen, Ruoming Pang, Ron J. Weiss, et al. 2017. Natural TTS synthesis by conditioning wavenet on mel spectrogram predictions. *CoRR*, abs/1712.05884.

Yushi Wang, Jonathan Berant, and Percy Liang. 2015. Building a semantic parser overnight. In *ACL*, pages 1332–1342, Beijing, China.

S. Young. 2007. Cued standard dialogue acts. Technical report, Cambridge University Engineering Dept.

Luke S. Zettlemoyer and Michael Collins. 2005. Learning to map sentences to logical form: Structured classification with probabilistic categorial grammars. In *Proceedings of the Twenty-First Conference on Uncertainty in Artificial Intelligence*, pages 658–666.

A Appendices

A.1 Dialog state tracking examples

After recognizing an utterance as a follow-up, we further classify the utterance into the following categories:

Request Entity is for utterances which provide a value, but do not specify the attribute or slot the provided value fills. The dialog state tracker decides which attribute the value belong to based on an ontology learned from semantic parser training data. For example.

1. User: Wake me up tomorrow
2. System: what time?
3. User: 8 am

This utterance is classified as *request entity* because it does not specify which attribute or slot the entity "8 am" fills. The corresponding logical form (LF1) for that utterance is:

```
1  {"action":{"follow_up":{"entity":
       "8 am"}}}
```

Self Correction is for utterances where the user corrects values they have previously supplied. For example:

1. User: Wake me up tomorrow at 8 am.
2. System: Done, you alarm at 8am tomorrow has been set.
3. User: Sorry make it 9 am please

The last utterance will be recognised as a *self correction* by the Semantic Parser. We execute this by rolling back the database execution, modifying the required value (i.e. from 8 am to 9 am) and executing the new logical form LF2. The corresponding logical form (LF1) is:

```
1  {"action":{"follow_up":{"entity":
       "9 am","self_correction":true}
   }}
```

And LF2 is:

```
1  {"action":{"create":{"when_day":"
       tomorrow","when_time":"9 am","
       self_correction":"true"}}}
```

Update Attribute is for utterances where the semantic parser can identify which attribute the user is referring to. For example,

1. User: create an alarm for tomorrow at 10 am.
2. System: Done, your alarm has been created.

3. User: call that alarm "meeting with Julie".

The semantic parser can extract the attribute (i.e. `name` in this example) and associated value (i.e. *meeting with Julie*) from the last utterance. Updating an attribute is a standard operation in dialog state tracking. The corresponding logical form (LF1) is:

```
1  {"action":{"follow_up":{"
       attribute":{"name":"meeting
       with Julie"}}}}
```

Confirmation is for utterances that semantic parser recognizes as a confirmation. The last utterance in the following dialog is an example of a confirmation:

1. User: Delete my alarm for tomorrow morning
2. System: You have 2 alarms for tomorrow, do you want to delete those?
3. User: Yes, do it.

The corresponding logical form (LF1) is

```
1  {"action":{"follow_up":{"
       confirmation":"yes"}}}
```

A.2 Execution return types

See table 1.

A.3 End-to-end examples

```
1  User: hey alarm clock, wake me up
       tomorrow
2  LF1 = LF2 :  {"action":{"create":
       {"when_day":"tomorrow"}}}
3  Execution: {"execution_results":[
       {"action":"create","error_code
       ":1,"error_attributes":["
       when_time"],"results":[]}]}
4  LF3: {"policy":[{"request":{"
       when_time":{}}}]}
5  NLG: When would you like it to
       ring?
6  ------------------
7  User: 6 am please
8  LF1: {"action":{"follow_up":{"
       entity":"6 am"}}}
9  LF2: {"action":{"create":{"
       when_day":"tomorrow","
       when_time":"6 am"}}}
10 Execution: {"execution_results":[
       {"action":"create","error_code
       ":0,"error_attributes":[],"
```

Return Types	Description
Execution success	Execution finishes successfully.
Expect zero got more	Execution expects no entity but got more. For example, create database entries that already exist.
Expect one got more	Execution expects exactly one entity but got more. For example, edit alarm by name but there are two alarms having the same name.
Expect at least one got zero	The value is not found. For example, query alarms by name but there aren't any alarms matching that name
Invalid values	The value is invalid. For example, create an alarm in the past.
Missing attributes	Missing attributes for execution. For example, create an alarm without specifying time.
Yes/no confirmation	Execution pauses to wait for confirmation from user for critical actions such as purchase, delete etc.
Execution fail	Execution fail for unknown reasons. This is useful for fallback policy.

Table 1: Execution return types.

```
      results":[{"id":"1","when_date
      ":"2019-04-11","when_time":"06
      :00"}]}]}
11 LF3: {"policy":[{"inform":{"
      action":"create","when_date":"
      2019-04-11","when_time":"06:00
      "}}]}
12 NLG: Your alarm will go off at 06
      :00 tomorrow.
```

LF1 and LF2 in line 2 above are the same because this is the start of a dialog, so the DST just passes through the LF1. The execution (line 3) returns error code = 1 (missing attribute). The user provides the missing information (line 7) and execution is successful (error code = 0 in line 10).

The following is a more complicated dialog with negation and self correction.

```
1 User: hey alarm clock, could you
      create alarms called feed the
      dog for every weekdays except
      Friday at 8 am
2 LF1 = LF2 :  {"action":{"create":
      {"interval":"1w","name":"feed
      the dog","when_day":["weekdays
      ","~friday"],"when_time":"8 am
      "}}}
3 Execution: {"execution_results":[
      {"action":"create","error_code
      ":0,"error_attributes":[],"
      results":[{"id":"2","interval"
      :"1w","name":"feed the dog","
      when_day":"monday,tuesday,
      wednesday,thursday","when_time
      ":"08:00"}]}]}
4 LF3: {"policy":[{"inform":{"
      action":"create","interval":"1
      w","name":"feed the dog","
      when_day":"monday,tuesday,
      wednesday,thursday","when_time
      ":"08:00"}}]}
5 NLG: Your weekly alarm called
      feed the dog will ring every
      monday, tuesday, wednesday and
      thursday at 08:00.
6 --------------------
7 User: hey alarm clock, sorry i
      meant 9 am
8 LF1: {"action":{"follow_up":{"
      entity":"9 am","
      self_correction":true}}}
9 LF2: {"action":{"create":{"
      interval":"1w","name":"feed
      the dog","when_day":["weekdays
      ","~friday"],"when_time":"9 am
      ","self_correction":"true"}}}
10 Execution: {"execution_results":[
      {"action":"edit","error_code":
      0,"error_attributes":[],"
      results":[{"id":"2","interval"
      :"1w","name":"feed the dog","
      when_day":"monday,tuesday,
```

```
     wednesday,thursday","when_time
     ":"08:00","when_time_new":"09:
     00"}]}]}
11 LF3: {"policy":[{"inform":{"
     action":"edit","interval":"1w"
     ,"name":"feed the dog","
     when_day":"monday,tuesday,
     wednesday,thursday","when_time
     ":"08:00","when_time_new":"09:
     00"}}]}
12 NLG: Your recurring monday,
     tuesday,wednesday and thursday
     alarm called feed the dog has
     been moved from 08:00 to 09:0
     0
```

AlpacaTag: An Active Learning-based Crowd Annotation Framework for Sequence Tagging

Bill Yuchen Lin[†*] **Dong-Ho Lee**[†*] **Frank F. Xu**[‡] **Ouyu Lan**[†] and **Xiang Ren**[†]

{yuchen.lin,dongho.lee,olan,xiangren}@usc.edu, frankxu@cmu.edu

[†]Computer Science Department   [‡]Language Technologies Institute
University of Southern California   Carnegie Mellon University

Abstract

We introduce an open-source web-based data annotation framework (AlpacaTag) for sequence tagging tasks such as named-entity recognition (NER). The distinctive advantages of AlpacaTag are three-fold. **1) Active intelligent recommendation**: dynamically suggesting annotations and sampling the most informative unlabeled instances with a back-end active learned model; **2) Automatic crowd consolidation**: enhancing real-time inter-annotator agreement by merging inconsistent labels from multiple annotators; **3) Real-time model deployment**: users can deploy their models in downstream systems while new annotations are being made. AlpacaTag is a comprehensive solution for sequence labeling tasks, ranging from rapid tagging with recommendations powered by active learning and auto-consolidation of crowd annotations to real-time model deployment.

1 Introduction

Sequence tagging is a major type of tasks in natural language processing (NLP), including *named-entity recognition* (detecting and typing entity names), *keyword extraction* (e.g. extracting aspect terms in reviews or essential terms in queries), *chunking* (extracting phrases), and *word segmentation* (identifying word boundary in languages like Chinese). State-of-the-art supervised approaches to sequence tagging are highly dependent on numerous annotations. New annotations are usually necessary for a new domain or task, even though transfer learning techniques (Lin and Lu, 2018) can reduce the amount of them by reusing data of other related tasks. However, manually annotating sequences can be time-consuming, expensive, and thus hard to scale.

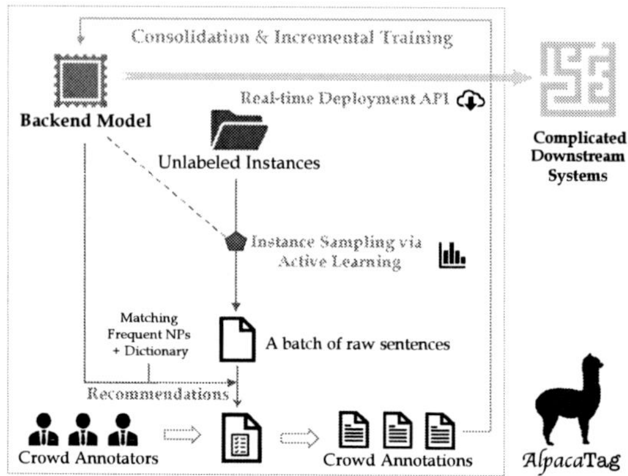

Figure 1: Overview of the AlpacaTag framework.

Therefore, it is still an important research question that how we can develop a better annotation framework to largely reduces human efforts.

Existing open-source sequence annotation tools (Stenetorp et al., 2012; Druskat et al., 2014a; de Castilho et al., 2016; Yang et al., 2018a) mainly focus on enhancing the friendliness of user interfaces (UI) such as data management, fast tagging with shortcut keys, supporting more platforms, and multi-annotator analysis. We argue that there are still three important yet underexplored directions of improvements: 1) active intelligent recommendation, 2) automatic crowd consolidation, 3) real-time model deployment. Therefore, we propose a novel web-based annotation tool named AlpacaTag[1] to address these three problems.

Active intelligent recommendation (§3) aims to reduce human efforts at both instance-level and corpus-level by learning a back-end sequence tagging model incrementally with incoming human annotations. At the instance-level, AlpacaTag applies the *model predictions* on current unlabeled sentences as tagging suggestions. Apart from that,

---

*Both authors contributed equally.

[1]The source code is publicly available at http://inklab.usc.edu/AlpacaTag/.

Proceedings of the 57th Annual Meeting of the Association for Computational Linguistics-System Demonstrations, pages 58–63
Florence, Italy, July 28 - August 2, 2019. ©2019 Association for Computational Linguistics

we also greedily match *frequent noun phrases* and a dictionary of *already annotated spans* as recommendations. Annotators can easily confirm or decline such recommendations with our specialized UI. At the corpus-level, we use active learning algorithms (Settles, 2009) for selecting next batches of instances to annotate based on the model. The goal is to select the most *informative* instances for human to tag and thus to achieve a more cost-effective way of using human efforts.

Automatic crowd consolidation (§4) of the annotations from multiple annotators is an underexplored topic in developing crowd-sourcing annotation frameworks. As a crowdsourcing framework, AlpacaTag collects annotations from multiple (non-expert) contributors with lower cost and a higher speed. However, annotators usually have different confidences, preferences, and biases in annotating, which leads to possibly high inter-annotator disagreement. It is shown very challenging to train models with such noisy crowd annotations (Nguyen et al., 2017; Yang et al., 2018b). We argue that consolidating crowd labels during annotating can lead annotators to achieve real-time consensus, and thus decrease disagreement of annotations instead of exhausting post-processing.

Real-time model deployment (§5) is also a desired feature for users. We sometimes need to deploy a state-of-the-art sequence tagging model while the crowdsourcing is still ongoing, such that users can facilitate the developing of their tagging-required systems with our APIs.

To the best of our knowledge, there is no existing annotation framework enjoying such three features. AlpacaTag is the first unified framework to address these problems, while inheriting the advantages of existing tools. It thus provides a more comprehensive solution to crowdsourcing annotations for sequence tagging tasks.

In this paper, we first present the high-level structure and design of the proposed AlpacaTag framework. Three key features are then introduced in detail: *active intelligent recommendation* (§3), *automatic crowd consolidation* (§4), and *real-time model deployment* (§5). Experiments (§6) are conducted for showing the effectiveness of the proposed three features. Comparisons with related works are discussed in §7. Section §8 shows conclusion and future directions.

2 Overview of AlpacaTag

As shown in Figure 1, AlpacaTag has an actively learned back-end model (top-left) in addition to a front-end web-UI (bottom). Thus, we have two separate servers: a back-end **model server** and a front-end **annotation server**. The model server is built with PyTorch and supports a set of APIs for communications between the two servers and model deployment. The annotation server is built on Django in Python, which interacts with administrators and annotators.

To start annotating for a domain of interest, admins should login and create a new project. Then, they need to further import their raw corpus (with CSV or JSON format), and assign the tag space with associated *colors* and *shortcut keys*. Admins can further set the batch size to sample instances and to update back-end models. Annotators can login and annotate (actively sampled) unlabeled instances with tagging suggestions. We further present our three key features in the next sections.

3 Active Intelligent Recommendation

This section first introduces the back-end model (§3.1) and then presents how we use the back-end model for both instance-level recommendations (tagging suggestions, §3.2) as well as corpus-level recommendations (active sampling, §3.3).

3.1 Back-end Model: BLSTM-CRF

The core component of the proposed AlpacaTag framework is the back-end sequence tagging model, which is learned with an incremental active learning scheme. We use the state-of-the-art sequence tagging model as our back-end model (Lample et al., 2016; Lin et al., 2017; Liu et al., 2018), which is based on bidirectional LSTM networks with a CRF layer (BLSTM-CRF). It can capture character-level patterns, and encode token sequences with pre-trained word embeddings, as well as using CRF layers to capture structural dependencies in tagging. In this section, we assume the model is fixed as we are talking about how to use it for infer recommendations. How to update it by consolidating crowd annotations is illustrated in the Section §4.

3.2 Tagging Suggestions (Instance-level Rec.)

Apart from the inference results from the back-end model on the sentences, we also include two other kinds of tagging suggestions mentioned in

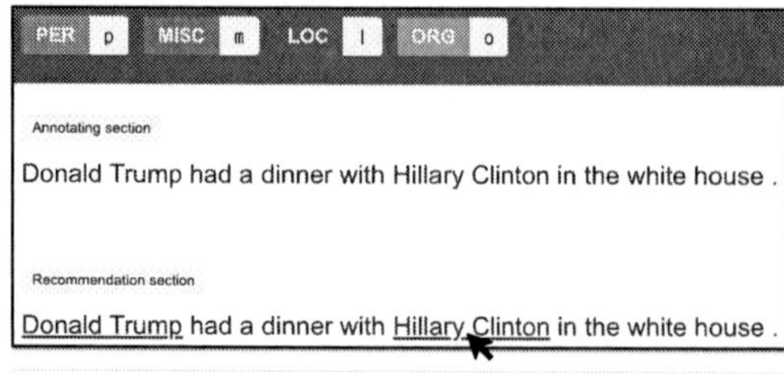

(a) the sentence and annotations are at the upper section; tagging suggestions are shown as underlined spans in the lower section.

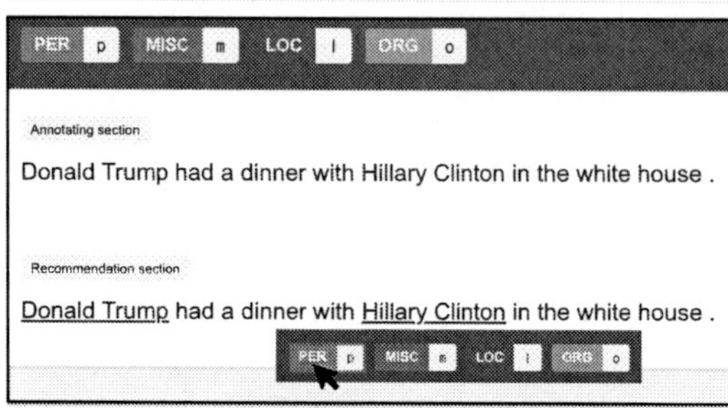

(b) after click on a suggested span, a floating window will show up near for confirming the types (suggested type is bounded with red line).

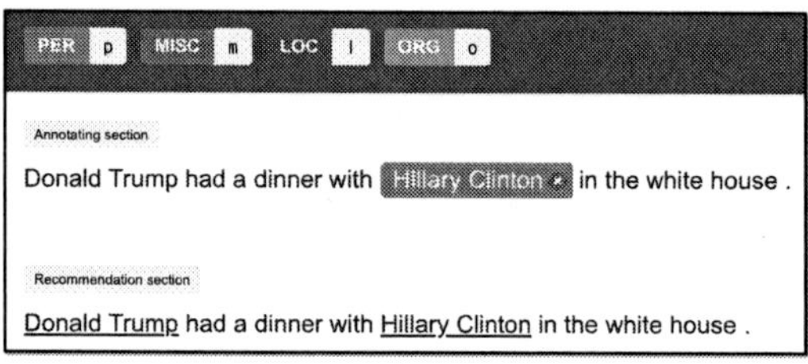

(c) after click a suggested type or press a shortcut key (e.g. 'p'), confirmed annotations will show up in the upper annotation section.

Figure 2: The workflow for annotators to confirm a given tagging suggestion ("Hillary Clinton" as PER).

Fig. 1: *(frequent) noun phrases* and the dictionary of already tagged spans. Specifically, after admins upload raw corpora, AlpacaTag runs a phrase mining algorithm (Shang et al., 2018) to gather a list of frequent noun phrases, which are more likely to be entities. Admins can also optionally enable the framework to consider all noun phrases by chunking as span candidates. These suggestions are not typed. Additionally, we also maintain a dictionary mapping from already tagged spans in previous sentences to their majority tagged types. Frequent noun phrases and dictionary entries are matched by the greedy forward maximum matching algorithm. Therefore, the final tagging suggestions are merged from three sources with the fol-

lowing priority (ordered by their precision): dictionary matches > back-end model inferences > (frequent) noun phrases, while the coverage of the suggestions are in the opposite order.

Figure 2 illustrates how AlpacaTag presents the tagging suggestions for the sentence "Donald Trump had a dinner with Hillary Clinton in the white house.". The two suggestions are shown in the bottom section as underscored spans "Donald Trump" and "Hilary Clinton" (Fig. 2a). When annotators want to confirm "Hilary Clinton" as a true annotation, they first click the span and then click the right type in the appearing float window (Fig. 2b). They can also press the customized shortcut key for fast tagging. Note that the PER button is underscored in Fig. 2b, meaning that it is a recommended type for annotators to choose. Fig. 2c shows that after confirming, it is added into final annotations. We want to emphasize that our designed UI well solves the problem of confirming and declining suggestions. The float windows reduce mouse movement time very much and let annotators easily confirm or change types by clicking or pressing shortcuts to correct suggested types.

What if annotators want to tag spans not recommended? Normally annotating in AlpacaTag is as friendly as other tools: annotators can simply select the spans they want to tag in the upper section and click or press the associated type (Fig. 3). We implement this UI design based on an open-source Django framework named *doccano*[2].

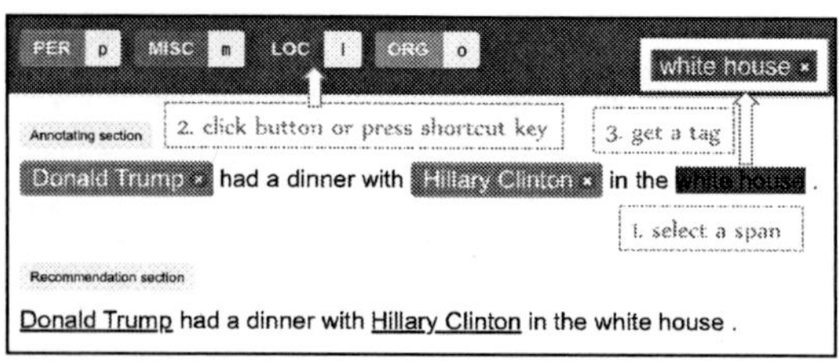

Figure 3: Annotating a span without recommendations.

3.3 Active Sampling (Corpus-level Rec.)

Tagging suggestions are at the instance level, while what instances we should ask annotators to label is also very important to save human efforts. Thus, the research question here is how to actively sample a set of the most *informative* instances from the whole unlabeled sentences, which is named active learning. The measure of informativeness is usually specific

[2]http://doccano.herokuapp.com/

to an existing model, which means what instances (if labeled correctly) can improve the model performance. A typical example of active learning is called *Least Confidence* (Culotta and McCallum, 2005), which applies the model on all the unlabeled sentences and treats the inference confidence as the negative of informativeness $(1 - \max_{y_1,...,y_n} \mathbb{P}[y_1, \ldots, y_n | \{\mathbf{x}_{ij}\}])$. For `AlpacaTag`, we apply an improved version named Maximum Normalized Log-Probability (MNLP) (Shen et al., 2018), which eliminates the effect of length of sequences by averaging:

$$\max_{y_1,...,y_n} \frac{1}{n} \sum_{i=1}^{n} \log \mathbb{P}[y_i | y_1, \ldots, y_{n-1}, \{\mathbf{x}_{ij}\}]$$

Simply put, we manage to utilize the current back-end model for measuring the informativeness of unlabeled sentences and then sample the optimal next batch for annotators to label.

4 Automatic Crowd Consolidation

As a crowd-sourcing annotation framework, `AlpacaTag` aims to reduce inter-annotator disagreement while keeping their individual strengths in labeling specific kinds of instances. We achieve this by applying annotator-specific back-end models ("personal models") and consolidate them into a shared back-end model named "consensus model". Personal models are used for personalized active sampling, such that annotators will label the regions of data space that are most important to be labeled by them respectively.

Assume there are K annotators, we refer them as $\{A_1, \ldots, A_K\}$. For each annotator A_i, we refer the corresponding sentences and annotations processed by it to be $\mathbf{x}_i = \{x_{i,j}\}_{j=1}^{l_i}$ and $\mathbf{y}_i^{A_i} \in \mathcal{Y}^{l_i}$. The target of consolidation is to generate predictions for the test data $\mathbf{x}$, while the resulting labels are referred as $\hat{\mathbf{y}}$. Note that annotators may annotate different portions of the data and sentences can have inconsistent crowd labels.

As shown in Fig. 4, we model the behavior of every annotator by constructing annotator representation matrices $\mathbf{C}^k$ from the network parameters of *personal back-end models*. The personal models share the same BLSTM layers for encoding sentences and avoiding overparameterizing. They are incrementally updated every batch, which usually consists of $50 \sim 100$ sentences sampled actively by the algorithms mentioned in §3.3. We further merge the crowd repre-

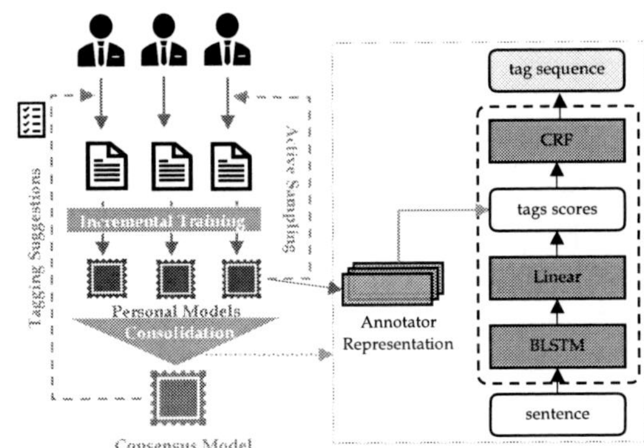

Figure 4: Reducing inter-annotator disagreement by training personal models for personalized active sampling and constructing consensus models.

sentation $\mathbf{C}^k$ into a representation matrix $\mathbf{C}$, and thus construct a consensus model by using $\mathbf{C}$ to generate tag scores in the BLSTM-CRF architecture, which is improved from the approach proposed by Nguyen et al. (2017).

In summary, `AlpacaTag` periodically updates the back-end consensus model by consolidating crowd annotations for annotated sentences through merging personal models. The updated back-end model continues to offer suggestions in future instances for all the annotators, and thus the consensus can be further solidified with recommendation confirmations.

5 Real-time Model Deployment

Waiting for a model to be trained with ready human annotations can be a huge bottleneck for developing complicated pipeline systems in information extraction. Instead, users may want a sequence tagging model that can be constantly updated, even when the annotation process is still undergoing. `AlpacaTag` naturally enjoys this feature since we maintain a back-end tagging model with incremental active learning techniques.

Thus, we provide a suite of APIs for interacting with the back-end consensus model server. They can work for both communication with the annotation server and real-time deployment of the back-end model. One can obtain inference results for their developing complicated systems by querying such APIs for downstream applications.

6 Experiments

To investigate the performance of our implemented back-end model with incremental active learning and consolidation, we conduct a prelim-

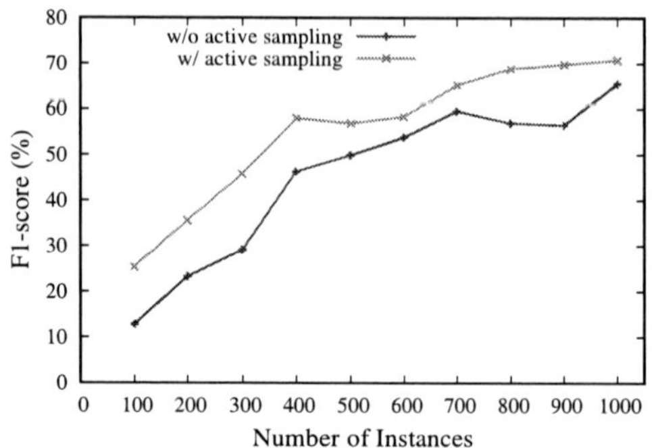

Figure 5: Effectiveness of incremental updating with and without active sampling.

inary experiment on the *CoNLL2003* dataset. We set iteration step size as 100 with the default order for single-user annotation, and incrementally update the back-end model for 10 iterations. Then, we apply our implementation for active sampling the optimal batches of samples to annotate dynamically. All results are tested on the official test set.

As shown in Fig. 5, the performance with active learning is indeed improved by a large margin over vanilla training effectively. We also find that with active sampling, using annotations of about 35% training data can achieve the performance of using 100%, confirming the reported results of previous studies (Siddhant and Lipton, 2018).

For consolidating multiple annotations, we test our implementation with the real-world crowd-sourced data collected by Rodrigues et al. (2013) using Amazon Mechanical Turk (AMT). Our methods outperform existing approaches including MVT-SLM (Wang et al., 2018) and Crowd-X (Nguyen et al., 2017) (see Tab. 1).

7 Related Works

Many sequence annotation tools have been developed (Ogren, 2006; Bontcheva et al., 2013; Chen and Styler, 2013; Druskat et al., 2014b) for basic annotation features including data management, shortcut key annotation, and multi-annotation presentation and analysis. However,

Methods	Precision(%)	Recall(%)	F_1(%)
MVT-SLM	88.88($\pm$0.25)	65.04($\pm$0.80)	75.10($\pm$0.44)
Crowd-Add	**89.74**($\pm$0.10)	64.50($\pm$1.48)	75.03($\pm$1.02)
Crowd-Cat	89.72($\pm$0.47)	63.55($\pm$1.20)	74.39($\pm$0.98)
Ours	88.77($\pm$0.25)	**72.79**($\pm$0.04)	**79.99**($\pm$0.08)
Gold	92.12($\pm$0.31)	91.73($\pm$0.09)	91.92($\pm$0.21)

Table 1: Comparisons of consolidation methods.

few of them enjoys the above-introduced three features of AlpacaTag. It is true that a few existing tools also support tagging suggestions (instance-level recommendations) as follows:

- BRAT (Stenetorp et al., 2012) and GATE (Bontcheva et al., 2013) can offer suggestions with a fixed tagging model like CoreNLP (Manning et al., 2014). However, it is hardly helpful when users need to annotate sentences with customized label set specific to their interested domains, which is the most common motivation for people to use an annotation framework.
- YEDDA (Yang et al., 2018a) simply generates suggestions by exact matching against a continuously updated lexicon of *already annotated spans*. In comparison, this is a subset of AlpacaTag's recommendations. Note that YEDDA cannot suggest any unseen spans.
- WebAnno (Yimam et al., 2013) integrates a learning component for suggestions, which is based on hand-crafted features and generic online learning framework (MIRA). Nonetheless, the back-end model is too far away from the state-of-the-art methods for sequence tagging and hard to customize for consolidation and real-time deployment.

AlpacaTag's tagging suggestions are more comprehensive since they are from state-of-the-art BLSTM-CRF architecture, annotation dictionary, and frequent noun phrase mining. An unique advantage is that it also supports active learning to sample instances that are most worth labeling to reduce human efforts. In addition, AlpacaTag further attempts to reduce inter-annotator disagreement during annotating by automatically consolidating personal models to consensus models, which pushes further than just presenting inter-annotator agreement without doing anything helpful.

While recent papers have shown the power of deep active learning with simulations (Siddhant and Lipton, 2018), a practical annotation framework with active learning is missing. AlpacaTag is not only an annotation framework but also a practical environment for evaluating different active learning methods.

8 Conclusion and Future Directions

To sum up, we propose an open-source web-based annotation framework AlpacaTag that provides users with more advanced features for reducing human efforts in annotating, while keeping the existing basic annotation functions like shortcut keys. Incremental active learning of back-end models with crowd consolidation facilities intelligent recommendations and reduce disagreement.

Future directions include supporting annotation of other tasks, such as relation extraction and event extraction. We also plan to design a real-time console for showing the status of back-end models based on *TensorBoard*, such that admins can better track the quality of deployed models and early stop annotating to save human efforts.

References

Kalina Bontcheva, Hamish Cunningham, Ian Roberts, Angus Roberts, Valentin Tablan, Niraj Aswani, and Genevieve Gorrell. 2013. Gate teamware: a web-based, collaborative text annotation framework. In *Proc. of LREC*.

Richard Eckart de Castilho, Éva Mújdricza-Maydt, Seid Muhie Yimam, Silvana Hartmann, Iryna Gurevych, Anette Frank, and Christian Biemann. 2016. A web-based tool for the integrated annotation of semantic and syntactic structures. In *Proc. of LT4DH@COLING*.

Wei-Te Chen and Will Styler. 2013. Anafora: a web-based general purpose annotation tool. In *Proc. of NAACL-HLT*.

Aron Culotta and Andrew McCallum. 2005. Confidence estimation for information extraction. In *Proc. of AAAI*.

Stephan Druskat, Lennart Bierkandt, Volker Gast, Christoph Rzymski, and Florian Zipser. 2014a. Atomic: an open-source software platform for multi-level corpus annotation. In *KONVENS*.

Stephan Druskat, Lennart Bierkandt, Volker Gast, Christoph Rzymski, and Florian Zipser. 2014b. Atomic: An open-source software platform for multi-level corpus annotation.

Guillaume Lample, Miguel Ballesteros, Sandeep Subramanian, Kazuya Kawakami, and Chris Dyer. 2016. Neural architectures for named entity recognition. In *Proc. of NAACL-HLT*.

Bill Y. Lin, Frank F. Xu, Zhiyi Luo, and Kenny Q. Zhu. 2017. Multi-channel bilstm-crf model for emerging named entity recognition in social media. In *NUT@EMNLP*.

Bill Yuchen Lin and Wei Lu. 2018. Neural adaptation layers for cross-domain named entity recognition. In *Proc. of EMNLP*.

Liyuan Liu, Jingbo Shang, Frank F. Xu, Xiang Ren, Huan Gui, Jian Peng, and Jiawei Han. 2018. Empower sequence labeling with task-aware neural language model. In *Proc. of AAAI*.

Christopher D. Manning, Mihai Surdeanu, John Bauer, Jenny Rose Finkel, Steven Bethard, and David McClosky. 2014. The stanford corenlp natural language processing toolkit. In *Proc. of ACL*.

An Thanh Nguyen, Byron C. Wallace, Junyi Jessy Li, Ani Nenkova, and Matthew Lease. 2017. Aggregating and predicting sequence labels from crowd annotations. *Proc. of ACL*.

Philip V Ogren. 2006. Knowtator: a protégé plug-in for annotated corpus construction. In *Proc. of NAACL-HLT*.

Filipe Rodrigues, Francisco C. Pereira, and Bernardete Ribeiro. 2013. Sequence labeling with multiple annotators. *Machine Learning*.

Burr Settles. 2009. Active learning literature survey. Technical report, University of Wisconsin-Madison Department of Computer Sciences.

Jingbo Shang, Jialu Liu, Meng Jiang, Xiang Ren, Clare R. Voss, and Jiawei Han. 2018. Automated phrase mining from massive text corpora. *Proc. of TKDE*.

Yanyao Shen, Hyokun Yun, Zachary C Lipton, Yakov Kronrod, and Animashree Anandkumar. 2018. Deep active learning for named entity recognition. In *Proc. of ICLR*.

Aditya Siddhant and Zachary Chase Lipton. 2018. Deep bayesian active learning for natural language processing: Results of a large-scale empirical study. In *Proc. of EMNLP*.

Pontus Stenetorp, Sampo Pyysalo, Goran Topić, Tomoko Ohta, Sophia Ananiadou, and Jun'ichi Tsujii. 2012. brat: a web-based tool for NLP-assisted text annotation. In *Proc. of EACL*.

Xuan Wang, Yu Zhang, Xiang Ren, Yuhao Zhang, Marinka Zitnik, Jingbo Shang, Curtis P. Langlotz, and Jiawei Han. 2018. Cross-type biomedical named entity recognition with deep multi-task learning. *Bioinformatics*.

Jie Yang, Yue Zhang, Linwei Li, and Xingxuan Li. 2018a. Yedda: A lightweight collaborative text span annotation tool. In *Proc. of ACL*.

YaoSheng Yang, Meishan Zhang, Wenliang Chen, Wei Zhang, Haofen Wang, and Min Zhang. 2018b. Adversarial learning for chinese ner from crowd annotations. In *Proc. of AAAI*.

Seid Muhie Yimam, Iryna Gurevych, Richard Eckart de Castilho, and Christian Biemann. 2013. Webanno: A flexible, web-based and visually supported system for distributed annotations. In *Proc. of ACL*.

ConvLab: Multi-Domain End-to-End Dialog System Platform

Sungjin Lee[†]   Qi Zhu[‡]   Ryuichi Takanobu[‡]   Zheng Zhang[‡]   Yaoqin Zhang[‡]   Xiang Li[‡]
Jinchao Li[†]   Baolin Peng[†]   Xiujun Li[†]   Minlie Huang[‡]   Jianfeng Gao[†]
[†]Microsoft Research, USA   [‡]Tsinghua University, China
[‡]{zhu-q18,gxly15,z-zhang15,zhangyq17}@mails.tsinghua.edu.cn
[†]{sule,jincli,xiul,jfgao}@microsoft.com   [‡]aihuang@tsinghua.edu.cn

Abstract

We present *ConvLab*, an open-source multi-domain end-to-end dialog system platform, aiming to enable researchers to quickly set up experiments with reusable components and compare a large set of different approaches, ranging from conventional pipeline systems to end-to-end neural models, in common environments. ConvLab offers a set of fully annotated datasets and the associated pre-trained reference models. As a showcase, we extend the MultiWOZ dataset with user dialog act annotations to train all component models and demonstrate how ConvLab makes it easy and effortless to conduct complicated experiments in multi-domain end-to-end dialog settings.

1 Introduction

Despite decades of research on dialog and increasingly large amounts of (annotated) dialog datasets, it is still challenging for any team who is new to the area to quickly develop a reasonable baseline system for task-oriented dialog due to the lack of a well-structured, easy-to-use open-source system that allows researchers to build and evaluate dialog bots. ConvLab is aimed to fill the gap. ConvLab is an open-source multi-domain end-to-end dialog system that allows researchers to automatically train dialog models, build and evaluate task-completion dialog bots. Such open-source systems have been instrumental in many AI research breakthroughs. For example, among many, Moses (Koehn, 2007), HTK (Young et al., 2002) and CoreNLP (Manning et al., 2014) have been widely used to facilitate subsequent research in machine translation, speech recognition and natural language processing, respectively.

ConvLab consists of a rich set of modeling tools and runtime engines for building task-oriented bots of different types, and an end-to-end evaluation platform. There are roughly two architectures of dialog systems (Gao et al., 2019): (1) a modular architecture (the top layer in Figure 2), consisting of natural language understanding (NLU), dialog state tracker (DST), dialog policy (POL) and natural language generation (NLG) components; and (2) a fully end-to-end neural architecture (the bottom layer in Figure 2) to minimize laborious hand-coding and error propagation down the pipeline. There also have emerged some models in-between (Wen et al., 2016; Mrkšić et al., 2016). Due to the wide range of approaches and different metrics used in prior studies, it is been impractical to perform a rigorous comparative study under the same condition. ConvLab is the first dialog research platform that covers a full range of trainable statistical models with fully annotated datasets, differing from previous toolkits whose focus is largely concentrated on the system policy component while other components are mostly limited to pre-fixed baseline models (Ultes, 2017; Miller et al., 2017; Li et al., 2018).

There is also an increasing interest in building bots that seamlessly intertwine multiple sub-domains to accomplish high-level user goals (Peng et al., 2017; Budzianowski et al., 2018). The development of multi-domain dialog system adds additional complexities to both data collection and annotation, and the models for dialog system components. For the former, Budzianowski et al. (2018) collected the MultiWOZ dataset, a dialog corpus with dialogs ranging over multiple domains for the trip information setting, whereas there is no open-platform yet that is designed to handle multi-domain, multi-intent phenomena. To foster multi-domain dialog research, ConvLab features the MultiWOZ task and offers a complete set of reference models ranging from individual components to end-to-end models that are trained on the MultiWOZ data with additional annotation for user dialog acts which is missing from the original

Proceedings of the 57th Annual Meeting of the Association for Computational Linguistics-System Demonstrations, pages 64–69
Florence, Italy, July 28 - August 2, 2019. ©2019 Association for Computational Linguistics

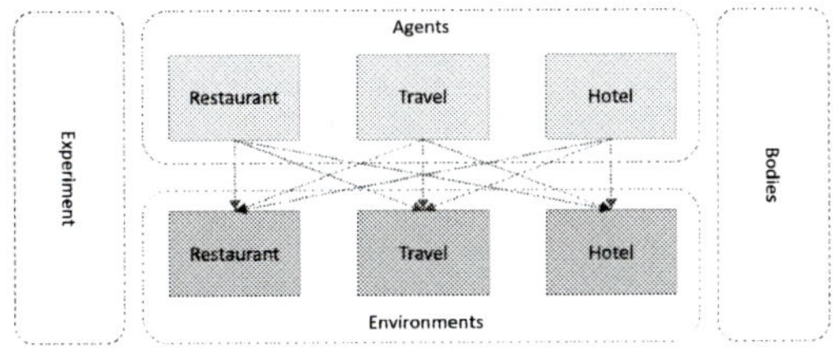

Figure 1: Overall design of ConvLab.

MultiWOZ dataset. Furthermore, ConvLab will be the standard platform for the multi-domain end-to-end task-completion dialog track in DSTC8[1].

Finally, to support end-to-end evaluation, ConvLab offers two complementary modules: Amazon Mechanical Turk integration for human evaluation and simulated users for automated evaluation. For user simulation, ConvLab provides both rule-based simulators and data-driven simulators. As data-driven user simulation recently gains more traction, ConvLab makes another contribution as a research platform for advancing user simulation technologies.

The summary of the unique contributions of ConvLab is:

- To the best of our knowledge, ConvLab is the first open-source multi-domain end-to-end dialog system that covers a full range of trainable statistical models with associated annotated datasets.

- ConvLab provides a rich set of tools and recipes to develop dialog systems of different types, enabling researchers to compare widely different approaches under the same condition.

- ConvLab provides end-to-end evaluation via both human and simulators.

- We are organizing DSTC8 and releasing ConvLab to the public.

2 ConvLab

This section details the design of ConvLab and its flexibility to support a wide range of experiments.

2.1 Overall Design

At a high level, to support flexible architectures for multi-domain dialog, ConvLab embraces the

[1]https://sites.google.com/dstc.community/dstc8/home

Agents-Environments-Bodies (AEB) design (illustrated in Figure 1) with the following semantics (Wah Loon Keng, 2017):

Agent an instance of dialog agent.

Environment an instance of user simulator or human evaluation component.

Body an incarnation of an agent in the environment – each body stores data that is specific to the associated agent and environment (indicated by the edges in Figure 1): states, actions, rewards, done flags.

With the AEB design, besides the usual single agent and single environment setting, a variety of advanced research experiments, such as multi-agent learning, multi-task learning and role-play, can be conducted without requiring specialized code for each case.

Multi-agent learning A centralized agent maps the joint observation of all domains to a joint action. A major drawback of this approach is its exponential growth in the observation-action space with the number of domains. One can address this intractability by factoring the centralized spaces into multi-agent systems (including hierarchical reinforcement learning agents). For example, in Figure 1, the centralized agent *Travel* can be decomposed into two separate domain agents *Restaurant* and *Hotel*.

Multi-task learning An agent can have multiple bodies in different environments for the sake of transfer learning. For example, any agent in Figure 1 can have its bodies not only in the corresponding environment but also in other environments to learn common knowledge across multiple domains. For example, in Figure 1, each agent can learn from all available environments.

Role play Recently, there has been increased interest in leveraging self-play as an alternative way of training reinforcement learning agents (et al., 2017). Following the same spirit, for task-completion dialogs, one can devise a role play – one agent plays the role of the system while the other agent the user. Such a role play setting can be readily achieved by having two agents talk to each other though a round-robin environment.

To perform systematic comparisons of agents and environments, and to automate hyper-parameter search, ConvLab makes use of SLM Lab (Wah Loon Keng, 2017) and Ray[2] for the experiment component in Figure 1 which provides multi-level control layers, i.e. Session, Trial and Experiment, and produces evaluation reports for each layer.

Session Each session initializes the agents and environments and then runs for a pre-defined number of episodes.

Trial Each trial holds a fixed set of parameter values and runs multiple sessions with random seeds. The trial then analyzes the sessions and takes the average.

Experiment An experiment is a study where the hyper-parameters are treated as input variables, and the outcome is measured by task-specific metrics such as success rate and average reward. Search is then automatically conducted to find the hyper-parameters that yield best performance.

ConvLab also helps avoid specifying complicated command line parameters and writing scripts by enabling users to control all relevant functionality via JSON configuration files. A configuration file specifies the model and its parameters for each component of the agent and environment for a given experiment. Thanks to the flexible configuration layer, researchers can build an array of different agents (Section 2.2) and environments (Section 2.3) with only slight modifications in the configuration file. Some example configuration files are presented in Section 4.

2.2 Dialog Agent Configuration

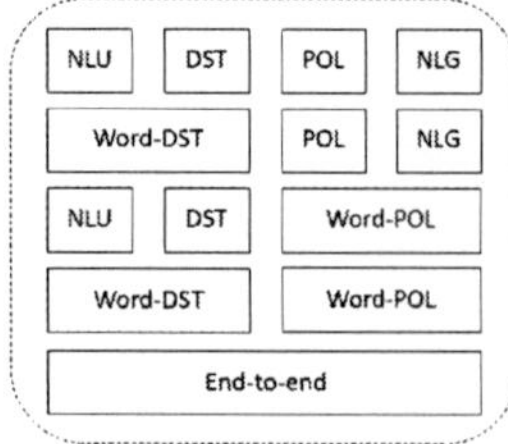

Figure 2: A dialog system configuration view.

In Figure 2, each layer represents a different way of constructing a dialog system. The top

layer, for example, corresponds to the conventional pipeline architecture consisting of NLU, DST, POL and NLG. Recently, researchers have introduced some models that merge some of the typical components such as word-level dialog state tracking, word-level dialog policy and end-to-end models, resulting in various possible combinations for building a dialog system as shown from the second layer in Figure 2. However, comparison among these possibilities in an end-to-end setting has been largely overlooked, partly due to the burden of implementing all comparative systems. With ConvLab, researchers can now focus on any particular component in Figure 2 while testing the algorithm in an end-to-end setting by simply creating a configuration file with a specification of other components.

2.3 Environment Configuration

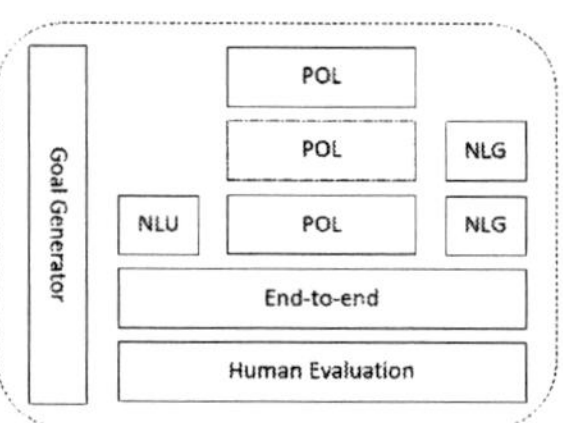

Figure 3: An environment configuration view.

As shown in Figure 3, there are also many different ways of combining components to build an environment. For example, the top layer corresponds to a user simulator operating at the dialog act level which is the typical setting of prior works focusing on developing reinforcement learning methods for dialog policy optimization. As with dialog agent, there are recent attempts on end-to-end approaches to avoid requiring expensive annotation (Kreyssig et al., 2018). For human evaluation, ConvLab also provides an integration of crowd source platform such as Amazon Mechanical Turk[3] as shown in the bottom layer.

2.4 Reference Models

This section describes a set of reference models for each component that are available in the initial release. As we will keep adding new state-of-the-art models, the set of reference models available in ConvLab will be extended.

---

[2]https://github.com/ray-project/ray

[3]ConvLab makes use of ParlAI's MTurk library (http://parl.ai/static/docs/mturk.html).

Natural Language Understanding For natural language understanding, ConvLab provides three reference models: Semantic Tuple Classifier (STC) (Mairesse et al., 2009), OneNet (Kim et al., 2017) and Multi-intent LU (MILU). STC can handle multi-domain, multi-intent dialog acts but cannot detect out-of-vocabulary (OOV) values. While OneNet can capture OOVs, it cannot handle multi-intent dialog acts. Thus, ConvLab offers a new MILU model which extends OneNet to process multi-intent dialog acts. For more details on MILU, please refer to the ConvLab site.

Dialog State Tracking The dialog state tracker is responsible for updating the belief state. ConvLab provides a rule-based tracker similar to the baselines in DSTCs (Williams et al., 2013) that are adapted to handle multi-domain interactions.

Word-level Dialog State Tracking Word-level DSTs directly take system and user natural language as inputs and update dialog state. ConvLab imports MDBT (Ramadan et al., 2018) model which jointly identifies the domain and tracks the belief states by utilizing the semantic similarity between dialog utterances and ontology terms.

System Policy For system policy, ConvLab provides three classes of implementations: handcrafted policy, supervised learning policy and reinforcement learning policy. For reinforcement learning, ConvLab supports a set of popular algorithms: DQN (Mnih et al., 2013) and its variants, REINFORCE (Williams, 1992), PPO (Schulman et al., 2017) and its self-imitation variant (Oh et al., 2018) . For multi-domain dialog, ConvLab initially offers centralized policies where the policy maps the joint observation of all domains to a joint action and will feature decentralized multi-agent approaches as well as hierarchical reinforcement learning approaches (Peng et al., 2017).

Natural Language Generation ConvLab provides a template-based model and SC-LSTM (Wen et al., 2015) for natural language generation. Each model is able to take the multi-domain, multi-intent dialog acts as input.

Word-level Policy Following Wen et al. (2016), word-level policy directly maps a context to response. ConvLab imports the baseline implementation released for the benchmarking purpose by Budzianowski et al. (2018)[4]. The baseline model extends a sequence-to-sequence model (Sutskever et al., 2014) with a dialog state encoding and a database query result encoding as additional features to the decoder.

User Policy For user policy, ConvLab provides an agenda-based (Schatzmann et al., 2007) user model and data-driven approaches such as HUS and its variational variants (Gur et al., 2018). Similar to the system side, each model works at the dialog act level, and can be pipelined with NLU and NLG modules to construct a whole user simulator.

End-to-end Model ConvLab makes available two end-to-end dialog system models: Mem2Seq (Madotto et al., 2018) and Sequicity (Lei et al., 2018). To support multi-domain intents, Sequicity resets the belief span when the model predicts a topic shift between domains.

3 Domains

The initial release of ConvLab offers two domains of differing complexity: MultiWOZ and Movie.

MultiWOZ The main task of the MultiWOZ domain is to help a tourist in a various situations involving multiple sub-domains such as requesting basic information about attractions and booking a hotel room. Specifically, there are 7 sub-domains - `Attraction, Hospital, Police, Hotel, Restaurant, Taxi, Train`. The annotated data consists of 10,438 dialogs. The average number of turns are 8.93 and 15.39 for single and multi-domain dialogs, respectively. ConvLab features additional annotations for user dialog acts and pre-trained reference models for all dialog system components and user simulators. Furthermore, ConvLab provides a set of end-to-end neural dialog models that are trained on the data.

Movie ConvLab imports the `Movie` domain from Microsoft Dialog Challenge (Li et al., 2018), encouraging researchers to continue working on the movie ticket booking task with enhanced tools. The annotated dataset consists of 2,890 dialogs, with approximately 7.5 turns per dialog on average. ConvLab offers a complete reference set of

---

[4]`https://github.com/budzianowski/multiwoz`

models trained on the data for both agent and user simulator.

We plan to add more domains such as the `Taxi` and `Restaurant` domains from Microsoft Dialog Challenge.

4 Demo

To demonstrate a glimpse of some working systems, this section presents two end-to-end experiments: 1) a comparison between NLU with rule-based DST and word-level DST; 2) a comparison between rule-based policy with NLG and word-level policy.

Experiment 1 Word-level DSTs often have shown higher performance than typical DSTs that take input from NLU (Ramadan et al., 2018; Mrkšić et al., 2016), but none of prior works confirmed the performance improvement in an end-to-end setting. Thanks to the flexible configuration interface and pre-trained reference models, with ConvLab, one can easily set up end-to-end experiments by simply modifying a few lines in the config files as listed in Table 1. While the overall accuracies of the rule-based DST and the word-level DST are 90.2% and 89.7%, respectively, the end-to-end task success rates are 69.05% and 16.67%. This clearly shows the gap between component-level performance and end-to-end performance. A detailed analysis on this is left for future work.

Experiment 2 Though word-level policy obtains an increasing traction, most studies only report corpus-based metrics such as BLEU and pseudo-success rate (i.e. success means all requested attributes are answered). This makes it hard to compare such approaches with conventional policies that are typically evaluated with task success metrics. Due to the space limitations, we omit the experimental config which is largely the same as the config listed on the left column in Table 1 except that the `policy` and `nlg` sections under the `agent` section are now replaced with a corresponding `word_policy` section. While the reported pseudo-success rate on test data is 60.96%, the success rate with a user simulator is 16.16%. This is also much lower than 69.05%, the performance of its counterpart with rule-based policy and NLG. Thus, there is huge room for improvement of the word-level policy in end-to-end settings.

NLU and rule-based DST	Word-level DST

<pre>{"multiwoz": {
  "agent": [{
   "name": "DialogAgent",
    "nlu": {
     "name": "OneNet"
    },
   "dst": {
    "name": "RuleDST"
   },
   "policy": {
    "name": "ExternalPolicy",
    "algorithm": {
     "name": "RulePolicy"
    }
   },
   "nlg": {
    "name": "TemplateNLG",
    "is_user": false
   }
  }],
  "env": [{
   "name": "multiwoz",
   "nlu": {
    "name": "OneNet"
   },
   "policy": {
    "name": "UserPolicyAgenda"
   },
   "nlg": {
    "name": "TemplateNLG",
    "is_user": true
   }
   "max_t": 40,
   "max_tick": 20000,
  }],
  "body": {
   "product": "outer",
   "num": 1
  }}}</pre>
	<pre>{"multiwoz": {
	  "agent": [{
	   "name": "DialogAgent",
	   "word-dst": {
	    "name": "MDBT"
	   },
	   "policy": {
	    "name": "ExternalPolicy",
	    "algorithm": {
	     "name": "RulePolicy"
	    }
	   },
	   "nlg": {
	    "name": "TemplateNLG",
	    "is_user": false
	   }
	  }],
	  "env": [{
	   "name": "multiwoz",
	   "nlu": {
	    "name": "OneNet"
	   },
	   "policy": {
	    "name": "UserPolicyAgenda"
	   },
	   "nlg": {
	    "name": "TemplateNLG",
	    "is_user": true
	   }
	   "max_t": 40,
	   "max_tick": 20000,
	  }],
	  "body": {
	   "product": "outer",
	   "num": 1
	}}}</pre>

Table 1: Example configs for comparing a system using word-level DST (right) with one using NLU and rule-based DST (left).

5 Code and Resources

The ConvLab platform is publicly available from `http://convlab.github.io`. Datasets and other resources such as tutorials and documentations can be found in the site.

6 Conclusion

We presented *ConvLab*, an open-source multi-domain end-to-end dialog system platform, that enables researchers to quickly set up experiments and compare different approaches without much effort. We will keep extending ConvLab by adding new state-of-the-art models going forward. The multi-domain end-to-end task completion dialog track in DSTC8 will employ ConvLab as the challenge platform, giving rise to a reference use case.

References

Silver et al. 2017. Mastering the game of go without human knowledge. *Nature*, 550(7676):354.

Paweł Budzianowski, Tsung-Hsien Wen, Bo-Hsiang Tseng, Iñigo Casanueva, Stefan Ultes, Osman Ramadan, and Milica Gašić. 2018. Multiwoz-a large-scale multi-domain wizard-of-oz dataset for task-oriented dialogue modelling. *arXiv preprint arXiv:1810.00278*.

Jianfeng Gao, Michel Galley, and Lihong Li. 2019. Neural approaches to conversational ai. *Foundations and Trends® in Information Retrieval*, 13(2-3):127–298.

Izzeddin Gur, Dilek Hakkani-Tur, Gokhan Tur, and Pararth Shah. 2018. User modeling for task oriented dialogues. *arXiv preprint arXiv:1811.04369*.

Young-Bum Kim, Sungjin Lee, and Karl Stratos. 2017. Onenet: Joint domain, intent, slot prediction for spoken language understanding. In *ASRU*, pages 547–553. IEEE.

Philipp et al. Koehn. 2007. Moses: Open source toolkit for statistical machine translation. In *ACL*, pages 177–180.

Florian Kreyssig, Inigo Casanueva, Pawel Budzianowski, and Milica Gasic. 2018. Neural user simulation for corpus-based policy optimisation for spoken dialogue systems. *arXiv preprint arXiv:1805.06966*.

Wenqiang Lei, Xisen Jin, Min-Yen Kan, Zhaochun Ren, Xiangnan He, and Dawei Yin. 2018. Sequicity: Simplifying task-oriented dialogue systems with single sequence-to-sequence architectures. In *ACL*, pages 1437–1447.

Xiujun Li, Sarah Panda, Jingjing Liu, and Jianfeng Gao. 2018. Microsoft dialogue challenge: Building end-to-end task-completion dialogue systems. *arXiv preprint arXiv:1807.11125*.

Andrea Madotto, Chien-Sheng Wu, and Pascale Fung. 2018. Mem2seq: Effectively incorporating knowledge bases into end-to-end task-oriented dialog systems. *arXiv preprint arXiv:1804.08217*.

François Mairesse, Milica Gasic, Filip Jurcicek, Simon Keizer, Blaise Thomson, Kai Yu, and Steve Young. 2009. Spoken language understanding from unaligned data using discriminative classification models. In *ICASPP*, pages 4749–4752. IEEE.

Christopher Manning, Mihai Surdeanu, John Bauer, Jenny Finkel, Steven Bethard, and David McClosky. 2014. The stanford corenlp natural language processing toolkit. In *ACL*, pages 55–60.

Alexander H Miller, Will Feng, Adam Fisch, Jiasen Lu, Dhruv Batra, Antoine Bordes, Devi Parikh, and Jason Weston. 2017. Parlai: A dialog research software platform. *arXiv preprint arXiv:1705.06476*.

Volodymyr Mnih, Koray Kavukcuoglu, David Silver, Alex Graves, Ioannis Antonoglou, Daan Wierstra, and Martin Riedmiller. 2013. Playing atari with deep reinforcement learning. *arXiv preprint arXiv:1312.5602*.

Nikola Mrkšić, Diarmuid O Séaghdha, Tsung-Hsien Wen, Blaise Thomson, and Steve Young. 2016. Neural belief tracker: Data-driven dialogue state tracking. *arXiv preprint arXiv:1606.03777*.

Junhyuk Oh, Yijie Guo, Satinder Singh, and Honglak Lee. 2018. Self-imitation learning. *arXiv preprint arXiv:1806.05635*.

Baolin Peng, Xiujun Li, Lihong Li, Jianfeng Gao, Asli Celikyilmaz, Sungjin Lee, and Kam-Fai Wong. 2017. Composite task-completion dialogue policy learning via hierarchical deep reinforcement learning. *arXiv preprint arXiv:1704.03084*.

Osman Ramadan, Paweł Budzianowski, and Milica Gašić. 2018. Large-scale multi-domain belief tracking with knowledge sharing. *arXiv preprint arXiv:1807.06517*.

Jost Schatzmann, Blaise Thomson, Karl Weilhammer, Hui Ye, and Steve Young. 2007. Agenda-based user simulation for bootstrapping a pomdp dialogue system. In *NAACL*, pages 149–152.

John Schulman, Filip Wolski, Prafulla Dhariwal, Alec Radford, and Oleg Klimov. 2017. Proximal policy optimization algorithms. *arXiv preprint arXiv:1707.06347*.

Ilya Sutskever, Oriol Vinyals, and Quoc V Le. 2014. Sequence to sequence learning with neural networks. In *NIPS*, pages 3104–3112.

Stefan et al. Ultes. 2017. Pydial: A multi-domain statistical dialogue system toolkit. *ACL, System Demonstrations*, pages 73–78.

Laura Graesser Wah Loon Keng. 2017. Slm-lab. `https://github.com/kengz/SLM-Lab`.

Tsung-Hsien Wen, Milica Gasic, Nikola Mrkšić, Pei-Hao Su, David Vandyke, and Steve Young. 2015. Semantically conditioned lstm-based natural language generation for spoken dialogue systems. In *EMNLP*, pages 1711–1721.

Tsung-Hsien Wen, David Vandyke, Nikola Mrksic, Milica Gasic, Lina M Rojas-Barahona, Pei-Hao Su, Stefan Ultes, and Steve Young. 2016. A network-based end-to-end trainable task-oriented dialogue system. *arXiv preprint arXiv:1604.04562*.

Jason Williams, Antoine Raux, Deepak Ramachandran, and Alan Black. 2013. The dialog state tracking challenge. In *SIGDIAL*, pages 404–413.

Ronald J Williams. 1992. Simple statistical gradient-following algorithms for connectionist reinforcement learning. *Machine learning*, 8(3-4):229–256.

Steve Young, Gunnar Evermann, Mark Gales, Thomas Hain, Dan Kershaw, Xunying Liu, Gareth Moore, Julian Odell, Dave Ollason, Dan Povey, et al. 2002. The htk book. *Cambridge university engineering department*, 3:175.

Demonstration of a Neural Machine Translation System with Online Learning for Translators

Miguel Domingo[1], Mercedes García-Martínez[2], Amando Estela[2], Laurent Bié[2], Alexandre Helle[2], Álvaro Peris[1], Francisco Casacuberta[1], and Manuel Herranz[2]

[1]PRHLT Research Center - Universitat Politècnica de València
{midobal, lvapeab, fcn}@prhlt.upv.es
[2]Pangeanic / B.I Europa - PangeaMT Technologies Division
{m.garcia, a.helle, a.estela, l.bie, m.herranz}@pangeanic.com

Abstract

We introduce a demonstration of our system, which implements online learning for neural machine translation in a production environment. These techniques allow the system to continuously learn from the corrections provided by the translators. We implemented an end-to-end platform integrating our machine translation servers to one of the most common user interfaces for professional translators: SDL Trados Studio. Our objective was to save post-editing effort as the machine is continuously learning from human choices and adapting the models to a specific domain or user style.

1 Introduction

Productivity is crucial in the translation industry. Nowadays, translation companies must be more competitive than ever and meet fast commercial demands. Thus, they need to produce high quality translations in shorter periods of time. Machine translation (MT) can help them to achieve this goal: instead of a linguist thinking out or "creating" translations from scratch, "humanizing" automatic translations has become a common process in the industry. This is known as post-editing (PE) and it has been shown to be effective in many cases (Arenas, 2008; Hu and Cadwell, 2016). As MT systems are continuously improving their capabilities (e.g. Hassan et al., 2018; Wu et al., 2016), this workflow has become of major relevance in the translation industry. Nonetheless, MT technology is still far from perfect (Dale, 2016; Koehn and Knowles, 2017), and there is still room for improvement.

Inherently to the PE process, new bilingual data is continuously generated (the post-edited samples). This data is typically used for the creation of domain-specific corpora, useful for adapting systems from a broader domain into a specific domain, client or style. The online learning (OL) paradigm aims to perform this adaptation during the PE process: each time the user validates a post-edited translation, the system is updated as this data is taken into account. Therefore, when the next translation is produced, the system will consider the previous post-editions. It is assumed that better translations (or translations more suited to the human post-editor preferences) will be produced.

The OL paradigm has quickly attracted the attention of researchers and industry. The CasMaCat (Alabau et al., 2013) and MateCat (Federico et al., 2014) projects—where phrase-based statistical MT systems were adapted incrementally from the user post-edits—achieved many advances in this direction. More recently, OL techniques were also applied to neural machine translation (NMT) systems (Peris et al., 2017; Turchi et al., 2017; Kothur et al., 2018; Wuebker et al., 2018; Peris and Casacuberta, 2018).

In this paper, we introduce a demo system of our in-house OL framework, in which we integrated our translation servers with the translators user-friendly interface SDL Trados Studio.

The rest of this document is structured as follows: Section 2 introduces the online learning paradigm. Next, in Section 3, we describe in detail our in-house architecture in which this paradigm is implemented. Finally, Section 4 summarizes the demo system.

2 Adapting a NMT system via online learning

We are interested in benefiting from the post-edits generated by the user during the PE process. To that end, we update the system on-the-fly, i.e, as soon as a sentence has been validated by the post-editor. Right after the user confirms a post-edit,

Proceedings of the 57th Annual Meeting of the Association for Computational Linguistics-System Demonstrations, pages 70–74
Florence, Italy, July 28 - August 2, 2019. ©2019 Association for Computational Linguistics

we update the models of our NMT system, using the source sentence and the post-edit as a training pair. This adaptation can be done following gradient descent, the regular training method for neural networks.

3 Architecture

Our in-house architecture of the OL framework is composed of three main modules: the MT engine, the user interface and the translation server which links both.

Moreover, we added a logging option to keep user tracking information as keystrokes, time and mouse movements. Fig. 1 illustrates this architecture.

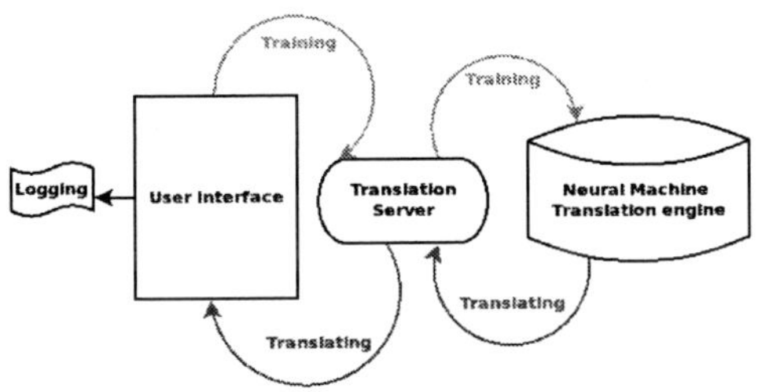

Figure 1: Architecture of our in-house OL framework. Red arrows represent how the correction made by the user arrives to the Machine Translation engine to be retrained. Blue arrows represent how machine translation is delivered to the user.

The translation process consists of delivering machine translations to the user interface and the training process retrains the MT engine with the feedback provided by the user. Both processes are performed through client-server communication. Next, we describe each module in detail.

3.1 Machine Translation Engine

The core of the MT engine is composed by the models generating translations, which can be retrained when required. Each translation project has its own model, whose architecture is set according to the project's need. All models are neural-based and are trained using `OpenNMT-py` (Klein et al., 2017).

Each MT model has its own configuration file, which contains personalized translation and OL options, such as tokenization, subword segmentation, learning rate, etc.

3.2 Translation Server

A translation server communicates with the MT models in order to generate translations and adapt the systems based on the user's post editions. This server is based on `OpenNMT-py`'s REST server and uses the HTTP protocol to define the messages in order to serve user's requests. The code of our translation server is open and available[1]. We created a branch in `OpenNMT-py` that features this server and is compatible with all its different models.

The communication between the user interface and the MT engine is performed by means of GET and POST requests. The server waits for translation requests. When received, these requests are sent to the machine translation engine in a JSON format. When a machine translation segment is corrected by the user, the correction is sent to the translation engine.

3.3 User Interface

In the translation industry, the most common user interface for translators is SDL Trados Studio[2]. Fig. 2 shows the user interface. The user gets the machine translation outputs automatically when the target part of the segment in the interface is clicked. Then, the user post-edits the segment and, when the translation is corrected, confirms it.

SDL allows the development of plugins for Trados Studio to enhance and extend the tool. Moreover, it has a large developer community[3] helping the software with add-ons and apps. We incorporated our adaptive framework as a Trados Studio plugin, that connected the user interface with Trados Studio with our translation server. As the user confirms a post-edit, the reviewed segment is sent back to the MT engine to be retrained with this new information.

In order to set up this plugin, the user fills the credentials with a username, password and URL pointing to the server (see Fig. 3 top left box). Also, the user fills the required languages and clicks in the "use machine translation" option (see Fig. 3 top right box). Finally, all the options

---

[1] `https://github.com/midobal/`
`OpenNMT-py/tree/OnlineLearning`

[2] `https://www.sdl.com/`
`es/software-and-services/`
`translation-software/sdl-trados-studio/`

[3] `https://community.sdl.com/`
`developers-more/developers/`
`language-developers`

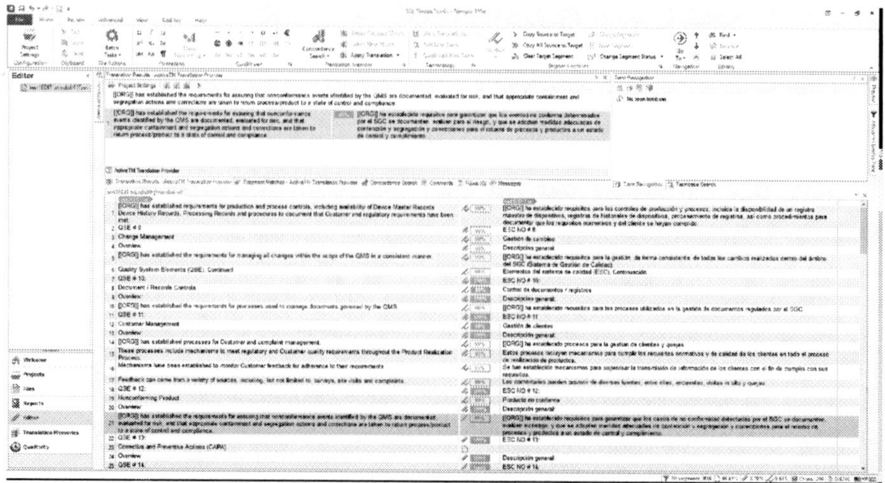

Figure 2: User Interface from Trados Studio SDL.

have to be enabled in the translation provider plugin (see Fig. 3 bottom box) in the Trados Studio project settings.

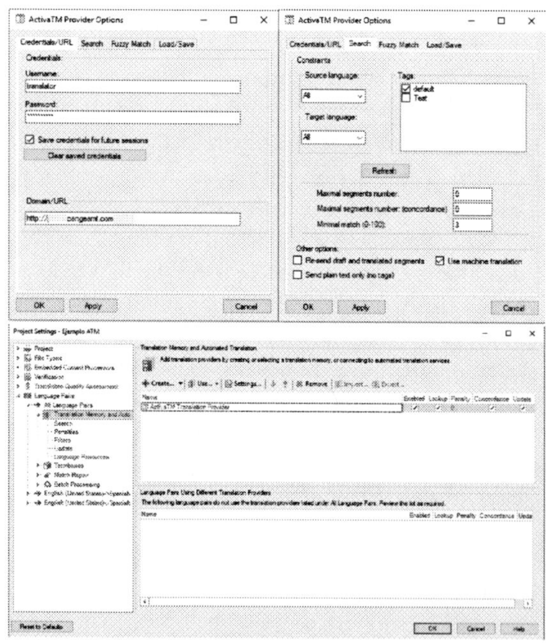

Figure 3: Machine translation plugin configuration.

3.4 Logging

In order to measure the productivity and effectiveness of OL during the PE process, we integrated tools to log the time, keystrokes and mouse movements involved in post-editing a given file. To achieve this, we incorporated the Qualitivity[4] plugin for Trados. This plugin generates an XML logging file, which contains all the keystrokes time information per segment. An example of this logging is shown in Figure 4.

With all this log information, we can measure the effort required to post-edit a file using MT with OL. Preliminary experiments in simulated and real environments with professional translators (Domingo et al., 2019), reported significant improvements of the quality of the translations generated by the MT systems (up to 5.3 points according to hTER, and 7.8 points according to hBLEU), and a significant reduction of the PE time (up to 7.5 second per sentence).

4 Summary

We have introduced a demonstration of Pangeanic's translation framework, which incorporates on-the-fly system adaptation via online learning. This paradigm allows human translators /post-editors to produce more human-quality text, that is, be more productive—a fundamental issue in the translation industry—since the system is continuously learning from the user post-edits, avoiding repetition of the same errors. We have integrated our MT servers into the SDL Trados Studio user interface which is one of the most used in the translation industry. This system aims to improve human translators' work by saving

---

[4]`https://community.sdl.com/`
`product-groups/translationproductivity/`
`w/customer-experience/2251.qualitivity`

```xml
<contentText>
  <source>[[ORG]] has established requirements for production and process controls, including availability of Device Master
    Records, Device History Records, Processing Records and procedures to document that Customer and regulatory requirements
    have been met.</source>
  <targetOriginal>[[ORG]] ha establecido requisitos para el control de la producción y el proceso, incluida la disponibilidad de Amo
    de Dispositivo, Device History Records, Processing Records y procedimientos para documentar el cumplimiento de los
    requisitos normativos y reglamentarios.</targetOriginal>
  <targetUpdated>[[ORG]] ha establecido requisitos para los controles de producción y procesos, incluida la disponibilidad de un
    registro maestro de Dispositivo, Device History Records, Processing Records y procedimientos para documentar el
    cumplimiento de los requisitos normativos y reglamentarios.</targetUpdated>
</contentText>
<qualityMetrics/>
<keyStrokes>
  <ks created="2019-04-03T12:47:15.309" match="" origin="" system="" selection="e" text="" key="[Delete]" SHIFT="False" CTRL="False" ALT="False"/>
  <ks created="2019-04-03T12:47:15.410" match="" origin="" system="" selection="" text=" " key="[Delete]" SHIFT="False" CTRL="False" ALT="False"/>
  <ks created="2019-04-03T12:47:16.486" match="" origin="" system="" selection="" text="l " key="L" SHIFT="False" CTRL="False" ALT="False"/>
  <ks created="2019-04-03T12:47:16.597" match="" origin="" system="" selection="" text="o" key="O" SHIFT="False" CTRL="False" ALT="False"/>
  <ks created="2019-04-03T12:47:16.673" match="" origin="" system="" selection="" text="s" key="S" SHIFT="False" CTRL="False" ALT="False"/>
  <ks created="2019-04-03T12:47:18.399" match="" origin="" system="" selection="" text="e" key="E" SHIFT="False" CTRL="False" ALT="False"/>
  <ks created="2019-04-03T12:47:18.606" match="" origin="" system="" selection="" text="s" key="S" SHIFT="False" CTRL="False" ALT="False"/>
  <ks created="2019-04-03T12:47:23.661" match="" origin="" system="" selection="a" text="" key="[Back]" SHIFT="False" CTRL="False" ALT="False"/>
  <ks created="2019-04-03T12:47:23.778" match="" origin="" system="" selection="l " text=" " key="[Back]" SHIFT="False" CTRL="False" ALT="False"/>
```

Figure 4: Example of Qualitivity's logging file.

time and effort.

Acknowledgments

The research leading to these results has received funding from the Spanish Centre for Technological and Industrial Development (Centro para el Desarrollo Tecnológico Industrial) (CDTI) and the European Union through Programa Operativo de Crecimiento Inteligente (Project IDI-20170964). We gratefully acknowledge the support of NVIDIA Corporation with the donation of a GPU used for part of this research.

References

Vicent Alabau, Ragnar Bonk, Christian Buck, Michael Carl, Francisco Casacuberta, Mercedes García-Martínez, Jesús González-Rubio, Philipp Koehn, Luis A. Leiva, Bartolomé Mesa-Lao, Daniel Ortiz-Martínez, Hervé Saint-Amand, Germán Sanchis-Trilles, and Chara Tsoukala. 2013. CASMACAT: An open source workbench for advanced computer aided translation. *The Prague Bulletin of Mathematical Linguistics*, 100:101–112.

Ana Guerberof Arenas. 2008. Productivity and quality in the post-editing of outputs from translation memories and machine translation. *Localisation Focus*, 7(1):11–21.

Robert Dale. 2016. How to make money in the translation business. *Natural Language Engineering*, 22(2):321–325.

Miguel Domingo, Mercedes García-Martínez, Álvaro Peris, Alexandre Helle, Amando Estela, Laurent Bié, Francisco Casacuberta, and Manuel Herranz. 2019. Incremental adaptation of NMT for professional post-editors: A user study. In *Proceedings of the Machine Translation Summit*. Under publication.

Marcello Federico, Nicola Bertoldi, Mauro Cettolo, Matteo Negri, Marco Turchi, Marco Trombetti, Alessandro Cattelan, Antonio Farina, Domenico Lupinetti, Andrea Martines, Alberto Massidda, Holger Schwenk, Loïc Barrault, Frederic Blain, Philipp Koehn, Christian Buck, and Ulrich Germann. 2014. The matecat tool. In *Proceedings of the 25th International Conference on Computational Linguistics: System Demonstrations*, pages 129–132.

Hany Hassan, Anthony Aue, Chang Chen, Vishal Chowdhary, Jonathan Clark, Christian Federmann, Xuedong Huang, Marcin Junczys-Dowmunt, William Lewis, Mu Li, et al. 2018. Achieving human parity on automatic chinese to english news translation.

Ke Hu and Patrick Cadwell. 2016. A comparative study of post-editing guidelines. In *Proceedings of the 19th Annual Conference of the European Association for Machine Translation*, pages 34206–353.

Guillaume Klein, Yoon Kim, Yuntian Deng, Jean Senellart, and Alexander M. Rush. 2017. OpenNMT: Open-source toolkit for neural machine translation. In *Proceedings of the Association for the Computational Linguistics*, pages 67–72.

Philipp Koehn and Rebecca Knowles. 2017. Six challenges for neural machine translation. In *Proceedings of the First Workshop on Neural Machine Translation*, pages 28–39.

Sachith Sri Ram Kothur, Rebecca Knowles, and Philipp Koehn. 2018. Document-level adaptation for neural machine translation. In *Proceedings of the 2nd Workshop on Neural Machine Translation and Generation*, pages 64–73.

Álvaro Peris and Francisco Casacuberta. 2018. Online learning for effort reduction in interactive neural machine translation. *Accepted in Computer Speech & Language*.

Álvaro Peris, Luis Cebrián, and Francisco Casacuberta. 2017. Online learning for neural machine translation post-editing. *arXiv:1706.03196*.

Marco Turchi, Matteo Negri, M Amin Farajian, and Marcello Federico. 2017. Continuous learning from human post-edits for neural machine translation. *The Prague Bulletin of Mathematical Linguistics*, 108(1):233–244.

Y. Wu, M. Schuster, Z. Chen, Q. V. Le, M. Norouzi, W. Macherey, M. Krikun, Y. Cao, Q. Gao, K. Macherey, J. Klingner, A. Shah, M. Johnson, X. Liu, Ł. Kaiser, S. Gouws, Y. Kato, T. Kudo, H. Kazawa, K. Stevens, G. Kurian, N. Patil, W. Wang, C. Young, J. Smith, J. Riesa, A. Rudnick, O. Vinyals, G. Corrado, M. Hughes, and J. Dean. 2016. Google's neural machine translation system: Bridging the gap between human and machine translation. *arXiv:1609.08144*.

Joern Wuebker, Patrick Simianer, and John DeNero. 2018. Compact personalized models for neural machine translation. In *Proceedings of the 2018 Conference on Empirical Methods in Natural Language Processing*, pages 881–886.

FASTDial: Abstracting Dialogue Policies for Fast Development of Task Oriented Agents

Serra Sinem Tekiroğlu and **Bernardo Magnini** and **Marco Guerini**
Fondazione Bruno Kessler, Via Sommarive 18, Povo, Trento, Italy
`tekiroglu@fbk.eu, magnini@fbk.eu, guerini@fbk.eu`

Abstract

We present a novel abstraction framework called FASTDial for designing task oriented dialogue agents, built on top of the OpenDial toolkit. This framework is meant to facilitate prototyping and development of dialogue systems from scratch also by non tech savvy, especially when limited training data is available. To this end, we use a generic and simple frame-slots data-structure with pre-defined dialogue policies that allows for fast design and implementation at the price of some flexibility reduction. Moreover, it allows for minimizing programming effort and domain expert training time, by hiding away many implementation details.

1 Introduction

In recent years, there has been an increasing demand for a new generation of conversational systems that are able to naturally interact and assist humans in a number of scenarios, including - but not limited to - virtual coaches, personal assistants and automatic help desks. However, when dealing with applications or commercial scenarios, technological complexity should be abstracted away since domain knowledge is often held by non tech savvy. Moreover, systems should be 'transparent' to easily allow for modification or scaling when needed, such as error fixing or new intents/objects/requirements integration.

To this end, several solutions have appeared on the market. On one side, there are open source tools/frameworks, such as OpenDial (Lison and Kennington, 2016), PyDial (Ultes et al., 2017) and DeepPavlov (Burtsev et al., 2018) that are very flexible and allow many integrations. While these tools are designed with the target of computer scientists in mind, they would still need domain expertise to design proper dialogues. On the other side of the spectrum, several commercial tools

aim at hiding dialogue implementation complexity, for example by using intuitive graphical interfaces to help also non technical experts build their own dialogues. This comes to the price of loosing some flexibility, integration capabilities, and control over the system.

However, constructing flexible multi-intent dialogue agents while keeping the implementation complexity minimal is not a trivial task both on commercial and open source tools. Considering that there are several domains requiring such dialogue systems (e.g. banking, e-commerce etc.), we aim at providing a framework that is easy to use but at the same time is still as flexible as possible.

To this end, we tried to merge the best of both worlds (commercial and open source tools) by designing and implementing a generalization architecture on top of OpenDial. OpenDial is a Java-based, domain-independent framework for developing probabilistic rule-based dialogue systems. While keeping the rule-based approach of OpenDial, our architecture, named FASTDial, abstracts away dialogue policies in a generic dialogue model that drastically reduces design effort and code complexity. This generic dialogue model starts with an intent recognition phase that is user initiative. Once the intent is recognized the interaction is converted to system initiative for filling the required slots. Still, the user is given an active part by allowing universal interruptions such as calling help or canceling the task (Jurafsky and Martin, 2017). In our view, most task oriented domains can be easily adapted to this schema. This allows for speeding up the prototyping of complex multi-intent dialogue scenarios. It allows easy integration of new languages and new intents, by prioritizing efficiency and extensibility to facilitate developing dialogue systems from scratch and with limited training data available. Scalabil-

Proceedings of the 57th Annual Meeting of the Association for Computational Linguistics-System Demonstrations, pages 75–80
Florence, Italy, July 28 - August 2, 2019. ©2019 Association for Computational Linguistics

ity can be quickly obtained also by non-experts since the technical implementation of the dialogue flow is abstracted away. Therefore, instead of focusing on a graphical interface approach, we abstracted the dialogue policy in order to make dialogue building simpler:

- non-experts can easily be trained to write dialogues - or better - to provide the information needed to automatically establish a dialogue.

- new intents can be quickly added.

- dialogues can be quickly and easily ported to new languages.

- by using API interface to separate dialogue from actual data we can increase the modularity in the applications.

However, generalizing the dialogue flow into certain logical patterns brings along the restriction in the dialogue policy flexibility such that the agent can only handle informable slot types and a single slot per turn.

The remainder of the paper is structured as follow: Section 2 presents the architecture of our system with its main components, while Section 3 presents our running example in the banking scenario. Finally, in Section 4 and 5 we evaluate our approach and discuss future developments.

2 Architecture

In the FASTDial architecture[1], the main conversational ability of the agent is encoded in a generalized dialogue policy mechanism that is fed with a *frame-slots data-structure* (FSDS). By abstracting the policy away, we manage a systematic way to load new intents (tasks/goals) to the agent represented only as slots, data_types, api calls, and pre-defined system utterances to produce relevant dialogues with the user.

In this scenario, each intent relevant to a given domain (e.g. 'make a money transfer', 'check account balance', 'block credit card') is represented by one FSDS data structure. After recognizing the user intent, the agent loads the corresponding FSDS from an external resource (i.e. json files) and interactively fills the slots by asking related questions to the user, making sure that all the constraints associated with each slot are fulfilled. By

---

[1]FASTDial code can be downloaded at the following link: `https://github.com/serrasinem/FASTDial`

design, the agent performs single-intent at a time and after each execution, the user can request a new intent. An intent can be categorized as either a query intent or an action intent. Regarding the banking domain, requesting information on the *Account Balance* is a query intent, while making a *Money Transfer* is categorized as an action intent.

The architecture has been designed to be handy especially in the application scenarios where many user intents must be implemented in a very short time and the training dialogue data is really scarce. The main framework is designed as a module on top of OpenDial toolkit. The architecture of the dialogue agent consists of 5 components; namely, Dialogue Manager, Integration Interface, Natural Language Understanding, Natural Language Generation, and Intent Manager.

2.1 Dialogue Manager Module

The dialogue manager is responsible of the intermodule communication and controlling the dialogue flow through dialogue states. In FASTDial, once the user intent is identified, the dialogue is led by the system. With respect to the slot order in the FSDS of the intent, the system asks the slot filling questions and processes the respective user utterance to retrieve the slot values. After the slot value is extracted, the DM module sends it to the API module for validation. If the value is valid, the DM module either activates the next slot state or finalizes the dialogue if all the mandatory slots are filled. If the value is not valid, the DM reformulates the machine utterance with the corresponding validation error and asks the slot filling question again. In Figure 1, we give an example dialogue demonstrating the aforementioned DM functioning.

Although FASTDial is designed to be system initiative during slot filling, slots can be expressed by the user at the intent utterance state, which is the initial stage of the conversation, (e.g. "I would like to transfer *AMOUNT* euros to *NAME*"). For this reason all slots described in the FSDS are also searched in the intent utterance. Consequently, as well as detecting the *Money Transfer* intent in the example above, the system would capture the values for the *transfer destination* and the *amount* slots. The system validates the detected values and if no error occurs the system skips the corresponding slot filling questions, i.e. *SKIPPED_TURN* in Figure 1.

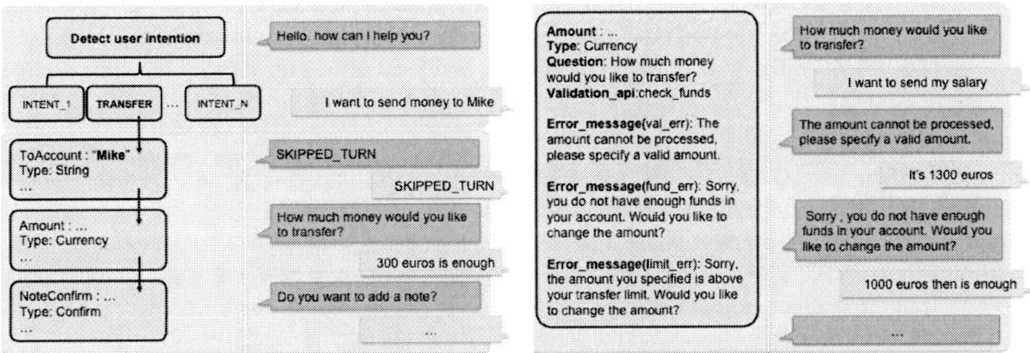

Figure 1: Example of dialogue with FASTDial in a multi-intent banking scenario. On the left: Upper section is intent recognition (user initiative). Once the intent has been recognized the system takes the lead and ask one slot at a time (lower section). On the right: a complex sub-dialogue due to validation errors for the amount slot.

FASTDial reduces the dialogue management complexity and provides a set of predefined dialogue policies, which most dialogue scenarios can be fitted into. However, the reduction of the dialogue flow complexity brings some restrictions to the flexibility of the dialogue management. We provide a list of restrictions and their alternatives in FASTDial dialogue flow as follows:

- system initiative dialogue flow: once the user intent is identified, the system tries to fill all necessary slots and in case of an unexpected user utterance, it changes the state to either repeating the question or finalizing the dialogue. This would prevent the system answering the mid-dialogue user questions, i.e. requestable slots (Henderson et al., 2013). As an example, in the *Money Transfer* intent, the user may ask about her account balance before specifying the amount of money she wants to send. The DM cannot change the intent to *Account Balance* query in this scenario.

- one slot per turn: a slot turn can only be for a single slot value. Multiple information must be asked in different questions as different slots. For instance, in a food ordering scenario, food type and number of orders should be defined as different slot turns. Still, both slots can be identified in the intent sentence if specified by the user.

2.2 Integration Interface

The dialogue agent can be used as an external tool to any application through its web service interface. Similar to the dialogue bAbI tasks (Bordes et al., 2016), the interface creates either a machine response or a functional call to its client. The responses of these functional calls, in a "variable:value format", are directed to the NLG module to transform the response values into suitable natural text shown to the user. In addition, for demo purposes, the framework has a simple Telegram application that requires a knowledge base implementation as a backend. Unlike the web service interface, Telegram app only produces machine utterances and connects to the backend knowledge base when necessary.

2.3 Natural Language Understanding

The task of the Natural Language Understanding component is twofold: first to recognize the user intent and then fill the corresponding FSDS that has been loaded by the Intent Module and active at the moment. While understanding the intent type is implemented as a model interface, the slot recognition task is handled by each slot type separately. The intent identification model is generated during the initialization of the agent, by retrieving the intent keys from all registered intents.

Each slot type has its own slot filling method and the type-specific slot constraints are employed to match the values from the user utterance. Therefore, the agent can employ different NLU approaches for different data types. Similar to the strategy in OpenDial, while a simple regular expression model is applied to retrieve numbers, a more complex deep learning recognition model can be applied to other slots. This approach allows integrating new slot filling models, such as Named Entity Recognition models (Louvan and

Magnini, 2018) or RNN (Mesnil et al., 2015), easily by overloading the matching function in the abstract class of the slot object.

2.4 Natural Language Generation

The machine utterances shown to the user throughout the dialogue are supplied by the Natural Language Generation module whose main responsibility is to select the correct machine response to lead the dialogue to successfully fulfill a user intent. In the startup of the agent, the NLG model is generated by using the intent descriptions retrieved from all the registered FSDSs and language-specific generic texts. API responses are also integrated into machine utterances whenever necessary. The machine utterances include the user greetings, the slot filling questions, confirmation requests, the output of the user intent executions, error messages (i.e. erroneous slot values, incomprehensible user utterances, and translation of the API responses with error codes).

2.5 Intent Manager

Intent Manager loads the intent frame (i.e. FSDS) on-the-fly when the user intent is detected by the NLU module. All possible FSDS, including their metadata and slot descriptions, are registered when the agent starts up. The intent frame descriptions reside in the FSDS Knowledge Base (KB), currently a simple folder containing json files of all registered intents. A new intent can be registered to the dialogue agent by adding it to the FSDS KB folder after the following properties are defined:

- name: defines the name of the intent.

- keys: defines the keywords that are necessary for understanding the user intent. It is a comma separated list of regular expressions. In addition, a more complex NLU function, such as any defined slot filling model, can be assigned to be called in this variable.

- confirmation: a boolean value determines if the execution of the intent requires a confirmation from the user. For instance, certain actions such as payments or, more generally, the tasks that require the user's complete awareness of the consequences should be finalized after the user's confirmation.

- confirmation question : if a confirmation is required for the execution of the intent, the confirmation question must be saved in this parameter.

- execution call: the final execution APICall. API formalism should be agreed upon with the middleware.

- success & error messages: the messages to be shown to the user when the execution of the intent is successful and when the execution of the intent is failed.

- slots: the 'ordered' list of slot objects that need to be filled to execute the intent.

A slot object can be in the type of String, List of Strings, Date, Time, Currency, Numeric, and Confirmation. Although we provide a pre-implemented list of possible slot types, the slot implementation has been designed as an abstract object that can be extended easily into new types of slots depending on the specific requirements of a new domain. For instance, a Named Entity slot that holds any given named entity can be implemented by employing a deep NER model. A slot object can be added to the slot list of an intent by defining the following variables.

- slot name: should be unique for intent.

- slot type: holds a slot type.

- constraint: type dependent. It determines the slot filling conditions necessary for the NLU.

- question: It holds the question to be asked to the user to fill the slot value.

- validation api: Each slot should be verified after receiving the value from the user in order to continue to the next slot, unless specified with the key "NoValidate". This variable holds the validation api function name to call after filling the slot value.

- error message: The error machine utterances and the error codes are defined in a list of "error_code:utterance" format.

- mandatory: This variable is a boolean value determining if the slot must be filled in order to execute the user intent.

- regex: We can define a list of regular expressions for extracting a slot value. Each regex should contain "{slot}" string, which is the filler for the expected slot value, e.g. "my {slot} card". While "keys" parameter predefines a set of slot values to be exactly matched, "regex" parameter defines a set of patterns to extract the unknown slot values from the user utterance.

- dependency: The possible values that a slot can take sometimes depend on a previous slot. In this condition, dependency variable is required to hold a slot name which is defined prior to the current slot.

3 Banking Domain

Considering the data scarcity, Banking dialogues could be one of the hardest datasets to retrieve due to security requirements. Not only the real user interaction dialogues, but also the KB structure or the logical structure of a banking action would not completely and easily been shared. In this scenario, training a model with the actual banking data or dialogue samples would not be possible. Keeping these requirements and limitations in mind, we generated FSDSs for various banking tasks, such as *Money Transfer*, *Account History Search*, *Account Balance* query, *Card Limit* query, *Canceling a Transfer*, and *Blocking a Card*, from scratch with the help of a domain expert. In this domain, intent types and almost all slot values detected in the user utterances are validated through API calls and the dialogue flow can change accordingly. In Listing 1, we provide the json object of a sample FSDS registered to accomplish a *Money Transfer*. It is worthwhile to mention that to give the ability of establishing dialogues for the *Money Transfer* intent, all required information resides in this single json object. Additionally, in Table 1, we show a simple *Account Balance* dialogue with the required API interaction.

```
{"name":"Transfer",
"keys":"make *transfer,send *money...",
"confirmation":true,
"confirmation_question":"Do you confirm
    sending {Amount} to {ToAccount}?",
"execution_call":"execute_transfer",
"slots": [
    {"slot_name":"ToAccount",
        "slot_type":"StringList",
        "constraint":"_keys_:
            recipient_list",
        "question":"What is the name of
            the recipient?",
        "validation_api":"
            check_recipient",
        "error_message":{"val_err":"
            There is no saved recipient
            with the name you provided.
            Please enter one of the
            options among: "},
        "mandatory":true,
        "regex": "money to {slot}"},
    {"slot_name":"Amount",
        "slot_type":"Currency",
        "constraint":"€",
        "dependency":"FromAccount",
        "question":"How much money would
            you like to transfer?",
        "validation_api":"
            check_funds_limit",
        "error_message":{"val_err":"The
            amount cannot be processed,
            please specify a valid
            amount.", "fund_err":"Sorry,
            you do not have enough
            funds in your account. Would
            you like to change the
            amount?","limit_err":"Sorry,
            the amount you specified is
            above your transfer limit.
            Would you like to change the
            amount?"},
        "mandatory": true},
    {"slot_name":"NoteConfirm",
        "slot_type":"Confirmation",
        "constraint":"yes,ok,sure,
            correct,right,positive;no,
            not now,not today,negative;
            action:skipNext",
        "question":"Do you want to add a
            note to your transfer?",
        "validation_api":"NoValidate",
        "error_message":{"val_err":"I
            couldn't understand your
            request. Could you please
            confirm or reject adding a
            note?"},
        "mandatory":true},
    {"slot_name":"Note",
        "slot_type":"String",
        "constraint":"",
        "question":"Please type your
            note.",
        "validation_api":"savePost",
        "error_message":{"val_err":"
            There is a problem with your
            request. Your note could
            not be saved."},
        "mandatory":false }],
"success_message":"OK, your transfer is
    done. Can I help you with anything
    else?",
"error_message":"Your transfer cannot be
    executed. {ErrorMessage} Can I help
    you with anything else?"}
```

Listing 1: json FSDS for *Money Transfer*

4 System Evaluation

Since one of our main claims is that our abstraction framework can drastically reduce dialogue design and code complexity - as compared to Open-Dial - we set up a comparison task. In this task we re-implemented three of the intent of the bank-

B:	Hello, how can I help you with ?
U:	I would like to check my account balance.
A$_C$:	MESSAGE: ACCOUNT_LIST, INTENT: AC-COUNTBALANCE
A$_R$:	[CHECKING, SAVINGS]
B:	You have Checking, Savings accounts. Which one would you like to query?
U:	savings, please
A$_C$:	INFO_TYPE: CHECK_ACCOUNT, MES-SAGE: SAVINGS
A$_R$:	STATE: INFO_CHECK_SUCCESS
A$_C$:	MESSAGE: EXECUTE_INTENT
A$_R$:	MESSAGE: {AMOUNT:100, CURRENCY-TYPE:€}, STATE: EXECUTE_SUCCESS
B:	The current balance on your Savings account is 100 €. Can I help you with anything else?

Table 1: An excerpt of an *Account Balance* dialogue generated from its FSDS toghether with the API calls. **B** is Bot, **U** is User, **A**$_C$ is API call, **A**$_R$ is API response.

ing scenario into the native OpenDial representation. The code reduction was of two orders of magnitude (on average from 2000 lines of XML code to 80 lines of json format FSDS description). Note that for this comparison we relied on a developer, so we excluded the time needed to learn the tool, that for OpenDial is expected to be much higher. As a second task, we ported the language-specific generic NLU/NLG definitions and original 9 Banking Domain intents to two new languages (Italian and Hungarian): on average setting up a completely functional dialogue agent with all 9 intents required from 3 to 4 hours. In this case we did not use a programmer but a native speaker per language with good knowledge of English.

5 Conclusion and Future Work

We presented FASTDial, a dialogue policy abstraction framework built on top of OpenDial that allows for fast prototyping and significant code complexity reduction in building conversational agents. We are planning to expand our framework with new features (e.g. new data types, multiple slots per turn), and also to build a version that allows for user driven dialogues. This new version would require some changes in the underlying logic. Moreover we are planning to integrate some available models for NLU and NLG into our FSDS structure to replace simple regular expres-

sion matching and template filling.

Acknowledgement

This work has been partially supported by the Conversational Banking Front-end EIT-Digital project (ID. 18039).

References

Antoine Bordes, Y-Lan Boureau, and Jason Weston. 2016. Learning end-to-end goal-oriented dialog. *arXiv preprint arXiv:1605.07683*.

Mikhail Burtsev, Alexander Seliverstov, Rafael Airapetyan, Mikhail Arkhipov, Dilyara Baymurz-ina, Nickolay Bushkov, Olga Gureenkova, Taras Khakhulin, Yuri Kuratov, Denis Kuznetsov, Alexey Litinsky, Varvara Logacheva, Alexey Lymar, Valentin Malykh, Maxim Petrov, Vadim Polulyakh, Leonid Pugachev, Alexey Sorokin, Maria Vikhreva, and Marat Zaynutdinov. 2018. Deeppavlov: Open-source library for dialogue systems. In *Proceedings of ACL 2018, System Demonstrations*, pages 122–127. Association for Computational Linguistics.

Matthew Henderson, Blaise Thomson, and Jason Williams. 2013. Dialog state tracking challenge 2&3.

Daniel Jurafsky and James H Martin. 2017. Dialog systems and chatbots. *Speech and language processing*.

P. Lison and C. Kennington. 2016. Opendial: A toolkit for developing spoken dialogue systems with probabilistic rules. In *Proceedings of the 54th Annual Meeting of the Association for Computational Linguistics (Demonstrations)*, pages 67–72, Berlin, Germany. Association for Computational Linguistics.

Samuel Louvan and Bernardo Magnini. 2018. Exploring named entity recognition as an auxiliary task for slot filling in conversational language understanding. In *Proceedings of the 2018 EMNLP Workshop SCAI: The 2nd International Workshop on Search-Oriented Conversational AI*, pages 74–80.

Grégoire Mesnil, Yann Dauphin, Kaisheng Yao, Yoshua Bengio, Li Deng, Dilek Hakkani-Tur, Xiaodong He, Larry Heck, Gokhan Tur, Dong Yu, et al. 2015. Using recurrent neural networks for slot filling in spoken language understanding. *IEEE/ACM Transactions on Audio, Speech, and Language Processing*, 23(3):530–539.

Stefan Ultes, Lina M Rojas Barahona, Pei-Hao Su, David Vandyke, Dongho Kim, Inigo Casanueva, Paweł Budzianowski, Nikola Mrkšić, Tsung-Hsien Wen, Milica Gasic, et al. 2017. Pydial: A multi-domain statistical dialogue system toolkit. *Proceedings of ACL 2017, System Demonstrations*, pages 73–78.

A Neural, Interactive-predictive System for Multimodal Sequence to Sequence Tasks

Álvaro Peris and **Francisco Casacuberta**
Pattern Recognition and Human Language Technology Research Center
Universitat Politcnica de Valncia, Valncia, Spain
`{lvapeab, fcn}@prhlt.upv.es`

Abstract

We present a demonstration of a neural interactive-predictive system for tackling multimodal sequence to sequence tasks. The system generates text predictions to different sequence to sequence tasks: machine translation, image and video captioning. These predictions are revised by a human agent, who introduces corrections in the form of characters. The system reacts to each correction, providing alternative hypotheses, compelling with the feedback provided by the user. The final objective is to reduce the human effort required during this correction process.

This system is implemented following a client–server architecture. For accessing the system, we developed a website, which communicates with the neural model, hosted in a local server. From this website, the different tasks can be tackled following the interactive-predictive framework. We open-source all the code developed for building this system. The demonstration in hosted in `http://casmacat.prhlt.upv.es/interactive-seq2seq`.

1 Introduction

The sequence to sequence problem involves the transduction of an input sequence $\mathbf{x}$ into an output sequence $\hat{\mathbf{y}}$ (Graves, 2012). In the last years, many tasks have been tackled under this perspective using neural networks with extraordinary results: neural machine translation (NMT; Sutskever et al., 2014; Bahdanau et al., 2015), speech recognition and translation (Chan et al., 2016; Niehues et al., 2018), image and video captioning (Xu et al., 2015; Yao et al., 2015), among others.

These systems are usually based on the statistical formalization of pattern recognition (e.g. Bishop, 2006). Following this probabilistic framework, the objective is to find most likely output se-

quence $\hat{\mathbf{y}}$, given an input sequence $\mathbf{x}$, according to a model Θ:

$$\hat{\mathbf{y}} = \arg\max_{\mathbf{y}} \ p(\mathbf{y} \mid \mathbf{x}; \Theta) \qquad (1)$$

In the last years, Θ has been frequently implemented as a deep neural network, trained in an end-to-end way. These neural systems have consistently outperformed other alternatives in the aforementioned problems. However and despite these impressive advances, the systems are not perfect, and still make errors (Koehn and Knowles, 2017).

In several scenarios, and especially in machine translation, fully-automatic systems are usually used for providing initial predictions to the input objects. These predictions are later revised by a human expert, who corrects the errors made by the system. This is known as post-editing and, in some scenarios, it increases the productivity with respect to performing the task from scratch (Alabau et al., 2016; Arenas, 2008; Hu and Cadwell, 2016).

1.1 Interactive-predictive pattern recognition

As an alternative to the static, decoupled post-editing, other strategies have been proposed, aiming to improve the productivity of the correction phase. Among them, the interactive-predictive pattern recognition (Foster et al., 1997) results particularly interesting. Under this framework, the static correction stage shifts to an iterative human-computer collaboration process.

The user interacts with the system by means of a feedback signal f. The system suggests then an alternative hypothesis $\bar{\mathbf{y}}$, compatible with the feedback. The inclusion of the feedback into the general pattern recognition rewrites Eq. (1) introduc-

Proceedings of the 57th Annual Meeting of the Association for Computational Linguistics-System Demonstrations, pages 81–86
Florence, Italy, July 28 - August 2, 2019. ©2019 Association for Computational Linguistics

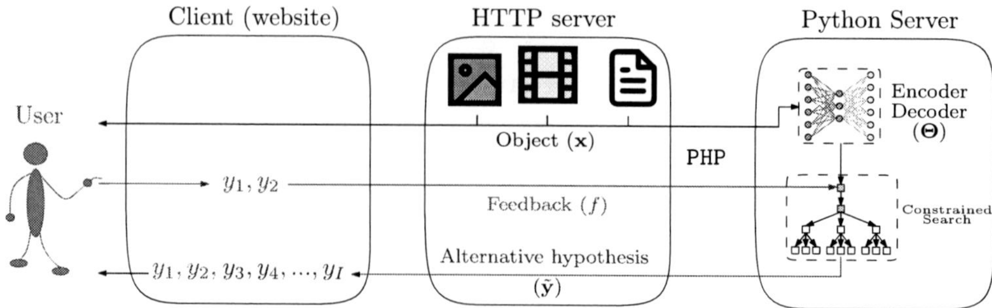

Figure 1: System architecture. The client, a website, presents the user several input objects (images, videos or texts) and a prediction. The user then introduces a feedback signal, for correcting this prediction. After being introduced, the feedback signal is sent to the server—together with the input object—for generating an alternative hypothesis, which takes into account the user corrections.

ing a restriction on the search space:

$$\tilde{\mathbf{y}} = \argmax_{\mathbf{y} \text{ compatible with } f} p(\mathbf{y} \mid \mathbf{x}, f; \Theta) \qquad (2)$$

The most paradigmatic application of the interactive-predictive pattern recognition framework is machine translation. The addition of interactive protocols to foster productivity of translation environments have been studied for long time, for phrase-based models (Alabau et al., 2013, 2016; Barrachina et al., 2009; Federico et al., 2014; Green et al., 2014) and also for NMT systems (Knowles and Koehn, 2016; Peris et al., 2017; Peris and Casacuberta, 2019; Wuebker et al., 2016).

The system we are presenting in this work is an extended version of Peris and Casacuberta (2019), who presented a NMT system that accepted a prefix feedback: the user corrected the first wrong character of the sentence. Hence, the system reacted to the feedback by providing an alternative suffix. This protocol can be implemented as a constrained beam search. Moreover, the system can be retrained incrementally, as soon as a corrected sample is validated, following an online learning scenario.

We generalize this interactive-predictive NMT system to cope with alternative input modalities, namely images and videos. The system can be accessed following a client–server interface. We developed a client website, that access to our servers, in which the interactive-predictive systems are deployed. A live demo of the system can be accessed in: `http://casmacat.prhlt.upv.es/interactive-seq2seq`.

In the following sections, we describe the main architecture, features and usage of our interactive-predictive system. We also describe the frontend of our demonstration website and present an example of interactive session.

2 System description

The core of our system is a neural sequence to sequence model, developed with NMT-Keras (Peris and Casacuberta, 2018). This library is built upon Keras (Chollet et al., 2015) and works for the Theano (Theano Development Team, 2016) and Tensorflow (Abadi et al., 2016) backends. The system is deployed as a Python-based HTTP server that waits for requests. The user interactions are introduced through a (client) HTML website. The website is hosted on a Nginx server that manages the interactions using Javascript and communicates with the Python server, using the PHP curl tool. All code is open-source and publicly available[1,2].

NMT-Keras extends the (already extensive) Keras functionalities, providing a flexible, easy to use framework upon which build neural models. Among the features brought by NMT-Keras, some of them are particularly useful for sequence-to-sequence tasks: extended recurrent neural networks, with embedded attention mechanisms and conditional LSTM/GRU units (Sennrich et al., 2017), multi-head attention layers, positional encodings and position-wise feed-forward networks for building Transformer models (Vaswani et al.,

---

[1]Python server source code: `https://github.com/lvapeab/interactive-keras-captioning`.

[2]HTML server source code: `https://github.com/lvapeab/inmt_demo_web`.

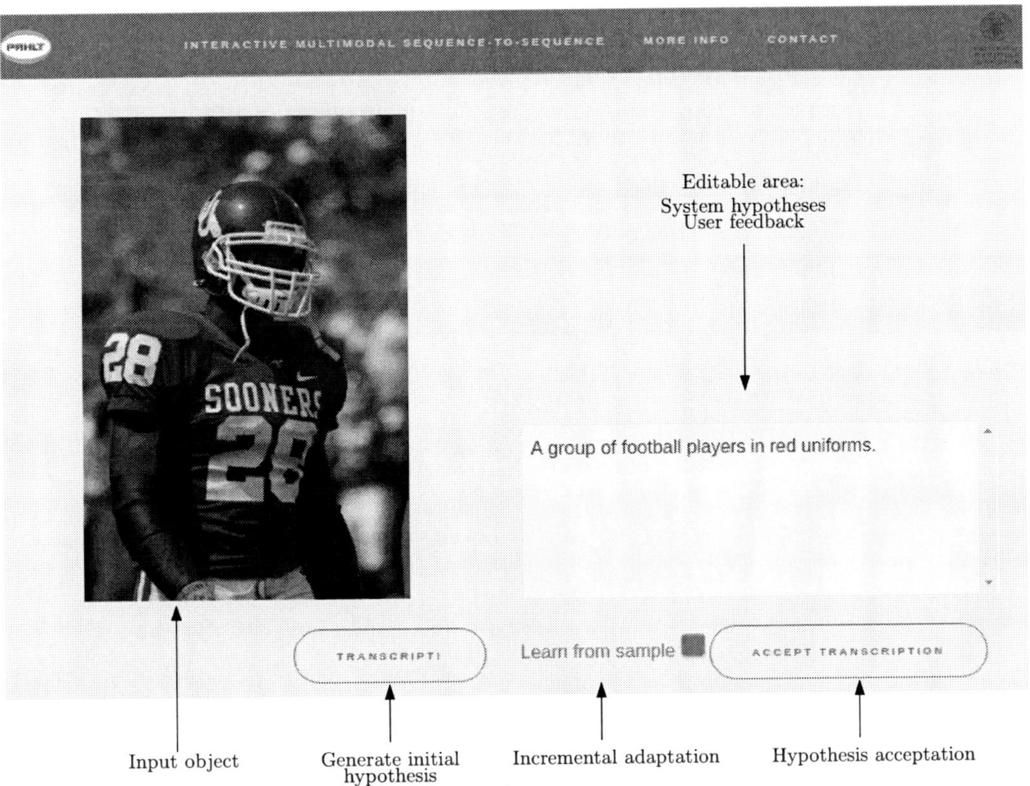

Figure 2: Frontend of the client website. As the button "Transcript!" is clicked, an initial hypothesis for the input object—in this case, an image—appears in the right area. The user then introduces corrections of this text. The system reacts to each translation, producing alternative hypotheses, always compliant with the user feedback. Once a correct caption of the image is reached, the user clicks in the "Accept translation" button, validating the hypothesis.

2017) and a modular handler for processing different data modalities, including text, images, videos or categorical labels.

Within this framework, we built our neural systems, which are leveraged via our interactive client–server application. The neural systems are deployed in a server, waiting for requests. When the client ask for a prediction, they react, generate the prediction and deliver it back to the client.

2.1 Usage of the interactive system

Our interactive-predictive system works as follows: initially, an input object is presented to the user in the client website. The user requests an automatic prediction of it. Next, the client communicates the server via PHP. The server queries the neural system, which produces an initial hypothesis applying Eq. (1). The hypothesis is then sent back to the client website.

Next, the interactive-predictive process starts: the user searches in this hypothesis the first er-

ror, and introduces a correction with the keyboard (writing one or more characters). When the user stops typing the correction, the system reacts, sending to the server a request containing the input object and the user feedback (the sequence of characters that conform the correct prefix). Then, the neural model implements Eq. (2) and produces an alternative hypothesis, such that it completes the correct prefix. This is implemented as a constrained beam search, as described in Peris et al. (2017); Peris and Casacuberta (2019). This iteration of the process is illustrated in Fig. 1.

This protocol is repeated until the user finds satisfactory the hypothesis given by the system. Then, it is validated. As soon as the sentence is validated, the system can be incrementally updated with this sample, following an online learning setup (Peris and Casacuberta, 2019). Hence, in future interactions, the system will be progressively updated, tailoring to a given domain or to the user preferences. These adaptive systems have

0	**System**	A group of football players in red uniforms.
1	**User**	*A* $\boxed{f}$ group of football players in red uniforms.
	System	*A f*ootball player in a red uniform is holding a football.
2	**User**	*A football player in a red uniform is* $\boxed{w}$ holding a football.
	System	*A football player in a red uniform is w*earing a football.
3	**User**	*A football player in a red uniform is wearing a* $\boxed{h}$ football.
	System	*A football player in a red uniform is w*earing a helmet.
4	**User**	*A football player in a red uniform is wearing a helmet.*

Figure 3: Interactive-predictive session for correcting the caption generated in Fig. 2. At each iteration, the user introduces a character correction (boxed). The system modifies its hypothesis, taking into account this feedback: keeping the correct prefix (green) and generating a compatible suffix.

shown to be effective for reducing the human effort spent in the process (Karimova et al., 2018).

3 System showcase

To show the interactive-predictive protocol described in the previous sections, we developed a website which hosts a demonstration of the system. Our demonstration system handles three different problems, regarding three different data modalities: text-to-text (NMT), image-to-text (image captioning) and video-to-text (video captioning). For tackling these tasks, we use a similar model: a neural encoder–decoder, based on recurrent neural networks with attention (Bahdanau et al., 2015; Xu et al., 2015; Yao et al., 2015). Our framework has also support for Transformer-like architectures (Vaswani et al., 2017).

The NMT task regards the translation of texts from a medical domain. The system is similar to the one used by Peris and Casacuberta (2019), and was trained on the UFAL corpus (Bojar et al., 2017). The image and video captioning systems were trained on the Flickr8k (Hodosh et al., 2010) and MSVD (Chen and Dolan, 2011) datasets, respectively. The images were encoded using an Inception convolutional neural network (Szegedy et al., 2016) trained on the ILSVRC dataset (Russakovsky et al., 2015). The decoder receives the representation previous to the fully-connected work. In the case of the video captioning system, we applied a 3D convolutional neural network (Tran et al., 2015), for obtaining time-aware features.

Finally, as aforementioned in previous sections, the systems can be retrained after the validation of each sample. In our demonstration, the systems are updated via gradient descent, but using a learning rate of 0, which prevents a degradation of the model due to accidental misuse.

3.1 Example: image captioning

We show and analyze an image captioning example. The NMT and video captioning tasks are similar. Fig. 2 shows the demo website, for the image captioning task. In the left part of the screen, the input object is shown, in this case, an image. As the user clicks in the "Transcript!" button, the system generates a caption of the image, displaying it in an editable area on the right part of the screen. The user can then introduce the desired corrections to this hypothesis. As a correction is introduced, the system reacts, providing an alternative caption, but always considering the feedback given by the user.

As can be seen in Fig. 2, the caption generated by the system has some errors. Fig. 3 an shows the interactive-predictive captioning session, for obtaining a correct sample. With three interactions, the system was able to obtain a correct caption for the image.

It is particularly interesting to observe that the system correctly accounts for the singular/plural concordance of the clause *in red uniform(s)*, depending on the subject (*A football player*/*A group of football players*).

4 Conclusions and future work

We presented a demonstration of a interactive-predictive neural system for multimodal sequence to sequence tasks. We described its client–server architecture and developed a website for ease the usage of the system.

As future work, we would like to improve the frontend of our website. Inspecting the attributes of black-box neural models is a relevant research topic, and it is under active development (e.g. Zeiler and Fergus, 2014; Ancona et al., 2017). Visualizing these relevant attributes would help to understand the model predictions and behavior.

Moreover, a more sophisticated frontend would allow to implement interesting features, such as mapping the attention weights through the input sequence or the implementation of more complex interaction protocols, such as touch-based interaction (Marie and Max, 2015) or segment-based interaction (Peris et al., 2017). We intend to offer the different functionalities of the toolkit as REST services, for improving the reusability of the code. It is also planned to release the library in a Docker container in order to ease the deployment of future applications.

Acknowledgments

We acknowledge the anonymous reviewers for their helpful suggestions. The research leading to these results has received funding from the Generalitat Valenciana under grant PROMETEOII/2014/030 and from TIN2015-70924-C2-1-R. We also acknowledge NVIDIA Corporation for the donation of GPUs used in this work.

References

Martín Abadi, Paul Barham, Jianmin Chen, Zhifeng Chen, Andy Davis, Jeffrey Dean, Matthieu Devin, Sanjay Ghemawat, Geoffrey Irving, Michael Isard, et al. 2016. Tensorflow: A system for large-scale machine learning. In *Proceedings of the 12th USENIX Symposium on Operating Systems Design and Implementation*, volume 16, pages 265–283.

Vicent Alabau, Ragnar Bonk, Christian Buck, Michael Carl, Francisco Casacuberta, Mercedes García-Martínez, Jesús González-Rubio, Philipp Koehn, Luis A. Leiva, Bartolomé Mesa-Lao, Daniel Ortiz-Martínez, Hervé Saint-Amand, Germán Sanchis-Trilles, and Chara Tsoukala. 2013. CASMACAT: An open source workbench for advanced computer aided translation. *The Prague Bulletin of Mathematical Linguistics*, 100:101–112.

Vicent Alabau, Michael Carl, Francisco Casacuberta, Mercedes Garca-Martnez, Jess Gonzlez-Rubio, Bartolom Mesa-Lao, Daniel Ortiz-Martnez, Moritz Schaeffer, and Germn Sanchis-Trilles. 2016. *New Directions in Empirical Translation Process Research*, New Frontiers in Translation Studies, chapter Learning Advanced Post-editing.

Marco Ancona, Enea Ceolini, Cengiz Öztireli, and Markus Gross. 2017. Towards better understanding of gradient-based attribution methods for deep neural networks. *arXiv:1711.06104*.

Ana Guerberof Arenas. 2008. Productivity and quality in the post-editing of outputs from translation memories and machine translation. *Localisation Focus*, 7(1):11–21.

Dzmitry Bahdanau, Kyunghyun Cho, and Yoshua Bengio. 2015. Neural machine translation by jointly learning to align and translate. *arXiv:1409.0473*.

Sergio Barrachina, Oliver Bender, Francisco Casacuberta, Jorge Civera, Elsa Cubel, Shahram Khadivi, Antonio Lagarda, Hermann Ney, Jesús Tomás, Enrique Vidal, and Juan-Miguel Vilar. 2009. Statistical approaches to computer-assisted translation. *Computational Linguistics*, 35(1):3–28.

Christopher M. Bishop. 2006. *Pattern Recognition and Machine Learning (Information Science and Statistics)*. Springer.

Ondej Bojar, Barry Haddow, David Mareek , Roman Sudarikov, Aleš Tamchyna, and Duan Vari. 2017. Report on building translation systems for public health domain (deliverable D1.1). Technical Report H2020-ICT-2014-1-644402, Health in my Language (HimL).

William Chan, Navdeep Jaitly, Quoc Le, and Oriol Vinyals. 2016. Listen, attend and spell: A neural network for large vocabulary conversational speech recognition. In *Proceedings of the IEEE International Conference on Acoustics, Speech and Signal Processing*, pages 4960–4964.

David L Chen and William B Dolan. 2011. Collecting highly parallel data for paraphrase evaluation. In *Proceedings of the 49th Annual Meeting of the Association for Computational Linguistics*, pages 190–200.

François Chollet et al. 2015. Keras. `https://github.com/keras-team/keras`. GitHub repository.

Marcello Federico, Nicola Bertoldi, Mauro Cettolo, Matteo Negri, Marco Turchi, Marco Trombetti, Alessandro Cattelan, Antonio Farina, Domenico Lupinetti, Andrea Martines, Alberto Massidda, Holger Schwenk, Loïc Barrault, Frederic Blain, Philipp Koehn, Christian Buck, and Ulrich Germann. 2014. The matecat tool. In *Proceedings of the 25th International Conference on Computational Linguistics: System Demonstrations*, pages 129–132.

George Foster, Pierre Isabelle, and Pierre Plamondon. 1997. Target-text mediated interactive machine translation. *Machine Translation*, 12:175–194.

Alex Graves. 2012. Sequence transduction with recurrent neural networks. *arXiv:1211.3711*.

Spence Green, Jason Chuang, Jeffrey Heer, and Christopher D. Manning. 2014. Predictive translation memory: A mixed-initiative system for human language translation. In *Proceedings of the Annual Association for Computing Machinery Symposium on User Interface Software and Technology*, pages 177–187.

Micah Hodosh, Peter Young, Cyrus Rashtchian, and Julia Hockenmaier. 2010. Cross-caption coreference resolution for automatic image understanding. In *Proceedings of the Fourteenth Conference on Computational Natural Language Learning*, pages 162–171.

Ke Hu and Patrick Cadwell. 2016. A comparative study of post-editing guidelines. In *Proceedings of the 19th Annual Conference of the European Association for Machine Translation*, pages 34206–353.

Sariya Karimova, Patrick Simianer, and Stefan Riezler. 2018. A user-study on online adaptation of neural machine translation to human post-edits. *Machine Translation*, 32(4):309–324.

Rebecca Knowles and Philipp Koehn. 2016. Neural interactive translation prediction. In *Proceedings of the Association for Machine Translation in the Americas*, pages 107–120.

Philipp Koehn and Rebecca Knowles. 2017. Six challenges for neural machine translation. In *Proceedings of the First Workshop on Neural Machine Translation*, pages 28–39.

Benjamin Marie and Aurélien Max. 2015. Touch-based pre-post-editing of machine translation output. In *Proceedings of the Conference on Empirical Methods in Natural Language Processing*, pages 1040–1045.

Jan Niehues, Ngoc-Quan Pham, Thanh-Le Ha, Matthias Sperber, and Alex Waibel. 2018. Low-latency neural speech translation. In *Proceedings of the 19th Annual Conference of the International Speech Communication Association*, pages 1293–1297.

Álvaro Peris and Francisco Casacuberta. 2018. NMT-Keras: a very flexible toolkit with a focus on interactive NMT and online learning. *The Prague Bulletin of Mathematical Linguistics*, 111:113–124.

Álvaro Peris and Francisco Casacuberta. 2019. Online learning for effort reduction in interactive neural machine translation. *Computer Speech & Language*, 58:98–126.

Álvaro Peris, Miguel Domingo, and Francisco Casacuberta. 2017. Interactive neural machine translation. *Computer Speech & Language*, 45:201–220.

Olga Russakovsky, Jia Deng, Hao Su, Jonathan Krause, Sanjeev Satheesh, Sean Ma, Zhiheng Huang, Andrej Karpathy, Aditya Khosla, Michael Bernstein, et al.

2015. Imagenet large scale visual recognition challenge. *International Journal of Computer Vision*, 115(3):211–252.

Rico Sennrich, Orhan Firat, Kyunghyun Cho, Alexandra Birch, Barry Haddow, Julian Hitschler, Marcin Junczys-Dowmunt, Samuel Läubli, Antonio Valerio Miceli Barone, Jozef Mokry, and Maria Nadejde. 2017. Nematus: a toolkit for neural machine translation. In *Proceedings of the Software Demonstrations at the 15th Conference of the European Chapter of the Association for Computational Linguistics*, pages 65–68.

Ilya Sutskever, Oriol Vinyals, and Quoc V. Le. 2014. Sequence to sequence learning with neural networks. In *Proceedings of the Advances in Neural Information Processing Systems*, volume 27, pages 3104–3112.

Christian Szegedy, Vincent Vanhoucke, Sergey Ioffe, Jon Shlens, and Zbigniew Wojna. 2016. Rethinking the inception architecture for computer vision. In *Proceedings of the IEEE Conference on Computer Vision and Pattern Recognition*, pages 2818–2826.

Theano Development Team. 2016. Theano: A Python framework for fast computation of mathematical expressions. *arXiv:1605.02688*.

Du Tran, Lubomir Bourdev, Rob Fergus, Lorenzo Torresani, and Manohar Paluri. 2015. Learning spatiotemporal features with 3d convolutional networks. In *Proceedings of the IEEE international conference on computer vision*, pages 4489–4497.

Ashish Vaswani, Noam Shazeer, Niki Parmar, Jakob Uszkoreit, Llion Jones, Aidan N Gomez, Łukasz Kaiser, and Illia Polosukhin. 2017. Attention is all you need. In *Advances in Neural Information Processing Systems*, pages 5998–6008.

Joern Wuebker, Spence Green, John DeNero, Sasa Hasan, and Minh-Thang Luong. 2016. Models and inference for prefix-constrained machine translation. In *Proceedings of the 54th Annual Meeting of the Association for Computational Linguistics*, volume 1, pages 66–75.

Kelvin Xu, Jimmy Ba, Ryan Kiros, Kyunghyun Cho, Aaron Courville, Ruslan Salakhutdinov, Richard Zemel, and Yoshua Bengio. 2015. Show, attend and tell: Neural image caption generation with visual attention. In *Proceedings of the International Conference on Machine Learning*, pages 2048–2057.

Li Yao, Atousa Torabi, Kyunghyun Cho, Nicolas Ballas, Christopher Pal, Hugo Larochelle, and Aaron Courville. 2015. Describing videos by exploiting temporal structure. In *Proceedings of the International Conference on Computer Vision*, pages 4507–4515.

Matthew D Zeiler and Rob Fergus. 2014. Visualizing and understanding convolutional networks. In *Proceedings of the European Conference on Computer Vision*, pages 818–833.

NeuralClassifier: An Open-source Neural Hierarchical Multi-label Text Classification Toolkit

Liqun Liu, **Funan Mu,** **Pengyu Li, Xin Mu, Jing Tang,**
Xingsheng Ai, Ran Fu, Lifeng Wang, Xing Zhou
Advertising and Marketing Services, Tencent Inc.
{liqunliu, marvinmu, perrypyli, anmarsmu, jamesjtang,
felixai, ranfu, fandywang, leostarzhou}@tencent.com

Abstract

In this paper, we introduce NeuralClassifier, a toolkit for neural hierarchical multi-label text classification. NeuralClassifier is designed for quick implementation of neural models for hierarchical multi-label classification task, which is more challenging and common in real-world scenarios. A salient feature is that NeuralClassifier currently provides a variety of text encoders, such as FastText, TextCNN, TextRNN, RCNN, VDCNN, DPCNN, DRNN, AttentiveConvNet and Transformer encoder, etc. It also supports other text classification scenarios, including binary-class and multi-class classification. Built on PyTorch[1], the core operations are calculated in batch, making the toolkit efficient with the acceleration of GPU. Experiments show that models built in our toolkit achieve comparable performance with reported results in the literature.

1 Introduction

Text classification is an important task in Natural Language Processing with many applications, such as web search, information retrieval, ranking and document classification (Deerwester et al., 1990; Pang et al., 2008). As a result of the great success of deep neural networks, a series of classification models based on neural networks that achieve very good performance in practice have been proposed (Kim, 2014; Lai et al., 2015; Joulin et al., 2016; Conneau et al., 2016; Liu et al., 2016; Johnson and Zhang, 2017; Vaswani et al., 2017; Yin and Schütze, 2017; Wang, 2018; Qiao et al., 2018; Guo et al., 2019).

The problem of Hierarchical Multi-label Classification (HMC) is a branch of classification problem. It is a more challenging classification problem in real-world scenarios. Unlike traditional flat

---

[*]Equal contribution

[1]https://pytorch.org/

```
"task_info": {
    "label_type": "multi-label",
    "hierarchical": true,
    "hierar_taxonomy": "rcv1.taxonomy",
    "hierar_penalty": 0.0001
}
"model_name": "TextCNN",
"device": "cuda",
"checkpoint_dir": "checkpoint/",
"data": {
    "train_files": ["/data/rcv1_train.json"],
    "validate_files": ["/data/rcv1_val.json"],
    "test_files": ["/data/rcv1_test.json"],
}
```

Figure 1: Configuration file segment.

and single-label text classification, it aims at considering the interrelationships among labels and classifying the text document into multiple labels, which are organized into a hierarchical structure of tree or DAG (Directed Acyclic Graph). Regularizing the deep architecture with the dependency among labels adopted by the existing solutions (Gopal and Yang, 2013; Peng et al., 2018) is more naturally for solving hierarchical multi-label text classification problem, especially for large scale datasets. It has a wide variety of real-world applications such as question answering (Qu et al., 2012), online advertising (Agrawal et al., 2013), and scientific literature organization (Peng et al., 2016).

There exist several open-source statistical hierarchical or multi label text classification toolkits, such as scikit-multilearn[2], sklearn-hierarchical-classification[3], which provide users with various hierarchical or multi-label classification modules based on scikit-learn's interfaces and conventions. On the other hand, there is limited choice for neural hierarchical multi-label text classification toolkits. Although many researchers have released their codes along with their hierarchical or multi-

---

[2]https://github.com/scikit-multilearn/scikit-multilearn
[3]https://github.com/globality-corp/sklearn-hierarchical-classification

Proceedings of the 57th Annual Meeting of the Association for Computational Linguistics-System Demonstrations, pages 87–92
Florence, Italy, July 28 - August 2, 2019. ©2019 Association for Computational Linguistics

Toolkits	Neural	Multi-label	Hierarchical	Feature Richness	Model Richness
scikit-multilearn	×	✓	×	×	✓
sklearn-hierarchical-classification	×	✓	✓	×	✓
HDLTex	✓	×	✓	×	×
HR-DGCNN	✓	✓	✓	×	×
NeuralClassifier	✓	✓	✓	✓	✓

Table 1: Toolkit Comparison.

```
Macro_average:
Overall: P: 0.926780, R: 0.926938, F1: 0.926859,
level_1: P: 1.000000, R: 0.983000, F1: 0.991427,
level_2: P: 0.988596, R: 0.972668, F1: 0.980567,
level_3: P: 0.946699, R: 0.937501, F1: 0.942077,
level_4: P: 0.925209, R: 0.926333, F1: 0.925771,


Micro_average:
Overall: P: 0.967359, R: 0.978000, F1: 0.972650,
         right: 978, predict: 1011, standard: 1000
level_1: P: 1.000000, R: 0.983000, F1: 0.991427,
         right: 983, predict: 983, standard: 1000
level_2: P: 0.979042, R: 0.981000, F1: 0.980020,
         right: 981, predict: 1002, standard: 1000
level_3: P: 0.973604, R: 0.980573, F1: 0.977076,
         right: 959, predict: 985, standard: 978
level_4: P: 0.962560, R: 0.976716, F1: 0.969586,
         right: 797, predict: 828, standard: 816
```

Figure 2: An illustration of evaluation outputs. "level 1" to "4" are the results of each level in hierarchical classification. Evaluation metrics are macro and micro.

label text classification papers (Kowsari et al., 2017; Peng et al., 2018), but the implementations are mostly focused on specific model structures and specific tasks, which greatly limit their extensions for other similar tasks.

In this paper, we introduce an open-source toolkit, NeuralClassifier[4], a neural hierarchical multi-label text classification toolkit based on PyTorch. It is designed for solving the hierarchical multi-label text classification problem with effective and efficient neural models. It provides a variety of models and features, users can utilize a comfortable configuration file with neural feature design and utilization. We take the layerwise implementation, which includes input layer, embedding layer, encoder layer and output layer. To our best knowledge, our work is the first neural hierarchical multi-label text classification toolkit with rich models. For the details, we give a summary comparison with existing toolkits in Table 1. NeuralClassifier is:

- **Rich in models and features:** An important feature of our work is that, compared with existing toolkits, NeuralClassifier reimplements a very large number of the state-of-the-art text encoders, including FastText (Joulin et al., 2016), TextCNN

(Kim, 2014), TextRNN (Liu et al., 2016), RCNN (Lai et al., 2015) , VDCNN (Conneau et al., 2016), DPCNN (Johnson and Zhang, 2017) , AttentiveConvNet (Yin and Schütze, 2017), DRNN (Wang, 2018), Transformer encoder (Vaswani et al., 2017), Star-Transformer encoder (Guo et al., 2019). Meanwhile, NeuralClassifier involves a variety of useful features or widgets, i.e., word-based and char-based input, optimizers, loss functions, embedding methods and attention mechanisms, etc. All those above can be configured through a configuration file. Figure 1 shows a segment of configuration file. Note that users can configure different text encoders and features through the configuration file, and can easily modify the source code to achieve more advanced developments.

- **Suitable for almost all text classification tasks:** NeuralClassifier is designed for hierarchical and multi-label classification, which naturally also supports binary-class and multi-class classification, so it can be considered a universal toolkit for text classification tasks. Especially in hierarchical multi-label classification task, the taxonomy can be organized in the form of a tree or DAG, and instances are multi-labeled during training and testing. It also provides a complete evaluation mechanism. An illustration with results is shown in Figure 2. Users can choose their task types only through a comfortable configuration file without any code work.

- **Effective and efficient:** We conduct the experiments based on a variety of models and features provided by NeuralClassifier. Experiments show models built in our toolkit output comparable performance with reported results in the literature. Furthermore, NeuralClassifier is implemented using batch calculation that can be accelerated using GPU. Our experiments demonstrate that NeuralClassifier is an effective and efficient toolkit.

The rest of this paper is organized as follows: Section 2 describes the detail of architecture of

---

[4]Code is available at `https://github.com/liqunhit/NeuralClassifier`

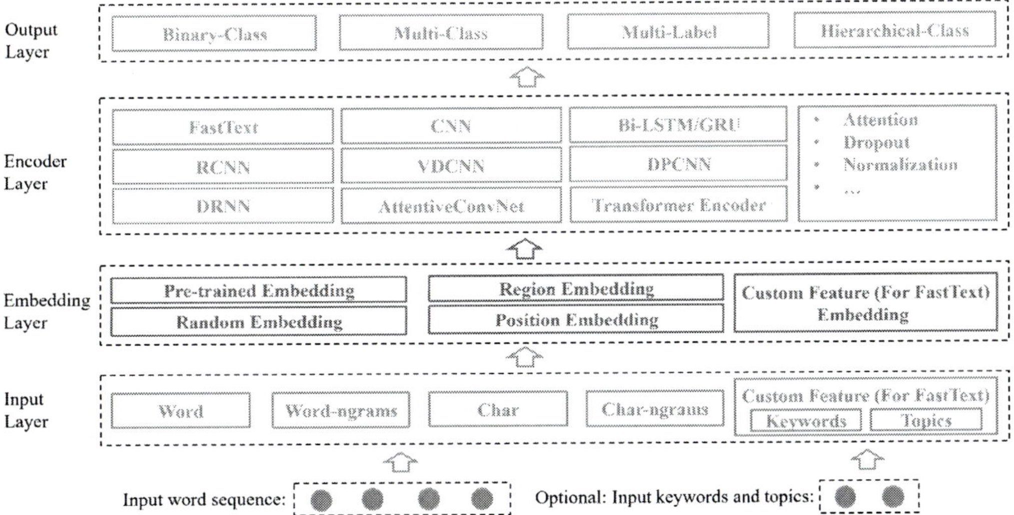

Figure 3: Architecture of NeuralClassifier. There are four layers: an input layer, an embedding layer, an encoder layer and output layer.

NeuralClassifier. The experimental evaluations and results are discussed in Section 3. Finally, Section 4 concludes this paper.

2 NeuralClassifier Architecture

The framework of NeuralClassifier is shown in Figure 3. It is composed of four layers: *input layer, embedding layer, encoder layer* and *output layer*. At the first layer (*input layer*), the input word sequence will be organized and processed as words, characters, or corresponding n-grams. For FastText, custom features such as keywords and topics are also supported. The embedding of input data will be generated at the embedding layer, subsequently be encoded at encoder layer. On top of the system, the different loss functions are constructed in the output layer to serve the different real-world tasks, i.e., binary-class, multi-class, multi-label and hierarchical multi-label classification. The user can deploy it through a comfortable configuration file without any code work. Note that a salient feature is that users can easily utilize and integrate any widgets in the NeuralClassifier to construct their own structure to satisfy any requirements.

The following will describe the pertinent details of the four layers and the user interface.

2.1 Layer Units

• **Input Layer.** The input text sequence will be processed at input layer. Input text sequence in the form of token (`word`) can be processed into

```
{
  "doc_label": ["Computer--MachineLearning--DeepLearning",
                "Neuro--ComputationalNeuro"],
  "doc_token": ["I", "love", "deep", "learning"],
  "doc_keyword": ["deep learning"],
  "doc_topic": ["AI", "Machine learning"]
}
```

Figure 4: An example of input data. Multiple levels of hierarchy are separated with '--'.

words and characters, along with their n-grams. Custom feature inputs such as keywords and topics are also supported when the text encoder is FastText. All the above can be flexibly configured by the users. Besides, reading input data can be accelerated with multiple processes. See Figure 4 for an example of input data.

• **Embedding Layer.** Various embeddings are processed at this layer. There are four embedding types can be chosen, which are random embedding, pre-trained embedding, region embedding and position embedding. Embedding can be initialized randomly or from a pre-trained embedding input. Region embedding (Qiao et al., 2018) is a supervised enhanced word embedding method that the representation of a word or char has two parts, the embedding of the word itself, and a weighting matrix to interact with the local context, referred to as local context unit. Position embedding (Vaswani et al., 2017) is an embedding method that considers position information in the input sequence.

- **Encoder Layer.** We reimplement a very large number of state-of-the-art text encoders at encoder layer, including FastText, TextCNN, TextRNN, RCNN, VDCNN, DPCNN, DRNN, Transformer encoder, Star-Transformer encoder and AttentiveConvNet. Each encoder has its own hyperparameters that can be configured by users.

- **Output Layer.** This layer determines the specific classification tasks, including binary-class, multi-class, multi-label and hierarchical-class. For the single-label (binary-class and multi-class) classification task, we provide three candidate loss functions, which are `SoftmaxCrossEntopy`, `BCLoss` and `SoftmaxFocalLoss` (Lin et al., 2017). For the hierarchical multi-label classification task, we use `BCELoss` or `SigmodFocalLoss` as the loss function for multi-label classification and add a recursive regularization (Gopal and Yang, 2013; Peng et al., 2018) for hierarchical classification. Using this regularization framework, we can incorporate the hierarchical dependencies between the class-labels into the regularization structure of the parameters thereby encouraging classes nearby in the hierarchy to share similar model parameters. In addition, such a regularization approach is more suitable for large-scale hierarchical multi-label classification task. Users can easily use above functions through the configuration file.

2.2 User Interface

NeuralClassifier provides abundant configuration interfaces, including the common settings, input settings, training settings and network structure settings. Through the configuration file, users can construct most state-of-the-art neural hierarchical multi-label text classification models. `JSON` is used as the configuration file format.

The configuration file has four major parts:

- **Common settings** include the type of classification tasks, which are single-labeled and multi-labeled, whether it is hierarchical (`task_info`), which running device to use (`device`), the specified model (`model_name`), directories of input and output data (`data`), how many subprocesses to use for data loading (`num_worker`), etc.

- **Input settings** include various configurations about input data, such as maximum input sequence length (`max_token_len`), minimum input token count (`min_token_count`), dictionary size (`max_token_dict_size`),

pre-trained embeddings of input data (`token_pretrained_file`), etc.

- **Training settings** include the batch size (`batch_size`), type of loss function (`loss_type`), optimizer (`optimizer_type`), learning rate (`learning_rate`), number of epochs (`num_epochs`), which GPUs to use (`visible_device_list`), etc.

- **Network structure settings** specify which text encoders to use, such as TextCNN, TextRNN, RCNN, Transformer, etc. For each text encoder, there are corresponding hyperparameters that can be configured. Take TextCNN as an example, users can configure the size and number of convolution kernels and the number of tops in the pooling (`kernel_sizes`, `num_kernels`, `top_k_max_pooling`).

2.3 Extension

Users can write their own custom modules on all those layers, and self-defined modules can be integrated into the toolkit easily. For example, if a user wants to implement a new classifier model, he/she only needs to implement the part at encoder layer. All the other network structures can be used and controlled through the configuration file.

3 Evaluation

In this section, we conduct several experiments to evaluate the performance of NeuralClassifier using datasets from two public benchmarks, namely, RCV1 (Lewis et al., 2004) and Yelp[5]. The experiments consist of three parts: (1) Results of using rich models and features in Section 3.1; (2) influence of hierarchical information in Section 3.2; (3) speed with batch size in Section 3.3.

3.1 Results of using rich models and features

We use the ability of various models and features provided by our toolkit to illustrate the performance of NeuralClassifier on hierarchical multi-label text classification problem. Concretely, we select a best model through coarse-grained experiments on each of the two benchmarks and fix it, and then fine-tune the features and hyperparameters, such as model structures, input representations, activation functions, optimizers, learning rate, etc. The best performance models[6] are as

---

[6]Note that the released settings are preliminary attempt so far, we will continue to update the optimization of parameter selection.

Models	RCV1 Micro-F1	Yelp Micro-F1
HR-DGCNN (Peng et al., 2018)	0.7610	–
HMCN (Wehrmann et al., 2018)	0.8080	0.6640
Our best models	**0.8099**	**0.6704**

Table 2: Results on the two benchmarks.

Encoders	RCV1 Micro-F1	RCV1 Macro-F1	Yelp Micro-F1	Yelp Macro-F1
TextCNN	0.7608	0.4649	0.6179	0.3851
TextRNN	0.7883	0.4972	**0.6704**	0.4059
RCNN	**0.8099**	**0.5332**	0.6569	0.3951
FastText	0.6887	0.2701	0.5386	0.1817
DRNN	0.7601	0.4523	0.6174	0.3835
DPCNN	0.7439	0.4141	0.5671	0.2393
VDCNN	0.7263	0.3860	0.6079	0.3427
AttentiveConvNet	0.7533	0.4373	0.6367	0.4040
Region embedding	0.7780	0.4888	0.6601	**0.4514**
Transformer	0.7603	0.4274	0.6533	0.4121
Star-Transformer	0.7668	0.4840	0.6293	0.3977

Table 3: Results of different text encoders.

follows: (1) RCNN with two-layers Bi-GRU and one-layer CNN for RCV1 dataset (input = word, optimizer = Adam, learning rate = 0.008); (2) TextRNN with one-layer Bi-GRU for Yelp dataset (input = word, optimizer = Adam, learning rate = 0.008). Table 2 shows the results of the best models on the two benchmarks. The best models can achieve comparable results with the state-of-the-art HMC models. The results shows the effectiveness of our implementation, and usability of a variety of models and features. Table 3 shows performances of different text encoders. In particular, we can use different combinations of strategies to guide the setup of model for better performance in the real applications.

3.2 Influence of hierarchical information

Hierarchical classification problems can also be solving by flat methods, which regard the hierarchical classification as a flat classification, regardless of the hierarchical relationship between labels. As mentioned before, our toolkit is configurable, we can easily set different loss functions by configuration. In this section, we discuss the influence of hierarchical information. Table 4 shows the results of setting the HMC loss function (Hierarchical) and the traditional multi-label loss function (Flat). As can been seen from the results, hierarchical information can greatly improve performance. It also demonstrates the effectiveness of

Encoders	Hierarchical Micro-F1	Hierarchical Macro-F1	Flat Micro-F1	Flat Macro-F1
TextCNN	0.7608	0.4649	0.7367	0.4224
TextRNN	0.7883	0.4972	0.7546	0.4505
RCNN	**0.8099**	**0.5332**	**0.7955**	**0.5123**
FastText	0.6887	0.2701	0.6865	0.2816
DRNN	0.7601	0.4523	0.7506	0.4450
DPCNN	0.7439	0.4141	0.7423	0.4261
VDCNN	0.7263	0.3860	0.7110	0.3593
AttentiveConvNet	0.7533	0.4373	0.7511	0.4286
Region embedding	0.7780	0.4888	0.7640	0.4617
Transformer	0.7603	0.4274	0.7602	0.4339
Star-Transformer	0.7668	0.4840	0.7618	0.4745

Table 4: Results of hierarchical and flat classification on RCV1.

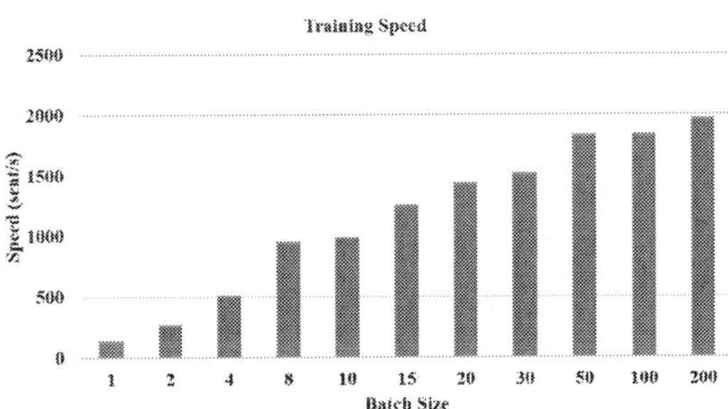

Figure 5: Results of speed with batch size.

our implementation.

3.3 Speed with Batch Size

As NeuralClassifier is implemented on bathed calculation, it can be greatly accelerated through parallel computing through GPU. We test the system speed on training process on RCV1 using a Nvidia Tesla P40 GPU. As shown in Figure 5, the training speed can be significantly accelerated through a large batch size, demonstrating the efficiency of our implementation.

4 Conclusion

This paper presents NeuralClassifier, an open-source neural hierarchical multi-label text classification toolkit. NeuralClassifier provides a large variety of text encoders and features. Users can design their models for different text classification tasks easily through the configuration file. We conduct a series of experiments and the results show that models built on NeuralClassifier can achieve state-of-the-art results with an efficient running speed.

References

Rahul Agrawal, Archit Gupta, Yashoteja Prabhu, and Manik Varma. 2013. Multi-label learning with millions of labels: Recommending advertiser bid phrases for web pages. In *Proceedings of the 22nd International Conference on World Wide Web*, pages 13–24.

Alexis Conneau, Holger Schwenk, Loïc Barrault, and Yann Lecun. 2016. Very deep convolutional networks for text classification. *arXiv preprint arXiv:1606.01781*.

Scott Deerwester, Susan T Dumais, George W Furnas, Thomas K Landauer, and Richard Harshman. 1990. Indexing by latent semantic analysis. *Journal of the American Society for Information Science*, 41(6):391–407.

Siddharth Gopal and Yiming Yang. 2013. Recursive regularization for large-scale classification with hierarchical and graphical dependencies. In *Proceedings of the 19th ACM SIGKDD International Conference on Knowledge Discovery and Data Mining*, pages 257–265.

Qipeng Guo, Xipeng Qiu, Pengfei Liu, Yunfan Shao, Xiangyang Xue, and Zheng Zhang. 2019. Star-transformer. *arXiv preprint arXiv:1902.09113*.

Rie Johnson and Tong Zhang. 2017. Deep pyramid convolutional neural networks for text categorization. In *Proceedings of the 55th Annual Meeting of the Association for Computational Linguistics (Volume 1: Long Papers)*, pages 562–570.

Armand Joulin, Edouard Grave, Piotr Bojanowski, and Tomas Mikolov. 2016. Bag of tricks for efficient text classification. *arXiv preprint arXiv:1607.01759*.

Yoon Kim. 2014. Convolutional neural networks for sentence classification. *arXiv preprint arXiv:1408.5882*.

Kamran Kowsari, Donald E Brown, Mojtaba Heidarysafa, Kiana Jafari Meimandi, Matthew S Gerber, and Laura E Barnes. 2017. Hdltex: Hierarchical deep learning for text classification. In *2017 16th IEEE International Conference on Machine Learning and Applications (ICMLA)*, pages 364–371.

Siwei Lai, Liheng Xu, Kang Liu, and Jun Zhao. 2015. Recurrent convolutional neural networks for text classification. In *29th AAAI Conference on Artificial Intelligence*.

David D Lewis, Yiming Yang, Tony G Rose, and Fan Li. 2004. Rcv1: A new benchmark collection for text categorization research. *Journal of Machine Learning Research*, 5:361–397.

Tsung-Yi Lin, Priya Goyal, Ross Girshick, Kaiming He, and Piotr Dollár. 2017. Focal loss for dense object detection. In *Proceedings of the IEEE International Conference on Computer Vision*, pages 2980–2988.

Pengfei Liu, Xipeng Qiu, and Xuanjing Huang. 2016. Recurrent neural network for text classification with multi-task learning. *arXiv preprint arXiv:1605.05101*.

Bo Pang, Lillian Lee, et al. 2008. Opinion mining and sentiment analysis. *Foundations and Trends® in Information Retrieval*, 2(1–2):1–135.

Hao Peng, Jianxin Li, Yu He, Yaopeng Liu, Mengjiao Bao, Lihong Wang, Yangqiu Song, and Qiang Yang. 2018. Large-scale hierarchical text classification with recursively regularized deep graph-cnn. In *Proceedings of the 2018 World Wide Web Conference on World Wide Web*, pages 1063–1072.

Shengwen Peng, Ronghui You, Hongning Wang, Chengxiang Zhai, Hiroshi Mamitsuka, and Shanfeng Zhu. 2016. Deepmesh: deep semantic representation for improving large-scale mesh indexing. *Bioinformatics*, 32(12):i70–i79.

Chao Qiao, Bo Huang, Guocheng Niu, Daren Li, Daxiang Dong, Wei He, Dianhai Yu, and Hua Wu. 2018. A new method of region embedding for text classification. In *International Conference on Learning Representations*.

Bo Qu, Gao Cong, Cuiping Li, Aixin Sun, and Hong Chen. 2012. An evaluation of classification models for question topic categorization. *Journal of the American Society for Information Science and Technology*, 63(5):889–903.

Ashish Vaswani, Noam Shazeer, Niki Parmar, Jakob Uszkoreit, Llion Jones, Aidan N Gomez, Łukasz Kaiser, and Illia Polosukhin. 2017. Attention is all you need. In *Advances in Neural Information Processing Systems*, pages 5998–6008.

Baoxin Wang. 2018. Disconnected recurrent neural networks for text categorization. In *Proceedings of the 56th Annual Meeting of the Association for Computational Linguistics (Volume 1: Long Papers)*, pages 2311–2320.

Jonatas Wehrmann, Ricardo Cerri, and Rodrigo Barros. 2018. Hierarchical multi-label classification networks. In *International Conference on Machine Learning*, pages 5225–5234.

Wenpeng Yin and Hinrich Schütze. 2017. Attentive convolution. *arXiv preprint arXiv:1710.00519*.

ADVISER: A Dialog System Framework for Education & Research

Daniel Ortega, Dirk Väth, Gianna Weber, Lindsey Vanderlyn,
Maximilian Schmidt, Moritz Völkel, Zorica Karacevic and Ngoc Thang Vu*
Institute for Natural Language Processing (IMS), University of Stuttgart
`thangvu@ims.uni-stuttgart.de`

Abstract

In this paper, we present ADVISER[1] - an open source dialog system framework for education and research purposes. This system supports multi-domain task-oriented conversations in two languages. It additionally provides a flexible architecture in which modules can be arbitrarily combined or exchanged - allowing for easy switching between rules-based and neural network based implementations. Furthermore, ADVISER offers a transparent, user-friendly framework designed for interdisciplinary collaboration: from a flexible back end, allowing easy integration of new features, to an intuitive graphical user interface supporting non-technical users.

1 Introduction

Dialog systems can be open-ended, e.g. small talk systems (Weizenbaum, 1966), or designed for a specific task, such as booking flights or finding restaurants (Bobrow et al., 1977; Wen et al., 2017). In this paper, we focus on task-oriented dialog systems, although our framework allows easy integration of non-task dialog systems (Vinyals and Le, 2015) and their combination (Yu et al., 2017). Task-oriented dialog systems are generally comprised of sequential modules addressing the varying subtasks required to facilitate a natural language dialog (Williams et al., 2016). A standard architecture implements this with a natural language understanding (NLU) unit which is responsible for parsing the user input (De Mori et al., 2008), a belief state tracker (BST) module (Mrkšić et al., 2017) that holds the state of the dialog, a policy module (Williams and Young, 2007) which determines the system's next action,

and a natural language generation (NLG) module which transforms the system act into natural language. Recently, there has been increasing interest in multi-domain, task-oriented dialog systems because of their ability to help users achieve more complex goals, which may not be cleanly divided into single-domain objectives (Mrkšić et al., 2015; Ultes et al., 2017). This increased freedom for users, however, requires increasingly sophisticated system architectures to effectively handle cross-domain actions or transitions between active domains.

During the last years, several toolkits (Bohus and Rudnicky, 2009; Skantze and Moubayed, 2012; Baumann and Schlangen, 2012; Lison and Kennington, 2016; Ultes et al., 2017; Miller et al., 2017) have been introduced to accelerate the development and testing process of goal-oriented dialog systems, for both single-domain and multi-domain systems. Almost all of them have been developed for fast prototyping, where new domains can be developed by swapping in new implementations for each module following the toolkit's architecture. However, generating natural and effective dialogs requires linguistic knowledge to be integrated throughout the system design, and most of these toolkits are primarily designed for technical users, which can limit the ease of collaboration with linguists and may thus affect the quality of the system's output.

To address these shortcomings, we propose a multilingual multi-domain dialog system with two parallel goals: 1) to provide a highly flexible research framework not only for technique oriented developers but also for non-technical oriented developers such as linguists and 2) to provide an interdisciplinary educational tool.

---

[1]Website: `https://www.ims.uni-stuttgart.de/forschung/ressourcen/werkzeuge/adviser.html`

* All authors contributed equally.

93

Proceedings of the 57th Annual Meeting of the Association for Computational Linguistics-System Demonstrations, pages 93–98
Florence, Italy, July 28 - August 2, 2019. ©2019 Association for Computational Linguistics

2   Related Work

During the last decade, several toolkits have been developed to facilitate the rapid implementation of goal-oriented dialog systems. RavenClaw (Bohus and Rudnicky, 2009) aimed to separate domain-specific aspects from domain-independent conversational skills, letting developers focus solely on describing the dialog task control logic. However, the most recent techniques like a statistical BST or a reinforcement learning (RL)-based policy are not compatible.

Our approach is inline with InproTK (Baumann and Schlangen, 2012), where high-level modules (such as NLU and dialog manager) communicate by networks created via configuration files. In ADVISER, there is no distinction between high or low-level modules, but they are similarly designed separately and our `DialogSystem` class defines the pipeline interaction between them, allowing them to easily be replaced with newer versions.

OpenDial (Lison and Kennington, 2016) relies on probabilistic rules and easily integrates external modules. We were inspired by this work to make the rules-based dialog systems fully domain-independent in ADVISER by storing the NLU rules and NLG templates in external files.

PyDial (Ultes et al., 2017), a multi-domain dialog toolkit, follows the classic approach for modular dialog systems. Although PyDial offers rules-based and statistical implementations for the modules, the overall structure is rather difficult to manipulate, if the pipeline needs to be modified.

3   Framework Design

Our goal with this system is to provide both a highly modular research platform and an interdisciplinary educational tool.

Use Cases   To accomplish this, we address the needs of the following three user groups: 1) technical users such as machine learning researchers 2) non-technical researchers such as linguists and 3) multidisciplinary students.

Design Criteria   The main *objectives* of the framework are threefold: 1) to maximise the ease for technical developers when exploring new architectures or extending system functionality with new techniques, e.g. machine learning. 2) To minimise the workload on code bases for non-technical users (e.g. linguists) allowing them to

focus on their main goals, e.g. exploring the dialog flow for new domains, or languages or investigating human language variations when interacting with a dialog system. 3) To provide an engaging way for multidisciplinary students to learn how dialog systems work.

From this, our framework is designed to optimise the following criteria:

Modularity: For each module in a classic dialog system pipeline (NLU, BST, dialog policy and NLG), we provide a handcrafted baseline module, additionally we provide a machine learning based implementation for the BST and policy (see section 4.2). These can be used to quickly assemble a working dialog system or as implementation guidelines for custom modules. Additionally, because all modules inherit from the same abstract class, technical users can also easily write their own implementations or combinations of modules.

Flexibility: In contrast to a more static dialog system pipeline, we propose a graph structure where the user is in control of the modules and their order. This level of control allows users to realise anything from pipelines to end-to-end systems. Even branching scenarios are possible as demonstrated by our meta policy which combines multiple parallel subgraphs into a single dialog.

Transparency: Inputs to and outputs from each module are captured by automatically generated XML interface descriptions, providing a transparent view of data flow through the dialog system.

User-friendly at different levels: technical users have the full flexibility to explore and extend the back end; non-technical users can use our defined modules for building systems; students from different disciplines could easily learn the concepts and explore human machine interaction.

4   Modules

4.1   Graphical User Interface

Graphical user interfaces (GUIs) allow users to access a system in an easy, clear and appealing fashion. Thus, in addition to a console, ADVISER provides two separate graphical interfaces: a GUI to chat with the dialog system and a gamelike interface for study purposes.

Chat interface   Our GUI is implemented as a module, which is called by the dialog system once at the beginning and once at the end of each turn. In the first turn, the GUI is initialised and loaded.

At the beginning of each turn, it blocks the processing pipeline until the user has entered a message. The message is displayed inside the GUI and then passed to succeeding modules, e.g. the NLU module. At the end of the turn, the module takes the output of the NLG and displays it inside the GUI.

Gamelike interface for study purposes Handcrafted NLU modules are often based on regular expressions (regexes), which aim to find patterns inside a user utterance in order to identify possible user acts. The module's developers try to cover as many user act realisations (UARs) as possible. However, due to the versatile nature of human language, many regexes are needed to yield a high coverage. In ADVISER, we provide an interface which supports collaboration between computer scientists and linguists to yield a higher quality of the NLU module. To motivate both sides, we frame this challenge as a game - the CrossTick game - in which computer scientists try to achieve high regex coverage and linguists try to write uncovered UARs. First, the user has to select the domain for which UARs are written and the NLU module that should be evaluated. After a UAR is created, it is analysed by the specified module and the user is informed via a tick (✓) or a cross (×) whether the user acts were detected correctly. The user can save and load files in JSON format.

4.2 Components of Dialog Systems

Input Up to now, only text is supported but our tool could be easily extendable to other modalities such as speech and vision. Currently text can either be entered through the console or our GUI.

NLU We implemented a domain-independent rules-based NLU that loads regexes from a JSON file. The regexes are split into three categories - general acts (e.g. *Hello*, *RequestAlternatives* and *Affirm*), domain-specific inform acts and domain-specific request acts. We supported both, English and German rules. The NLU module receives the user input as string and checks it across all regexes, creating a list of possible user acts. If no act is found, then it is assumed that the NLU was not capable of understanding and the user act is interpreted as a *BadAct*. We additionally resolve some ambiguities using the belief state, i.e. the dialog history. If a non-contextualised *Affirm* or *Deny* act is found, the system attempts to use the dialog history to contextualise it.

BST The belief state tracker maintains a representation of the current dialog state. The rules-based BST receives a list of user acts from the NLU that are decoded and stored with probabilities in the belief state. The BST also detects the presence of discourse acts, e.g. *Hello*, *Repeat*, *Inform* and *Request*. Moreover, it stores information from the system history including the last requested slot and last entity offered.

Our machine learning based belief state tracker is trained to predict the belief state directly from text without the need for an NLU. To track the constraints and requests issued by the user, we feed system actions and user input turn-wise into a recurrent network and concatenate the resulting hidden states of both inputs before predicting the final belief state (Jagfeld and Vu, 2017).

Policy The rules-based policy aims to provide users with a single entity matching the constraints they have specified. After each turn, the policy verifies that the user has not ended the dialog. It then reads the current belief state and generates a suitable query for the database. If there are multiple results, the next system act will request more information from the user to disambiguate. Otherwise, the system is able to make an offer – directly informing the user about a specific entity – or to give more details about a current offer.

Our machine learning policy is trained using deep RL. Similar to the Deep Q-learning algorithm (Mnih et al., 2013), an action-value function is approximated by a neural network which outputs a value for each possible system action given the vectorised representation of a turn's belief state as input. The neural network is constructed following the duelling architecture (Wang et al., 2016), consisting of two separate calculation streams. Each stream has its own layers, where one stream calculates the value function and the other an advantage function so that their combination in a special final layer yields the action-value function again. Additionally, an updated copy of this network is used to evaluate the agent's actions while the original up-to-date network is accessed to choose the agent's greedy actions (Van Hasselt et al., 2016). For the agent's efficient off-policy batch-training, we make use of prioritised experience replay (Schaul et al., 2015) by assigning experienced dialog turns a sampling probability proportional to errors in the action-value estimates.

NLG In the natural language generation module, the semantic representation of the system act is transformed into natural language. In the handcrafted NLG module, each possible system act is mapped to exactly one utterance. To reduce the potentially large number of mappings, templates are used which allow multiple mappings from system acts to their respective utterance at once. By specifying placeholders for a system acts slots and/or values, the utterance can be formulated independent of the actual realisations (e.g. `inform(name={X}, ects={Y}) → The course {X} is worth {Y} ECTS.`). During the dialog, the system iterates through the templates and chooses the first one for which the system act fits the template's signature. For each domain we present here, we created both German and English templates.

User Simulator To support automatic evaluation and enable RL, we implemented a user simulator to provide user actions at the intention level. For this purpose, we integrated the Agenda-based (Schatzmann et al., 2007) user simulator into our framework. The task of the system is to fulfil the user's goal within the course of the dialog. For this purpose, we populated our agendas with actions requesting information and informing about the constraints based on the specified goal. For the design of a user simulator, we additionally considered that its objective was not only to fulfil the user's goal but also to support the RL policy in the learning process. Therefore, it was not sufficient to answer the system's request and fulfil the user's goal, but also to force the system to answer with suitable actions. In the context of RL, we achieved this by delaying a dialog turn if the system's answer was not an expected action or completely nonsense, because it reduces the reward the policy receives for the ongoing dialog. In addition, several parameters influence the user simulator's behaviour. Those are manually crafted and chosen with a suitable probability wherever variation to the user makes sense.

Meta Policy In a multi-domain dialog system, intelligently switching between or combining individual domains is necessary to provide the user a unified experience. However, the best way to accomplish this remains unclear. In our system, we propose an architecture where all domains are allowed to run in parallel and the resulting output is processed by a Meta Policy. The meta policy is responsible for tracking which domains are active and, if necessary, combining their output. In the case where a user utterance cannot be directly handled in the context of a single domain, the meta policy is also responsible for rewriting it into one or more single-domain utterances. If this happens, rather than outputting something for that turn or asking for user input, the system steps through an additional turn, using the rewritten utterance as the new user input. In this way the meta policy is able to intelligently coordinate switching or combining domains, preserving as much information as possible to make as informed of a decision as possible. This architecture can be seen in figure 1.

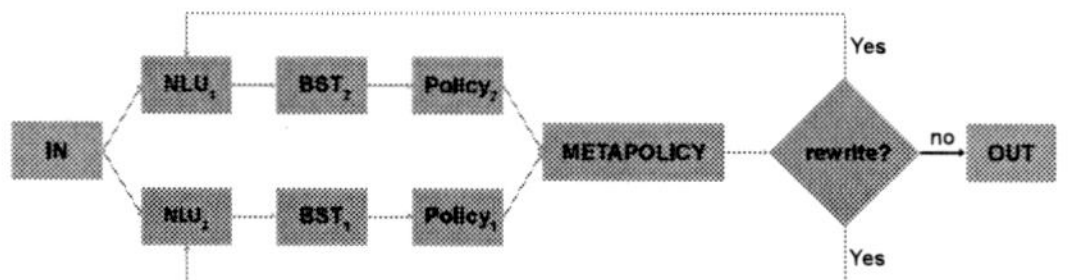

Figure 1: Multi-domain system architecture, showing how information is passed between each module and the final system output is coordinated by the meta policy.

5 Proof-of-Concept Showcases

In order to feedback on the quality, functionality, and usefulness of the ADVISER system, we conducted two experiments: we first investigated user experiences with a student support dialog system and second explored the effectiveness of using a game within a multidisciplinary practical course.

5.1 Student Support Dialog System

Multilingual and multi-domain As a real-world use case, we implemented a dialog system, using our ADVISER framework, to help students navigate through the course and module selection at the Institute for Natural Language Processing (IMS) at the University of Stuttgart. This task consists of three domains for asking information about lecturers, for locating courses, and for collecting information about modules. Students can freely switch between or combine the domains in order to find the information they need. Additionally because of the students' backgrounds, our system supports NLU and NLG in both, English and German.

Evaluation and Results We evaluated our dialog policies automatically on two domains: the new domain - IMS modules and the benchmark domain - Cambridge restaurants (Ultes et al., 2017). Table 1 shows the performance of the supported policies tested against the user simulator. Each result was obtained by averaging across ten different random seeds with 500 test dialogs each.

Agent	CamRestaurants		IMS modules	
	Suc.	Turns	Suc.	Turns
RL	97.5%	5.03	91.6%	5.25
HDC	100%	4.75	99.8%	7.0

Table 1: Percentage of successful dialogs and average dialog length for Cambridge restaurants and IMS modules domains evaluated with a RL policy and a handcrafted policy (HDC).

To gain a better understanding of how AD-VISER works under real-world conditions, we asked 13 volunteers to conduct a series of five conversations with the system. Participants were required to chat with ADVISER via text input in English to find modules offered by the IMS. For each dialog, participants were given a list of goals, detailing constraints to inform the system about and to request from the system. These included information such as responsible lecturer, the term within which the module was offered, and whether the module was related to a particular discipline, e.g. linguistics and statistics.

After each dialog, participants were asked to rate their chat with ADVISER, considering the quality of the respective dialog in terms of naturalness and coherence as well as how successful ADVISER was in processing the information provided by the user and how comfortable it was to use. Overall, participants rated the quality of dialog with the RL policy a 4.3 similar to the results obtained from dialogs using the rules-based policy (4.48 points on average) on a scale from 1 (very bad) to 7 (very good), confirming the functionality of the system. Considering the system's success in processing the user information correctly, on a scale from 1 (very bad) to 5 (very good), participants again found ADVISER to be slightly above average. This result applies to both dialogs which were generated using the rules-based policy (3.52 on average) and those using the RL policy (3.52 point average). 61.5 % of the participants reported that they would use ADVISER for their own pur-

poses. Moreover, asking participants to rate the comfort of using the system on a scale from 1 (very bad) to 5 (very good), an average comfort level was 3.69, indicating that most users felt comfortable with the system.

5.2 Multidisciplinary Practical Course

To test ADVISER as a tool for study purposes, we evaluated the CrossTick game, where linguistics and computer science students work to develop and gain a better understanding of the NLU in a dialog system.

CrossTick game Given a user act, linguistics students/researchers work to find as many UARs as possible which are not recognised by the system. On the other side, computer science students/researchers minimise the system errors by developing either new rules or machine learning models to handle more natural language variations of the user inputs.

Evaluation In order to test the efficiency and the user's opinion about the game, the same 13 participants from the previous evaluation were given 10 tasks. Per task, users were asked to take the linguist's perspective, and given intent, slots, and values to generate natural language for. In this case *intent* corresponds to the type of sentence (e.g. *Inform/Request*), *slot* to the type of information a user is giving/requesting and *value* describes the actual information given. If participants succeeded in creating natural language variations that were not covered by the system's NLU, they saw a cross mark ($\times$) next to their input, and points were added to their score. Otherwise, they obtained a check mark ($\checkmark$), worth 0 points. Although users could reach an infinite number of points per task, they were encouraged to be more productive and creative by telling them to beat the high score another user previously scored.

During the survey, 84.6% of the participants stated that the game was effective for educational purposes. Further, on a scale from 1 (completely useless) to 5 (very useful) the CrossTick Game received on average 3.69 points, suggesting that most users learned the NLU module's functionality. Overall, participants enjoyed using the game. Some participants especially liked the challenge to beat the high score, while others enjoyed that they were rewarded with points for uncovered sentences.

6 Conclusions

In this paper, we presented ADVISER - an open source dialog system which supports multilingual, multi-domain human-machine task-oriented conversations. It supports modules which can easily be interchanged between rules-based and machine learning implementations –including deep learning and RL. Our preliminary human study shows that with our toolkit one can easily build a useful dialog system. Furthermore, the CrossTick game offers an appealing interface for education purposes for different study disciplines.

Acknowledgments

We would like to thank all the voluntary students at the University of Stuttgart for their participation in the evaluation. This work was funded by the Carl Zeiss Foundation.

References

Timo Baumann and David Schlangen. 2012. The inprotk 2012 release. In *NAACL-HLT Workshop on Future Directions and Needs in the Spoken Dialog Community: Tools and Data*.

Daniel G. Bobrow, Ronald M. Kaplan, Martin Kay, Donald A. Norman, Henry Thompson, and Terry Winograd. 1977. GUS: a Frame-Driven Dialog System. *Artificial Intelligence*, 8.

Dan Bohus and Alexander I. Rudnicky. 2009. The ravenclaw dialog management framework: Architecture and systems. *Comput. Speech Lang.*

Renato De Mori, Frédéric Bechet, Dilek Hakkani-Tur, Michael McTear, Giuseppe Riccardi, and Gokhan Tur. 2008. Spoken language understanding. *IEEE Signal Processing Magazine*.

Glorianna Jagfeld and Ngoc Thang Vu. 2017. Encoding word confusion networks with recurrent neural networks for dialog state tracking. In *Proceedings of the Workshop on Speech-Centric Natural Language Processing*.

Pierre Lison and Casey Kennington. 2016. Opendial: A toolkit for developing spoken dialogue systems with probabilistic rules. In *Proceedings of ACL*.

Alexander Miller, Will Feng, Dhruv Batra, Antoine Bordes, Adam Fisch, Jiasen Lu, Devi Parikh, and Jason Weston. 2017. Parlai: A dialog research software platform. In *Proceedings of EMNLP*.

Volodymyr Mnih, Koray Kavukcuoglu, David Silver, Alex Graves, Ioannis Antonoglou, Daan Wierstra, and Martin Riedmiller. 2013. Playing atari with deep reinforcement learning. In *NIPS Deep Learning Workshop*.

Nikola Mrkšić, Diarmuid Ó Séaghdha, Blaise Thomson, Milica Gasic, Pei-Hao Su, David Vandyke, Tsung-Hsien Wen, and Steve Young. 2015. Multi-domain dialog state tracking using recurrent neural networks. In *Proceedings of ACL*.

Nikola Mrkšić, Diarmuid O Séaghdha, Tsung-Hsien Wen, Blaise Thomson, and Steve Young. 2017. Neural belief tracker: Data-driven dialogue state tracking. In *Proceedings of ACL*.

Jost Schatzmann, Blaise Thomson, Karl Weilhammer, Hui Ye, and Steve Young. 2007. Agenda-based user simulation for bootstrapping a pomdp dialogue system. In *Proceedings of NAACL*.

Tom Schaul, John Quan, Ioannis Antonoglou, and David Silver. 2015. Prioritized experience replay. In *Proceedings of ICLR*.

Gabriel Skantze and Samer Al Moubayed. 2012. Iristk: a statechart-based toolkit for multi-party face-to-face interaction. In *ICMI*.

Stefan Ultes, Lina M. Rojas Barahona, Pei-Hao Su, David Vandyke, Dongho Kim, Iñigo Casanueva, Paweł Budzianowski, Nikola Mrkšić, Tsung-Hsien Wen, Milica Gasic, and Steve Young. 2017. PyDial: A Multi-domain Statistical Dialogue System Toolkit. In *Proceedings of ACL*.

Hado Van Hasselt, Arthur Guez, and David Silver. 2016. Deep reinforcement learning with double q-learning. In *Proceedings of AAAI*.

Oriol Vinyals and Quoc Le. 2015. A neural conversational model. In *Proceedings of ICML*.

Ziyu Wang, Tom Schaul, Matteo Hessel, Hado Van Hasselt, Marc Lanctot, and Nando De Freitas. 2016. Dueling network architectures for deep reinforcement learning. In *Proceedings of ICML*.

Joseph Weizenbaum. 1966. ELIZA: A Computer Program for the Study of Natural Language Communication Between Man and Machine. *Communications of the ACM*, 9(1).

Tsung-Hsien Wen, David Vandyke, Nikola Mrkšić, Milica Gašić, Lina M Rojas-Barahona, Pei-Hao Su, Stefan Ultes, and Steve Young. 2017. A network-based end-to-end trainable task-oriented dialogue system. In *Proceedings of EACL*.

Jason Williams, Antoine Raux, and Matthew Henderson. 2016. The dialog state tracking challenge series: A review. *Dialogue & Discourse*.

Jason Williams and Steve Young. 2007. Partially observable markov decision processes for spoken dialog systems. *Computer Speech & Language*.

Zhou Yu, Alexander Rudnicky, and Alan Black. 2017. Learning conversational systems that interleave task and non-task content. In *Proceedings of IJCAI*.

KCAT: A Knowledge-Constraint Typing Annotation Tool

Sheng Lin[1], Luye Zheng[1], Bo Chen[1], Siliang Tang[1]*, Yueting Zhuang[1],
Fei Wu[1], Zhigang Chen[2], Guoping Hu[2] & Xiang Ren[3]
[1]Zhejiang University
[2]iFLYTEK Research, [3]University of Southern California,
{shenglin, antlar, chenbo123}@zju.edu.cn,
{siliang, yzhuang, wufei}@zju.edu.cn,
{zgchen, gphu}@iflytek.com,
xiangren@usc.edu

Abstract

Fine-grained Entity Typing is a tough task which suffers from noise samples extracted from distant supervision. Thousands of manually annotated samples can achieve greater performance than millions of samples generated by the previous distant supervision method. Whereas, it's hard for human beings to differentiate and memorize thousands of types, thus making large-scale human labeling hardly possible. In this paper, we introduce a Knowledge-Constraint Typing Annotation Tool (KCAT[1]), which is efficient for fine-grained entity typing annotation. KCAT reduces the size of candidate types to an acceptable range for human beings through entity linking and provides a Multi-step Typing scheme to revise the entity linking result. Moreover, KCAT provides an efficient Annotator Client to accelerate the annotation process and a comprehensive Manager Module to analyse crowdsourcing annotations. Experiment shows that KCAT can significantly improve annotation efficiency, the time consumption increases slowly as the size of type set expands.

1 Introduction

Recent years Natural Language Processing community has seen a surge of interests in fine-grained entity typing (**FET**) as it serves as an important cornerstone of several nature language processing tasks including relation extraction (Mintz et al., 2009), entity linking (Raiman and Raiman, 2018), and knowledge base completion (Dong et al., 2014). Given an entity mention (i.e. a sequence of token spans representing an entity) in the corpus, **FET** aims at uncovering its context-dependent type. Table 1 includes Fine-grained

Entity Typing datasets in recent years, the target types often form a type hierarchy.

The difficulty of FET and FET Annotation both increase rapidly with the growth of type hierarchy's depth. Previous research work mainly focus on generating train corpus with distant supervision (Ling and Weld, 2012; Gillick et al., 2014; Ren et al., 2016a; Choi et al., 2018). In spite of its efficiency, distant supervision brings the problem of noisy labels, for example, {*Other, brand*} are noisy labels for '*Kobe*' in "*Kobe scored 60 points in the final game.*". According to (Choi et al., 2018), 6000 manually labeled samples achieved greater performance than millions of samples generated by distant supervision. (Onoe and Durrett, 2019) observed that noisy samples may even cause damage to the performance of FET model. (Ren et al., 2016b; Onoe and Durrett, 2019) proposed label noise reduction methods, which are pretty complicated and hard to migrate.

Thus the annotation corpus for FET is important and necessary. However, it is not easy to annotate a corpus for FET since it's hard for human beings to differentiate and memorize thousands of types.

To solve this extremely hard annotation task, we use Entity Linking (EL) to constrain the candidate types of the entity mention. Entity Linking, which tries to link entity mention to a unique entity in a specific knowledge base (i.e. Yago or Freebase), has been studied for years. The state-of-the-art EL system yields 0.93 F1 score in Conll2003(Sang and Buchholz, 2000), while the F1 scores of FET vary from 0.40 (Onoe and Durrett, 2019) to 0.79 (Abhishek et al., 2017) on different datasets. With the help of EL, the candidate types of a mention can be greatly reduced as shown in the Table 1. Based on this observation, we develop a Knowledge-Constraint Typing Annotation Tool (KCAT). KCAT uses an external entity linking tool to constrain the candidate types of

---

*Corresponding Author.
[1]Code is available at https://github.com/donnyslin/KCAT

Proceedings of the 57th Annual Meeting of the Association for Computational Linguistics-System Demonstrations, pages 99–104
Florence, Italy, July 28 - August 2, 2019. ©2019 Association for Computational Linguistics

Dataset	Depth	#Types	#KC Types	Ratio.%
BBN	2	47	2.1	4.3%
FIGER	2	110	2.3	2.1%
TAC 2018	14	7309	8.5	0.1%

Table 1: Size of Candidate Types before and after **Knowledge-Constraint** on Different Datasets, and the ratio of the latter to the former

mentions. Because errors made by Entity Linking are inevitable, we provide an EL revision extension in KCAT which can also help the annotation of Entity Linking. The extension uses the coarse-grained type of mention to constrain the candidate entities of mention, which greatly saves the time of revising EL result. The details of the annotation interaction are described in section 3. Besides using the Knowledge Constraint technology to make the annotation of FET easier, KCAT provides other 4 functions to further improve the annotation efficiency: Hierarchical Structure Visualization, Annotation Hint, Annotation Modification and Annotation Export. In brief, KCAT has the advantages as follows:

- **Knowledge-Constraint:** it visualizes candidate types hierarchically, which is extracted from Knowledge Base and reduced by entity linking.
- **Efficient:** it supports multiple shortcuts to improve annotation efficiency; entity description of the wiki and type description to help distinguish candidate types.
- **Portable:** it is only required to replace a few json files to complete the migration of different datasets.
- **Comprehensive:** it supports crowdsourcing results comparison and integration.

The rest of the paper is organized as: Section 2 briefly describes recent research in FET. Section 3 introduces the overview of our framework. Section 4 describes the architecture of KCAT and its detail functions. Section 5 analyses the efficiency comparison and annotation quality in different annotation mode. Finally, Section 6 concludes this paper.

2   Related Works

Named Entity Recognition (NER) has been studied for several decades, which classifies coarse-grained types (e.g. person, location). In order to reduce the cost of obtaining fine-grained typing corpus, distant supervision has been widely used in FET (Ling and Weld, 2012; Gillick et al., 2014; Ren et al., 2016a; Choi et al., 2018). Inevitably, distant supervision brings the unique challenge of noisy labels in FET which seriously slows down the research process in this field. Many researchers focus on noise reduction of label(Ren et al., 2016b,a; Onoe and Durrett, 2019). The costliness of annotated corpus and the problem of noisy labels greatly hurt the usability of FET technique. Previous entity typing annotation tools (Stenetorp et al., 2012; Yang et al., 2018) focus on the coarse-grained types and is hard to migrate to fine-grained types. A specific and carefully designed annotation tool is urgently needed for FET. To the best of our knowledge, KCAT is the first Fine-grained Entity Typing Annotation tool.

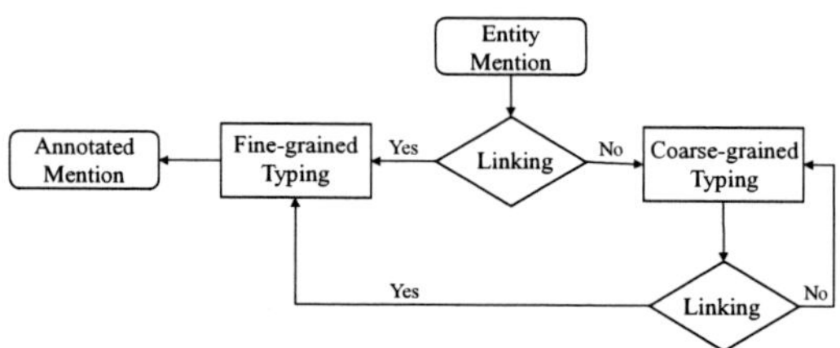

Figure 1: The framework of KCAT

3   Overview

This section overviews the proposed framework as shown in Figure 1. KCAT leverages **Type Hierarchy from Knowledge Base**, and reduces the size of candidate types to a small range through **Entity Linking**. Furthermore, KCAT proposes a **Multistep Typing** scheme because the result from Entity Linking may be incorrect. As shown in Figure 1, given an entity mention, KCTA links it to entity in Knowledge Base by EL model. Fine-grained type can be directly labeled if this result from model is correct, otherwise KCTA provides entity linking revision by coarse-grained type constraint to filter out candidates entities with inconsistent types and finally labels fine-grained type. The details will be described following.

3.1   Type Hierarchy and Knowledge Base

Given a set of types $\mathcal{T} = \{t_1, ..., t_N\}$, these types usually form a Directed Acyclic Graph (DAG) or more commonly a tree. Each entity e in Knowledge Base $\mathcal{K}$ has only several types, $\mathcal{T}_e = \{t_1, ..., t_M\} \subset \mathcal{T}$. In general, the size $|\mathcal{T}_e|$ is far less than the size $|\mathcal{T}|$. As shown in Table 1, the average size $\overline{|\mathcal{T}_e|}$ maintains in a small range as $|\mathcal{T}|$ expands. Therefore, EL, as a Knowledge Constraint method, helps to reduce the candidate size significantly.

3.2 Entity Linking

Given a set of entity mentions $\mathcal{M} = \{m_1, ..., m_T\}$ in corpus $\mathcal{D}$, Entity Linking aims to link each mention m_t to its corresponding gold entity e_i^* in $\mathcal{K}$. Such process is usually divided into two steps: *Candidate generation* first collects a set of possible candidate entities $\mathcal{E}_i = \{e_i^1, ..., e_i^{|\mathcal{E}_i|}\}$ for m_i; *Candidate ranking* is then applied to rank all candidates. The linking system selects the top ranked candidate as the predicted entity $\hat{e}_i$. Given a mention in text, our system firstly links it to $\mathcal{K}$ by state-of-the-art Entity Linking system (Le and Titov, 2018), which yields 0.93 F1 score on Conll 2003 dataset. As shown in Figure 2, *Kobe* is an entity mention which can be linked to "Kobe Bean Bryant" in $\mathcal{K}$, whose types only contain *person* and its descendant, we only need to type on the subtree. Whereas, after EL there are still 7% wrong linked mentions which need to be manually revised. Hence, for each mention, we provide the candidate entities with top 20 ranked score from EL system as the revision choices. In current EL systems, ground truth entity coverage can reach 0.98 (Ganea and Hofmann, 2017) which ensuring the recall of revision choices.

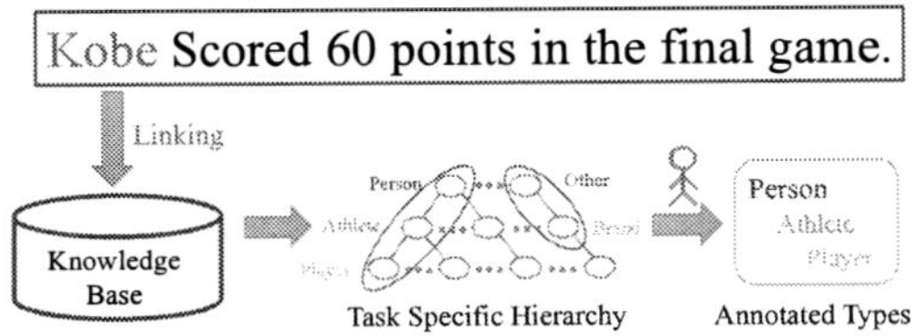

Figure 2: The Process of Knowledge Constraint by Entity Linking

Even though, the revision progress can be tough as The context may be ambiguous for manually linking mentions. Distinguishing different entities can be time-consuming and difficult for an amateurish annotator. To accelerate the revision progress, KCAT uses multi-step typing to reduce the number of candidate entities.

3.3 Multi-step Typing

Entity Linking and **Entity Typing** are mutually improved: a) EL helps to reduce the size of can-

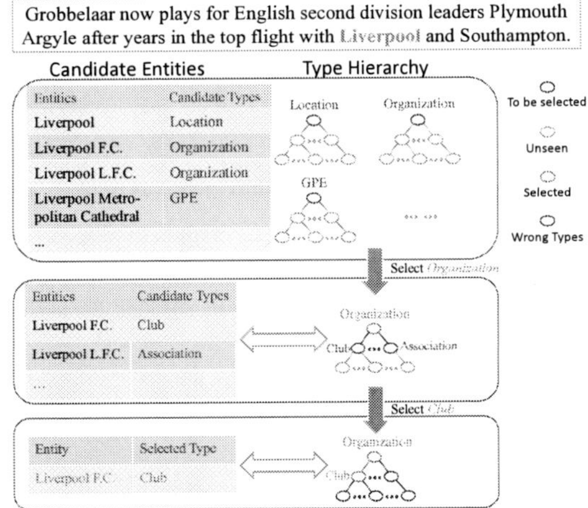

Figure 3: Interaction between Typing and Linking

didate types of ET; b) ET helps to filter out irrelevant candidate entities of EL with inconsistent types. Based on this observation, we propose a Multi-step Typing scheme. Figure 3 demonstrates the interaction between entity typing and linking. The left part shows the candidate entities in every step and the right part shows the candidate types constrained by candidates entities. The red words"*Liverpool*" is an entity mention "*Liverpool*", EL mistakenly links football *Club* "*Liverpool F.C.*" to "*Liverpool City*". It's tough for human to label the mention as *Club* without professional knowledge, but it's easy to label it as *Organization*. In our scheme, the user firstly selects the coarse-grained type *Organization*, and observes that the candidate entities which contain *Organization*. Gold entity, "Liverpool F.C.", and *Club* can be easily picked out. Through hierarchy type selection, the user focus on a few candidate entities, which can prompt user to do deeper type selection.

4 KCAT

KCAT is developed based on standard Python GUI library Tkinter, hence it only needs Python installation as prerequisite. It provides user-friendly interfaces for annotators. KCAT contains two main modules: **Annotator Client** and **Manager Module**.

- **Annotator Client:** With the help of Knowledge Constraint, KCAT makes the impossible annotation of FET possible. An Annotation Client is designed to further accelerate the annotation

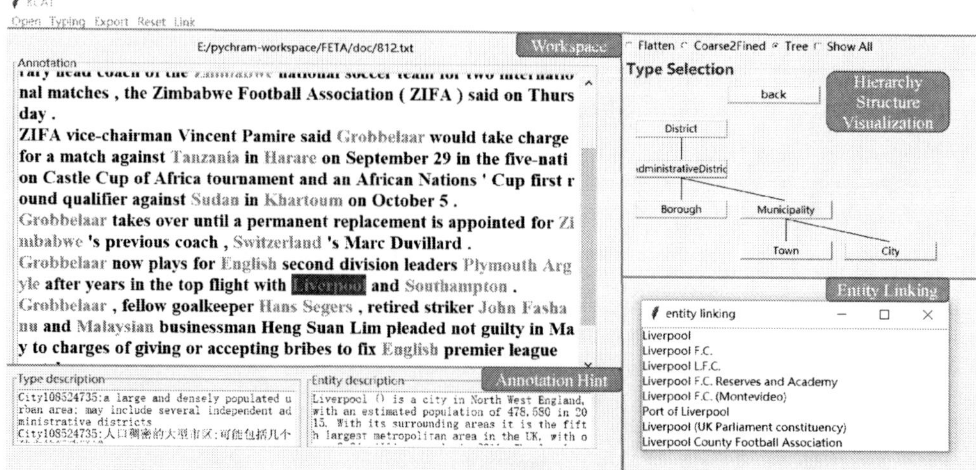

Figure 4: A Screenshot of KCAT (different parts are seperated by bold red line)

process. It provides 4 practical functions to reduce annotation time: **a) Hierarchical Structure Visualization, b) Annotation Hint, c) Annotation Modification, d) Annotation Export**.

- **Manager Module:** KCAT also provides a Manager Module to analyse the annotation results.

We will introduce these two modules in following sections respectively.

4.1 Annotator Client

Figure 4 shows the interface of Annotator Client. The interface consists of 5 parts. The toolbar contains some basic functions for **Annotation Modification** and **Annotation Export**. The main area in the upper left is the text in annotating, in which mentions are colored by red and types are colored by blue. The upper right area shows the **Hierarchical Structure Visualization** and the bottom left area shows the **Annotation Hint** which helps annotators to know more about the type and entity information. The children window titled as "entity linking" in the bottom right shows the candidate entities ranked by entity linking system.

a) Hierarchical Structure Visualization

On most entity typing datasets, types can be formed by hierarchical structure, hence Directed Acyclic Graph (DAG) is a good view to represent this structure. By this hierarchical structure, KCAT supports up-down searching without scanning irrelevant types in other subgraph.

b) Annotation Hint

Annotator may not memorize all the definitions of types and descriptions of entities. Therefore, prompting type definitions and entity descriptions will contribute to the labeling process. KCAT provides the definition of type extracted from WordNet(Fellbaum, 2012) and the first paragraph of Wikipedia page related to entity to help the annotator further acquainted with the type and entity.

c) Annotation Modification

Sometimes users need to revise the annotation when they make mistakes. KCAT provides several efficient modification actions to revise these incorrect annotations.

Action Undo and Redo: annotators can cancel their previous actions or redo their canceled actions to return to any previous states by press the shortcut key Ctrl+z and Ctrl+y respectively.

Label Modify and Reset: if an entity mention receives an incorrect type, annotator only needs to put the cursor inside the span and restart labeling. In addition, annotator can reset the annotations by shortcut key Ctrl+r.

d) Annotation Export

KCAT provides the "Export" function, which exports the annotated text as standard format (ended with txt) or json format so that it's easy to be processed by users.

4.2 Manager Module

The Manager Module aims to evaluate the quality of annotated files, analyzes the detailed disagreements of different annotators and integrates all annotation results from multiple annotators.

Multiple Annotators Comparison

The annotations from multiple annotators are inconsistent, in order to evaluate the quality of annotations, KCAT provides a Multiple Annotator Comparison interface to generate the accuracy matrix to measure consistency among multiple annotators, which is illustrated in Figure 5.

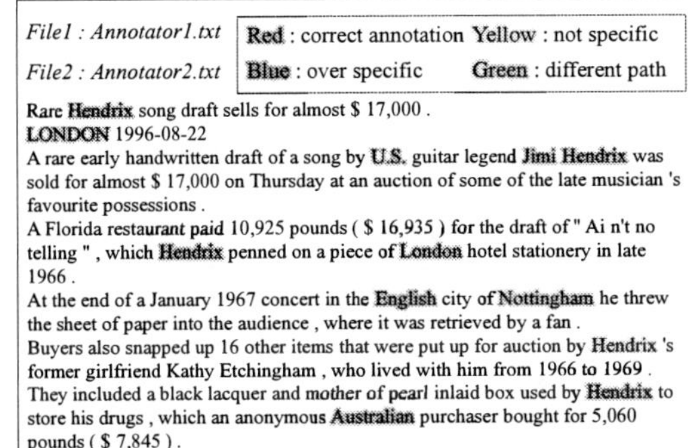

Figure 5: Multiple Annotator Analysis

Rare **Hendrix** song draft sells for almost $ 17,000 .
LONDON 1996-08-22
A rare early handwritten draft of a song by **U.S.** guitar legend **Jimi Hendrix** was sold for almost $ 17,000 on Thursday at an auction of some of the late musician 's favourite possessions .
A Florida restaurant paid 10,925 pounds ($ 16,935) for the draft of " Ai n't no telling " , which **Hendrix** penned on a piece of **London** hotel stationery in late 1966 .
At the end of a January 1967 concert in the **English** city of **Nottingham** he threw the sheet of paper into the audience , where it was retrieved by a fan .
Buyers also snapped up 16 other items that were put up for auction by **Hendrix** 's former girlfriend Kathy Etchingham , who lived with him from 1966 to 1969 . They included a black lacquer and **mother of pearl** inlaid box used by **Hendrix** to store his drugs , which an anonymous **Australian** purchaser bought for 5,060 pounds ($ 7,845) .

Figure 6: Error Analysis

Error Analysis

There are three common error patterns in entity typing task: (a) Over Specific; mislabeling parent type as child type (i.e., annotated as athlete while the ground truth type is person). (b)Not Specific; in contrary to former (a). (c)Incorrect Path; labeling the wrong child type (i.e., entity is annotated as athlete while the ground truth type is artist and they are both child type of person). KCAT provides an interface to generate the error analysis report in ".tex" format, as shown in Figure 6, different errors are rendered in different colors.

Annotations Integration

The Annotations Integration interface provides a method to integrate all annotation results from crowdsourcing annotations to generate final labels by voting.

5 Experiment

In order to verify the efficiency of KCAT, we conduct a mock annotation experiment. 100 sentences are extracted from the English dataset of Conll 2003 (Sang and Buchholz, 2000) as the corpus to be annotated. The entity mention spans in these sentences have been annotated. Type hierarchy is extracted from following three datasets: (1) Conll 2003; (2) BBN(Ren et al., 2016a); (3) FIGER(Ling and Weld, 2012); and YAGO Knowledge Base(Heng et al., 2018). The mappings between entity and its related types are provided by these datasets. We have chosen two annotation modes: (a) without pre-linking, directly through top-down search or flatten search; (b) filtering out types that are inconsistent with entity types through entity linking.

Annotation Efficiency. In Table 2, we compare the labeling time in aforementioned two modes and calculate the percentage of time saved with Entity Linking on different type set. It can be observed that with the number of types increases, time consumption increases slowly with entity linking, while without entity linking, time consumption increases exponentially. The percentage of time saved also increases as the number of types expands on different datasets. When there are thousands of types in Knowledge Base, such as YAGO Knowledge Base(Heng et al., 2018), which contains 7309 types, it's impossible for human to annotate.

Type Set	#types	depth	Time		
			w/ EL	w/o EL	Rel%
Conll	5	1	**5**	6	6.3%
BBN	47	2	**8**	17	52.9%
FIGER	112	2	**10**	30	66.7%
YAGO	7309	14	**13**	-	-

Table 2: Time Consumption (minute) of Annotating 60 Sentences on Different Datasets

Annotation Quality. Pairwise accuracy is used to measure the consistence between arbitrary two annotators. For multiple annotators, we can generate a heat map, each element of the heat map represents pairwise accuracy, darker color means higher accuracy. In Figure 7, the User 1, 2, and 3 adopt the mode (b), and the User 4, 5 and 6 adopts the mode (a), and it can be observed that the labeling quality of 1, 2, and 3 is significantly better than 4, 5, 6 as the former have higher consistency.

6 Conclusion

In this paper, we propose an efficient Knowledge Constraint Fine-grained Entity Typing Annotation Tool, which further improves entity typing process through entity linking together with some practical functions.

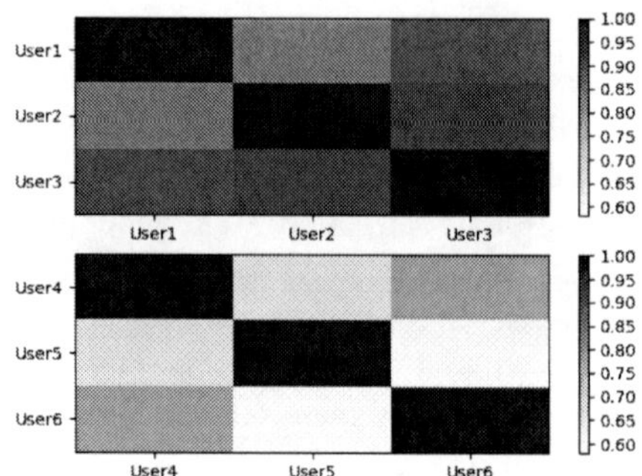

Figure 7: A Comparison of Multiple Annotators in Accuracy

7 Acknowledgement

This work has been supported in part by NSFC (No.61751209, U1611461), Zhejiang University-iFLYTEK Joint Research Center, Chinese Knowledge Center of Engineering Science and Technology (CKCEST), Engineering Research Center of Digital Library, Ministry of Education. Xiang Ren's research has been supported in part by National Science Foundation SMA 18-29268.

References

Abhishek Abhishek, Ashish Anand, and Amit Awekar. 2017. Fine-grained entity type classification by jointly learning representations and label embeddings. In *Proceedings of the 15th Conference of the European Chapter of the Association for Computational Linguistics: Volume 1, Long Papers*, pages 797–807, Valencia, Spain. Association for Computational Linguistics.

Eunsol Choi, Omer Levy, Yejin Choi, and Luke Zettlemoyer. 2018. Ultra-fine entity typing. *arXiv preprint arXiv:1807.04905*.

Xin Dong, Evgeniy Gabrilovich, Geremy Heitz, Wilko Horn, Ni Lao, Kevin Murphy, Thomas Strohmann, Shaohua Sun, and Wei Zhang. 2014. Knowledge vault: A web-scale approach to probabilistic knowledge fusion. In *Proceedings of the 20th ACM SIGKDD international conference on Knowledge discovery and data mining*, pages 601–610. ACM.

Christiane Fellbaum. 2012. Wordnet. *The Encyclopedia of Applied Linguistics*.

Octavian-Eugen Ganea and Thomas Hofmann. 2017. Deep joint entity disambiguation with local neural attention. *arXiv preprint arXiv:1704.04920*.

Dan Gillick, Nevena Lazic, Kuzman Ganchev, Jesse Kirchner, and David Huynh. 2014. Context-dependent fine-grained entity type tagging. *arXiv preprint arXiv:1412.1820*.

Ji Heng, Sil Avirup, Trang Dang Hoa, J. Goldschen Alan, Duncan Jason, Getman Jeremy, Nothman Joel, Onyshkevych Boyan, Soboroff Ian, and Strassel Stephanie. 2018. Tac kbp2018 entity discovery and linking for 7,309 entity types. http://nlp.cs.rpi.edu/kbp/2018/ EDL2018TaskSpec_V2.0.pdf.

Phong Le and Ivan Titov. 2018. Improving entity linking by modeling latent relations between mentions. *arXiv preprint arXiv:1804.10637*.

Xiao Ling and Daniel S Weld. 2012. Fine-grained entity recognition. In *Twenty-Sixth AAAI Conference on Artificial Intelligence*.

Mike Mintz, Steven Bills, Rion Snow, and Dan Jurafsky. 2009. Distant supervision for relation extraction without labeled data. In *Proceedings of the Joint Conference of the 47th Annual Meeting of the ACL and the 4th International Joint Conference on Natural Language Processing of the AFNLP: Volume 2-Volume 2*, pages 1003–1011. Association for Computational Linguistics.

Yasumasa Onoe and Greg Durrett. 2019. Learning to Denoise Distantly-Labeled Data for Entity Typing. In *Proceedings of the 2019 Conference of the North American Chapter of the Association for Computational Linguistics: Human Language Technologies*.

Jonathan Raphael Raiman and Olivier Michel Raiman. 2018. Deeptype: multilingual entity linking by neural type system evolution. In *Thirty-Second AAAI Conference on Artificial Intelligence*.

Xiang Ren, Wenqi He, Meng Qu, Lifu Huang, Heng Ji, and Jiawei Han. 2016a. Afet: Automatic fine-grained entity typing by hierarchical partial-label embedding. In *Proceedings of the 2016 Conference on Empirical Methods in Natural Language Processing*, pages 1369–1378.

Xiang Ren, Wenqi He, Meng Qu, Clare R Voss, Heng Ji, and Jiawei Han. 2016b. Label noise reduction in entity typing by heterogeneous partial-label embedding. In *Proceedings of the 22nd ACM SIGKDD international conference on Knowledge discovery and data mining*, pages 1825–1834. ACM.

Erik F Sang and Sabine Buchholz. 2000. Introduction to the conll-2000 shared task: Chunking. *arXiv preprint cs/0009008*.

Pontus Stenetorp, Sampo Pyysalo, Goran Topić, Tomoko Ohta, Sophia Ananiadou, and Jun'ichi Tsujii. 2012. Brat: a web-based tool for nlp-assisted text annotation. In *Proceedings of the Demonstrations at the 13th Conference of the European Chapter of the Association for Computational Linguistics*, pages 102–107. Association for Computational Linguistics.

Jie Yang, Yue Zhang, Linwei Li, and Xingxuan Li. 2018. Yedda: A lightweight collaborative text span annotation tool.

An Environment for Relational Annotation of Political Debates

André Blessing[1], Nico Blokker[2], Sebastian Haunss[2],
Jonas Kuhn[1], Gabriella Lapesa[1], and Sebastian Padó[1]

[1]IMS, University of Stuttgart, Germany
[2]SOCIUM, University of Bremen, Germany

Abstract

This paper describes the MARDY corpus annotation environment developed for a collaboration between political science and computational linguistics. The tool realizes the complete workflow necessary for annotating a large newspaper text collection with rich information about *claims* (demands) raised by politicians and other actors, including claim and actor spans, relations, and polarities. In addition to the annotation GUI, the tool supports the identification of relevant documents, text pre-processing, user management, integration of external knowledge bases, annotation comparison and merging, statistical analysis, and the incorporation of machine learning models as "pseudo-annotators".

1 Introduction

Scalable text analysis techniques can open corpora to new questions in computational social sciences and digital humanities. This goal can be greatly facilitated with an environment for cross-disciplinary corpus access that supports the design and refinement of analysis categories and models – equally well at the conceptual and the natural language processing (NLP) level. It thus also invites a mixed-methods approach (Kuhn, to appear) towards more far-reaching research questions – combining the strengths of scalable computational models and the expert view on contextualized text instances.

This paper describes the MARDY tool, an interactive annotation environment for *political claims analysis* in computational political science (see Padó et al. (2019) for a task analysis and initial modeling results). The term claim is operationalized as a textual span containing a demand, proposal, criticism, or a decision made by actors active in the respective field (Koopmans and Statham, 1999). For example, a commentator may put forward the claim that the voting age be lowered to

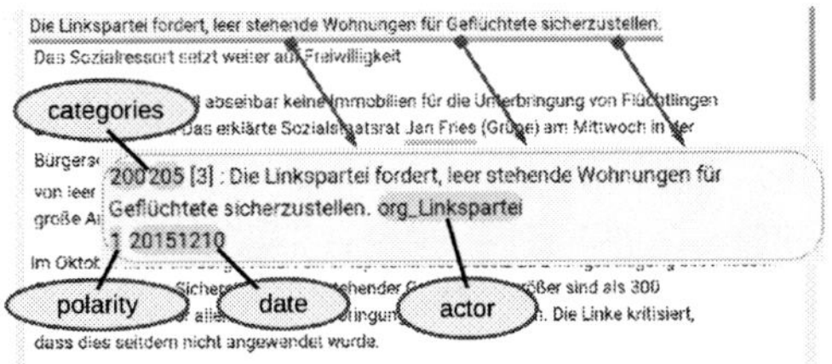

Figure 1: Annotation for the text span: "The Left Party demands that vacant flats be secured for refugees." which includes claim category 205 (forced occupancy), the actor *Linkspartei* (Left Party), and positive polarity.

16; a political party may propose that a government help (or deter) refugees. Figure 1 shows a typical example of a claim from a German domestic politics debate on immigration: A sentence is identified as containing a claim, the claim is categorized according to an annotation scheme, and assigned an actor, a polarity, and a date.

Political Science Background. Understanding the structure and evolution of political debates is central to understanding democratic decision making (Haunss and Hofmann, 2015). Therefore, an important research strand in political science aims at modeling and analyzing the exact mechanisms of political discourse, such as the formation of *discourse coalitions* out of *actors* (Hajer, 1993).

Discourse network analysis (Leifeld, 2016) builds on top of claims analysis (Koopmans and Statham, 1999), representing debates as graphs and analyzing their structure and dynamics. Actors and claims are represented as the two classes of nodes in a bipartite *affiliation network*. In Figure 2, actors are circles, claims are squares, and they are linked by edges that indicate support (green) or opposition (orange). A discourse coalition is the projection of the affiliation network on the actor side (dotted edges), while the projection on the concept side yields argumentative clusters. Affiliation networks open up a systematic view on conjectured discur-

Proceedings of the 57th Annual Meeting of the Association for Computational Linguistics-System Demonstrations, pages 105–110
Florence, Italy, July 28 - August 2, 2019. ©2019 Association for Computational Linguistics

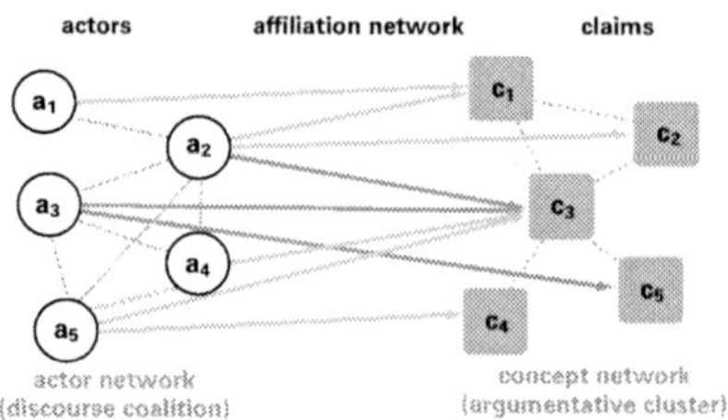

Figure 2: Actor, affiliation, and concept networks

sive patterns, e.g. regarding the stability/variability of coalition configurations in response to external events. To warrant a sufficiently focused analysis of discursive patterns, it is common to restrict attention to the debate in a given topical issue field. In the issue field of internal security policy, e.g., a recurring pattern could be hypothesized as follows: whenever a terrorist network is on the news, claims are made that police should receive more funding.

Annotating debates in corpora. To establish an empirical basis for research into the dynamics of political discourse, a systematic annotation methodology (*coding*, in the social science terminology) needs to be defined. The overarching goal is to identify and label claims brought forward by specific actors in a corpus covering public discourse, of the news coverage thereof, from a predefined time span. Within this scope, it is important to come as close as possible to discovering and annotating all claims made during the researched period. The granularity of distinct claim types adopted in the analysis has to be carefully chosen to ensure that different formulations of the same claim (claims with the same *substance*) are aggregated, while related claims have to be differentiated when this is relevant for the evolution of discourse dynamics. A debate-independent inventory of claim categories is hence impossible, and the development of a so-called *codebook* specifying annotation guidelines for relevant claim types is a crucial part of every issue-specific study (typically going through a cycle of revisions before freezing the claim types).

Manual vs. automatic annotation. To ensure reliability in the face of complex statements and of ambiguities only resolvable with world knowledge, annotation for political claims analysis has traditionally proceeded almost exclusively manually. There is however considerable potential for computer-aided annotation approaches that may increase the speed and consistency of annotations. This contribution demonstrates a technical architec-

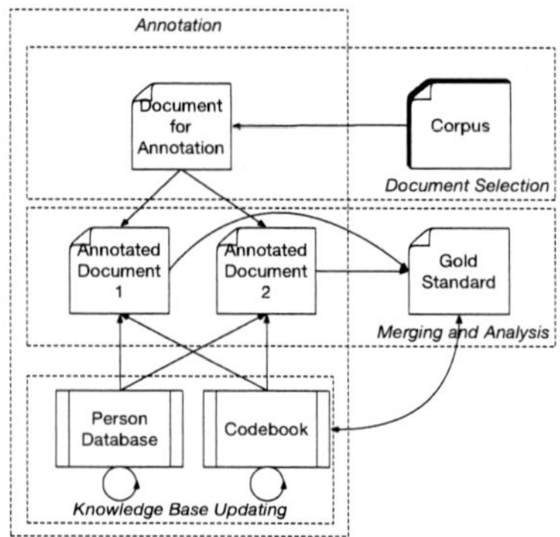

Figure 3: Workflow for Political Claims Annotation

ture supporting researchers from political science in the full cycle of corpus selection, codebook development, (parallel) annotation, annotation adjudication and consistency checking. Although various tools for annotation-related subtasks in corpus linguistics and NLP development exist, the specific interleaving of the various workflow steps in corpus-based social science and digital humanities calls for an integrated architecture.

The MARDY tool we present is a general environment for annotating of articles for political claims analysis. It extends ideas and components from earlier computational social science and digital humanities projects.[1] In a usability study on German newspaper texts (see Section 4), users reported improved guidance over traditional annotation procedures, and the integration of Machine Learning (ML) predictions as (pseudo-)annotators provides a unified interface for experiments with manual and automatic annotation.

2 Annotation Workflow Requirements

Figure 3 shows a typical annotation workflow that applies to political claims analysis as well as to related annotation tasks (see Section 5). The four dashed boxes with labels in italics show the major tasks involved, each of which comes with a number of desiderata.

Document Selection. We assume that annotation is performed on the basis of a potentially large overall corpus where full annotation of all documents is not feasible or desired. Thus, the first task is the *selection of relevant documents* for annotation. This is essentially an information retrieval task, where keyword-based approaches face the typical prob-

---

[1]Specifically, *e-Identity* (Blessing et al., 2015) and CRETA (Blessing et al., 2017).

lem of resulting in either high recall–low precision scenarios (too few keywords) or low recall–high precision scenarios (too many keywords).

Annotation. Since projects typically involve several annotators, the environment should not just support *annotation* proper, but also *user administration* (user management, task assignment).

Assuming that we annotate relations between actors and their claims, the annotation links markables to external knowledge bases, specifically the actors to a database of persons and other relevant entities (parties, companies, geopolitical entities etc.) and the claims to an ontology of claim categories (the *codebook*). The environment should support the integration of external knowledge bases for this purpose as seamlessly as possible.

Merging and Evaluation. Following best practice in both political science and NLP, we carry out double annotation of the relevant documents. These independent annotations need to be combined into a gold standard and merged by an expert adjudicator where they diverge. Our merging system also allows the integration of automatic generated annotations, which is particularly useful to counteract oversights, thus improving recall (see Section 4).

Knowledge Base Update. To support an evolutionary process of the analytical categories, both the actor and the claims knowledge bases (KBs) must be modifiable. The actor KB is initialized with resources like Wikidata (Vrandečić and Krötzsch, 2014), but allows for manual extension to cover references to less known people. Similarly, some claims categories typically need to be refined or coarsened in the initial phase of annotating a new topic of debate. The dynamic nature of the KBs make it necessary for the environment to provide functionality for *data and error analysis* and for *versioning of KBs and data*.

Comparison to other annotation environments. In the NLP community, BRAT[2] and WebAnno[3] are the most prominent tools for web-based annotation. Both tools focus on annotation of linguistic items (tagging, named entities). They are not designed for the annotation of complete document collections, nor do they provide interfaces to integrate complex and dynamic codebooks. The same holds if we consider more general frameworks like UIMA[4] or

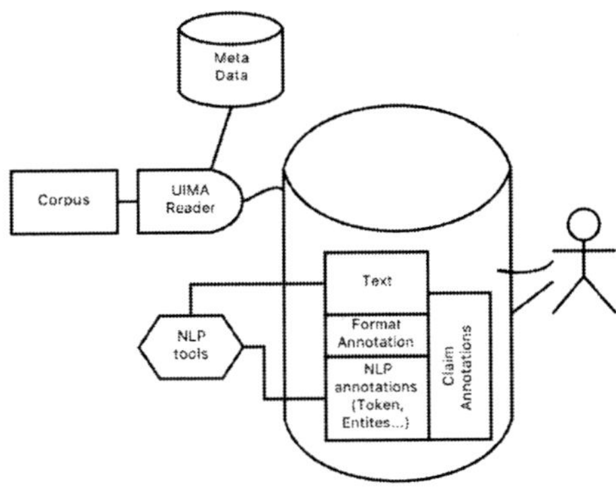

Figure 4: Technical structure of environment

GATE[5]: they cannot be used directly for complex annotation tasks, but need to be adapted (as we did for UIMA, cf. Section 3).

Established tools for qualitative data analysis (QDA) in political science are MAXQDA, NVivo and Atlas.ti (Friese, 2019; Rädiker and Kuckartz, 2019). These applications allow researchers to comfortably annotate a wide variety of textual data. However, their unit of analysis is always the text and not the annotated text segment. As a result, they do not retain the relational aspects of annotations: A text segment in which actor A makes claim X and actor B makes claim Y becomes indistinguishable from an annotation in which B claims X and A claims Y. Another tool, the discourse network analyzer (DNA) by Leifeld (2009), was developed specifically for the purpose of Discourse Network Analysis and solves this issue by focusing on the concept/actor relation as the unit of analysis. However, this application offers only very basic support for multiple annotators and does not enable parallel annotation of text. All annotations are always visible to the entire team, and there is no functionality to compare and merge annotations.

3 Design and Implementation

Figure 4 shows the technical structure and the frameworks used for the environment which we have developed to realize the workflow and desiderata from Section 2. The web page `https://mardy-spp.github.io/` contains a demo video, information concerning demo access, as well as a docker image for the annotation environment.

Document Preprocessing and Selection. Our environment builds on existing pipelines and web services using UIMA as data exchange formalism.

---

[2] `https://brat.nlplab.org/`
[3] `https://webanno.github.io/webanno/`
[4] `https://uima.apache.org/index.html`
[5] `https://gate.ac.uk/`

The input documents (in this case newspaper articles provided by the publisher) are encoded in a proprietary XML format. We developed a reader which parses and transforms the source articles into the UIMA representation defined by our type systems. That involves three tasks: i) identifying all relevant textual parts of the articles (e.g., embedded image captions have to be removed); ii) extracting meta data (e.g., date, author, title); iii) transforming format information (e.g., headings, footnotes). Afterwards, the text is passed through a generic pre-processing pipeline which calls several CLARIN webservices, namely tokenization and sentence boundary detection[6], POS tagging[7], and named entity recognition[8]. The analyzed documents are stored in an UIMA repository and an Elastic stack (`https://www.elastic.co/`).

Selecting a good sample has an high impact on the annotation process. MARDY starts off by using the Elastic stack's built-in keyword-based search to select relevant documents. This approach is complemented by a document classifier which can be trained as soon as some documents have been confirmed for annotation and some others rejected.

Annotation Frontend. Our core system is based on a client-server architecture. The Java server component interacts with the Elastic stack and the UIMA repository to store and retrieve annotated documents. The front-end is implemented with AngularJS (`https://angularjs.org/`).

The GUI for article view and annotation is implemented in Annotatorjs (`http://annotatorjs.org/`), a framework which enables text span annotation. Once the annotator has selected the relevant textual span, an input widget (Figure 5) displays claim categories (as defined by the annotation schema) as well as a suggestion list of potential actors, dates, and polarity (see below for details). This reduces annotation in most cases to selection among a small number of options and is crucial to increase annotation speed. Annotations are stored in a JSON-based format which is integrated by our back-end into the UIMA standoff format.

The tool supports user management for article assignment, as well as for checking the progress

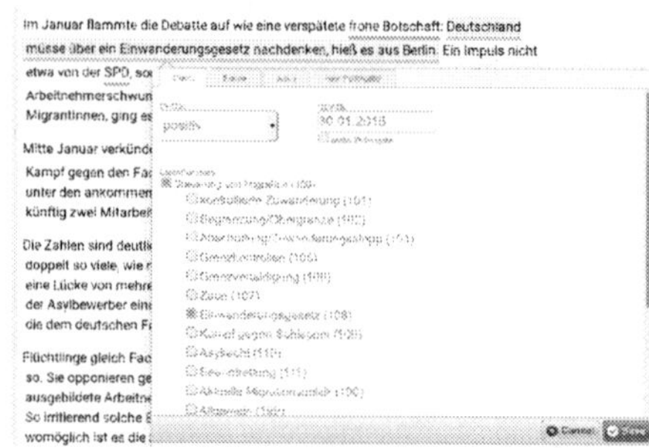

Figure 5: Annotation interface

of the annotation (documents are displayed as in progress, still awaiting annotation, or finished).

Merging. Figure 6 shows the view which enables experts to merge annotations into the gold standard. The experts decide for each row (same background color) if the detected text snippet is a claim and, if it is, then it is copied to the right column which shows the gold annotations. Each gold annotation can be further modified to adjust categories, actors and polarity of the claim. Usually, the annotations listed on the left are by human annotators, which are identified by IDs shown in square brackets ([7] in Figure 6). MARDY allows the users to integrate the predictions of a machine learning classifier which are then displayed in the merging view, marked as [AI] and with a lighter background color. Figure 6 illustrates an evaluation scenario for the [AI] pseudo-annotator. In the first row, [AI] has spotted a claim that the manual annotator had missed; moreover, it has identified the correct macro-category (700): the expert just needs to approve the claim and assign a finer-grained category. The [AI] annotator is, however, not perfect: the claim in the second row has been correctly identified only by the human annotator. In the third row, [AI] produced a false positive, probably because the candidate sentence contains the keyword *Lösung* (*solution*), which is a strong lexical cue for claims. In this case, though, only the need for a solution is stated, with no proposed action, leading the expert to reject the annotation.

Evaluation and Codebook Update. MARDY offers the possibility to evaluate annotation performance, thus providing valuable feedback to both annotators and specialists. The evaluation view reports performance (TP, FP, FN, precision, recall, and F1) aggregated per annotator and per category. The former is useful for training purposes, the latter particularly informative for the incremental re-

---

[6]`http://hdl.handle.net/11858/00-247C-0000-0007-3736-B`

[7]`http://hdl.handle.net/11858/00-247C-0000-0022-D906-1`

[8]`http://hdl.handle.net/11858/00-247C-0000-0022-DDA1-3`

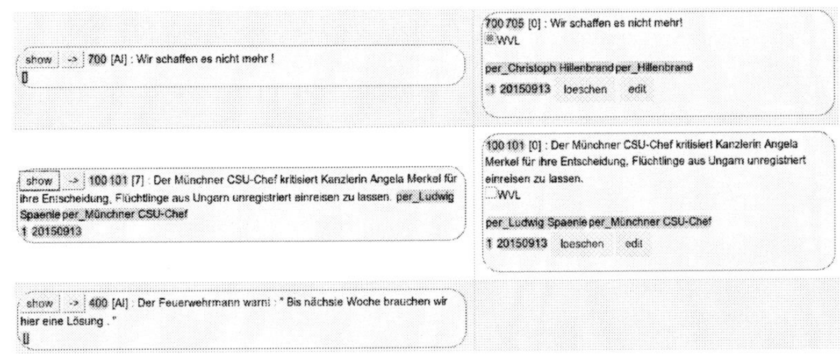

Figure 6: Left: user annotation or AI predictions; Right: approved annotations

finement of the codebook in the light of corpus evidence: categories that are often confounded are either ill-defined, or they stand in a systematic relationship (equivalence, subsumption, negation). Both cases may indicate the need for a redefinition of such categories. Versioning of data and codebook is available to later reconstruct how the annotation schema evolved during the project.

Actor Annotation and Update. In order to increase the speed and consistency of actor annotation, MARDY presents a set of plausible actors. This is achieved by attempting to link each named entity of type person or organization to a Wikidata entry. These entries provide canonical names (*Angela Merkel*) from which we derive variants (*A. Merkel, Frau Merkel*). We also exploit encyclopedic information to identify phrases that likely refer to these actors (e.g., *Kanzlerin (chancellor), CDU-Vorsitzende (CDU chairwoman)*). Given that Wikidata does not provide exhaustive coverage, the actor KB is extended whenever an annotator identifies an unknown actor.

4 Usability Study

In this section, we show how MARDY has been employed in a political science study targeting one of the major topics of German politics of 2015: the domestic debate on (im)migration policy. So far, we annotated 423 newspaper articles from *TAZ* (http://www.taz.de/), with a total of 982 claims (Padó et al., 2019).

The first step is **document selection**. The whole TAZ corpus contains more than 140.000 articles for the year 2015. The keyword-based search was used with a high recall objective in mind and resulted in 3112 articles. From the 423 annotated documents from this sample, approximately 58% was found to be off-topic. In the future, the second ML-based selection stage (cf. Section 3) should improve precision and thus reduce annotator load (fewer irrelevant articles to go through).

For **annotation**, each article was assigned to two annotators. 20 articles were used for annotator training and therefore assigned to all annotators. Note that the order in which the articles were shown to the annotators was randomized and thus not chronological. Multiple annotators could work simultaneously on the same article, while being monitored and compared by the researchers in real time. These features simplify and improve instructions and supervision, thus being more time-efficient than traditional approaches. Additionally, the fact that actor and claim categories are presented directly to annotators in the tool without laborious switching between applications led to a quicker and more comfortable annotation experience. Particularly helpful for high recall was the **integration of ML-based pseudo-annotators**: the identification of claims is a hard task for human coders, so that even the merging of several independent human annotations does not guarantee full coverage. We found that relatively simple neural sequence classifiers were already good enough to substantially boost the recall during the merging phase (Padó et al., 2019).

After several training rounds, we proceeded to a first **evaluation**. The quality of the human annotations was assessed in comparison to the gold standard. We computed annotation reliability for two parts of the annotation: claim detection and claim classification. For claim detection, we use Cohen's Kappa: For each sentence we compare whether the two annotators classified the sentence as part of a claim or not. We obtained a Kappa value of 0.58. Since claim classification is a multi-label task, Kappa cannot be used. We therefore computed Macro-F1 for all nine categories, obtaining an average F1 score of 63.5%.

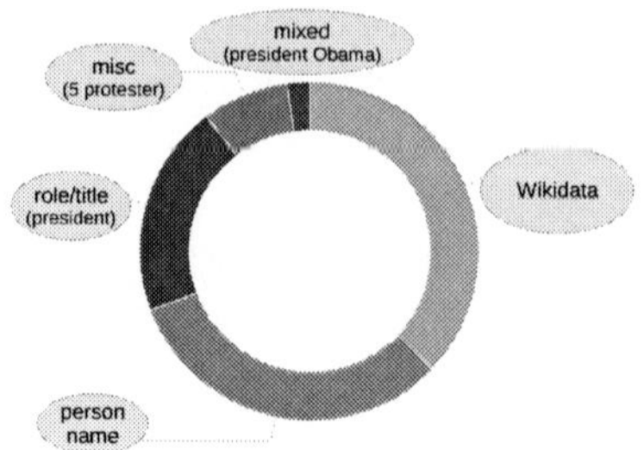

Figure 7: Actor Linkage: Distribution of categories.

Our annotation workflow greatly benefited from **integration with the claim category and actor KBs**. Indeed, the codebook was subject to many changes throughout the annotation process, as expected: Several iterations of reading articles and applying annotations were needed before convergence on a final version. Regarding the actor KB, Figure 7 illustrates the distribution of the actor categories annotated in the TAZ documents. The green portion are those person names that occur directly in Wikidata (roughly one third). Another third is composed of roles and titles (*Kanzlerin* (chancellor)) and mixed mentions (*Kanzlerin Merkel*), which may or may not be covered in Wikidata. The last third (light blue) are person names lacking completely in Wikidata. This underscores the need to easily and seamlessly extend the actor KB.

5 Outlook

We introduced an annotation environment whose features have been shaped by the goal of annotating German political debates to support discourse network analysis. Our tool is, however, highly flexible. First of all, its use is not restricted to German and it can be linked to any NLP pipeline. Moreover, it is not restricted to a specific document type: it can be employed, for example, for annotation targeting fewer layers (e.g., just claims and polarity, like in forum discussions). Finally, the framework can be (and has been, in the CRETA project (Blessing et al., 2017)) adapted to a broader range of text analysis contexts: e.g., it can be employed in literary studies to identify textual spans associated to characters, or having specific stylistic features. Finally, from a NLP perspective, our tool is a straightforward evaluation platform for classification models.

Acknowledgments

We acknowledge funding by Deutsche Forschungsgemeinschaft (DFG) through MARDY (Modeling Argumentation Dynamics) within SPP RATIO and by Bundesministerium für Bildung und Forschung (BMBF) through the Center for Reflected Text Analytics (CRETA).

References

André Blessing, Nora Echelmeyer, Markus John, and Nils Reiter. 2017. An end-to-end environment for research question-driven entity extraction and network analysis. In *Proc. of LaTeCH*, pages 57–67.

André Blessing, Fritz Kliche, Ulrich Heid, Cathleen Kantner, and Jonas Kuhn. 2015. Computerlinguistische Werkzeuge zur Erschließung und Exploration großer Textsammlungen aus der Perspektive fachspezifischer Theorien. In C. Baum and T. Stäcker, editors, *Grenzen und Möglichkeiten der Digital Humanities (= Sonderband der ZfdG 1)*.

Susanne Friese. 2019. *Qualitative data analysis with ATLAS*. SAGE Publications Limited.

Maarten A Hajer. 1993. Discourse Coalitions and the Institutionalization of Practice: The Case of Acid Rain in Britain. In *The Argumentative Turn in Policy Analysis and Planning*, pages 43–76. Duke University Press.

Sebastian Haunss and Jeanette Hofmann. 2015. Entstehung von Politikfeldern – Bedingungen einer Anomalie. *dms – der moderne staat*, 8(1):29–49.

Ruud Koopmans and Paul Statham. 1999. Political Claims Analysis: Integrating Protest Event And Political Discourse Approaches. *Mobilization*, 4(2):203–221.

Jonas Kuhn. to appear. Computational text analysis within the humanities: How to combine working practices from the contributing fields? *Language Resources and Evaluation*.

Philip Leifeld. 2009. Die Untersuchung von Diskursnetzwerken mit dem Discourse Network Analyzer (DNA). In *Politiknetzwerke. Modelle, Anwendungen und Visualisierungen*, pages 391–404. VS Verlag für Sozialwissenschaften, Opladen.

Philip Leifeld. 2016. Discourse Network Analysis: Policy Debates as Dynamic Networks. In *The Oxford Handbook of Political Networks*. Oxford University Press.

Sebastian Padó, André Blessing, Nico Blokker, Erenay Dayanik, Sebastian Haunss, and Jonas Kuhn. 2019. Who sides with whom? towards computational construction of discourse networks for political debates. In *Proceedings of ACL*, Florence, Italy.

Stefan Rädiker and Udo Kuckartz. 2019. *Analyse qualitativer Daten mit MAXQDA: Text, Audio und Video*. VS Verlag.

Denny Vrandečić and Markus Krötzsch. 2014. Wikidata: A free collaborative knowledgebase. *Commun. ACM*, 57(10):78–85.

GLTR: Statistical Detection and Visualization of Generated Text

Sebastian Gehrmann
Harvard SEAS
gehrmann@seas.harvard.edu

Hendrik Strobelt
IBM Research
MIT-IBM Watson AI lab
hendrik.strobelt@ibm.com

Alexander M. Rush
Harvard SEAS
srush@seas.harvard.edu

Abstract

The rapid improvement of language models has raised the specter of abuse of text generation systems. This progress motivates the development of simple methods for detecting generated text that can be used by and explained to non-experts. We develop GLTR, a tool to support humans in detecting whether a text was generated by a model. GLTR applies a suite of baseline statistical methods that can detect generation artifacts across common sampling schemes. In a human-subjects study, we show that the annotation scheme provided by GLTR improves the human detection-rate of fake text from 54% to 72% without any prior training. GLTR is open-source and publicly deployed, and has already been widely used to detect generated outputs.

1 Introduction

The success of pretrained language models for natural language understanding (McCann et al., 2017; Devlin et al., 2018; Peters et al., 2018) has led to a race to train unprecedentedly large language models (Radford et al., 2019). These large language models have the potential to generate textual output that is indistinguishable from human-written text to a non-expert reader. That means that the advances in the development of large language models also lower the barrier for abuse.

Instances of malicious autonomously generated text at scale are rare but often high-profile, for instance when a simple generation system was used to create fake comments in opposition to net neutrality (Grimaldi, 2018). Other scenarios include the possibility of generating false articles (Wang, 2017) or misleading reviews (Fornaciari and Poesio, 2014). Forensic techniques will be necessary to detect this automatically generated text. These techniques should be accurate, but also easy to convey to non-experts and require little setup cost.

Human-Written

The programme operates on a weekly elimination process to find the best all-around baker from the contestants, who are all amateurs.

Generated

The first book I went through was The Cook's Book of New York City by Ed Mirvish. I've always loved Ed Mirvish's recipes and he's one of my favorite chefs.

Figure 1: The top-k overlay within GLTR. It is easy to distinguish sampled from written text. The real text is from the Wikipedia page of The Great British Bake Off, the fake from GPT-2 large with temperature 0.7.

In this work, we argue that simple statistical detection methods for generated/fake text can be applied within a visual tool to assist in detection. The underlying assumption is that systems over generate from a limited subset of the true distribution of natural language, for which they have high confidence. In a white-box setting where we have access to the system distribution, this property can be detected by computing the model density of generated output and comparing it to human-generated text. We further hypothesize that these methods generalize to black-box scenarios, as long as the fake text follows a similar sampling assumption and is generated by a large language model.

We develop a visual tool, GLTR, that highlights text passages based on these metrics, as shown in Figure 1[1]. We conduct experiments to empirically test these metrics on a set of widely-used language models and show that real text uses a wider subset of the distribution under a model. This is noticeable especially when the model distribution is low-entropy and concentrates most

---

[1]Our tool is available at http://gltr.io.
The code is provided at https://github.com/HendrikStrobelt/detecting-fake-text

111

Proceedings of the 57th Annual Meeting of the Association for Computational Linguistics-System Demonstrations, pages 111–116
Florence, Italy, July 28 - August 2, 2019. ©2019 Association for Computational Linguistics

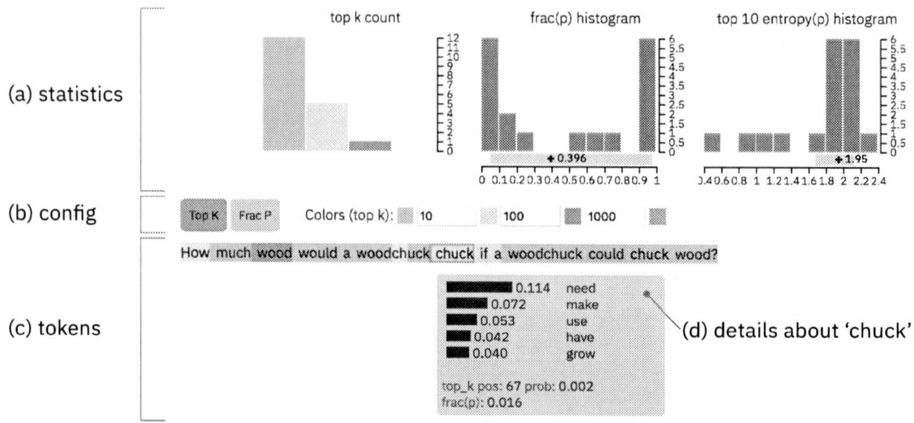

Figure 2: User interface for GLTR. On the top, we show three graphs with global information (a). Below the graphs, users can switch between two different annotations and customize the top-k thresholds (b). On the bottom, each token is shown with the associated annotation as heatmap (c). The tooltip (d) highlights information about the current prediction when hovering over the word "chuck".

probability in a few words. We demonstrate in a human-subjects study that without the tool, subjects can differentiate between human- and model-generated text only 54% of the time. With our tool, subjects were able to detect fake text with an accuracy of over 72% without any prior training. By presenting this information visually, we also hope the tool teaches users to notice the artefacts of text generation systems.

2   Method

Consider the generation detection task as deciding whether a sequence of words $\hat{X}_{1:N}$ have been written by a human or generated from a model. We do not have supervision for this task, and instead, want to use distributional properties of the underlying language. In the white-box case, we are also given full access to the language model distribution, $p(X_i \mid X_{1:i-1})$, that was used in generation. In the general case, we assume access to a different learned model of the same form. This approach can be contextualized in the evaluation framework proposed by Hashimoto et al. (2019) who find that human-written and generated text can be discriminated based on the model likelihood if the human acceptability is high.

The underlying assumption of our methods is that to generate natural looking text, most systems sample from the head of the distribution, e.g., through max sampling (Gu et al., 2017), k-max sampling (Fan et al., 2018), beam search (Chorowski and Jaitly, 2016; Shao et al.,

2017), temperature-modulated sampling (Dagan and Engelson, 1995), or even implicitly with rule-based templated approaches. These techniques are biased, but seem to be necessary for fluent output and are widely used. We therefore propose three simple tests, using a detection model, to assess whether text is generated in this way: (**Test 1**) the probability of the word, e.g. $p_{\text{det}}(X_i = \hat{X}_i|X_{1:i-1})$, (**Test 2**) the absolute rank of a word, e.g. rank in $p_{\text{det}}(X_i|X_{1:i-1})$, and (**Test 3**) the entropy of the predicted distribution, e.g. $-\sum_w p_{\text{det}}(X_i = w|X_{1:i-1})\log p_{\text{det}}(X_i = w|X_{1:i-1})$. The first two test whether a generated word is sampled from the top of the distribution and the last tests whether the previously generated context is well-known to the detection system such that it is (overly) sure of its next prediction.

3   GLTR: Visualizing Outliers

We apply these tests within our tool GLTR (pronounced Glitter) – a **G**iant **L**anguage model **T**est **R**oom. GLTR aims to both teach users what to be aware of when assessing whether a text is real, and to assist them in performing forensic analyses. It works on a per-instance basis for *any* textual input.

The backend supports multiple detection models. Our publicly deployed version uses both BERT (Devlin et al., 2018) and GPT-2 117M (Radford et al., 2019). Since GPT-2 117M is a standard left-to-right language model, we compute $p_{\text{det}}(X_i \mid X_{1...i-1})$ at each position i in a text X. BERT is trained to predict a masked

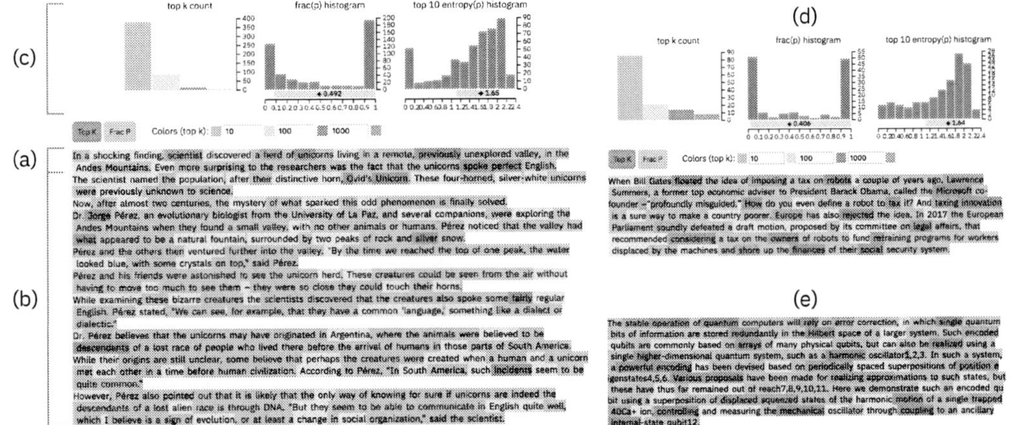

Figure 3: On the left, we analyze a generated sample (a-c) with GLTR that is generated from a non-public GPT-2 model. The first sentence (a) is the prompt given to the model. We can observe that the generated text (b) is mostly highlighted in green and yellow, which strongly hints at a generated text. The histograms (c) show additional hints at the automatic generation. On the right, we show samples from a real NYT article (d) and a scientific abstract (e). Compared to the "unicorn" example, the fraction of red and purple words is much higher.

token, given a bidirectional context. Thus, we iteratively mask out each correct token $\hat{X}_i$ and use a context of 30 words to each side as input to estimate $p_{\text{det}}(X_i|X_{i-30...i-1}, X_{i+1...X_i+30})^2$.

The central feature of the tool is the overlay function, shown in Figure 2c, which can render arbitrarily chosen top-k buckets (Test-2) as an annotation over the text. By default, a word that ranks within the top 10 is highlighted in green, top 100 in yellow, top 1,000 in red, and the rest in purple. GLTR also supports an overlay for Test-1 that highlights the probability of the chosen word in relation to the one that was assigned the highest probability. Since the two overlays provide evidence from two separate sources, their combination helps to form an informed assessment.

The top of the interface (Figure 2a), shows one graph for each of the three tests. The first one shows the distribution over the top-k buckets, the second the distribution over the values from the second overlay, and the third the distribution over the entropy values. For a more detailed analysis, hovering over a word (Figure 2d) shows a tooltip with the top 5 predictions, their probabilities, and the rank and probability of the following word.

The backend of GLTR is implemented in PyTorch and is designed to ensure extensibility. New detection models can be added by registering

themselves with the API and providing a model and a tokenizer. This setup will allow the front-end of the tool to continue to be used as improved language models are released.

Case Study We demonstrate the functionality of GLTR by analyzing three samples from different sources, shown in Figure 3. The interface shows the results of detection analysis with GPT-2 117M. The first example is generated from GPT-2 1.5B. Here the example is conditioned on a seed text.[3] The analysis shows that not a single token in the generated text is highlighted in purple and very few in red. Most words are green or yellow, indicating high rank. Additionally, the second histogram shows a high fraction of high-probability choices. A final indicator is the regularity in the third histogram with a high fraction of low-entropy predictions and an almost linear increase in the frequency of high-entropy words.

In contrast, we show two human written samples; one from a New York Times article and a scientific abstract (Figure 3d+e). There is a significantly higher fraction of red and purple (e.g. non-obvious) predictions compared to the generated example. The difference is also observable in the histograms where the fraction of low-probability words is higher and low-entropy contexts smaller.

---

[2]While BERT can handle inputs of length 512, we observed only minor differences between using the full and shortened contexts.

[3]*In a shocking finding, scientist discovered a herd of unicorns living in a remote, previously unexplored valley, in the Andes Mountains. Even more surprising to the researchers was the fact that the unicorns spoke perfect English*

Feature	AUC
Bag of Words	0.63 ±0.11
(Test 1 - GPT-2) Average Probability	0.71 ±0.25
(Test 2 - GPT-2) Top-K Buckets	0.87 ±0.07
(Test 1 - BERT) Average Probability	0.70 ±0.27
(Test 2 - BERT) Top-K Buckets	0.85 ±0.09

Table 1: Cross-validated results of fake-text discriminators. Distributional information yield a higher informativeness than word-features in a logistic regression.

4 Empirical Validation

We validate the detection features by comparing 50 articles for each of 3 generated and 3 human data sources. The first two sources are documents sampled from *GPT-2 1.5B* (Radford et al., 2019). We use a random subset of their released examples that were generated (1) with a temperature of 0.7 and (2) truncated to the top 40 predictions. As alternative source of generated text, we take articles that were generated by the autonomous Washington Post *Heliograf* system, which covers local sports results and gubernatorial races. As human-written sources, we choose random paragraphs from the bAbI task children book corpus (CBT) (Hill et al., 2015), New York Times articles (NYT), and scientific abstracts from the journals nature and science (SA). To minimize overlap with the training set, we constrained the samples to publication dates past or close to the release of the GPT-2 models.

Our first model uses the average probability of each word in a document as single feature (Test 1) and the second one the distribution over four buckets (highlight colors in GLTR) of absolute ranks of predictions (Test 2). As a baseline we consider a logistic regression over a bag-of-words representation of each document. We cross-validate the results by training on each combination of four of the sources (two real/fake) and testing on the remaining two.

Results As Table 1 illustrates, the GLTR features lead to better separation than word-features, both with and without access to the true generating model. The classifier that uses ranking information learns that real text samples from the tail of the distribution more frequently. The odds ratio for a word outside the top 100 predictions is

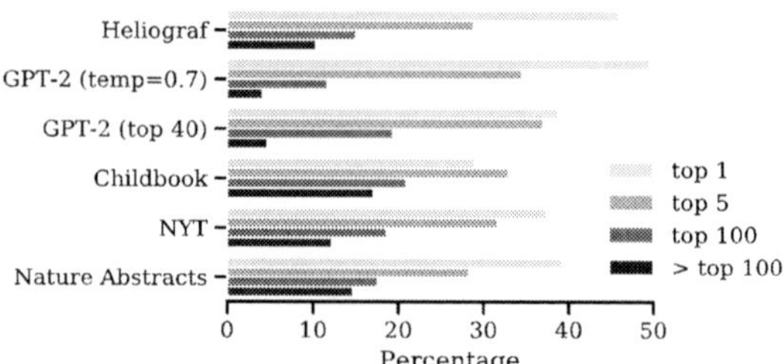

Figure 4: Distribution over the rankings of words in the predicted distributions from GPT-2. The real text in the bottom three examples has a consistently higher fraction of words from the tail of the distribution.

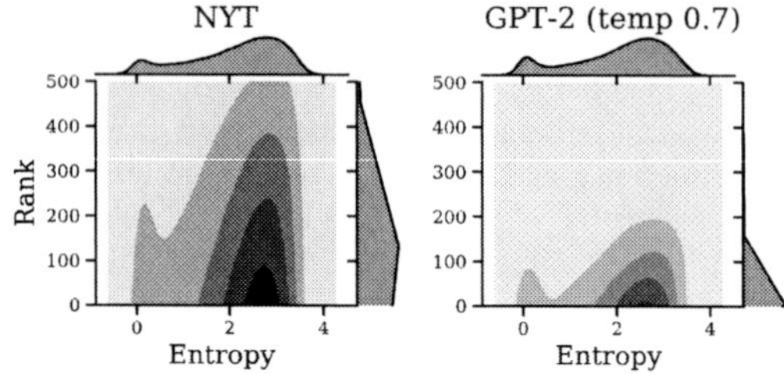

Figure 5: A kernel density estimate of the contextual entropy (Test 3) versus the next-word rank (Test 2) for NYT and GPT-2. Human-written text (NYT) is more likely to have high-rank words, even in low-entropy contexts.

5.32, while the odds ratio for being the top 1 prediction is 0.09. Figure 4 presents the distribution of rankings under GPT-2 and further corroborates this finding. Real texts use words outside of the top 100 predictions 2.41 times as frequently under GPT-2 (1.67 for BERT) as generated text, even compared to sampling with a lower temperature.

To get a better sense of how low-rank words enter into natural text, we look at the probability of each word compared to its relative rank. We hypothesize that human authors use low-rank words, even when the entropy is low, a property that sampling methods for generated text avoid. We compare the relationship of the entropy and rank of the next word by computing a Gaussian Kernel-density estimate over their distributions. As shown in Figure 5, human text uses high-rank words more frequently, regardless of the estimated entropy.

5 Human-Subjects Study

To evaluate the efficacy of the GLTR tool, we conducted a human-subjects study on 35 volunteer students in a college-level NLP class. Our goal was to both have students be able to tell generated text from real, but also to see which parts raised the suspicion of the students. In two rounds, students were first shown five texts without overlay and then five texts with overlay and were asked to assess which texts were real within 90 seconds. In between the rounds, we presented a brief tutorial on the overlay and showed the example in Figure 1 but did not disclose any information about the study. For each participant and round, we presented two texts generated from GPT-2 with 0.7 temperature, one from Heliograf, and two from NYT.[4] We alleviated bias from the text selection by randomly assigning texts to either of the two rounds between students.

Results The results demonstrate the ease of use of the overlay. Without the interface, the participants achieved an accuracy of 54.2%, barely above random chance. While only 40% of texts were real, they trusted 56.0% of texts, Heliograf at a higher rate than GPT-2 (68.6% vs. 51.4%, $p < 0.01$). The difficulty of the task without overlay was rated at 3.89 on a 5-point Likert scale, further supporting the need for assistive systems. With the interface, the performance improved to 72.3%. The average treatment effect shows an improvement of 18.1% with $p < 0.001$, even after controlling for whether a participant is a native speaker and how difficult they rated the task. 42.1% of the participants stated that the interface helped them be more accurate, and 37.1% found that it helped them to identify fakes faster.

Qualitative Findings The tool caused students to think about the properties of the fake text. While humans would vary expressions in real texts, models rarely generate synonyms or referring expressions for entities, which does not follow the theory of centering in discourse analysis (Grosz et al., 1995). An example of this is shown in the text in Figure 3b in which the model keeps generating the name Pérez and never refers to him as he. Another observation was that samples from Heliograf exhibit high parallelism in sentence structure. Since previous work has found that neural language models learn long linguistic structures as well, we imagine that sentence structure analysis can further be used for forensic analysis. We hope that automatic analysis and visualization like GLTR will help students better under-

---

[4]We randomly sampled one paragraph of text and resampled NYT if it was covering recent, well-known events.

stand the generation artifacts in current systems.

6 Related Work

While statistical detection methods have been applied in the past, the increase in language model power upends past assumptions in this area. Lavergne et al. (2008) introduce prediction entropy as an indicator of fake text. However, their findings are the opposite of ours (low entropy for generated text), a change which is indicative of language model improvements. Similar work finds that texts differ in perplexity under a language model (Beresneva, 2016), frequency of rare bigrams (Grechnikov et al., 2009), and n-gram frequencies (Badaskar et al., 2008). Similar methods that detect machine translation (Arase and Zhou, 2013). Hovy (2016) finds that a logistic regression model can detect generated product reviews at a higher rate than human judges, indicating that humans struggle with this task. Finally, we distinguish this task from detecting misinformation in text (e.g. Shu et al., 2017). We aim to understand the statistical signature and not the content of text.

7 Discussion and Conclusion

We show how detection models can be applied to analyze whether a text is automatically generated using only simple statistical properties. We apply the insights from the analysis to build GLTR, a tool that assists human readers and improves their ability to detect fake texts.

Impact GLTR aims to educate and raise awareness about generated text. To explain GLTR to non-NLP experts, we included a blog post on the web page with examples and an explanation of GLTR. Within the first month, GLTR had 30,000 page views for the demo and 21,000 for the blog. Numerous news websites and policy researchers reached out to discuss the ethical implications of language generation. The feedback from these discussions and in-person presentations helped us to refine our publicly released examples and explore the limits of our detection methods.

Future Work A core assumption of GLTR is that systems use biased sampling for generating text. One can imagine adversarial schemes that aim to fool our overlay; however, forcibly sampling from the tail decreases the coherence of a text which may make it harder to fool human readers. Another potential limitation are samples conditioned on a hidden seed text. A conditional distribution will look different, even if we have access to the model. Our preliminary qualitative investigations with GLTR show a relatively short-range memory on this seed, but it is crucial to conduct more in-depth evaluations on the influence of conditions in future work. The findings further motivate future work on how to use our methods as part of autonomous classifiers to assist moderators on social media or review platforms.

Acknowledgments

AMR gratefully acknowledges the support of NSF 1845664 and a Google research award.

References

Yuki Arase and Ming Zhou. 2013. Machine translation detection from monolingual web-text. In *Proceedings of the 51st Annual Meeting of the Association for Computational Linguistics (Volume 1: Long Papers)*, volume 1, pages 1597–1607.

Sameer Badaskar, Sachin Agarwal, and Shilpa Arora. 2008. Identifying real or fake articles: Towards better language modeling. In *Proceedings of the Third International Joint Conference on Natural Language Processing: Volume-II*.

Daria Beresneva. 2016. Computer-generated text detection using machine learning: A systematic review. In *International Conference on Applications of Natural Language to Information Systems*, pages 421–426. Springer.

Jan Chorowski and Navdeep Jaitly. 2016. Towards better decoding and language model integration in sequence to sequence models. *arXiv preprint arXiv:1612.02695*.

Ido Dagan and Sean P Engelson. 1995. Selective sampling in natural language learning. In *Proceedings of the IJCAI Workshop on New Approaches to Learning for Natural Language Processing*, pages 41–48.

Jacob Devlin, Ming-Wei Chang, Kenton Lee, and Kristina Toutanova. 2018. Bert: Pre-training of deep bidirectional transformers for language understanding. *arXiv preprint arXiv:1810.04805*.

Angela Fan, Mike Lewis, and Yann Dauphin. 2018. Hierarchical neural story generation. In *Proceedings of the 56th Annual Meeting of the Association for Computational Linguistics (Volume 1: Long Papers)*, volume 1, pages 889–898.

Tommaso Fornaciari and Massimo Poesio. 2014. Identifying fake amazon reviews as learning from crowds. In *Proceedings of the 14th Conference of the European Chapter of the Association for Computational Linguistics*, pages 279–287.

EA Grechnikov, GG Gusev, AA Kustarev, and A Raigorodsky. 2009. Detection of artificial texts. *RCDL2009 Proceedings. Petrozavodsk*, pages 306–308.

James V. Grimaldi. 2018. U.s. investigating fake comments on net neutrality. *The Wall Street Journal*.

Barbara J Grosz, Scott Weinstein, and Aravind K Joshi. 1995. Centering: A framework for modeling the local coherence of discourse. *Computational linguistics*, 21(2):203–225.

Jiatao Gu, Kyunghyun Cho, and Victor OK Li. 2017. Trainable greedy decoding for neural machine translation. *arXiv preprint arXiv:1702.02429*.

Tatsunori B Hashimoto, Hugh Zhang, and Percy Liang. 2019. Unifying human and statistical evaluation for natural language generation. *arXiv preprint arXiv:1904.02792*.

Felix Hill, Antoine Bordes, Sumit Chopra, and Jason Weston. 2015. The goldilocks principle: Reading children's books with explicit memory representations. *arXiv preprint arXiv:1511.02301*.

Dirk Hovy. 2016. The enemy in your own camp: How well can we detect statistically-generated fake reviews–an adversarial study. In *Proceedings of the 54th Annual Meeting of the Association for Computational Linguistics (Volume 2: Short Papers)*, volume 2, pages 351–356.

Thomas Lavergne, Tanguy Urvoy, and François Yvon. 2008. Detecting fake content with relative entropy scoring. *PAN*, 8:27–31.

Bryan McCann, James Bradbury, Caiming Xiong, and Richard Socher. 2017. Learned in translation: Contextualized word vectors. In *Advances in Neural Information Processing Systems*, pages 6294–6305.

Matthew E Peters, Mark Neumann, Mohit Iyyer, Matt Gardner, Christopher Clark, Kenton Lee, and Luke Zettlemoyer. 2018. Deep contextualized word representations. *arXiv preprint arXiv:1802.05365*.

Alec Radford, Jeff Wu, Rewon Child, David Luan, Dario Amodei, and Ilya Sutskever. 2019. Language models are unsupervised multitask learners.

Louis Shao, Stephan Gouws, Denny Britz, Anna Goldie, Brian Strope, and Ray Kurzweil. 2017. Generating high-quality and informative conversation responses with sequence-to-sequence models. *arXiv preprint arXiv:1701.03185*.

Kai Shu, Amy Sliva, Suhang Wang, Jiliang Tang, and Huan Liu. 2017. Fake news detection on social media: A data mining perspective. *ACM SIGKDD Explorations Newsletter*, 19(1):22–36.

William Yang Wang. 2017. " liar, liar pants on fire": A new benchmark dataset for fake news detection. *arXiv preprint arXiv:1705.00648*.

OpenKiwi: An Open Source Framework for Quality Estimation

Fábio Kepler
Unbabel

Jonay Trénous
Unbabel

Marcos Treviso[*]
Instituto de Telecomunicações

Miguel Vera
Unbabel

André F. T. Martins
Unbabel

`{kepler, sony, miguel.vera, andre.martins}@unbabel.com`
`marcosvtreviso@gmail.com`

Abstract

We introduce OpenKiwi, a PyTorch-based open source framework for translation quality estimation. OpenKiwi supports training and testing of word-level and sentence-level quality estimation systems, implementing the winning systems of the WMT 2015–18 quality estimation campaigns. We benchmark OpenKiwi on two datasets from WMT 2018 (English-German SMT and NMT), yielding state-of-the-art performance on the word-level tasks and near state-of-the-art in the sentence-level tasks.

1 Introduction

Quality estimation (QE) provides the missing link between machine and human translation: its goal is to evaluate a translation system's quality without access to reference translations (Specia et al., 2018b). Among its potential usages are: informing an end user about the reliability of automatically translated content; deciding if a translation is ready for publishing or if it requires human post-editing; and highlighting the words that need to be post-edited.

While there has been tremendous progress in QE in the last years (Martins et al., 2016, 2017; Kim et al., 2017; Wang et al., 2018), the ability of researchers to reproduce state-of-the-art systems has been hampered by the fact that these are either based on complex ensemble systems, complicated architectures, or require not well-documented pre-training and fine-tuning of some components. Existing open-source frameworks such as WCE-LIG (Servan et al., 2015), QuEST++ (Specia et al., 2015), Marmot (Logacheva et al., 2016), or DeepQuest (Ive et al., 2018), while helpful, are currently behind the recent best systems in WMT QE shared tasks. To address the shortcoming

above, this paper presents **OpenKiwi**,[1] a new open source framework for QE that implements the best QE systems from WMT 2015–18 shared tasks, making it easy to combine and modify their key components, while experimenting under the same framework.

The main features of OpenKiwi are:

- Implementation of four QE systems: QUETCH (Kreutzer et al., 2015), NuQE (Martins et al., 2016, 2017), Predictor-Estimator (Kim et al., 2017; Wang et al., 2018), and a stacked ensemble with a linear system (Martins et al., 2016, 2017);

- Easy to use API: can be imported as a package in other projects or run from the command line;

- Implementation in Python using PyTorch as the deep learning framework;

- Ability to train new QE models on new data;

- Ability to run pre-trained QE models on data from the WMT 2018 campaign;

- Easy to track and reproduce experiments via `YAML` configuration files and (optionally) MLflow;

- Open-source license (Affero GPL).

This project is hosted at `https://github.com/Unbabel/OpenKiwi`. We welcome and encourage contributions from the research community.[2]

2 Quality Estimation

The goal of **word-level QE** (Figure 1) is to assign quality labels (OK or BAD) to each *machine-translated word*, as well as to *gaps* between words

---

[1] `https://unbabel.github.io/OpenKiwi`.
[2] See `https://unbabel.github.io/OpenKiwi/contributing.html` for instructions for contributors.

---

* Work done during an internship at Unbabel in 2018.

117

Proceedings of the 57th Annual Meeting of the Association for Computational Linguistics-System Demonstrations, pages 117–122
Florence, Italy, July 28 - August 2, 2019. ©2019 Association for Computational Linguistics

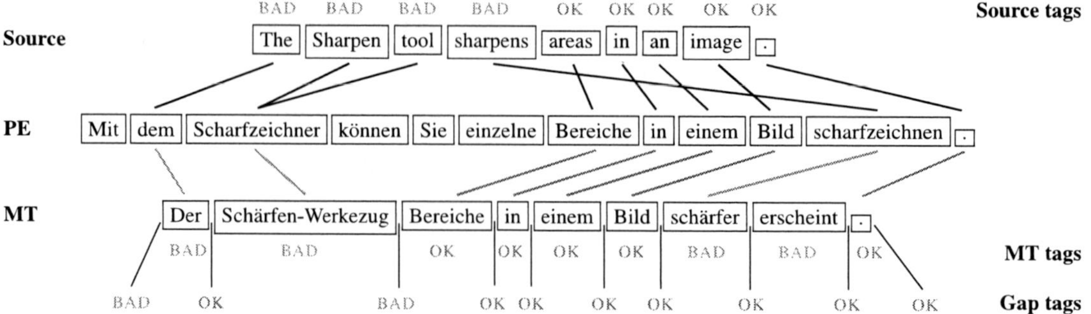

Figure 1: Example from the WMT 2018 word-level QE training set. Shown are the English source sentence (top), the German machine translated text (bottom), and its manual post-edition (middle). We show also the three types of word-level quality tags: MT (or target) tags account for words that are replaced or deleted, gap tags account for words that need to be inserted, and source tags indicate what are the source words that were omitted or mistranslated. For this example, the HTER sentence-level score (number of edit operations to produce PE from MT normalized by the length of PE) is $8/12 = 66.7\%$, corresponding to 4 insertions, 1 deletion, and 3 replacements out of 12 reference words.

(to account for context that needs to be inserted), and *source words* (to denote words in the original sentence that have been mistranslated or omitted in the target). In the last years, the most accurate systems that have been developed for this task combine linear and neural models (Kreutzer et al., 2015; Martins et al., 2016), use automatic post-editing as an intermediate step (Martins et al., 2017), or develop specialized neural architectures (Kim et al., 2017; Wang et al., 2018).

Sentence-level QE, on the other hand, aims to predict the quality of the whole translated sentence, for example based on the time it takes for a human to post-edit it, or on how many edit operations are required to fix it, in terms of HTER (Human Translation Error Rate) (Specia et al., 2018b). The most successful approaches to sentence-level QE to date are based on conversions from word-level predictions (Martins et al., 2017) or joint training with multi-task learning (Kim et al., 2017; Wang et al., 2018).

3 Implemented Systems

OpenKiwi implements four popular systems that have been proposed in the last years, which we now describe briefly.

QUETCH. The "QUality Estimation from scraTCH" system (Kreutzer et al., 2015) is designed as a multilayer perceptron with one hidden layer, non-linear *tanh* activation functions and a lookup-table layer mapping words to continuous dense vectors. For each position in the MT, a window of fixed size surrounding that position,

as well as a windowed representation of aligned words from the source text, are concatenated as model input.[3] The output layer scores OK/BAD probabilities for each word with a softmax activation. The model is trained independently to predict source tags, gap tags, and target tags. QUETCH is a very simple model and does not rely on any kind of external auxiliary data for training, only the shared task datasets.

NuQE. OpenKiwi also implements the NeUral Quality Estimation system proposed by Martins et al. (2016). Its architecture consists of a lookup layer containing embeddings for target words and their source-aligned words, in the same fashion as QUETCH. These embeddings are concatenated and fed into two consecutive sets of two feed-forward layers and a bi-directional GRU layer. The output contains a softmax layer that produces the final OK/BAD decisions. Like QUETCH, training is also carried independently for source tags, gap tags, and target tags. NuQE is also a blackbox system, meaning it is trained with the shared task data only (i.e., no auxiliary parallel or roundtrip data).

Predictor-Estimator. Our implementation follows closely the architecture proposed by Kim et al. (2017), which consists of two modules:

- a *predictor*, which is trained to predict each token of the target sentence given the source and

---

[3]The alignments are provided by the shared task organizers, which are computed with `fast_align` (Dyer et al., 2013).

the left and right context of the target sentence;

- an *estimator*, which takes features produced by the *predictor* and uses them to classify each word as OK or BAD.

Our predictor uses a bidirectional LSTM to encode the source, and two unidirectional LSTMs processing the target in left-to-right (LSTM-L2R) and right-to-left (LSTM-R2L) order. For each target token t_i, the representations of its left and right context are concatenated and used as query to an attention module before a final softmax layer. It is trained on the large parallel corpora provided as additional data by the WMT shared task organizers. The estimator takes as input a sequence of features: for each target token t_i, the final layer before the softmax (before processing t_i), and the concatenation of the i-th hidden state of LSTM-L2R and LSTM-R2L (after processing t_i). In addition, we train this system with a multi-task architecture that allows us to predict sentence-level HTER scores. Overall, this system is capable to predict sentence-level scores and all word-level labels (for MT words, gaps, and source words)—the source word labels are produced by training a predictor in the reverse direction.

Stacked Ensemble. The systems above can be ensembled by using a stacked architecture with a feature-based linear system, as described by Martins et al. (2017). The features are the ones described there, including lexical and part-of-speech tags from words, their contexts, and their aligned words and contexts, as well as syntactic features and features provided by a language model (as provided by the shared task organizers). This system is only used to produce word-level labels for MT words.

4   Design, Implementation and Usage

OpenKiwi is designed and implemented in a way that allows new models to be easily added and run, without requiring much concern about input data processing and output generation and evaluation. That means the focus can be almost exclusively put in adding or changing a `torch.nn.Module` based class. If new flags or options are required, all that is needed is to add them to the CLI parsing module.

Design. As a general architecture example, the training pipeline follows these steps:

- Each input data, like source text and MT text, is defined as a `Field`, which holds information about how data should be tokenized, how the inner vocabulary is built, how the mapping to IDs is done, and how a list of samples is padded into a tensor;

- A `Dataset` holds a set of input and output fields, and builds minibatches of samples, each containing their respective input and output data;

- A training loop iterates over epochs and steps, calling the model with each minibatch, computing the loss, backpropagating, evaluating on the validation set, and saving snapshots as requested;

- By default, the best model is kept and predictions on the validation set are saved as probabilities.

The flow rarely needs to be changed for the QE task, so all that is needed for quick experimentation is changing configuration parameters (check the **Usage** part below) or the model class.

Implementation. OpenKiwi supports Python 3.5 and later. Since reproducibility is important, it uses Poetry[4] for deterministic dependency management. To decrease the risk of introducing breaking changes with new code, a set of tests are also implemented and currently provide a code coverage close to 80%.

OpenKiwi offers support for tracking experiments with MLflow,[5] which allows comparing different runs and searching for specific metrics and parameters.

Usage. Training an OpenKiwi model is as simple as running the following command:

```
$ python kiwi train --config
      config.yml
```

where `config.yml` is a configuration file with training and model options.

OpenKiwi can also be installed as a Python package by running `pip install openkiwi`. In this case, the above command can be switched by

```
$ kiwi train --config config.yml
```

---

[4]https://poetry.eustace.io/
[5]https://mlflow.org/

source	the Sharpen tool sharpens areas in an image.
mt	der Schärfen-Werkezug Bereiche in einem Bild schärfer erscheint.

```
HTER: 0.5848351716995239
```


Figure 2: Interactive visualization of the system output. Words tagged as BAD as shown in *red*, and BAD gaps are denoted as red underscores ("_"). The Jupyter Notebook producing this output is available at `https://github.com/Unbabel/OpenKiwi/blob/master/demo/KiwiViz.ipynb`.

If used inside another Python project, OpenKiwi can be easily used like the following:

```python
import kiwi

config = 'config.yml'
run_info = kiwi.train(config)
```

After training, predicting on new data can be performed by simply calling

```python
model = kiwi.load_model(
    run_info.model_path
)
source = [
    'the Sharpen tool sharpens '
    'areas in an image .'
]
target = [
    'der Schärfen-Werkezug '
    'Bereiche in einem Bild '
    'schärfer erscheint .'
]
examples = [{
    'source': source,
    'target': target
}]
out = model.predict(examples)
```

Figure 2 shows an example of QE predictions using the framework.

5 Benchmark Experiments

Datasets. To benchmark OpenKiwi, we use the following datasets from the WMT 2018 quality estimation shared task, all English-German (En-De):

- Two quality estimation datasets of sentence triplets, each consisting of a source sentence (SRC), its machine translation (MT) and a human post-edition (PE) of the machine translation: a larger dataset of 26,273 training and 1,000 development triplets, where the MT is generated by a phrase-based statistical machine translation (SMT); and a smaller dataset of 13,442 training and 1,000 development triplets, where the MT is generated by a neural machine translation system (NMT). The data also contains word-level quality labels and sentence-level scores that are obtained from the post-editions using TERCOM (Snover et al., 2006).

- A corpus of 526,368 artificially generated sentence triplets, obtained by first cross-entropy filtering a much larger monolingual corpus for in-domain sentences, then using round-trip translation and a final stratified sampling step.

- A parallel dataset of 3,396,364 in-domain sentences used for pre-training of the predictor-estimator model.

Systems. In addition to the models that are part of OpenKiwi, in the experiments below, we also use Automatic Post-Editing (APE) adapted for QE (APE-QE). APE-QE has been used by Martins et al. (2017) as an intermediate step for quality estimation, where an APE system is trained on the human post-edits and its outputs are used as pseudo-post-editions to generate word-level quality labels and sentence-level scores in the same way that the original labels were created. Since OpenKiwi's focus is not on implementing a sequence-to-sequence model, we used an external software, OpenNMT-py (Klein et al., 2017), to train two separate translation models:

- SRC → PE: trained first on the in-domain corpus provided, then fine-tuned on the shared task data.

Model	En-De SMT					En-De NMT				
	MT	gaps	source	r	ρ	MT	gaps	source	r	ρ
QUETCH	39.90	17.10	36.10	48.32	51.31	29.18	13.26	28.91	42.84	49.59
NuQE	50.04	35.53	42.08	59.62	60.89	32.49	15.01	30.19	43.41	50.87
PRED-EST	57.29	43.68	33.02	70.95	74.49	39.25	21.54	29.52	50.18	55.66
APE-QE	55.12	47.04	51.11	58.01	60.58	37.60	21.78	**34.46**	35.23	38.88
ENSEMBLED	61.33	**53.05**	**51.11**	**72.89**	**76.37**	43.04	**24.74**	**34.46**	**52.34**	**56.98**
STACKED	**62.40**	–	–	–	–	**43.88**	–	–	–	–

Table 1: Benchmarking of the different models implemented in OpenKiwi on the WMT 2018 development set, along with an ensembled system (ENSEMBLED) that averages the predictions of the NuQE, APE-QE, and PRED-EST systems, as well as a stacked architecture (STACKED) which stacks their predictions into a linear feature-based model, as described by Martins et al. (2017). For each system, we report the five official scores used in WMT 2018: word-level F_1^{mult} for MT, gaps, and source tokens, and sentence-level Pearson's r and Spearman's ρ rank correlations.

Model	En-De SMT					En-De NMT				
	MT	gaps	source	r	ρ	MT	gaps	source	r	ρ
deepQUEST	42.98	28.24	<u>33.97</u>	48.72	50.97	30.31	<u>11.93</u>	<u>28.59</u>	38.08	48.00
UNQE	–	–	–	70.00	72.44	–	–	–	**<u>51.29</u>**	**<u>60.52</u>**
QE Brain	<u>62.46</u>	<u>49.99</u>	–	**<u>73.97</u>**	**<u>75.43</u>**	<u>43.61</u>	–	–	50.12	60.49
OpenKiwi	**62.70**	**52.14**	**48.88**	71.08	72.70	**44.77**	**22.89**	**36.53**	46.72	58.51

Table 2: Final results on the WMT 2018 test set. The first three systems are the official WMT18-QE winners (underlined): deepQUEST is the open source system developed by Ive et al. (2018), UNQE is the unpublished system from Jiangxi Normal University, described by Specia et al. (2018a), and QE Brain is the system from Alibaba described by Wang et al. (2018). Reported numbers for the OpenKiwi system correspond to best models in the development set: the STACKED model for prediction of MT tags, and the ENSEMBLED model for the rest.

- MT → PE: trained on the concatenation of the corpus of artificially created sentence triplets and the shared task data oversampled by a factor of 20.

These predictions are then combined in the ensemble and stacked systems as explained below.

Experiments. We show benchmark numbers on the two English-German WMT 2018 datasets. In Table 1, we compare different configurations of OpenKiwi on the development datasets. For the single systems, we can see that the predictor-estimator has the best performance, except for predicting the source and the gap word-level tags, where APE-QE is superior. Overall, ensembled versions of these systems perform the best, with a stacked architecture being very effective for predicting word-level MT labels, confirming the findings of Martins et al. (2017).

Finally, in Table 2, we report numbers on the official test set. We compare OpenKiwi

against the best systems in WMT 2018 (Specia et al., 2018a) and another existing open-source tool, deepQuest (Ive et al., 2018). Overall, OpenKiwi outperforms deepQuest for all word-level and sentence-level tasks, and attains the best results for all the word-level tasks.

6 Conclusions

We presented OpenKiwi, a new open source framework for QE. OpenKiwi is implemented in PyTorch and supports training of word-level and sentence-level QE systems on new data. It outperforms other open source toolkits on both word-level and sentence-level, and yields new state-of-the-art word-level QE results.

Since its release, OpenKiwi was adopted as the baseline system for the WMT 2019 QE shared task[6], Moreover, all the winning systems of the word-, sentence- and document-level tasks of the

---

[6]More specifically, the NuQE model: http://www.statmt.org/wmt19/qe-task.html

WMT 2019 QE shared task[7] (Kepler et al., 2019) used OpenKiwi as their building foundation.

Acknowledgments

The authors would like to thank Eduardo Fierro, Thomas Reynaud, and the Unbabel AI and Engineering teams for their invaluable contributions to OpenKiwi.

They would also like to thank the support provided by the European Union in the context of the PT2020 projects 027767 and 038510.

References

Chris Dyer, Victor Chahuneau, and Noah A Smith. 2013. A simple, fast, and effective reparameterization of IBM model 2. In *Proceedings of the 2013 Conference of the North American Chapter of the Association for Computational Linguistics: Human Language Technologies*, pages 644–648.

Julia Ive, Frédéric Blain, and Lucia Specia. 2018. DeepQuest: a framework for neural-based Quality Estimation. In *International Conference on Computational Linguistics (COLING)*.

Fábio Kepler, Jonay Trénous, Marcos Treviso, Miguel Vera, António Góis, M. Amin Farajian, António V. Lopes, and André F. T. Martins. 2019. Unbabel's Participation in the WMT19 Translation Quality Estimation Shared Task. In *Conference on Machine Translation (WMT)*.

Hyun Kim, Jong-Hyeok Lee, and Seung-Hoon Na. 2017. Predictor-Estimator using Multilevel Task Learning with Stack Propagation for Neural Quality Estimation. In *Conference on Machine Translation (WMT)*.

Guillaume Klein, Yoon Kim, Yuntian Deng, Jean Senellart, and Alexander M Rush. 2017. Opennmt: Open-source toolkit for neural machine translation. *arXiv preprint arXiv:1701.02810*.

Julia Kreutzer, Shigehiko Schamoni, and Stefan Riezler. 2015. QUality Estimation from ScraTCH (QUETCH): Deep Learning for Word-level Translation Quality Estimation. In *Workshop on Machine Translation (WMT)*.

Varvara Logacheva, Chris Hokamp, and Lucia Specia. 2016. Marmot: A toolkit for translation quality estimation at the word level. In *LREC*.

André F. T. Martins, Ramon Astudillo, Chris Hokamp, and Fábio Kepler. 2016. Unbabel's Participation in the WMT16 Word-Level Translation Quality Estimation Shared Task. In *Conference on Machine Translation (WMT)*.

André F. T. Martins, Marcin Junczys-Dowmunt, Fabio Kepler, Ramon Astudillo, Chris Hokamp, and Roman Grundkiewicz. 2017. Pushing the limits of translation quality estimation. *Transactions of the Association for Computational Linguistics (to appear)*.

Christophe Servan, Ngoc-Tien Le, Ngoc Quang Luong, Benjamin Lecouteux, and Laurent Besacier. 2015. An Open Source Toolkit for Word-level Confidence Estimation in Machine Translation. In *The 12th International Workshop on Spoken Language Translation (IWSLT'15)*, Da Nang, Vietnam.

Matthew Snover, Bonnie Dorr, Richard Schwartz, Linnea Micciulla, and John Makhoul. 2006. A study of translation edit rate with targeted human annotation. In *Proceedings of association for machine translation in the Americas*, volume 200.

Lucia Specia, Frédéric Blain, Varvara Logacheva, Ramón Astudillo, and André F. T. Martins. 2018a. Findings of the wmt 2018 shared task on quality estimation. In *Proceedings of the Third Conference on Machine Translation, Volume 2: Shared Task Papers*, pages 702–722, Belgium, Brussels. Association for Computational Linguistics.

Lucia Specia, Gustavo Paetzold, and Carolina Scarton. 2015. Multi-level translation quality prediction with quest++. In *ACL-IJCNLP 2015 System Demonstrations*, pages 115–120, Beijing, China.

Lucia Specia, Carolina Scarton, and Gustavo Henrique Paetzold. 2018b. Quality estimation for machine translation. *Synthesis Lectures on Human Language Technologies*, 11(1):1–162.

Jiayi Wang, Kai Fan, Bo Li, Fengming Zhou, Boxing Chen, Yangbin Shi, and Luo Si. 2018. Alibaba Submission for WMT18 Quality Estimation Task. In *Conference on Machine Translation (WMT)*.

---

[7] http://www.statmt.org/wmt19/qe-results.html

Microsoft ICECAPS: An Open-Source Toolkit for Conversation Modeling

Vighnesh Leonardo Shiv, Chris Quirk, Anshuman Suri, Xiang Gao,
Khuram Shahid, Nithya Govindarajan, Yizhe Zhang, Jianfeng Gao,
Michel Galley, Chris Brockett, Tulasi Menon, Bill Dolan
Microsoft Corporation
```
{vishiv, chrisq, ansuri, xiag, khurams,
   nigovind, yizzhang, jfgao, mgalley,
chrisbkt, tulasim, billdol}@microsoft.com
```


Abstract

The Intelligent Conversation Engine: Code and Pre-trained Systems (Microsoft ICECAPS) is an upcoming open-source natural language processing repository. ICECAPS wraps Tensor-Flow functionality in a modular component-based architecture, presenting an intuitive and flexible paradigm for constructing sophisticated learning setups. Capabilities include multitask learning between models with shared parameters, upgraded language model decoding features, a range of built-in architectures, and a user-friendly data processing pipeline. The system is targeted toward conversational tasks, exploring diverse response generation, coherence, and knowledge grounding. ICECAPS also provides pretrained conversational models that can be either used directly or loaded for fine-tuning or bootstrapping other models; these models power an online demo of our framework.

1 Introduction

Neural conversational systems have seen great improvements over the past several years, with current models able to generate surprisingly coherent dialogs (Gao et al., 2019a). Business applications, games, and potentially other settings can benefit from intelligent conversational agents, inviting users to interact intuitively with complex systems.

Although a range of open-source tools is available to train neural network models for natural language processing (Vaswani et al., 2018; Gardner et al., 2018; Klein et al., 2017), only a few emphasize multi-turn conversational settings (Miller et al., 2017; Burtsev et al., 2018). Conversations present distinct challenges. They generally consist of many turns, and agents need to contextualize responses in these multi-turn contexts. Agents may also need to contextualize their responses in other cues, such as style, intent, and external knowledge, while retaining a conversational flow.

We present ICECAPS[1], a conversation modeling toolkit developed to bring together these desirable characteristics. ICECAPS is built on top of TensorFlow functionality wrapped in a user-friendly paradigm. Users can build agents with induced personalities, capable of generating diverse responses, grounding those responses in external knowledge, and avoiding particular phrases. Our toolkit's foundation is an extensible framework based on composable model structures, supporting complex configurations with component chaining and multi-task training schedules. We also provide large pre-trained conversational systems to support fast exploration.

2 Architecture

ICECAPS is designed for modularity, flexibility, and ease of use. Modules are built on top of Ten-sorFlow Estimators, making them easy for developers to use and extend flexibly. ICECAPS supports arbitrary architectures of modules chained together within versatile multi-task configurations.

2.1 Component chaining

Sequence-to-sequence models can be abstracted as chains of sequence encoders and sequence decoders. Our library implements various encoders and decoders, which can be chained together to form a single, end-to-end functional model. This chaining paradigm allows users to flexibly combine components and create topologies including multiple models with shared components. Chaining also allows users to bootstrap new models from components of previously trained models.

2.2 Multi-task learning

Multi-task learning is a powerful training paradigm that promotes robust feature represen-

---

[1] `https://github.com/microsoft/icecaps`

Proceedings of the 57th Annual Meeting of the Association for Computational Linguistics-System Demonstrations, pages 123–128
Florence, Italy, July 28 - August 2, 2019. ©2019 Association for Computational Linguistics

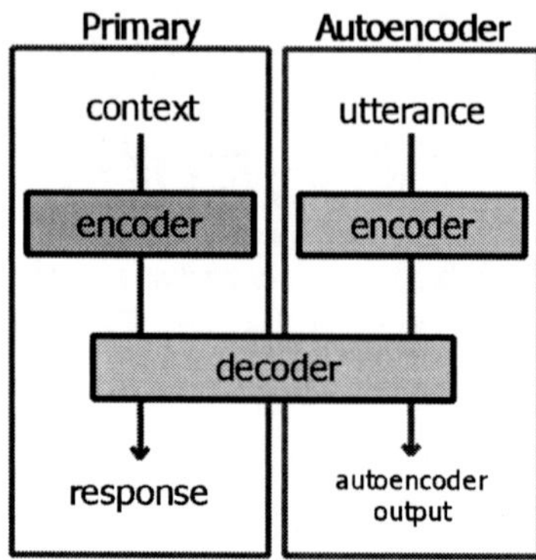

Figure 1: An example of a basic multi-task configuration. Two encoder-decoder chains share a common decoder, alternately trained on separate datasets.

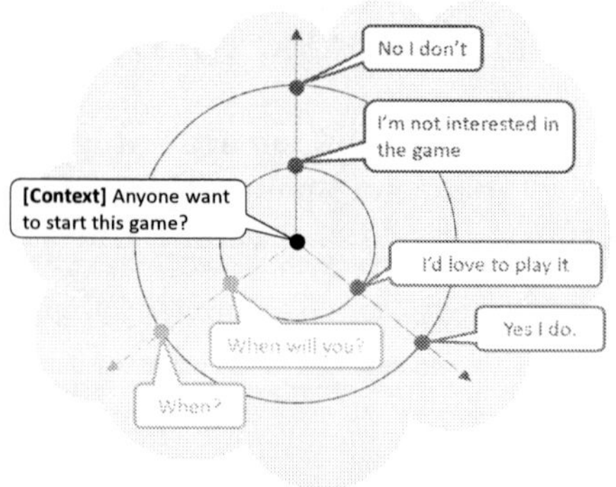

Figure 2: Illustration of latent space under SpaceFusion. The distance between predicted response vectors and contexts represents relevance; the angle between them represents intent. Figure from (Gao et al., 2019b).

tations (Gao et al., 2019b; Liu et al., 2019). By unifying a conversational sequence-to-sequence model and an autoencoder with a shared decoder, multi-task learning can personalize the conversational model (Luan et al., 2017). Multi-task learning has potentially many other powerful applications for inducing biases in conversational systems. ICECAPS allows users to build arrays of models with arbitrary sharing of components, and place them in a multi-task learning environment. Users can construct arbitrary multi-task training schedules, assigning different tasks or balances among tasks per training step.

3 Built-in modules and configurations

ICECAPS provides several built-in modules and configurations. Most standard NLP architectures are available, including transformers (Vaswani et al., 2017), LSTM-based seq2seq models (Sutskever et al., 2014) with attention (Bahdanau et al., 2015; Luong et al., 2015), n-gram convolutional language models, and deep convolutional networks for baseline image grounding. Where applicable, these are implemented as chains of simpler components as per our design philosophy. We also provide features that target conversational scenarios, from individual chainable components to custom multi-task learning presets.

3.1 Personality grounding

Inspired by recent work on modeling personality differences in conversational systems (Li et al., 2016b), ICECAPS provides implementations of personality-grounded seq2seq and transformer de-

coders. This architecture consists of additional personality embeddings, which are provided to the decoder alongside token embeddings at each time-step of decoding. Grounding generated responses helps condition outputs based on a given personality embedding: for the same query, the system learns to generate responses in different styles, all while preserving the underlying context.

3.2 SpaceFusion

SpaceFusion (Gao et al., 2019b) is a learning paradigm that aligns latent spaces learned by different models trained over different datasets. Of particular interest is its application to neural conversation modelling, where SpaceFusion can optimize the relevance and diversity of generated responses jointly. ICECAPS implements a SpaceFusion preset that extends its multi-task capabilities. SpaceFusion constructs a multi-task environment of two seq2seq models with a shared decoder, as in (Luan et al., 2017). It distinguishes itself by modifying the multi-task objective function with several regularization terms. These extra terms encourage responses for the same context to be placed nearby in latent space and aligning semantically related responses along straight lines in latent space. This induces a structure in the latent space such that distance and direction from a predicted response vector roughly correspond to relevance and diversity, respectively, as in Figure 2.

3.3 Knowledge grounding

A critical task in building intelligent conversational agents is grounding their responses in an external knowledge base. This allows agents to provide informed responses with context about the real world, without needing comprehensive paired conversational data to embody that information. We provide an extension of stochastic answer networks (Liu et al., 2018), a machine reading comprehension system, that acts as a full knowledge-grounded conversation model (Qin et al., 2019), hybridizing machine reading comprehension with a response generation model. At a high level, this model consists of two deep biLSTMs in parallel that encode conversational context and knowledge, respectively. The information from these encoders is then combined using cross-attention, the output of which forms the basis of a memory cell that powers a response generator.

4   Decoding features

ICECAPS provides a custom beam search decoder that extends TensorFlow's native beam search decoder by introducing several useful features.

4.1   Diverse generation with MMI re-ranking

Generative language systems are notorious for generating bland, uninteresting samples. Although generated hypotheses generally have high scores on metrics used to approximate context and relevance of generated texts (e.g. perplexity and BLEU), these metrics fail to measure diversity, a highly desirable trait for responses generated by conversational systems.

To alleviate this, we provide an implementation of the maximum mutual information (MMI) scoring function (Li et al., 2016a). We extend and modify the TensorFlow TrainingHelper and BasicDecoder classes for our implementation. MMI employs a separately trained model that learns to predict queries from given responses: the inverse map of the conversational model. Using the MMI model, for a given set of hypotheses, we calculate the log-probability of a given query per hypothesis: $P(query|hypothesis)$. This approximates response diversity, as frequent and repetitive hypotheses would be associated with many possible queries, thus generating a lower probability for any specific query. This score is weighted and used to re-rank hypotheses, pushing blander responses below context-unique responses.

4.2   Token filtering

Models trained on real-world data may utter undesirable words or phrases. Users may want the agent to avoid profanities or other offensive language. Likewise, the system should avoid obvious ungrammatical outputs, such as broken abbreviations or nonsensical punctuation marks.

ICECAPS supports several filters, including a general censor-list and a start-token censor-list. The general censor-list contains a list of tokens to disable during response generation; probabilities associated with these tokens are clamped to zero. The start-token censor-list is similar, but only masks the response's first token. We also support infrequency filters; users may restrict the decoder from generating responses with rare words.

4.3   Modified beam search decoding

The standard beam-search implementation in TensorFlow works by iteratively generating tokens, generating a constant number of hypotheses at the end of the decoding phase. ICECAPS implements a modified beam search decoder with a different criterion for exploring complete hypotheses. Rather than considering a completion of every hypothesis, this decoder only considers a complete version of a hypothesis if the END token is one of the top k options for the next token. This version of beam-search decoding may result more more or less than k final hypotheses, depending on how often the decoder produced an END token.[2] This form of decoding can sometimes produce cleaner hypotheses than the standard beam-search implementation, perhaps because END is only allowed when the model score is high. This helps increase the quality of generated sequences, as they tend to have improved grammatical coherence, though the number of returned outputs is often less than k.

4.4   Repetition penalty

The ICECAPS custom decoder also includes a repetition penalty, used in the scoring function employed during the beam search phase. This penalty helps avoid the well-known problem of decoders generating repetitive responses and getting stuck in loops. The repetition penalty is calculated as:

$$\log\left(\min\left(1, \frac{uniq(s)}{\lceil(A \times \|s\|)\rceil}\right)\right) \qquad (1)$$

for a given response s, where A is the repetition allowance and $uniq(s)$ is the number of unique tokens in s.

---

[2]If no responses are generated by the last time-step, we return all hypotheses generated in the last time-step, ensuring that the decoder always produces at least one response.

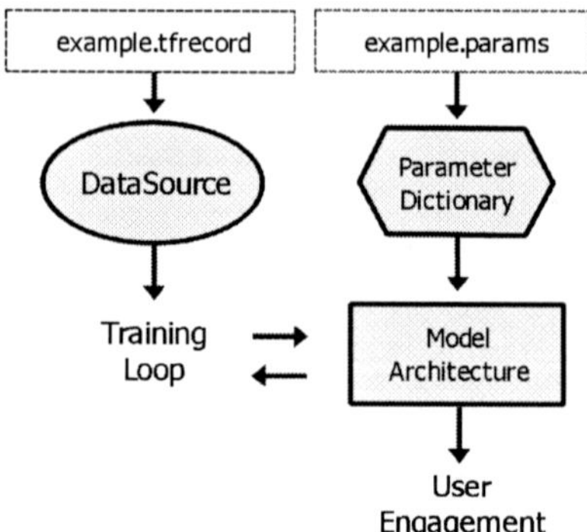

Figure 3: The five-phase pattern underlying ICECAPS training configurations. Hyperparameters are extracted into a dictionary from a file, which are used to initialize the model architecture. Data files initialize DataSource objects, which feed the training loop. The user can engage with the system once trained.

5 Building systems

ICECAPS is designed to make building complex dialogue systems intuitive for the end user.

5.1 Text data processing

TensorFlow estimators expect to read data from TFRecord binary files for efficient processing. We provide a script TEXT_DATA_PROCESSING.PY for converting text data into TFRecords, equipped with several useful preprocessing transformations. Our script can sort data within local windows so that batches fed during training have minimal padding inefficiency. These batches can be shuffled amongst each other to mitigate any biases induced by sorting. We provide token preprocessing through byte pair encoding (Sennrich et al., 2016), which builds a token set at a level of abstraction between characters and words. This often allows for faster training and improved generalization. Another feature focused on conversational scenarios is fixed-length context extraction. Conversational data often contains large, potentially unwieldy multi-turn contexts; we can limit our data samples to a desired context length. We also provide an option for annotating datasets with topic grounding information, by analyzing the data for unique tokens to use as topic markers.

5.2 Training configurations

ICECAPS training configurations follow a basic five-phase pattern. We include example training scripts that users may use as templates.

Loading hyperparameters. We supply hyperparameters to the model architecture via .PARAMS files. These files follow a simple, readable format: each line pairs the name of a hyperparameter with its supplied value, separated by a colon. Every ICECAPS estimator is equipped with a set of expected hyperparameters, and their associated default values when those hyperparameters are not provided. Users can view these hyperparameters through a static API call. In systems with multiple modules, users can add prefixes to hyperparameters to properly assign them to the right modules.

Building model architecture. Architectures are built by composing modules, chaining them and placing them in EstimatorGroups as appropriate. They are initialized with the loaded dictionaries of hyperparameters.

Connecting data sources. We now connect TFRecord files to our architecture via an input pipeline. We provide a high-level wrapper around TensorFlow's native Dataset-based pipelining. Users initialize DataSource objects with TFRecord files and produce input pipelines from those files. Our DataSource class also provides methods for combining multiple input pipelines from DataSource objects, either by randomly interleaving them or by combining them in parallel to feed multi-task configurations.

Training the system. The system is now ready to train: a single call to the training function with the desired number of batches or epochs is sufficient. However, users can construct more elaborate training schedules, consisting of sequences of training function calls with different arguments. This is particularly useful in multi-task scenarios, where we may want to train the system with different balances across tasks in different steps. For instance, one could first pre-train a single task, then shift to multi-task learning evenly distributed across two tasks.

The user can now engage with the trained system. Users can run their system on an evaluation set, collecting appropriate metrics and decoded responses. They can also interact with the system directly. ICECAPS provides a command-line interactive session for users to have conversations with their agents and directly observe their responses. Response generation is powered by the custom decoder described in Section 4. While the command-line session is useful for quick testing, for convenience we also provide a simple GUI-based inter-active session in which users can load their trained models. The GUI makes it easy to view multiple turns of conversation history alongside a top-k list of generated responses with associated scores.

6 Pre-trained models

ICECAPS comes packaged with pre-trained systems for conversation modeling based on the features described in Section 3. Users can either employ these systems to load conversational agents for immediate use or to bootstrap the training process for new configurations.

The largest-scale pre-trained system we currently offer is a deep Transformer-based architecture trained on real-world conversational data. Our model employs 12 layers with layer normalization, a modified initialization scheme that accounts for model depth, and byte pair encodings (Sennrich et al., 2016) for the tokenizer. We trained this system on a large corpus of conversations scraped from Reddit. The data was extracted from Reddit comment chains spanning from 2005 till 2017. The dataset consists of hundreds of millions of paired instances of contexts and responses with billions of tokens. Our model uses a vocabulary size of 50,257, and was trained on eight Nvidia V100 machines with NVLink.

We provide a set of trained personality embeddings for implementing diverse personality chatbots. These embeddings were learned through multi-task learning between paired conversation data and unpaired utterances categorized by speaker. These embeddings define a personality space; users may use the provided embeddings for their applications or train new personality embeddings within this space.

We also provide a demo of a conversational agent that combines a number of key features discussed in this paper. This agent is powered by an LSTM-based seq2seq model built on the Space-Fusion paradigm. Our agent demonstrates the improvements to conversational response generation made possible by a combination of multi-task learning and our improved beam search decoder.

7 Related toolkits

Several NLP-oriented toolkits have been open-sourced. Tensor2Tensor (Vaswani et al., 2018), maintained by Google Brain, extends TensorFlow with an array of state-of-the-art baseline deep learning models. It places a strong emphasis on sequence modeling baselines. AllenNLP (Gardner et al., 2018) is a PyTorch library developed by AI2 for natural language processing tasks, notable for an open-source release of ELMo (Peters et al., 2018). OpenNMT (Klein et al., 2017) is a popular neural machine translation toolkit originally developed for LuaTorch that now has implementations in PyTorch and TensorFlow. MarianNMT (Junczys-Dowmunt et al., 2018) is another framework for neural machine translation developed between the Adam Mickiewicz University in Pozna and the University of Edinburgh. It is built in C++ and designed for fast training in multi-GPU systems. Texar (Hu et al., 2018) is a text generation toolkit affiliated with Carnegie Mellon University, featuring a similar emphasis on modularity to ICECAPS. It includes reinforcement learning capabilities alongside its sequence modelling tools.

A few other toolkits have a dialog emphasis. DeepPavlov (Burtsev et al., 2018) is a deep learning library with a focus on task-oriented dialogue. It provides demos and pre-trained models for tasks such as question answering and sentiment classification. Affiliated with DeepPavlov is the ConvAI2 challenge (Dinan et al., 2019), a general dialogue competition featuring a synthetic personalized conversational dataset. ParlAI (Miller et al., 2017) is a library centered around task-oriented dialogue, compiling a number of popular datasets for NLP tasks as well as pre-trained models for knowledge-grounded dialog agents trained on crowd-sourced data.

8 Conclusion

Microsoft ICECAPS is a new open-source NLP library focused on building intelligent conversation agents that can communicate naturally with humans. Our release contributes key conversation modeling features to the open-source community, including personalization, knowledge grounding, diverse response modeling and generation, and more generally a multi-task architecture for inducing biases in conversational agents. Built for modularity and ease of use, ICECAPS allows users to extend our conversational technologies in novel ways for their agents. We provide the community with a number of pre-trained conversational systems trained on real-world data. Planned future directions for ICECAPS include multi-modality grounding and semantic parsing.

References

D. Bahdanau, K. Cho, and Y. Bengio. 2015. Neural machine translation by jointly learning to align and translate. In *3rd International Conference on Learning Representations, ICLR 2015, San Diego, CA, USA, May 7-9, 2015, Conference Track Proceedings*.

M. Burtsev, A. Seliverstov, R. Airapetyan, M. Arkhipov, D. Baymurzina, N. Bushkov, O. Gureenkova, T. Khakhulin, Y. Kuratov, D. Kuznetsov, A. Litinsky, V. Logacheva, A. Lymar, V. Malykh, M. Petrov, V. Polulyakh, L. Pugachev, A. Sorokin, M. Vikhreva, and M. Zaynutdinov. 2018. DeepPavlov: Open-source library for dialogue systems. In *Proceedings of the 56th Annual Meeting of the Association for Computational Linguistics-System Demonstrations*.

E. Dinan, V. Logacheva, V. Malykh, A. Miller, K. Shuster, J. Urbanek, D. Kiela, A. Szlam, I. Serban, R. Lowe, S. Prabhumoye, A. W. Black, A. Rudnicky, J. Williams, J. Pineau, M. Burtsev, and J. Weston. 2019. The second conversational intelligence challenge (convai2).

J. Gao, M. Galley, and L. Li. 2019a. Neural approaches to conversational AI. *Foundations and Trends® in Information Retrieval*.

X. Gao, S. Lee, Y. Zhang, C. Brockett, M. Galley, J. Gao, and B. Dolan. 2019b. Jointly optimizing diversity and relevance in neural response generation. In *NAACL-HLT 2019*.

M. Gardner, J. Grus, M. Neumann, O. Tafjord, P. Dasigi, N. F. Liu, M. Peters, M. Schmitz, and L. S. Zettlemoyer. 2018. Allennlp: A deep semantic natural language processing platform. In *Proceedings of Workshop for NLP Open Source Software*.

Z. Hu, H. Shi, Z. Yang, B. Tan, T. Zhao, J. He, W. Wang, L. Qin, D. Wang, et al. 2018. Texar: A modularized, versatile, and extensible toolkit for text generation. *arXiv preprint arXiv:1809.00794*.

M. Junczys-Dowmunt, R. Grundkiewicz, T. Dwojak, H. Hoang, K. Heafield, T. Neckermann, F. Seide, U. Germann, A. Fikri Aji, N. Bogoychev, A. F. T. Martins, and A. Birch. 2018. Marian: Fast neural machine translation in C++. In *Proceedings of ACL 2018 System Demonstrations*.

G. Klein, Y. Kim, Y. Deng, J. Senellart, and A. M. Rush. 2017. OpenNMT: Open-source toolkit for neural machine translation. In *Proc. ACL*.

J. Li, M. Galley, C. Brockett, J. Gao, and B. Dolan. 2016a. A diversity-promoting objective function for neural conversation models. In *Proceedings of the 2016 Conference of NAACL-HLT*.

J. Li, M. Galley, C. Brockett, G. P. Spithourakis, J. Gao, and B. Dolan. 2016b. A persona-based neural conversation model. In *Proceedings of the 54th Annual Meeting of ACL*.

X. Liu, P. He, W. Chen, and J. Gao. 2019. Multi-task deep neural networks for natural language understanding. *arXiv preprint arXiv:1901.11504*.

X. Liu, Y. Shen, K. Duh, and J. Gao. 2018. Stochastic answer networks for machine reading comprehension. In *Proceedings of the 56th Annual Meeting of the Association for Computational Linguistics (Volume 1: Long Papers)*.

Y. Luan, C. Brockett, B. Dolan, J. Gao, and M. Galley. 2017. Multi-task learning for speaker-role adaptation in neural conversation models. In *Proceedings of the The 8th International Joint Conference on Natural Language Processing*.

T. Luong, H. Pham, and C. D. Manning. 2015. Effective approaches to attention-based neural machine translation. In *Proceedings of the 2015 Conference on Empirical Methods in Natural Language Processing, EMNLP 2015, Lisbon, Portugal, September 17-21, 2015*.

A. H. Miller, W. Feng, A. Fisch, J. Lu, D. Batra, A. Bordes, D. Parikh, and J. Weston. 2017. ParlAI: A dialog research software platform. In *Proceedings of the 2017 EMNLP System Demonstration*.

M. E. Peters, M. Neumann, M. Iyyer, M. Gardner, C. Clark, K. Lee, and L. Zettlemoyer. 2018. Deep contextualized word representations. In *Proc. of NAACL*.

L. Qin, M. Galley, C. Brockett, X. Liu, X. Gao, B. Dolan, Y. Choi, and J. Gao. 2019. Contentful neural conversation with on-demand machine reading. In *ACL 2019*.

R. Sennrich, B. Haddow, and A. Birch. 2016. Neural machine translation of rare words with subword units. In *Proceedings of the 54th Annual Meeting of ACL (Volume 1: Long Papers)*.

I. Sutskever, O. Vinyals, and Q. V. Le. 2014. Sequence to sequence learning with neural networks. In *Advances in Neural Information Processing Systems 27*. Curran Associates, Inc.

A. Vaswani, S. Bengio, E. Brevdo, F. Chollet, A. N. Gomez, S. Gouws, L. Jones, Ł. Kaiser, N. Kalchbrenner, N. Parmar, R. Sepassi, N. Shazeer, and J. Uszkoreit. 2018. Tensor2tensor for neural machine translation. *CoRR*, abs/1803.07416.

A. Vaswani, N. Shazeer, N. Parmar, J. Uszkoreit, L. Jones, A. N. Gomez, Ł. Kaiser, and I. Polosukhin. 2017. Attention is all you need. In *Advances in NIPS 30*. Curran Associates, Inc.

PERSPECTROSCOPE: A Window to the World of Diverse Perspectives

Sihao Chen, Daniel Khashabi, Chris Callison-Burch, Dan Roth
University of Pennsylvania
{sihaoc,danielkh,ccb,danroth}@cis.upenn.edu

Abstract

This work presents PERSPECTROSCOPE, a web-based system which lets users query a discussion-worthy natural language claim, and extract and visualize various perspectives in support or against the claim, along with evidence supporting each perspective. The system thus lets users explore various perspectives that could touch upon aspects of the issue at hand. The system is built as a combination of retrieval engines and learned textual-entailment-like classifiers built using a few recent developments in natural language understanding. To make the system more adaptive, expand its coverage, and improve its decisions over time, our platform employs various mechanisms to get corrections from the users.

PERSPECTROSCOPE is available at github. com/CogComp/perspectroscope.[1]

1 Introduction

One key consequence of the information revolution is a significant increase and a contamination of our information supply. The practice of fact-checking won't suffice to eliminate the biases in text data we observe, as the degree of factuality alone does not determine whether biases exist in the spectrum of opinions visible to us. To better understand controversial issues, one needs to view them from a diverse yet comprehensive set of *perspectives*.

Understanding most nontrivial *claim*s requires insights from various *perspective*s. Today, we make use of search engines or recommendation systems to retrieve information relevant to a claim, but this process carries multiple forms of *bias*. In particular, they are optimized relative to the claim (query) presented, and the popularity of the relevant documents returned, rather than with respect

to the diversity of the *perspective*s presented in them or whether they are supported by evidence.

While it might be impractical to show an exhaustive spectrum of views with respect to a *claim*, cherry-picking a small but diverse set of *perspectives* could be a tangible step towards addressing the limitations of the current systems. Inherently this objective requires the understanding of the relations between each *perspective* and *claim*, as well as the nuance in semantic meaning between *perspective*s under the context of the *claim*.

This work presents a demo for the task of *substantiated perspective discovery* (Chen et al., 2019). Our system receives a *claim* and it is expected to present a *diverse* set of *well-corroborated perspectives* that take a *stance* with respect to the claim. Each perspective should be substantiated by *evidence* paragraphs which summarize pertinent results and facts.

A typical output of the system is shown in Figure 3. The input to the system is a *claim*: *Social media (like facebook or twitter) have had very positive effects in our life style.* There is no single, best way to respond to the claim, but rather there are many valid responses that form a spectrum of perspectives, each with a *stance* relative to this claim and, ideally, with evidence supporting it.

To support the input claim, one could refer to the observation that interactions between individuals has become easier through the social media. Or one can refer to the success they have brought to those in need of reaching out to masses (e.g., business individuals). On the contrary, one could oppose the given claim by pointing out its negative impacts on productivity and the increase in cyber-bullying. Each of these arguments, which we refer to as a *perspective* throughout the paper, is an opinion, possibly conditional, in support of a given *claim* or against it. A *perspective* thus con-

---

[1]A brief demo of the system: https://www. youtube.com/watch?v=MXBTR1Sp3Bs.

Proceedings of the 57th Annual Meeting of the Association for Computational Linguistics-System Demonstrations, pages 129–134
Florence, Italy, July 28 - August 2, 2019. ©2019 Association for Computational Linguistics

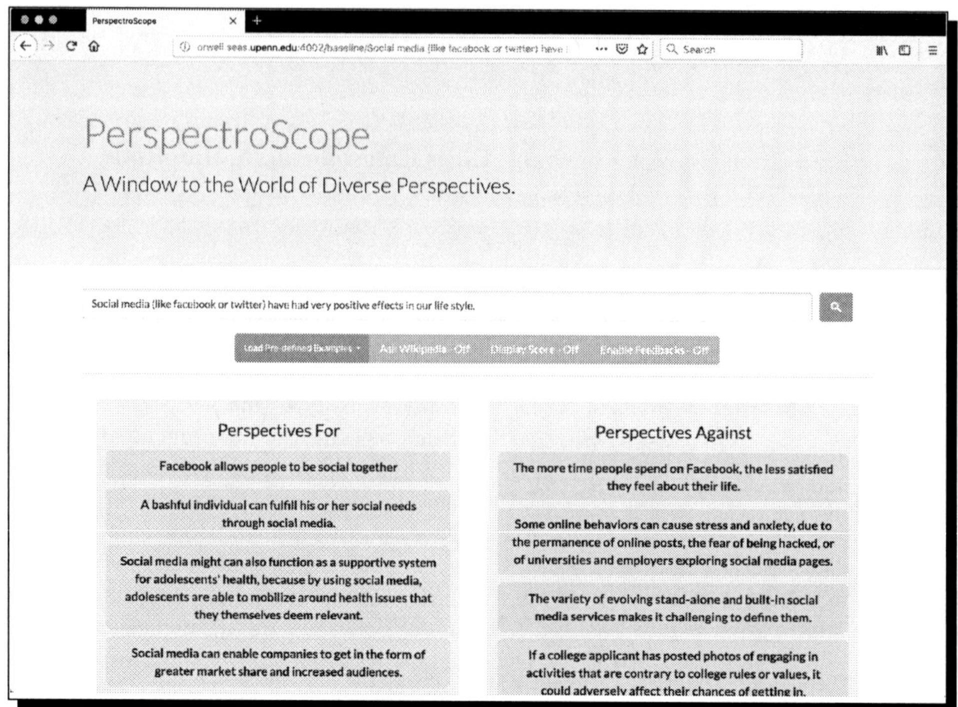

Figure 1: Given a *claim* as the input, our system is expected to discover various *perspectives* and their *stance* with respect to the claim. Each claim also comes with the relevant *evidence* that substantiates the given perspective.

stitutes a particular attitude towards a given *claim*. Additionally, each of these *perspective* has to be well-supported by *evidence* found in paragraphs that summarize findings and substantiations of different sources.

Overall, PERSPECTROSCOPE provides an interface to help individuals by providing a small but diverse set of *perspectives*. Our system is built upon a few recent developments in the field. In addition, our system is designed to be able to utilize feedback from the users of the system to improve its predictions. The rest of this paper is dedicated to delineating the details of PERSPECTROSCOPE.

2 PERSPECTROSCOPE

2.1 Core Design Structure

A high-level picture of the work is shown in Figure 2. Our system uses a mix of retrieval engines and learned classifiers to ensure both quality and efficiency. The retrieval systems extract candidates (perspectives or evidence paragraphs) which are later evaluated by carefully designed classifiers.

2.2 Learned Classifiers

In building PERSPECTROSCOPE we borrow the definitions and dataset provided by Chen et al. (2019). The provided dataset, PERSPECTRUM, is a crowdsourced collection of claims, perspectives and evidence extracted from online debate websites as well as other web content. We follow the same steps as Chen et al. (2019) to create classifiers for the following tasks:

C1: Relevant Perspective Extraction. This classifier is expected to return the collection of perspectives with respect to a given claim.

C2: Perspective Stance Classification. Given a claim, this classifier is expected to score a collection of perspectives with the degree to which it *supports* or *opposes* the given claim.

C3: Perspective Equivalence. This classifier is expected to decide whether two given perspectives are equivalent or not, in the context a given claim.

C4: Extraction of Supporting Evidence. This classifier decides whether a given document lends enough evidence for a given perspective to a claim.

In training the classifiers for each of the tasks,

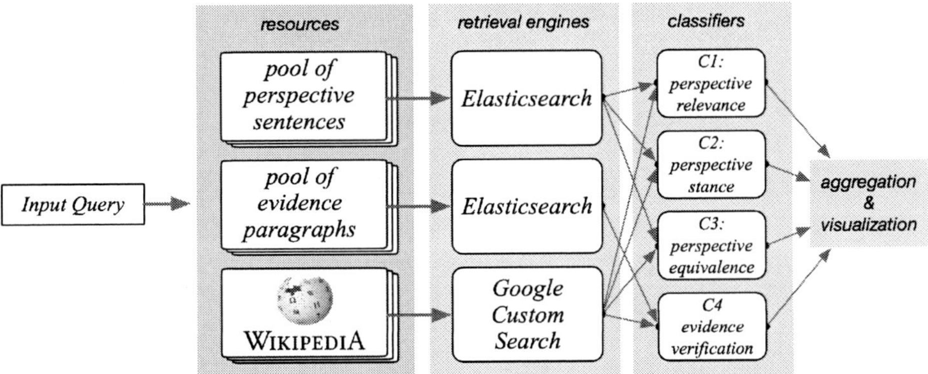

Figure 2: Overview of the system structure: given a query to the system, it extracts candidates from its internal knowledge

we use BERT (Devlin et al., 2019) and we follow the same steps described in Chen et al. (2019).

2.3 Candidate Retrieval

We use a retrieval (IR) system[2] to generate *perspective* and *evidence* candidates for the learned classifiers. We take $10k$ perspective sentences and $8k$ evidence paragraphs from Chen et al. (2019) and index them respectively in two independent retrieval engines. For each input claim, we query the claim and retrieve top-30 perspective candidates from the retrieval engine. Upon user request, we query the claim concatenated with a perspective candidate to retrieve top-20 evidence candidates from the pool of $8k$ evidence paragraphs.

To support a broader range of topics not covered by PERSPECTRUM, we use Wikipedia to retrieve extra candidate perspectives/evidence. Given an input claim from the user, we issue a query to the Google Custom Search API[3] and retrieve top 10 relevant Wikipedia pages. We clean up each page using newspaper3k[4] and use the first sentence of the paragraphs within each document as candidate perspectives, and the rest sentences in each paragraph as candidate evidence.

2.4 Minimal Perspective Discovery

The overall decision making is outlined in Algorithm 1. As mentioned earlier, the whole process is a pipeline starting with candidate generation via retrieval engines, and followed by scoring with the learned classifiers. The final step is to select a *min-*

imal set of perspectives with the DBSCAN clustering algorithm (Ester et al., 1996).

Algorithm 1: Minimal Perspective Extraction

Input: claim c.
Output: perspectives, their stances & evidence.
$\hat{P} \leftarrow \text{IR}(c)$ // candidate perspectives
$P = \{\}$
foreach $p \in \hat{P}$ **do**
    // perspective relevance
    if $C1(c,p) > T1$ *and* $abs(C2(c,p)) > T2$ **then**
        $e \leftarrow C2(c,p)$
        $\hat{E} \leftarrow \text{IR}(c,p)$ // candidate evidence
        $E = \{\}$
        foreach $e \in \hat{E}$ **do**
            // evidence verification
            if $C4(c,p,e) > T4$ **then**
                $E \leftarrow E \cup \{e\}$.
            end
        end
        $P \leftarrow P \cup \{(p,s,E)\}$.
    end
end
$P \leftarrow$ /* minimal perspectives after clustering with DBSCAN on the equivalence scores between any perspective pairs via $C3$. */

The parameters of this algorithm (e.g., the thresholds $T1, T2, ...$) are tuned manually on a held-out set.

2.5 Utilizing user feedback

User feedback/logs are valuable sources of information for many successful applications. In this work, we collect two forms of feedback signals from users. We record all queries of claims issued to the system. In addition, the users have the option to tell us whether a given perspective is a good or bad one (based on the quality of its relevance, stance or evidence prediction). It is important to

---

[2] www.elastic.co
[3] https://cse.google.com/cse/
[4] github.com/codelucas/newspaper

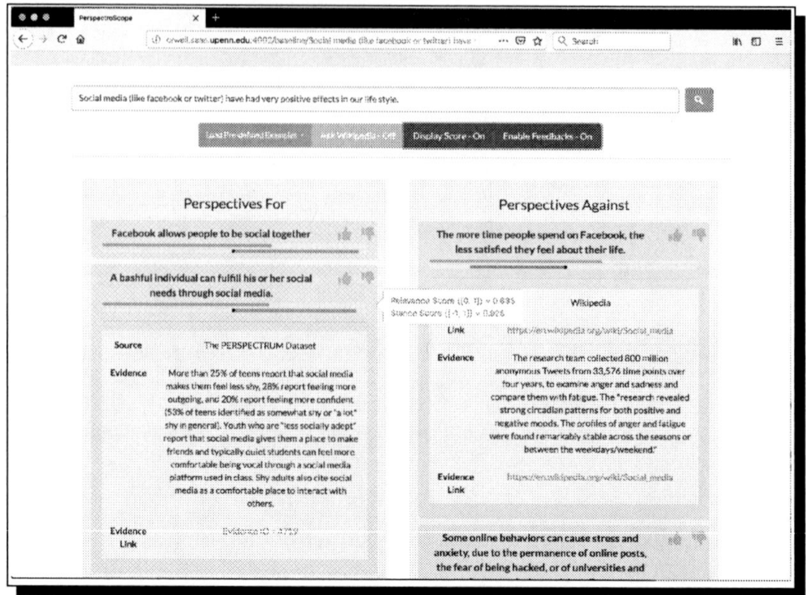

Figure 3: A demonstration of the system features. The grey and blue/red color bars (under each perspective) show the relevance and stance predictions, respectively. Upon user request, the system provides a paragraph of supporting evidence for each perspective. Users have the option to provide feedback to each perspective via the *thumbs-up* or *thumbs-down* button.

note that we are not collecting any personal information in the process.

The user annotations can provide extra supervision signals for task C1-C4 with a broader topical coverage. These annotations can in turn be used in the classifier training and iteratively improve our prediction results with increasing number of users.

3   Related Work

There are few related tools to this work. `args.me` is a platform that accepts natural language queries and returns links to the pages that contain relevant topics (Wachsmuth et al., 2017), which are split into *supporting & opposing* categories (screenshot in Figure 4). Similarly, `ArgumentText` (Stab et al., 2018a) takes a topic as input and returns *pro/con* arguments retrieved from the web. This work takes the effort one step further by employing language understanding techniques.

There is a rich line of work on using Wikipedia as source for argument mining or to assess the veracity of a claim (Thorne et al., 2018). For instance, `FAKTA` is a system that extracts relevant documents from Wikipedia, among other sources, to predict the factuality of an input claim (Nadeem et al., 2019).

Beyond published works, there are websites that employ similar technologies. For instance, `bing.com` has recently started a service that provides two different responses to a given argument (screenshot in Figure 4). Since there is no published work on this system, it is not clear what the underlying mechanism is.

There exist a number of online debate platforms that provide similar functionalities as our system: `kialo.com`, `procon.org`, `idebate.org`, among others. Such websites usually provide a wide range of debate topics and various arguments in response to each topic. These resources have been proven useful in a line of works in argumentation (Hua and Wang, 2017; Stab et al., 2018b; Wachsmuth et al., 2018), among many others. While they provide rich sources of information, their content is fairly limited in terms of either their topical coverage or data availability for academic research purposes.

There also exist a few other works in this direction that do not accompany a publicly available tool or demo. For instance, Hasan and Ng (2014); Levy et al. (2018) attempt to identify relevant arguments within web text in the context of a given topic.

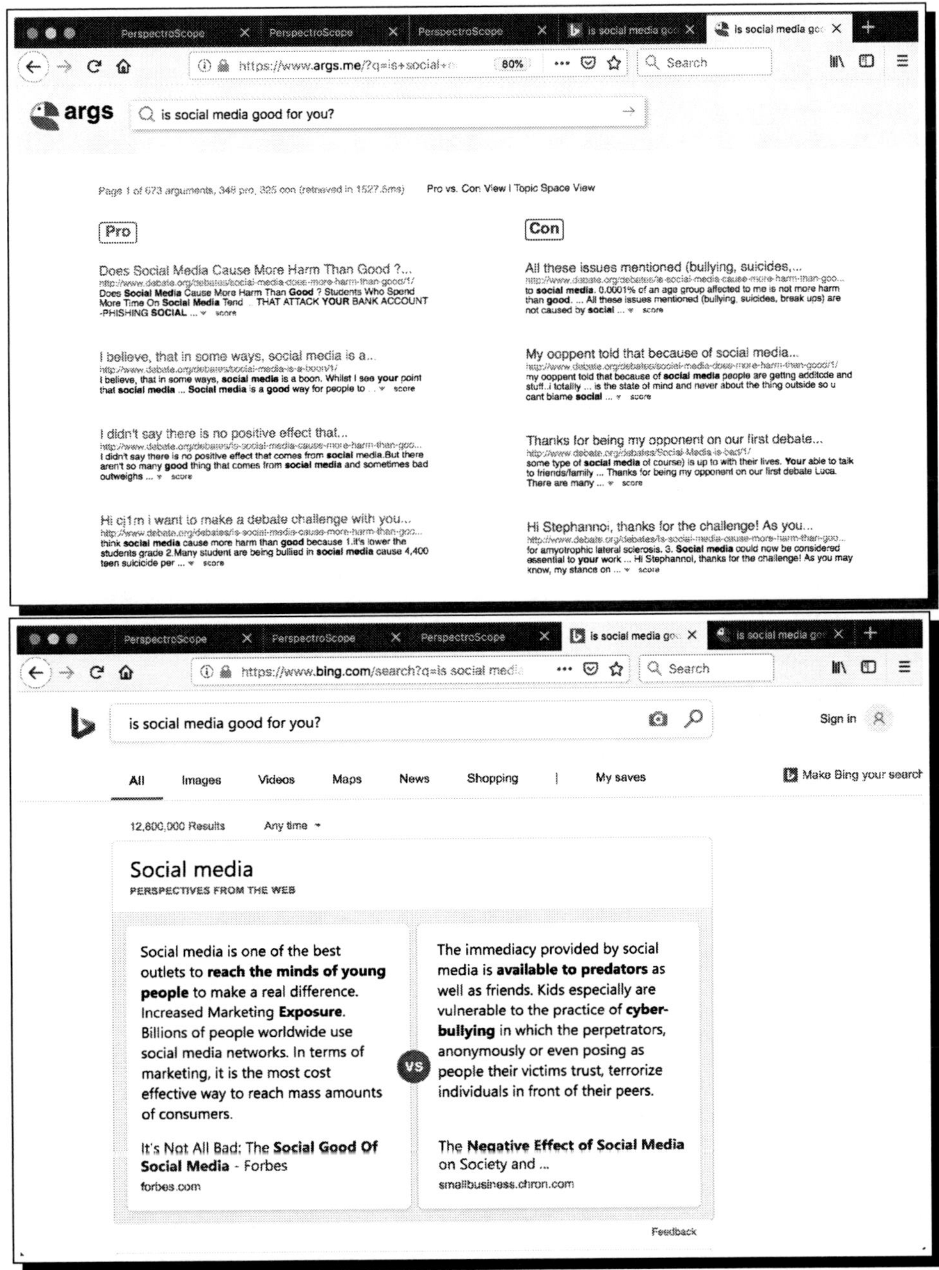

Figure 4: Related work: `args.me` an argument retrieval engine using arguments extracted from debate websites; `bing.com` search engine showing contrasting views on a debate topic.

4   Conclusion and Future Work

We have presented PERSPECTROSCOPE, a powerful interface for exploring different perspectives to discussion-worthy claims. The system is built with a combination of retrieval engines and learned classifiers to create a good balance between speed and quality. Our system is designed with the mindset of being able to get feedback from users of the system.

While this work offers a good step towards a higher quality and flexible interface, there are many issues and limitations that are not addressed here and are opportunities for future work. For instance, the system provided here does not provide any guarantees in terms of the *exhaustiveness* of the perspectives in the world, or levels of expertise and trustworthiness of the identified evidence. Moreover, any classifier trained on some annotated data (such as what we used here) could potentially contain hidden biases that might not be easy to see. We hope that some of these challenges and limitations will be addressed in future work.

Acknowledgments

This work was supported in part by a gift from Google and by Contract HR0011-15-2-0025 with the US Defense Advanced Research Projects Agency (DARPA). The views expressed are those of the authors and do not reflect the official policy or position of the Department of Defense or the U.S. Government.

References

S. Chen, D. Khashabi, W. Yin, C. Callison-Burch, and D. Roth. 2019. Seeing things from a different angle: Discovering diverse perspectives about claims. In *Proceedings of the 2019 Conference of the North American Chapter of the Association for Computational Linguistics: Human Language Technologies, Volume 1*, pages 542–557.

J. Devlin, M.-W. Chang, K. Lee, and K. Toutanova. 2019. Bert: Pre-training of deep bidirectional transformers for language understanding. In *Proceedings of the 2019 Conference of the North American Chapter of the Association for Computational Linguistics: Human Language Technologies, Volume 1*, pages 4171–4186.

M. Ester, H.-P. Kriegel, J. Sander, X. Xu, et al. 1996. A density-based algorithm for discovering clusters in large spatial databases with noise. In *Proceedings of 1996 Conference on Knowledge Discovery & Data Mining*, pages 226–231.

K. S. Hasan and V. Ng. 2014. Why are you taking this stance? identifying and classifying reasons in ideological debates. In *Proceedings of the 2014 Conference on Empirical Methods in Natural Language Processing*, pages 751–762.

X. Hua and L. Wang. 2017. Understanding and Detecting Supporting Arguments of Diverse Types. In *Proceedings of the 55th Annual Meeting of the Association for Computational Linguistics, Volume 2*, pages 203–208.

R. Levy, B. Bogin, S. Gretz, R. Aharonov, and N. Slonim. 2018. Towards an argumentative content search engine using weak supervision. In *Proceedings of the 27th International Conference on Computational Linguistics*, pages 2066–2081.

M. Nadeem, W. Fang, B. Xu, M. Mohtarami, and J. Glass. 2019. Fakta: An automatic end-to-end fact checking system. In *Proceedings of the 2019 Conference of the North American Chapter of the Association for Computational Linguistics (Demonstrations)*, pages 78–83.

C. Stab, J. Daxenberger, C. Stahlhut, T. Miller, B. Schiller, C. Tauchmann, S. Eger, and I. Gurevych. 2018a. Argumentext: Searching for arguments in heterogeneous sources. In *Proceedings of the 2018 Conference of the North American Chapter of the Association for Computational Linguistics: Demonstrations*, pages 21–25.

C. Stab, T. Miller, B. Schiller, P. Rai, and I. Gurevych. 2018b. Cross-topic argument mining from heterogeneous sources. In *Proceedings of the 2018 Conference on Empirical Methods in Natural Language Processing*, pages 3664–3674.

James Thorne, Andreas Vlachos, Christos Christodoulopoulos, and Arpit Mittal. 2018. FEVER: a Large-scale Dataset for Fact Extraction and VERification. In *Proceedings of the 2018 Conference of the North American Chapter of the Association for Computational Linguistics: Human Language Technologies, Volume 1 (Long Papers)*, volume 1, pages 809–819.

H. Wachsmuth, M. Potthast, K. Al Khatib, Y. Ajjour, J. Puschmann, J. Qu, J. Dorsch, V. Morari, J. Bevendorff, and B. Stein. 2017. Building an argument search engine for the web. In *Workshop on Argument Mining*.

H. Wachsmuth, S. Syed, and B. Stein. 2018. Retrieval of the best counterargument without prior topic knowledge. In *Proceedings of the 56th Annual Meeting of the Association for Computational Linguistics, Volume 1*, pages 241–251.

HEIDL: Learning Linguistic Expressions with Deep Learning and Human-in-the-Loop

Yiwei Yang[1], Eser Kandogan[2], Yunyao Li[2], Walter S. Lasecki[1], Prithviraj Sen[2]
[1]Computer Science and Engineering, University of Michigan - Ann Arbor
[2]IBM Research - Almaden, San Jose, CA
{yanyiwei, wlasecki}@umich.edu, {eser, yunyaoli, senp}@us.ibm.com

Abstract

While the role of humans is increasingly recognized in machine learning community, representation of and interaction with models in current human-in-the-loop machine learning (HITL-ML) approaches are too low-level and far-removed from human's conceptual models. We demonstrate HEIDL, a prototype HITL-ML system that exposes the machine-learned model through high-level, explainable linguistic expressions formed of predicates representing semantic structure of text. In HEIDL, human's role is elevated from simply evaluating model predictions to interpreting and even updating the model logic *directly* by enabling interaction with rule predicates themselves. Raising the currency of interaction to such semantic levels calls for new interaction paradigms between humans and machines that result in improved productivity for text analytics model development process. Moreover, by involving humans in the process, the human-machine co-created models generalize better to unseen data as domain experts are able to instill their expertise by extrapolating from what has been learned by automated algorithms from few labelled data.

1 Introduction

Machine learning (ML) is an inherently iterative process where humans, ML experts, play a central role. Experts decide which features to include, hyperparameters to tune, metrics to evaluate, and whether the desired level of quality has been attained, failing which they iterate all over. Traditionally, to understand a predictive model one usually begins by examining the model's predictions with little understanding of the inner workings of the learned, *black-box* model. More transparent representations of predictive models, such as first-order logic (a dialect with human-interpretable semantics), allows understanding the inner work-

ings of the learned model, but traditional techniques (Muggleton, 1996) to learning these are too brittle for real-world data, as they fail to learn anything unless there exists a logic program that can perfectly separate the data according to its labels. Deep learning has been used to successfully learn rule-based predictive models (Cohen et al., 2017; Yang et al., 2017; Evans and Grefenstette, 2018) from data with noisy labels. Besides interpretability and explainability, other advantages of learning a logical model include the promise of improved generalization to unseen data due to the strong inductive bias provided by the predicates employed (Evans and Grefenstette, 2018).

Human-in-the-loop machine learning (HITL-ML) approaches aim to provide humans with the ability to interact with the model that goes beyond simply examining model predictions. Humans need to be able to interpret, explain, and reason about models throughout the model development cycle, especially in domains where labeled training data is too limited to learn a model that generalizes well to unseen data, we need to be able to interpret and examine machine learning models. The above-mentioned works that utilize deep learning to learn a logical theory raise new opportunities and challenges since their precise syntax is more readily interpretable by humans that allows for new ways for humans to interact with machine learned models at levels that go far beyond just inspecting predictions.

In this demo, we describe a HITL-ML approach for text analytics that exposes the machine-learned model through abstract, semantic, explainable rules, and allows humans and domain experts to examine, interact, and even modify the model logic directly. We present *HEIDL* (Human-in-the-loop linguistic Expressions wIth Deep Learning), a system designed to help domain experts access the linguistic expressions or rules learned

Proceedings of the 57th Annual Meeting of the Association for Computational Linguistics-System Demonstrations, pages 135–140
Florence, Italy, July 28 - August 2, 2019. ©2019 Association for Computational Linguistics

with deep learning for text analytics, inspect them, show their inner workings by exposing how they operate on examples, and even breaking them apart into their constituent predicates and adding new ones to create new expressions in the process. HEIDL enables domain experts to instill their expertise into a machine-learned model thus resulting in a co-created one that has superior generalization performance than what is achievable by humans or machine learning optimization algorithms alone while incurring a fraction of human labor thus increasing the productivity of the overall text analytics model development process.

To evaluate HEIDL's efficacy, we conducted a user study where IBM's data scientists used HEIDL to improve linguistic expressions for classifying sentences extracted from real-world, legal contracts. Since contracts may be proprietary, the initial learned linguistic expressions fed as input to HEIDL were trained on IBM procurement contracts while the test set consisted of non-IBM procurement contract sentences. Within 30 minutes, each data scientist produced linguistic expressions with training set precision, recall upwards of 75% representing a significant reduction in model development time since trawling through $> 28,000$ training sentences to construct linguistic expressions from scratch would require multiple weeks of effort. In terms of prediction quality, while a black-box long short-term memory network trained by replacing tokens with GloVe embeddings (Pennington et al., 2014) produces 44% F1 on held out non-IBM procurement contract sentences, the linguistic expressions modified by data scientists via HEIDL produces 55% F1 translating to a 25% improvement in out-of-domain generalization performance. We emphasize that HEIDL is not specific to the task described here and may be useful for learning linguistic expressions for any classification task. Moreover, the main ideas embodied in HEIDL may be helpful for building tools to learn explainable models for applications beyond classification.

2   Related Work

Human computation integrates human effort into computational processes to complete tasks that cannot yet be done by computer. Prior work has focused on using crowdsourcing to facilitate and scale human computation. For instance, crowd-powered systems have been developed to sup-

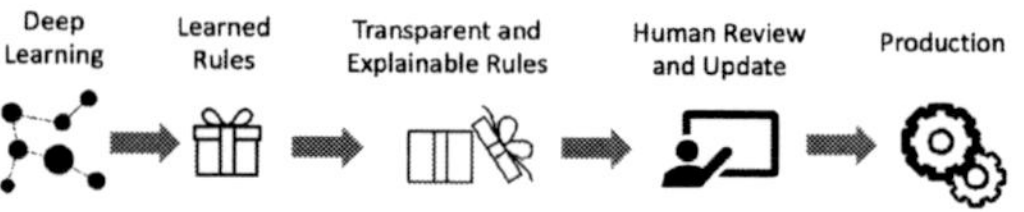

Figure 1: Overview of our approach

port continuous conversations (Lasecki et al.), edit rules governing UI behaviors described in natural language (Lee et al.), support natural language editing of papers (Bernstein et al.), and create novel stories (Kim et al.). There is also work on evaluating task design tradeoffs on crowdsourced text annotations(Snow et al.) and (Jiang et al.). Our approach draws on human computation by leveraging domain experts to create a more generalizable model even when data is scarce.

Prior work in HITL-ML has focused on eliciting knowledge from people to create more powerful models. For example, research has introduced ways to solicit examples from people for labels to strengthen the training data, e.g., through active learning (Settles and Craven) queries that select the most informative item from an oracle to reduce labeling effort. In SEER (Hanafi et al., 2017), people select few examples for the system to learn information extraction rules. In AnchorViz (Chen et al.), people explore semantically related examples to find feature blinded items. Other work has focused on interactive clustering where people guide the model by changing the clusters (Smith et al.) and providing keywords (Sherkat et al.), and on eliciting feedback from experts to select relevant features (Micallef et al.). We also elicit user input to improve a model, but our approach presents understandable output, allowing users to directly modify it by selecting trusted rules.

3   Approach

Fig.1 shows an overview of our approach where we begin by learning linguistic expressions from labeled data using deep learning followed by using our system to explain said expressions to domain experts so they can verify and modify these. We briefly explain how to derive predicates from semantic linguistic structures, then describe how deep learning is used to construct linguistic expressions before describing our system.

3.1   Semantic Linguistic Structure (SLS)

Each SLS refers to the shallow semantic representations corresponding to each sentence and generated automatically with natural language pro-

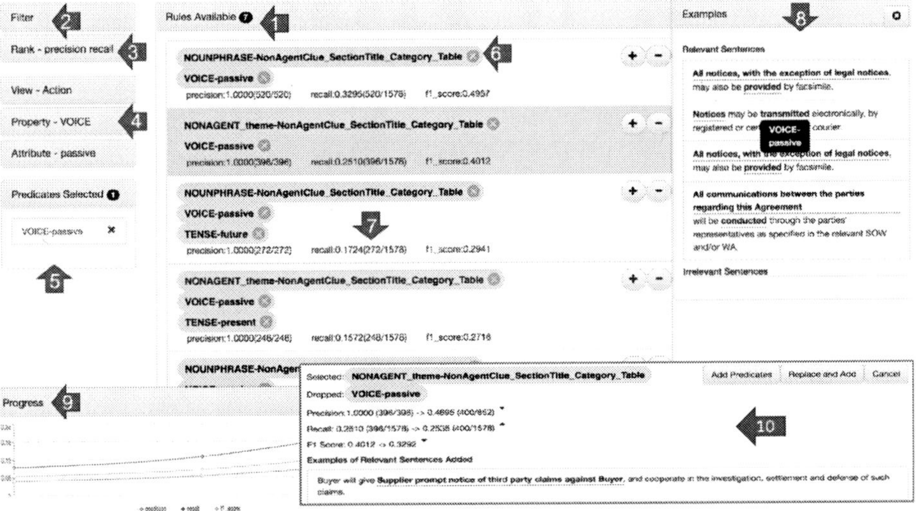

Figure 2: UI allows users (1) to get an overview of linguistic expressions (2) filter by precision, recall, and F1, (3) rank, (4,5) filter by predicates, (6) remove expressions by predicate, (7) examine metrics and (8) examples for each expression, (9) monitor overall progress as users add and remove expressions to their collection, and (10) provide a 'playground' allowing users to examine and modify expressions.

cessing techniques such as semantic role labeling and syntactic parsing. It captures "who is doing what to whom, when, where and how" described in a sentence as depicted by the following example (simplified for readability).

John bought daisy for Mary yesterday
agent action theme beneficiary context:temporal

SLSs may be used as predicates to form linguistic expressions. For sentence classification, we extract SLSs using SystemT's (Krishnamurthy et al., 2009) semantic role labeler including but not limited to actions/verbs and various arguments of the action such as agent (doer of the action), object of the action and manner in which it is performed. From these, we construct: 1) predicates that test properties of the action such as tense, aspect, mood, modalclass, voice and polarity, and 2) predicates generated by looking up the extracted verb (bases), agents, objects etc. in dictionaries. For the user study task, we have access to a multitude of hand-crafted dictionaries that contain surface forms for verb (bases), objects, themes etc. We emphasize that HEIDL is not specific to a particular set of predicates and can work with any set of predicates that allow us to learn initial, high quality linguistic expressions. Just like many other text analytics applications, and particularly for the domain of legal contracts, dictionary match predicates offer one way to achieve this.

3.2 Deep Learning Linguistic Expressions

As mentioned in Section 1, recent works use neural networks to learn a logical theory. Two powerful and extremely general formulations that can learn from noisy labeled data virtually any kind of logic program, including linguistic expressions for classification, are TensorLog (Cohen et al., 2017) and ∂ILP (Evans and Grefenstette, 2018). Describing the accompanying learning algorithms is out of scope for this demo proposal but we describe the *weighted rules* model representation to ground our system and better describe the input to HEIDL. Given predicates $\mathcal{P} = \{\mathrm{pred}_1, \ldots \mathrm{pred}_m\}$ and binary class labeled data $\mathcal{D} = \{(\mathbf{x}_1, y_1), \ldots (\mathbf{x}_n, y_n)\}$ such that each label $y_i \in \{0, 1\}$ and $\mathbf{x}_i$ denotes a sentence, the weighted rules model associates a non-negative weight with each rule or linguistic expression[1]:

$$w_1: \quad \ell(\mathbf{x}) \leftarrow \mathrm{pred}_1^1(\mathbf{x}) \wedge \ldots \mathrm{pred}_{k_1}^1(\mathbf{x})$$
$$\vdots$$
$$w_N: \quad \ell(\mathbf{x}) \leftarrow \mathrm{pred}_1^N(\mathbf{x}) \wedge \ldots \mathrm{pred}_{k_N}^N(\mathbf{x})$$

Intuitively, if sentence $\mathbf{x}$ satisfies a linguistic expression then $\mathbf{x}$ inherits the corresponding weight; the higher the weight the greater the chance of the sentence being assigned the label, i.e. $\ell(\mathbf{x})$

---

[1]Weighted rules are also popular in statistical relational learning (e.g., Markov logic networks (Richardson and Domingos, 2006)) and for learning closed paths in knowledge graphs (Yang et al., 2017), the latter being based on TensorLog (Cohen et al., 2017).

is true. While learning a model based on logic provides strong inductive bias that can help regularize the learned model and better generalize to unseen data, due to limited labeled data in many real-world applications (e.g., enterprise settings where privacy and proprietary ownership restricts the size of the training set) the risk of overfitting is not completely eliminated. Moreover, the presence of weights can hamper explainability since humans are much better at interpreting logical expressions. Our goal is to take a weighted rules model such as described above and modify it to a fully explainable, more generalizable model that consists of a set of linguistic expressions following simple yet powerful disjunctive semantics, in other words, sentence x is assigned the label if *any* of the expressions hold true for it, which is where HEIDL comes into the picture.

3.3   User Experience

Unlike classical HITL-ML, our approach allows people to interact with machine-learned linguistic expressions and facilitate co-operative model development. There are two primary challenges: (1) present users with a quick overview of learned expressions; enable them to organize, order, and navigate expressions effectively, (2) help understand each expression's semantics and quality through examples and statistics; deepen understanding by providing a 'playground' to verify and modify expressions while examining impact (see Fig.2). Below we describe some of the user experience features in more detail to address these challenges.

3.3.1   Overview, Rank, Filter

Initially, the system presents all machine-learned linguistic expressions along with their precision, recall, and F1 measures (relevant for classification tasks). Users can rank and filter to organize the expressions to process them. Ranking allows users to quickly see the expressions with high performance on training data and is especially useful when the list of expressions is large. Filtering allows users to narrow down to a small set of similar expressions without being overwhelmed. Users can filter expressions by setting a minimum threshold on multiple performance measures. Users can also filter expressions by their constituent predicates. Filtering by predicate is useful when the users reckon an expression potentially generalizable, and would like to see similar expressions that share common predicates.

3.3.2   Linguistic Expression Selection

The end goal of the system is to create a collection of trusted linguistic expressions. To do so, after evaluating an expression, users would add it to the 'approved' or 'disapproved' collection. When an expression is approved, the combined performance of all approved expressions is recomputed. This helps users to keep track of their overall progress. To help users assess expressions, HEIDL provides a random sample of up to 4 true positive and 4 false positive matching example sentences. Each example is decorated with annotations highlighting the constituent predicates that form part of the expression when the cursor hovers on it (Fig. 2).

While HEIDL shows the performance of each linguistic expression individually, they may be misleading as the sentences retrieved by the expression may be already covered by other expressions that have already been approved. HEIDL provides a 'look ahead' feature to see the potential 'delta' effect of adding the expression to the approved collection so users can see if approving the expression would be beneficial, in which case they can take a closer look by reading its associated examples, or examine it in 'Playground' mode.

3.3.3   Playground

HEIDL provides a Playground mode that allows users to inspect and modify linguistic expressions by adding or dropping predicates, and examine the effects. While playing with expressions, users can also examine the 'delta' examples. If a predicate is dropped, then the expression becomes more general, thus retrieving more sentences than it previously did. Conversely, if a predicate is added fewer sentences are retrieved and HEIDL shows examples of the difference. This is beneficial because it allows users to see the effect of individual predicates. Adding new predicates is especially useful if experts have a sense for which predicates are potentially good. Performance measures and examples are updated accordingly, helping users decide whether or not to keep the modification.

4   Salient Results from a User Study

To evaluate HEIDL's efficacy, we conducted a user study among IBM data scientists with NLP expertise and knowledge of legal contracts. We recruited 4 data scientists – a relatively large number given most teams in industry include only 1-2 data scientists. The task was to label sentences with *Communication* which implies some form of communication between the two parties involved in the contract. The training data consists of 28, 174 sentences extracted from 149 IBM procurement contracts and the held out, test data consists of 1259 sentences extracted from 11 non-IBM procurement contracts. The initial set of 188 weighted linguistic expressions learned using deep learning performed at 67% F1 (the harmonic mean of precision and recall) on the test set. Note that, as mentioned in Section 3.2, weights can lead to lack of explainability. Thus the data scientist's task is to use HEIDL to generate from this initial set of linguistic expressions, a smaller set expressed in pure first-order logic that achieves maximal performance on the out-of-domain test set. For each data scientist, we initialize HEIDL with the initial linguistic expressions, the training set sentences, and the corresponding predicates and dictionaries. Our baseline is a well established sentence classification neural network, based on bi-directional long short-term memory (LSTM). More precisely, the LSTM replaces the tokens in the input sentence with their corresponding 300-dimensional GloVe embedding, computes an intermediate hidden state which are then max-pooled, fed into a fully connected layer and ReLU activation before passing it through sigmoid activation to get a probability of predicting the label. To improve training of the LSTM, we employed a variety of dropout regularizations: variational dropout after the embedding lookup layer, weight dropout in the LSTM layer, and dropout in the fully connected layer.

Each user took roughly 30 minutes to build a model that performed to their satisfaction on the training set (recall that, data scientists did not have access to the held out test set) which is far less effort than what would be required if writing linguistic expressions from scratch (by our estimates, person-weeks to cover the close 30, 000 sentences in the training set). Moreover, users selected fewer expressions compared to deep learning's weighted rules (5-8 vs. 188) indicating that HEIDL helps learn parsimonious models thus aiding explainability. Most importantly, HEIDL improves generalization. We did a post-hoc analysis, measuring F1 for all combinations of sets of rules learned by the 4 participants. We report the averages and standard deviations respectively for teams sizes: 1: .32(SD=.17), 2: .46(SD=.1), 3: .52(SD=.06),

and 4: .55(SD=0), showing that F1 increases with team size. On average, teams of 3 produced a F1 of .52 on the test set, as compared to .44 produced by the LSTM, which lacks explainability. We can potentially create a model with less human effort if high expertise exists (i.e., one of our participants subsumed the others in all combinations), if we can determine expertise beforehand. We also chose the top-K best rules from the initial set of linguistic expressions (where K was determined by optimizing over the training set) which produced .41 on the test set. These results indicate that using HEIDL, data scientists can instill their domain expertise into learned linguistic expressions and achieve superior out-of-domain generalization than using supervised learning alone while incurring far less human effort than writing rules from scratch.

5 Demo Overview

Besides *Communication*, other useful labels for labeling sentences in legal contracts include *Term & Termination* (sentences that state contract termination clauses) and *Payment Terms* (sentences that mention payments). The demo will provide an opportunity for attendees to use HEIDL to solve such classification tasks by developing binary classifiers in the form of linguistic expressions. Attendees will be able to access the 28, 000 sentences extracted from IBM procurement contracts and explore the initial 188 linguistic expressions learned using deep learning formed out of 183 predicates along with their associated dictionaries to get a feel for what it takes for a data scientist to develop linguistic expressions for such a challenging real-world domain. In our experience, the first good linguistic expressions usually takes a few seconds of exploration to identify using HEIDL's ranking and filtering features. For example, consider the line: *Notices may be* **transmit***ted electronically*

Clearly, this sentence is referring to exchanging notices between the two parties involved in the contract and hence communication. Such sentences can be labeled with *Communication* via dictionary matching predicates where the dictionary checks for relevant verb (bases) such as such as 'notify' and 'transmit'. More complex linguistic expressions may require combining multiple predicates and entering 'Playground' mode or understanding how expressions work through examples shown by HEIDL. The accompanying video (`https://youtu.be/kicfGDMKu-w`) shows HEIDL in action.

6   Conclusion

Our taxonomy contains many more labels relevant to the contracts domain, each requiring development of linguistic expressions. Testimonies from data scientists confirm that for all labeling tasks, HEIDL was extremely useful. HEIDL is not specifically designed to work with a specific set of predicates nor with rules learned solely using deep learning. As long as the text analytics classification task provides a set of dictionary matching predicates from which a learner can produce accurate initial linguistic expressions, HEIDL can help domain experts instill further domain expertise into them. Even if the domain expert does not modify the linguistic expressions, tools such as HEIDL provide a useful control point that allows humans to verify the model before deploying it which should prove useful in enterprise settings. HEIDL's rule-centric interface provides an interesting counter-point to other HITL-ML methods such as active learning and SEER which are more example-centric. HEIDL is meant to improve productivity of domain experts and while we hope to perform further evaluations in future (on other tasks e.g., sentiment labeling), initial results have yielded promising results.

References

Michael S. Bernstein, Greg Little, Robert C. Miller, Björn Hartmann, Mark S. Ackerman, David R. Karger, David Crowell, and Katrina Panovich. Soylent: A word processor with a crowd inside. In *UIST*.

Nan-Chen Chen, Jina Suh, Johan Verwey, Gonzalo Ramos, Steven Drucker, and Patrice Simard. Anchorviz: Facilitating classifier error discovery through interactive semantic data exploration. In *IUI*.

William W. Cohen, Fan Yang, and Kathryn Rivard Mazaitis. 2017. Tensorlog: Deep learning meets probabilistic dbs. *CoRR*.

Richard Evans and Edward Grefenstette. 2018. Learning explanatory rules from noisy data. *JAIR*.

Maeda F. Hanafi, Azza Abouzied, Laura Chiticariu, and Yunyao Li. 2017. Synthesizing extraction rules from user examples with seer. In *SIGMOD*.

Youxuan Jiang, Catherine Finegan-Dollak, Jonathan K Kummerfeld, and Walter Lasecki. Effective crowdsourcing for a new type of summarization task. In *NAACL*.

Joy Kim, Justin Cheng, and Michael S. Bernstein. Ensemble: Exploring complementary strengths of leaders and crowds in creative collaboration. In *CSCW*.

Rajasekar Krishnamurthy, Yunyao Li, Sriram Raghavan, Frederick Reiss, Shivakumar Vaithyanathan, and Huaiyu Zhu. 2009. SystemT: A System for Declarative Information Extraction. *SIGMOD Record*.

Walter S. Lasecki, Rachel Wesley, Jeffrey Nichols, Anand Kulkarni, James F. Allen, and Jeffrey P. Bigham. Chorus: A crowd-powered conversational assistant. In *UIST*.

Sang Won Lee, Yujin Zhang, Isabelle Wong, Yiwei Yang, Stephanie D. O'Keefe, and Walter S. Lasecki. Sketchexpress: Remixing animations for more effective crowd-powered prototyping of interactive interfaces. In *UIST*.

Luana Micallef, Iiris Sundin, Pekka Marttinen, Muhammad Ammad-ud din, Tomi Peltola, Marta Soare, Giulio Jacucci, and Samuel Kaski. Interactive elicitation of knowledge on feature relevance improves predictions in small data sets. In *IUI*.

Stephen Muggleton. 1996. Learning from positive data. In *Worshop on ILP*.

Jeffrey Pennington, Richard Socher, and Christopher D Manning. 2014. Glove: Global vectors for word representation. In *EMNLP*.

Matthew Richardson and Pedro Domingos. 2006. Markov logic networks. *Machine Learning*.

Burr Settles and Mark Craven. An analysis of active learning strategies for sequence labeling tasks. In *EMNLP*.

Ehsan Sherkat, Seyednaser Nourashrafeddin, Evangelos E. Milios, and Rosane Minghim. Interactive document clustering revisited: A visual analytics approach. In *IUI*.

Alison Smith, Varun Kumar, Jordan Boyd-Graber, Kevin Seppi, and Leah Findlater. Closing the loop: User-centered design and evaluation of a human-in-the-loop topic modeling system. In *IUI*.

Rion Snow, Brendan O'Connor, Daniel Jurafsky, and Andrew Y. Ng. Cheap and fast—but is it good?: Evaluating non-expert annotations for natural language tasks. In *EMNLP*.

Fan Yang, Zhilin Yang, and William W. Cohen. 2017. Differentiable learning of logical rules for knowledge base reasoning. In *NIPS*.

My Turn To Read: An Interleaved E-book Reading Tool for Developing and Struggling Readers

Nitin Madnani   Beata Beigman Klebanov
Anastassia Loukina   Binod Gyawali   John Sabatini
Patrick Lange   Michael Flor
Educational Testing Service, Princeton, NJ, USA
`{nmadnani,bbeigmanklebanov,aloukina,bgyawali,`
`jsabatini,plange,mflor}@ets.org`

Abstract

Literacy is crucial for functioning in modern society. It underpins everything from educational attainment and employment opportunities to health outcomes. We describe My Turn To Read, an app that uses interleaved reading to help developing and struggling readers improve reading skills while reading for meaning and pleasure. We hypothesize that the longer-term impact of the app will be to help users become better, more confident readers with an increased stamina for extended reading. We describe the technology and present preliminary evidence in support of this hypothesis.

1 Introduction

According to the results of the 2017 National Assessment of Educational Progress (NAEP)[1], 32% of U.S. 4th graders read below the Basic level. Most such students lack foundational skills of oral reading fluency – accuracy, reading rate, and prosody. Furthermore, more than a million students *at* the Basic level are also relatively slow readers, have poor prosody, and make more errors than skilled readers (Sabatini et al., 2018).

The combination of low reading accuracy and slow reading rate likely take a toll on a young reader's engagement and motivation to read. While there are many interesting fiction and non-fiction books available to young readers, a slow, laborious reading process can make the act of reading feel like work, not pleasure. The problem is perhaps most acute for children who do not have adults to read with them. Children who do not acquire text fluency in school are left to their own devices to try to bootstrap it without the feedback and motivation usually provided by a knowledgeable and supportive teacher or caretaker.

My Turn To Read (MTTR) is an educational application designed to help such low-proficiency readers improve reading skills through sustained reading with technological support. To make the critical transition from word-by-word reading to fluency, readers need to be engaged in the flow and process of reading for meaning and pleasure, which cannnot occur if getting through every page is a struggle. MTTR can be thought of as a virtual reading companion who narrates part of the story to help enhance engagement and alleviate frustration during reading, and ultimately to help improve confidence, fluency, and reading stamina.

In the next section, we describe the idea of interleaved or turn-based reading and its hypothesized benefits (§2). Next, we describe the MTTR app itself – its features, components, and any NLP & Speech technologies (§3). Next, we discuss the results of trialing MTTR with two summer camps (§4). We conclude with our future plans for MTTR for both additional features as well as additional NLP & Speech technologies (§5).

2 Oral Reading with Turn-Taking

Listening to and engaging in oral reading pervades daily life – parents reading aloud to children, children receiving reading instruction in schools, and adults choosing audio narration (for books & podcasts) as the reading medium that best fits busy schedules. Oral reading fluency is also an important indicator of reading skill (Fuchs et al., 2001).

The main idea behind interleaved book reading is to allow the user to take turns reading aloud from a long, challenging, high-interest book with a virtual partner, realized, in our case, through an audiobook narration. The text of the book is split into paragraphs which are then allocated to alternating narrator and user turns[2]. During the

---

[1] `https://www.nationsreportcard.gov/reading_2017/nation/achievement?grade=4`

[2] The actual number of paragraphs in each turn may vary.

narrator turn, the user listens to the corresponding recording from the audiobook; during the user turns the user is prompted to read the text of the user turn aloud. The narrator and user turns do not overlap – the user continues reading from where the narrator left off, and vice versa.

We hypothesize that (a) the interest in the story and the quality of the narration increases enjoyment, and (b) the interleaving of effortful reading with the more relaxing experience of listening to a skilled narrator allows regular breaks for the user to rebuild stamina to continue reading. The combined effect of (a) and (b) is to make the process sufficiently easygoing and engaging for the user to continue reading the whole book with the app, thus gaining reading practice and boosting their skill, confidence, and enthusiasm as readers.

3   My Turn To Read App

In this section, we describe the current version of the MTTR application. The application is designed to be cross-platform – it works on the web as well as on the iOS and Android mobile platforms. It was particularly important to have mobile versions of the application since (a) it provides more flexibility to the users (i.e., kids can read on a computer or school tablet during school hours and continue reading on a different device at home) and (b) in our preliminary interviews with adult literacy learners – another target demographic of the app – a majority said that they used mobile phones as their *only* computing device.

Mobile versions of MTTR are built using Apache Cordova[3] – a cross-platform toolkit – with platform-specific modifications where necessary. The reading and listening components in all versions are built on top of Readium[4], a robust, standards-compliant, and open-source e-reader. Figure 1 shows a screenshot of the iOS version of MTTR.

As users read with MTTR, it logs information about their interactions. The audio from user turns is recorded and stored. The app also logs rich process data which allow reconstructing the timeline of a user's interaction with the app, such as timestamps for the beginning and end of each user and narrator turn and the answers given to reading comprehension questions (see §3.2). Other than the turn audio, no other personally identifying in-

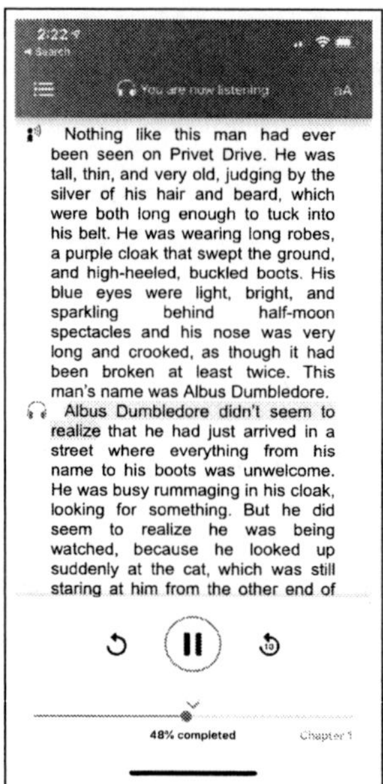

Figure 1: A screenshot of the iOS version of My Turn To Read (MTTR). Start of narrator turn is marked with the headphones & start of user turn is marked with speaker icon. Currently the narrator is reading (see status bar on top); the user can follow the narrator using the yellow highlight and also pause, replay, and rewind.

formation is collected and stored by the app. A separate, secure authentication server stores user-provided email used for registration. All collected data is stored in a secure database with strict access controls and no public access. The user is explicitly notified when the recording is about to start and via a status bar while it is in process.

Next, we describe the salient MTTR features along with the underlying NLP & Speech technologies, where appropriate. A video illustrating most of the user-facing features in action is currently available at https://www.youtube.com/watch?v=Efsl1ZMWFkE.

3.1   Read Aloud eBooks

In order to use a book with MTTR, we need to combine the eBook and the audiobook versions of the book into a new format such that every paragraph is assigned a unique ID and the text is synchronized with the audio in the audiobook. These are necessary to (a) transition between listening and reading and (b) highlight text fragments in the eBook corresponding to the audio being played during narrator turns (as shown in Figure 1). The default highlighting is at the sentence level

---

[3]https://cordova.apache.org
[4]https://readium.org

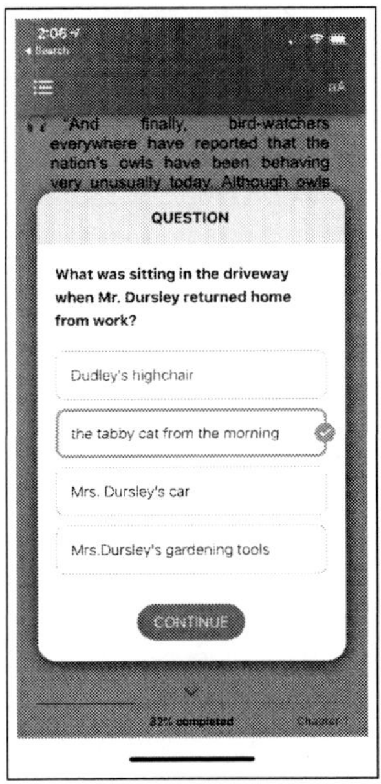
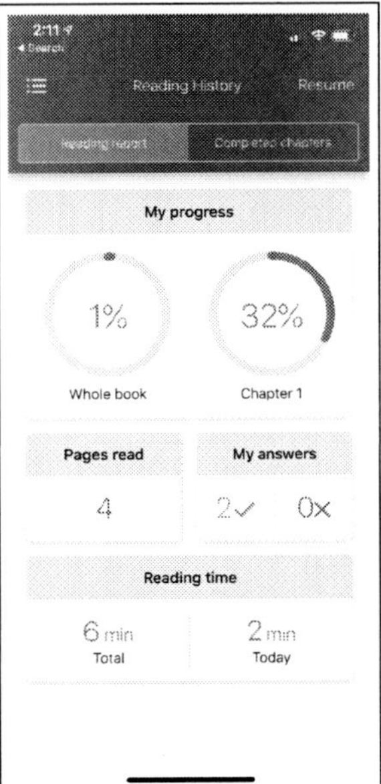
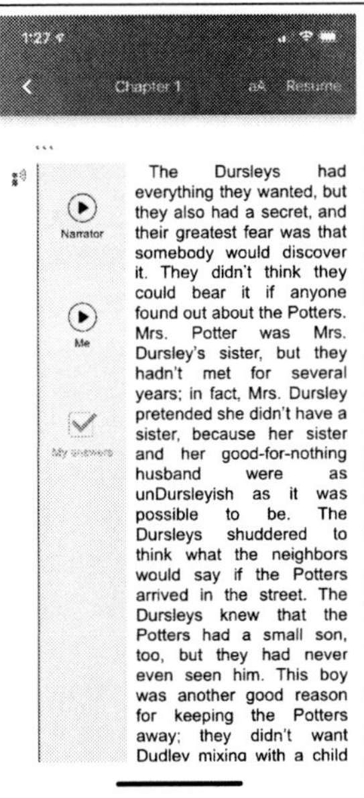

Figure 2: Screenshots illustrating reading comprehension questions and "Reading History" from MTTR: the first screen shows an example question, the second shows a report of the reading activity, and the third shows how readers can interact with already completed turns.

but we manually split long sentences into shorter spans based on syntax & narrator pauses and also make other adjustments to align with sometimes idiosyncratic narrator prosody. The purpose of the highlighting is to make it easier for a struggling reader to follow along during narrator turns, without the highlight moving so often as to be distracting (highlighting each word) or highlighting such large chunks of text as to defeat the purpose of closely following the narrator (highlighting complete sentences, no matter how long).

We use the EPUB format[5] to create what we call a "Read Aloud eBook" used by MTTR. To link the text in the book to the synchronized audio, we use SMIL (Synchronized Multimedia Integration Language), as defined in the EPUB Media Overlays specification. The complete process for generating a Read Aloud eBook is as follows:

1. We use `lxml`[6] to extract the plain text from the original eBook EPUB. We then break up paragraphs into sentences and create a mapping between sentence identifiers and token indices where sentences start and end.

2. We use forced alignment to align words in the normalized text of each chapter to the audio-book MP3 file for this chapter. The alignment is done using the Kaldi ASR toolkit (Povey et al., 2011) and the LibriSpeech acoustic models (Panayotov et al., 2015). The resulting word-level alignment is used to compute the beginning and end timestamps for each sentence. We use Sequitur G2P (Bisani and Ney, 2008) to phonetically transcribe out-of-vocabulary words. The transcriptions are checked manually and added to the lexicon used for forced alignment.

3. We use `ebooklib`[7] to generate a new EPUB file with sentences linked to time segments in the relevant MP3 file using SMIL.

4. We perform the splitting and other manual adjustments in the generated eBook to create subsentential highlighting spans as necessary. We then map any new spans back to the word-level alignment and regenerate the Read Aloud eBook with these spans as the highlighting units, linked via SMIL to audio timestamps. Subsentential spans can also be generated automatically (Parlikar and Black, 2012); we plan to use the manual splits to help improve automated splitting.

[5] http://www.idpf.org/epub
[6] https://github.com/lxml/lxml
[7] https://github.com/aerkalov/ebooklib

143

3.2 Reading Comprehension Questions

To check that users are paying attention to the story and to remind them of important story elements, we created approximately one reading comprehension question (RCQ) for every 100 words of running text. These are surface-level questions focused on the plot, on relationships between characters, on important descriptive details; the answers are usually stated in the text. Users are asked two questions after every other one of their turns. All questions are multiple choice with 2-4 options. Figure 2 shows an example.[8]

We also experimented with automated generation of RCQs using the semantic-role based system described in (Flor and Riordan, 2018). This system generated 1,350 questions for a 228-sentence excerpt from chapter 2 of *Harry Potter and the Sorcerer's Stone*. After removing all the questions that required resolution of pronominal or temporal anaphora to be sufficiently clear, as well as questions that contained incorrect information or were grammatically ill-formed, we were left with 280 questions for a closer examination. These questions were reviewed by an expert who has previously written RCQs used in the app. Of these, 75 (27%) were deemed usable as-is or with a small fix (Q: "Why did Dudley have a tantrum?" A: "because his knickerbocker glory didn't have enough ice cream on top" illustrates Dudley's character; Q: "What did Uncle Vernon shout about once a week?" A: "that Harry needed a haircut" points at something unusual about Harry). Out of 280 questions, 150 (53%) were deemed unacceptable because they asked about a marginal detail (Q: "Who started looking for socks?" A: "Harry"). The remaining 20% of the questions had various problems such as insufficient specificity (Q:"Was Harry punished?" A: "no" requires more precise description of what he was or was not punished for in the particular instance in question), easily answerable based on general knowledge without reading the book (Q: "Who is slithering to the floor?" A: "the great snake"), awkward phrasing (Q: "What did Harry see?" A: "a huge Dudley tantrum coming on"), and too long to be readable (Q: "Had Dudley's gang been chasing him as usual when, as much to Harry's surprise as anyone else's, there he was sitting on the chimney?", A: "yes"). These findings suggest that above and beyond the known challenges of correctness of information and of form and non-anaphoricity, the biggest issue when generating questions based on a 100-word excerpt from a long story is choosing what to ask about. For MTTR, we want questions to also serve as reminders about important plot elements, characterizations, etc., and not just pick up on any minutiae.

3.3 Reading History

MTTR provides a section called "Reading History" containing two sub-sections. "Reading Report" allows users to keep track of how much they have read with MTTR (number of minutes that day and overall), what percentage of the current chapter (and the book) they have completed, and how many RCQs they have answered correctly. "Completed Chapters" allows users to revisit the turns completed so far: they can listen again to the narrator read its own turns and also listen to their own recordings of their turns. In fact, it also allows them to listen to the narrator read *their* turns since the audiobook contains narration for all paragraphs. Listening to themselves and then the narrator allows users to locate areas for improvement. This section also allows users to examine their answers to the questions that have been asked based on a given turn. Figure 2 shows the "Reading History" section from the app.

MTTR contains other useful features not described here in detail due to space limitations. For example, it allows users to adjust turn sizes – a really struggling reader might rely more on the narrator early on but gain the confidence to read aloud more as the book progresses. MTTR also allows readers to *re-record* their turns via "Reading History" if they catch some errors in their reading or get inspired by listening to the narrator.

4 Extrinsic Evaluation

In order for *any* reading app to have an impact on readers' skills – something that develops slowly and gradually – it is necessary for them to actually use the app consistently over a substantial period of time, preferably willingly.

We trialed MTTR with two summer camp programs in the greater NYC area in June–August 2018. One program ran for 6 weeks and included a reading session with the app for 20-50 minutes four days a week, with fewer days in the first week of the camp. The second program ran for a total

---

[8]Figures 1 and 3 are used by permission of the copyright owner Educational Testing Service.

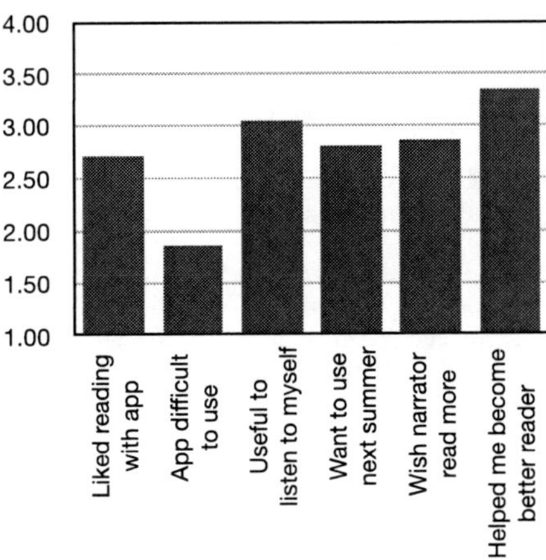

Figure 3: *[Top]* Children reading with MTTR in summer camps. *[Bottom]* Average ratings for MTTR survey questions from responses provided by 25 child participants in summer camp reading sessions. Each question was rated on a 4-point scale.

of 8 weeks (different children were enrolled for a different number of weeks) with a variable reading schedule depending on other camp activities; each reading session included about half an hour of reading and half an hour of related games and activities. All children read *Harry Potter and the Sorcerer's Stone* by J.K. Rowling, with narration by Jim Dale. Children used MTTR on tablets connected to consumer-grade headsets with built-in microphones in a fairly laid-back, informal atmosphere; see Figure 3. A total of 36 children aged 8–11 participated in the two trials.

In both camps, children had the option to stop using the app entirely and engage in another camp activity. Of course, they could also hold the device but not actually *use* the app, or go through the motions of tapping on buttons but not actually do any listening or reading. We found that not only did children use the app when an opportunity was provided (based on the camp program), they also largely engaged with the app productively. In total, we logged more than 61 hours of listening (2,978 narrator turns). Our initial analy-

sis of user turns showed that 1,580 of them were of reasonable duration to make complete bona-fide reading of the turn possible (see (Beigman Klebanov et al., 2019) for details on estimating reasonable turn durations); based on transcriptions of these turns, they in fact contained 111 read words per turn on average. Finally, we also logged 9.5 hours spent answering 2,104 comprehension questions with 65% questions answered correctly. We also asked the children to fill out a survey at the end about their experience with MTTR. Figure 3 shows the the results from the 25 children who completed the surveys.

The fact that an overwhelming majority of the children who started reading with MTTR continued to use it for the duration of their camp enrollment *and* also continued to read aloud is a promising result. Furthermore, the positive responses to survey questions – particularly the one that asked if they believed that MTTR helped them become better readers – also suggest that MTTR has the potential to support extended reading and thus have the hypothesized positive impact.

5 Discussion & Future Work

My Turn To Read is currently in beta and we plan to release freely-available web[9] and mobile (iOS & Android) versions in August of 2019 with the public-domain book *The Adventures of Pinocchio*. We plan to add more books in subsequent releases.

While the functionality implemented in MTTR has already yielded promising results, several avenues of future work are planned or underway.

We are already working on using automated speech recognition to track readers' progress and provide useful automated feedback when appropriate (Loukina et al., 2017). Our plan is to first investigate a server-based speech processing system which will receive the readers' speech over a (secure and encrypted) internet connection[10]. Based on our observations of the offline-vs-online usage and the latency profiles, we may decide that on-device speech processing is a better alternative.

We are working with users and teachers on determining what specific type of oral-reading-based feedback would be most useful (Kannan et al., 2019). Although automated processing of children's speech holds promise for estimating read-

---

[9] https://myturntoread.org.

[10] MTTR stores recordings on-device until an internet connection is available.

ing skill, especially if we aggregate measurements from multiple user turns (Loukina et al., 2018; Wang et al., 2019), feedback for individual user turns is likely to be difficult due to substantial behavioral and technical noise in recordings, e.g., background noise, equipment malfunction, cross-speaker interference, skipped turns, mumbling, etc. (Loukina et al., 2018, 2019). Furthermore, we want to ensure that the feedback does not discourage already struggling readers (e.g., providing fluency scores may not be the right approach).

We plan to continue our work on automated question generation which will help shorten the turn-around time for adding new books.

Finally, we are exploring a use case for MTTR in classrooms in an ongoing trial with grade 3–5 students in an NJ elementary school. Although the results haven't been analyzed quantitatively, preliminary anecdotal evidence shows very positive reactions from both teachers and students.

Our goal is to help students thrive as fluent, confident, and enthusiastic readers; our hope is to be able to demonstrate quantitatively that MTTR can be instrumental in achieving this goal and, eventually, reduce the persistently high proportion of struggling readers in U.S. schools and elsewhere.

6 Acknowledgements

We thank the Astea Solutions team for the app design and development work; K. Dreier, V. Liceralde, J. Bruno, C. Appel, and I. Blood for creating the comprehension questions and K. Dreier also for her help with evaluating the automatically generated questions; J. Lentini for help with the summer camp data collection; Y. Qian and A. Misra for help with ASR. We also thank the site administrators and instructors in the two summer camps for implementing the summer reading program with MyTurnToRead.

References

Beata Beigman Klebanov, Anastassia Loukina, Nitin Madnani, John Sabatini, and Jennifer Lentini. 2019. Would you? Could you? On a tablet? Analytics of Children's eBook reading. In *Proceedings of the 9th International Conference on Learning Analytics & Knowledge*.

Maximilian Bisani and Hermann Ney. 2008. Joint-Sequence Models for Grapheme-to-Phoneme Conversion. *Speech Communication*, 50(5):434 – 451.

Michael Flor and Brian Riordan. 2018. A Semantic Role-based Approach to Open-Domain Automatic Question Generation. In *Proceedings of the BEA Workshop*, pages 254–263.

Lynn S. Fuchs, Douglas Fuchs, Michelle K. Hosp, and Joseph R. Jenkins. 2001. Oral Reading Fluency as an Indicator of Reading Competence: A Theoretical, Empirical, and Historical Analysis. *Scientific Studies of Reading*, 5(3):239–256.

Priya Kannan, Beata Beigman Klebanov, Shiyi Shao, Colleen Appel, and Rodolfo Long. 2019. Evaluating Teachers' Needs for On-going Feedback from a Technology-based Book Reading Intervention. Presented at the Annual Meeting of the National Council on Measurement in Education.

Anastassia Loukina, Beata Beigman Klebanov, Patrick Lange, Binod Gyawali, and Yao Qian. 2017. Developing Speech Processing Technologies for Shared Book Reading with a Computer. In *Proceedings of the 6th International Workshop on Child Computer Interaction (WOCCI)*, pages 46–51.

Anastassia Loukina, Patrick Lange, Yao Qian, Beata Beigman Klebanov, Nitin Madnani, Abhinav Misra, and Klaus Zechner. 2019. The Impact of Ambient Noise on Measurement of Oral Reading Performance. Presented at the Annual Meeting of the National Council on Measurement in Education.

Anastassia Loukina, Beata Beigman Klebanov Nitin Madnani, Abhinav Misra, Georgi Angelov, and Ognjen Todic. 2018. Evaluating On-device ASR on Field Recordings from an Interactive Reading Companion. In *Proceedings of IEEE-SLT*.

Vassil Panayotov, Guoguo Chen, Daniel Povey, and Sanjeev Khudanpur. 2015. Librispeech: An ASR Corpus Based on Public Domain Audio Books. In *Proceedings of the International Conference on Acoustics, Speech and Signal Processing (ICASSP)*.

Alok Parlikar and Alan W. Black. 2012. Modeling Pause-duration for Style-specific Speech Synthesis. In *Proceedings of Interspeech*.

Daniel Povey, Arnab Ghoshal, Gilles Boulianne, Lukas Burget, Ondrej Glembek, ..., and Karel Vesely. 2011. The Kaldi Speech Recognition Toolkit. In *Proceedings of the IEEE Workshop on Automatic Speech Recognition and Understanding (ASRU)*.

John Sabatini, Zuowei Wang, and Tenaha O'Reilly. 2018. Relating Reading Comprehension to Oral Reading Performance in the NAEP Fourth-Grade Special Study of Oral Reading. *Reading Research Quarterly*, 54(2):253–271.

Zuowei Wang, John Sabatini, and Tenaha O'Reilly. 2019. Harry Potter Knows How Well You Read: Estimating Children's Reading Ability from Oral Novel Reading. Presented at the Annual Meeting of the National Council on Measurement in Education.

GrapAL: Connecting the Dots in Scientific Literature

Christine Betts[♠*], **Joanna Power**[♡], **Waleed Ammar**[♡]
♠Paul G. Allen School of Computer Science & Engineering,
University of Washington, Seattle, WA, USA
♡Allen Institute for Artificial Intelligence, Seattle, WA, USA
chrstn@cs.washington.edu, {joannap,waleeda}@allenai.org

Abstract

We introduce GrapAL (Graph database of Academic Literature), a versatile tool for exploring and investigating a knowledge base of scientific literature that was semi-automatically constructed using NLP methods. GrapAL fills many informational needs expressed by researchers. At the core of GrapAL is a Neo4j graph database with an intuitive schema and a simple query language. In this paper, we describe the basic elements of GrapAL, how to use it, and several use cases such as finding experts on a given topic for peer reviewing, discovering indirect connections between biomedical entities, and computing citation-based metrics. We open source the demo code to help other researchers develop applications that build on GrapAL.[1]

1 Introduction

Researchers rely on scientific literature to perform a wide variety of tasks such as searching for papers, assessing applicants for a research position and keeping track of papers published on topics of interest. Several software tools are available to help researchers perform these tasks. For example, many biomedical researchers use PubMed to find papers relevant for their studies,[2] Google Scholar allows researchers to verify and curate their user profiles,[3] and Semantic Scholar extracts research topics, figures, and tables from papers and links them to external content such as slides, videos and GitHub repositories.[4] However, such tools tend to only feature the most commonly used functionalities in order to keep the interface simple for users,

ignoring the long tail of informational needs such as finding experts on a given topic, identifying potential collaborators, assessing influence between research areas, and discovering connections between biological entities.

In this paper, we address these limitations by introducing a tool that provides a flexible and efficient way to query the Semantic Scholar knowledge base, a semi-automatically constructed knowledge base of scientific literature (Ammar et al., 2018). In addition to bridging the gap between available tools and informational needs of researchers, GrapAL demonstrates how semi-automatically constructed knowledge bases can be effectively used to solve real-world problems.

GrapAL is publicly available at `grapal.allenai.org`, along with documentation.[5] In the following section (§2), we introduce the schema and query language used in GrapAL and discuss how users can connect to the database. In §3, we show how GrapAL can be used to satisfy several compelling case studies. In §4, we discuss some of the design choices and the system architecture for GrapAL.

2 How to Use GrapAL

GrapAL is designed to satisfy many use cases requested by Semantic Scholar users who need to process scientific literature. To achieve this, we design GrapAL as a Neo4j property graph with an intuitive schema, making it queryable with the Cypher query language (Francis et al., 2018).

Schema. Fig. 1 demonstrates the schema of our graph database, which consists of 7 node types (displayed in turquoise) and 8 edge types (displayed in purple). The properties associated with

---

*Work done while at the Allen Institute for Artificial Intelligence.

[1] https://github.com/allenai/grapal-website
[2] https://www.ncbi.nlm.nih.gov/pubmed/
[3] https://scholar.google.com/
[4] https://www.semanticscholar.org/

[5] A screencast of the tool is available at https://www.youtube.com/watch?v=1ivX9sHw2RU&feature=youtu.be

Proceedings of the 57th Annual Meeting of the Association for Computational Linguistics-System Demonstrations, pages 147–152
Florence, Italy, July 28 - August 2, 2019. ©2019 Association for Computational Linguistics

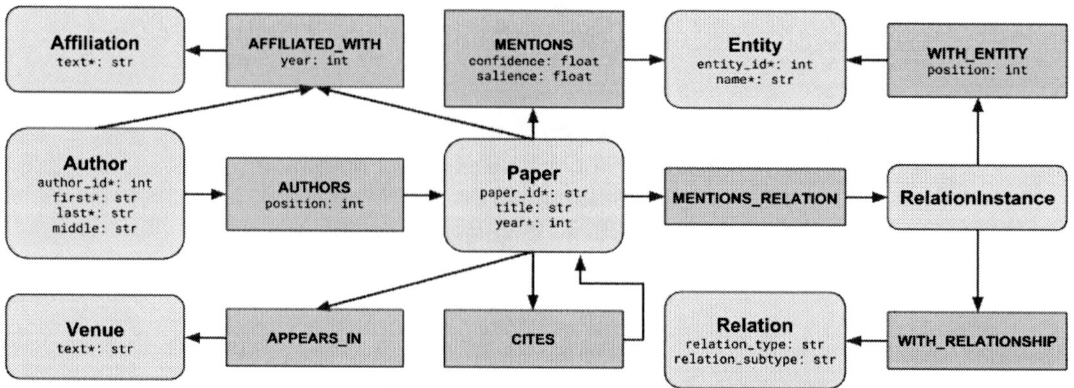

Figure 1: Overview of GrapAL schema. *denotes indexed property.

Node Type	Count	Edge Type	Count
Affiliation*	16M	AFFILIATED_WITH	119M
Author	17M	APPEARS_IN	67M
Entity	493K	AUTHORS	148M
Paper	46M	CITES	693M
Relation	51	MENTIONS	400M
RelationInstance	347K	MENTIONS_RELATION	73M
Venue*	78K	WITH_ENTITY	1M
		WITH_RELATIONSHIP	350K

Table 1: Approximate node and edge cardinalities. (*) indicates node types that are not canonicalized.

each node and edge type are listed. In order to avoid violating intellectual property of publishers, we do not include some information about papers such as the abstract and full text.

At the core of the graph is the `Paper` node. `Paper` nodes may connect to `Venue` nodes, `Author` nodes, `Affiliation` nodes, `Entity` nodes, `RelationInstance` nodes or other `Paper` nodes via APPEARS_IN edges, AUTHORS edges, AFFILIATED_WITH edges, MENTIONS edges, MENTIONS_RELATION edges and CITES edges, respectively. A `RelationInstance` node, e.g., CAUSES[SMOKING,CANCER], represents an n-ary relationship of type `Relation` (via a WITH_RELATIONSHIP edge) between two or more `Entity` nodes (via WITH_ENTITY edges). Details on how we extract entities and various metadata for each paper can be found in Ammar et al. (2018). The only schema changes introduced in this work are including `Affiliation` and `Venue` nodes (and corresponding edge types), and optimizing for query execution time. Table 1 provides the number of instances of each node and edge type in the schema at the time of this writing.

Query Language. Before we discuss realistic case studies in §3, we introduce the query lan-

guage used in GrapAL with a few toy examples:

First, consider the following query that matches arbitrary author nodes in GrapAL and returns the first 10:

```
// Find arbitrary authors.
MATCH (a:Author) RETURN a LIMIT 10
```

More often than not, we only want to match nodes with some desired properties. In the next example, we only match authors with first name 'Clarence' and last name 'Ellis'. Note the round brackets used to specify an instance of node type `Author`, and the curly brackets used to specify its properties.

```
// Find authors by name.
MATCH (a:Author {last: "Ellis", first:
↪   "Clarence"})
RETURN a
```

Alternatively, we could use a WHERE clause to specify the desired properties of matched nodes, as demonstrated in the following example that matches papers by their title. This example also shows how to match nodes by specifying their relation to another node, e.g., authors of a paper. Note the use of square brackets to specify edges and the arrow to specify edge direction.

```
// Find authors of a specific paper.
MATCH (a:Author)-[:AUTHORS]->(p:Paper)
WHERE p.title = "One-shot learning of
↪   object categories"
RETURN a
```

More information about the Cypher query language can be found in Francis et al. (2018).

Connecting to GrapAL. Users can query GrapAL in a variety of methods. First, an interactive graphical interface is available at `https://grapal.allenai.org:7473/browser/` that is suitable for interactive exploration of GrapAL with a relatively small number of results. We demonstrate how the interactive interface could be used in a screencast.[6]

Users can also build web applications that leverage GrapAL through the Neo4j HTTP endpoint.[7] As an example, we have developed a simple web-based application at `https://grapal.allenai.org/app` that can be used to load any of the case studies described in the next section.[8] Users can also type in arbitrary queries, share the queries with collaborators, and download the results in JSON format.

Users can also query the graph natively in their favourite programming language using one of the Neo4j language drivers. Neo4j officially supports five languages: .NET, Java, Javascript, Go and Python, but additional drivers are available.[9] We provide an example of using the Python driver to compute disruption scores as described in Wu et al. (2019).[10]

DOI and ArXivId Compatibility. Users can switch between Digital Object Identifiers (DOIs) or arXiv identifiers (ArXivId) and paper IDs with the Semantic Scholar API[11]. For example, we can look up the paper node corresponding to the DOI 10.1038/nrn3241 by first executing the HTTP query `https://api.semanticscholar.org/v1/paper/10.1038/nrn3241` that returns a JSON object with paper ID 931d6b6ee097eab80b8f89a313c8d3a6d5443cb2. Then, we execute the Cypher query:

```
// Look up paper by ID.
MATCH (p:Paper {paper_id:
  ↪ "931d6b6ee097eab80b8f89a313c8d3
  ↪ a6d5443cb2"})
RETURN p
```

In the future, we plan to add DOI properties and ArXivId properties to the knowledge base.

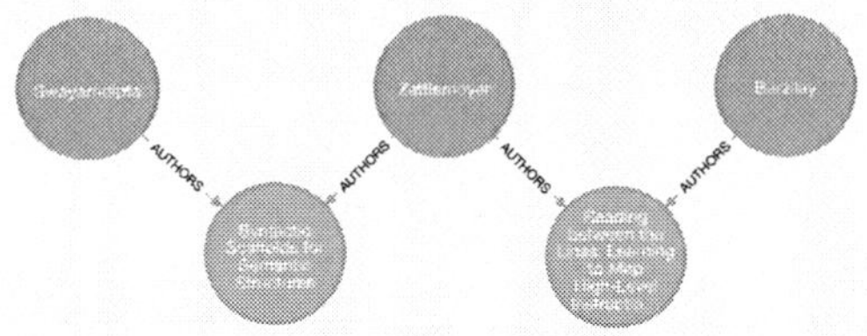

Figure 2: Shortest path between Swabha Swayamdipta and Regina Barzilay.

3   Case Studies

We interviewed computer science and biomedical researchers to better understand the kinds of questions they would like to answer from a knowledge base of scientific literature. In this section, we focus on some of the more compelling use cases that were identified in the interviews, and provide example queries to address them in GrapAL.

For each example we give a link to load the query in the query loader and the full text of the query. From the query loader, users can view or save the results of a query and also copy it to be pasted into the Neo4j browser, where users can view interactive visualizations of the query results.

Shortest Path. Consider a researcher **a** seeking an introduction or an endorsement to work with another researcher **b**. By finding the shortest path between the two researchers in GrapAL, researcher **a** can identify common collaborators connecting the two. The following query, for instance, matches a path connecting Swabha Swayamdipta and Regina Barzilay using authorship edges only, and returns a path that connects them via Luke Zettlemoyer who co-authored papers with both researchers (see Fig. 2).[12]

```
// Find shortest path between two
  ↪ researchers by name.
MATCH p=shortestPath((a:Author)-
  [:AUTHORS*0..6]-(b:Author))
WHERE a.first = "Swabha"
  AND a.last = "Swayamdipta"
  AND b.first = "Regina"
  AND b.last = "Barzilay"
RETURN p
```

In this example, we constrain the number and type of edges in the graph to a maximum of six AUTHORS edges. For authors with an ambiguous name, it may be necessary to specify the author by

---

149

their ID, which can be found by inspecting their author page URL on Semantic Scholar:[13]

```
// Find shortest path between two
↪    researchers, one by author ID.
MATCH p=shortestPath((a:Author)-
    [:AUTHORS*0..6]-(b:Author))
WHERE a.author_id = 2705113
    AND b.first = "Regina"
    AND b.last = "Barzilay"
RETURN p
```

Similar queries can be used to find colleagues who published at a given venue, or currently work at a given university or research lab.

Finding Experts. One of the pain points in organizing a conference is identifying reviewers who are knowledgeable about the research topics discussed in submitted papers. By querying GrapAL, members of the organizing committee will be able to find more competent reviewers, while relying less on their (often biased) professional network when deciding whom to invite for peer reviewing. For example, the following query can be used to find researchers who published the most on "Relationship extraction" since 2013.[14]

```
// Find authors who published the most
↪    on relation extraction since 2013.
MATCH (a:Author)-[:AUTHORS]->(p:Paper),
    (p)-[:MENTIONS]->
    (:Entity {name: "Relationship
        extraction"})
WHERE p.year > 2013
WITH a, count(p) as cp
RETURN a, cp
ORDER BY cp DESC
```

Here, we use ORDER BY cp DESC to sort the authors by the number of papers they published on this topic. In order to find the node that represents a topic of interest in GrapAL, users could use the search feature on semantic scholar and inspect the relevant topic page URL for the entity ID, or use regular expressions to query GrapAL, e.g.,[15]

```
// Fuzzy matching of entity names.
MATCH (e:Entity)
WHERE e.name =~ "(?i)relationship
    extraction"
RETURN e
```

---

[13]E.g., Swabha Swayamdipta's author page URL is https://www.semanticscholar.org/author/ Swabha-Swayamdipta/2705113

[14]This query can be loaded and modified at https:// grapal.allenai.org/app/?example=experts

[15]This query can be loaded and modified at https://grapal.allenai.org/app/?example= canonical-entity

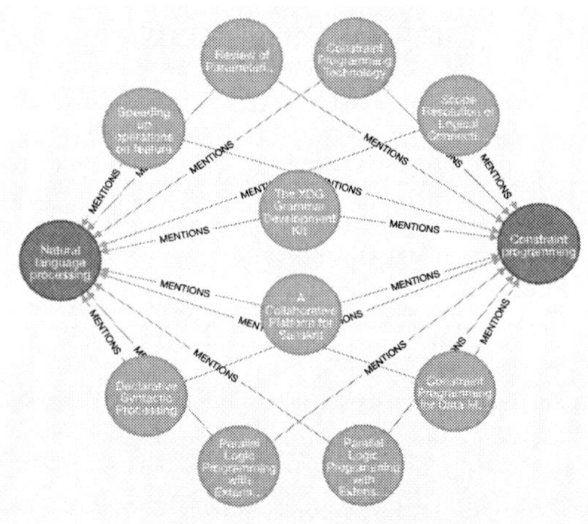

Figure 3: Ten papers that mention both 'Natural language processing' and 'Constraint programming.'.

Papers at the Intersection of Entities. Search engine results sometimes make it difficult to find papers that discuss multiple topics or fields. With GrapAL, we can return papers that discuss any number of entities of interest, e.g., "Constraint programming" and "Natural language processing". Fig. 3 shows a visualization of the results on the Neo4j browser, limited to 10 papers.[16]

```
// Find papers which mention both
↪    constraint programming and natural
↪    language processing.
MATCH (p:Paper)-[:MENTIONS]->
    (e1:Entity {name: "Constraint
        programming"}),
    (p:Paper)-[:MENTIONS]->
    (e2:Entity {name: "Natural language
        processing"})
RETURN p
```

Connecting Scientific Concepts. Some researchers wanted to explore direct and indirect connections between two scientific concepts (entities) of interest, e.g., the impact of 'adjuvant antiestrogen therapy (Arimidex)' on 'estrogen receptors'. Using GrapAL, we can find how two entities are indirectly connected via coded relationships and a chain of entities in the knowledge base, which can help generate new hypotheses or quickly assess the viability of a hypothesis before conducting expensive lab experiments.[17]

---

[16]This query can be loaded and modified at https://grapal.allenai.org/app/?example= intersecting-entities

[17]This query can be loaded and modified at https://grapal.allenai.org/app/?example= scientific-concepts

```
// Find path between Estrogen Receptors
↪    and Arimidex via coded
↪    relationships.
MATCH path=shortestPath(
    (er:Entity {name: "Estrogen
        Receptors"})-
    [:WITH_ENTITY*0..15]-
    (ar:Entity {name: "Arimidex"}))
WITH nodes(path) as ns
UNWIND ns as n
MATCH (n)-[:WITH_ENTITY {position: 0}]->
    (e0:Entity),
    (n)-[:WITH_ENTITY {position: 1}]->
        (e1:Entity),
    (n)-[:WITH_RELATIONSHIP]->
        (r:Relation)
RETURN e0, r, e1
```

This query returns a list of triples (e0, r, e1) that connect 'Arimidex' to 'Estrogen Receptors'. The UNWIND operator allows us to examine each node on the shortest path and process it as needed.

Citation-Based Metrics. Citations are often used as a proxy for the impact of papers, researchers or venues. In addition to computing traditional metrics such as h-index and i10-index, GrapAL can also be used to compute more granular metrics, e.g., to estimate the rate at which papers in one conference cite papers in another conference:[18]

```
// Find the number of times a NAACL
↪    paper cites a CVPR paper.
MATCH (p1:Paper)-[:APPEARS_IN]->
    (naacl:Venue),
(p2:Paper)-[:APPEARS_IN]->(cvpr:Venue),
path=((p1)-[:CITES]->(p2))
WHERE naacl.text =~ ".*NAACL.*"
AND cvpr.text =~ ".*CVPR.*"
RETURN count(path)
```

This query returns the number of times a NAACL paper cites a CVPR paper. We use the =~ operator to match on venue names by regular expression because venues are stored as unstructured strings.

4 System Design

Graph Database. Due to the high connectivity in the data and the nature of queries GrapAL is designed for, we opted to create GrapAL using a graph-native database instead of a more conventional relational database. Unlike a relational database, a graph database provides a natural and efficient way to query and traverse multi-hop relations without using computationally expensive join operations. Several graph database systems have recently become available, including AWS Neptune, Grakn.ai, dgraph and Neo4j. We decided to build GrapAL on Neo4j since it is one of the more mature platforms, has a strong community of developers, and is the most widely used graph database system as of the time of this writing.[19] One limitation of Neo4j is that it is not a distributed database system, but we were able to fit GrapAL on a single server.

Building and Deploying GrapAL. GrapAL is powered by the same data that powers the `semanticscholar.org` website, as described in Ammar et al. (2018). We use a *staging server* to read a snapshot of the data as Spark DataFrames from AWS S3 and write CSV files that match the property schema described earlier. Due to the sheer amount of records, we process different shards of the data in parallel before aggregating all shards into one CSV file for each node and edge type of the schema. Then, we use the Neo4j CSV import function to build the database. Once we've built the database, we start up a Neo4j server and run a Cypher script to create indexes. The staging server is an EC2 machine with instance type `r5.24xlarge`. This process takes around 6 hours and the resulting database is roughly 80 GB (including indexes).

Once the data is imported, the database files are copied over to a *production server* that serves the dataset publicly and has lower processor and memory requirements compared to the staging server. The staging server is an EC2 machine with instance type `r4.16xlarge`. We plan to rebuild GrapAL at a monthly cadence with new snapshots of the data.

5 Related Work

Related APIs are available to help researchers navigate scientific literature. Singh et al. (2018) provides an API to interact with the ACL anthology. However, it is limited to the areas of computational linguistics and natural langauge processing, and it uses a predefined list of query templates with placeholders for authors, papers and venues. Springer Nature SciGraph [20] provides an API for accessing publication metadata from the Springer Nature corpus, but it is limited to papers and books

---

[18]This query can be loaded and modified at
`https://grapal.allenai.org/app/?example=citation-metrics`

[19]`https://db-engines.com/en/ranking/graph+dbms`

[20]`https://scigraph.springernature.com/explorer`

published by Springer Nature. The Microsoft Academic Graph (Shen et al., 2018) is similarly an API for examining academic literature. As a relational database, it is hard to query with complex, multi-hop relations as discussed in §4. This work is also related to a line of NLP work focusing on scientific documents including citation prediction (e.g., Yogatama et al., 2011; Bhagavatula et al., 2018), author modeling (e.g., Sim et al., 2015), stylometry (e.g., Bergsma et al., 2012), bibliometrics (e.g., Foulds and Smyth, 2013; Weihs and Etzioni, 2017) and information extraction (e.g., Kergosien et al., 2018; Andruszkiewicz and Hazan, 2018).

6 Conclusion

GrapAL is a versatile tool for exploring and investigating scientific literature built on the Neo4j graph database framework. We describe the basic elements of GrapAL, how to use it, and use cases such as finding experts on a given topic for peer reviewing, discovering indirect connections between biomedical entities, and computing citation-based metrics.

Future improvements include more metadata and changes to the structure of affiliation and venue data. We intend to change the data pipeline architecture to perform event-based incremental updates rather than a regular batch build. We continue to improve the models used to populate GrapAL's nodes and edges (e.g., author disambiguation and entity extraction and linking).

Acknowledgments

We thank Khaled Ammar for his graph database suggestions, Michal Guerquin for his help in designing and building the pipeline, and Darrell Plessas for his technical assistance. We also thank Noah Smith and the Semantic Scholar team for their support.

References

Waleed Ammar, Dirk Groeneveld, Chandra Bhagavatula, Iz Beltagy, Miles Crawford, Doug Downey, Jason Dunkelberger, Ahmed Elgohary, Sergey Feldman, Vu Ha, Rodney Kinney, Sebastian Kohlmeier, Kyle Lo, Tyler Murray, Hsu-Han Ooi, Matthew E. Peters, Joanna Power, Sam Skjonsberg, Lucy Lu Wang, Chris Wilhelm, Zheng Yuan, Madeleine van Zuylen, and Oren Etzioni. 2018. Construction of the literature graph in semantic scholar. In *Proc. of NAACL*.

Piotr Andruszkiewicz and Rafal Hazan. 2018. Annotated corpus of scientific conference's homepages for information extraction. In *Proc. of LREC*.

Shane Bergsma, Matt Post, and David Yarowsky. 2012. Stylometric analysis of scientific articles. In *Proc. of NAACL*.

Chandra Bhagavatula, Sergey Feldman, Russell Power, and Waleed Ammar. 2018. Content-based citation recommendation. In *Proc. of NAACL*.

James Foulds and Padhraic Smyth. 2013. Modeling scientific impact with topical influence regression. In *Proc. of EMNLP*.

Nadime Francis, Alastair Green, Paolo Guagliardo, Leonid Libkin, Tobias Lindaaker, Victor Marsault, Stefan Plantikow, Mats Rydberg, Petra Selmer, and Andrés Taylor. 2018. Cypher: An evolving query language for property graphs. In *Proc. of SIGMOD*.

Eric Kergosien, Amin Farvardin, Maguelonne Teisseire, Marie-Noëlle Bessagnet, Joachim Schöpfel, Stéphane Chaudiron, Bernard Jacquemin, Annig Lacayrelle, Mathieu Roche, Christian Sallaberry, and Jean-Philippe Tonneau. 2018. Automatic identification of research fields in scientific papers. In *Proc. of LREC*.

Zhihong Shen, Hao Ma, and Kuansan Wang. 2018. A web-scale system for scientific knowledge exploration. In *Proc. of ACL*.

Yanchuan Sim, Bryan Routledge, and Noah A. Smith. 2015. A utility model of authors in the scientific community. In *Proc. of EMNLP*.

Mayank Singh, Pradeep Dogga, Sohan Patro, Dhiraj Barnwal, Ritam Dutt, Rajarshi Haldar, Pawan Goyal, and Animesh Mukherjee. 2018. Cl scholar: The acl anthology knowledge graph miner. In *Proc. of NAACL*.

Luca Weihs and Oren Etzioni. 2017. Learning to predict citation-based impact measures. In *Proc. of ACM/IEEE Joint Conference on Digital Libraries*, pages 49–58. IEEE Press.

Lingfei Wu, Dashun Wang, and James A. Evans. 2019. Large teams develop and small teams disrupt science and technology. *Nature*, 566:378–382.

Dani Yogatama, Michael Heilman, Brendan O'Connor, Chris Dyer, Bryan R. Routledge, and Noah A. Smith. 2011. Predicting a scientific community's response to an article. In *Proc. of EMNLP*.

ClaimPortal: Integrated Monitoring, Searching, Checking, and Analytics of Factual Claims on Twitter

Sarthak Majithia   Fatma Arslan   Sumeet Lubal
Damian Jimenez   Priyank Arora   Josue Caraballo   Chengkai Li
Department of Computer Science and Engineering
The University of Texas at Arlington

Abstract

We present ClaimPortal, a web-based platform for monitoring, searching, checking, and analyzing English factual claims on Twitter. We explain the architecture of ClaimPortal, its components and functions, and the user interface. While the last several years have witnessed a substantial growth in interests and efforts in the area of computational fact-checking, ClaimPortal is a novel infrastructure in that fact-checkers have largely skipped factual claims in tweets. It can be a highly powerful tool to both general web users and fact-checkers. It will also be an educational resource in helping cultivate a society that is less susceptible to falsehoods. While it currently focuses on politics-related tweets, it will be extended to include more general factual claims.

1 Introduction

The spreading of falsehoods on the web has adverse effects on a myriad of aspects in our society. Politicians are doubling down on claims that are demonstrably false because of the safety net that "fake news" affords them. These efforts to manipulate and distort public opinions in order to gain political leverage can have negative effects on a democracy, and they can even result in the potential manipulation of democratic election results.

At news organizations such as The Washington Post, New York Times and FactCheck.org, professional fact-checkers take on the hard battle to counter misinformation and disinformation. They vet claims by analyzing relevant data and documents and publishing their verdicts. For instance, PolitiFact.com gives factual claims truthfulness ratings such as true, half true, false, and even "pants on fire". However, there is simply far more misinformation on the web than what fact-checkers can keep up with. The process of fact-checking is laborious and intellectually demand-

ing, as it takes the professionals about one day to research and write a typical article about a factual claim (Hassan et al., 2015a). This difficulty leaves many harmful claims unchecked, since fact-checking organizations can only use their limited resources to focus on national events and prominent figures.

This problem of unchecked claims is exacerbated on social media. On the one hand, it is unlikely fact-checkers are able to check every social media post, due to limited resources and the sheer volume of data. [1] On the other hand, a large number of false claims, likely much more than those in traditional media, are being spread through social media. This can be due to the compounded effect of several factors: social media platforms have become increasingly important to public figures and organizations in engaging with voters and citizens; mobile devices have brought an age in which sharing and disseminating information is easy for anyone, including both malicious and unintentional creators of falsehoods; the falsehoods are further replicated and amplified by social media bots and clickbait articles. The consequence can be devastating. For instance, a recent study reports that a sample of 140,000 Twitter users in the battleground state of Michigan shared as many junk news items as professional news during the final ten days of the 2016 election, each constituting 23% of the web links they shared on Twitter in that period. [2]

In this paper we present ClaimPortal, a web-based platform for monitoring, searching, checking, and analytics of factual claims on Twitter. ClaimPortal is available at `https://idir.uta.edu/claimportal`. ClaimPortal continuously collects tweets and *monitors* factual

---

[1] `https://mashable.com/article/snopes-stops-fact-checking-for-facebook/`
[2] `http://politicalbots.org/?p=1064`

Proceedings of the 57th Annual Meeting of the Association for Computational Linguistics-System Demonstrations, pages 153–158
Florence, Italy, July 28 - August 2, 2019. ©2019 Association for Computational Linguistics

claims embedded in tweets. It is *integrated with fact-checking tools*, including a claim matcher which finds known fact-checks matching any given tweet, a claim spotter which scores each claim and the corresponding tweet based on their check-worthiness, i.e., how important it is to fact-check them. ClaimPortal provides an intuitive and convenient *search interface* that assists its users to sift through these factual claims in tweets using filtering conditions on dates, twitter accounts, content, hashtags, check-worthiness scores, and types of claims. ClaimPortal also provides simple *analytics and visualization* tools for discovering patterns pertinent to how certain twitter accounts make claims, how different types of claims are distributed, and so on.

The initial call to arms to research on computational fact-checking was made nearly a decade ago (Cohen et al., 2011). The last several years have witnessed a substantial growth in interests and efforts in this arena. These efforts tackle various fronts, from detecting important factual claims that are worth checking (Hassan et al., 2015b; Jimenez and Li, 2018), to using databases for discerning factual claims' robustness (Wu et al., 2017) and truthfulness (Ciampaglia et al., 2015; Shi and Weninger, 2016; Jo et al., 2019), to building end-to-end fact-checking systems (Babakar and Moy, 2016; Hassan et al., 2017a,b), and visualizing the spread of claims (Shao et al., 2016). ClaimPortal is a novel infrastructure in that fact-checkers have largely skipped factual claims in tweets, especially those from less prominent accounts, due to limited resources.

2 System Architecture and Components

2.1 System Architecture

ClaimPortal is composed of a front-end web based GUI, a MySQL database, an Elasticsearch [3] search engine, an API, and several decoupled batch data processing components (Figure 1). The system operates on two layers. The *front-end presentation layer* allows users to narrow down search results by applying multiple filters. Keyword search on tweets is powered by Elasticsearch which is coupled with querying the database to provide additional filters. Additionally, it provides numerous visualized graphs. The *back-end data collection and computation layer* performs pre-processing

---

[3]https://www.elastic.co/products/
elasticsearch

of tweets, computing check-worthiness scores of tweets using the public ClaimBuster API (Hassan et al., 2017a), Elasticsearch batch insertion, detecting claim types of tweets, and finding similar fact-checked claims for each tweet, using Claim-Buster API. ClaimPortal stays up-to-date with current tweets by periodically calling the Twitter REST API.

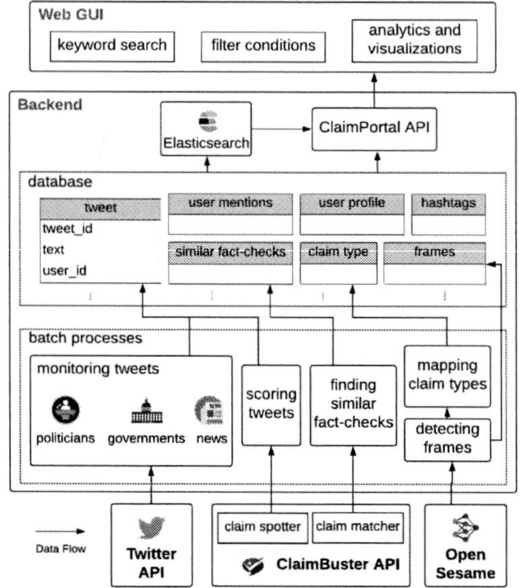

Figure 1: ClaimPortal system architecture.

2.2 Monitoring, Processing, and Storing Tweets

ClaimPortal at this moment focuses on politically-charged tweets, but will be expanded to eventually cover all types of tweets. We curated a list of prominent Tweet handles in U.S. politics that include but are not limited to house representatives and senators in the Congress, governors, city mayors, U.S. Cabinet members, other government officials, and political teams of news media. We then made use of the *user_timeline* endpoint of the Twitter REST API to navigate through each user's timeline and collected their tweets. More specifically, we navigated through the historic data of a user's timeline, which is a one-time process. We then keep our data up-to-date by continuously monitoring newly posted tweets. As of April 10, 2019, ClaimPortal monitors 3,200 Twitter handles and has collected approximately 3.3 million tweets after being deployed in mid-January 2019. We are working on substantially expanding the curated list of Twitter handles.

Claim Type	FrameNet Frames
Conflict	Invading, Attack, Explosion, Destroying, Hostile encounter, Use firearm, Shoot projectiles, Downing, Protest, Political actions
Life	Giving birth, Being born, Death, Killing, Forming relationships, Cause harm, Personal relationship, Dead or alive
Movement	Self motion, Inhibit movement, Travel, Departing, Arriving, Visiting, Motion, Cause motion, Bringing
Transaction	Import export scenario, Commerce buy, Commerce sell, Getting, Commerce pay, Borrowing, Giving
Business	Activity start, Conquering, Endeavor failure, Intentionally create, Business closure, Locale closure
Contact	Meet with, Discussion, Come together, Communication, Contacting, Communication means, Text creation, Request
Personnel	Take place of, Get a job, Hiring, Appointing, Removing, Firing, Quitting, Choosing, Becoming a member, Change of leadership
Justice	Arrest, Imprisonment, Detaining, Extradition, Breaking out captive, Try defendant, Pardon, Appeal, Verdict, Sentencing, Fining, Execution, Releasing, Notification of charges
Comparison	Comparing two entities, Comparing at two different points in time
Quantity	Change position on scale, Creating, Causation, Cause change of position on a scale, Occupy rank, Ratio
Stance	Taking sides, Opinion, Be in agreement on assessment, Vote, Oppose and Support Consistency
Speech	Statement, Affirm or deny, Telling

Table 1: Claim types and their corresponding FrameNet frames. Frames in red color are created by us.

ClaimPortal's back-end layer focuses on data processing and storage. The Twitter REST API provides us with the necessary data. However, the system does not require all of it. In fact, a lot of the API's response is discarded to keep our database small and yet sufficient enough to provide all necessary information for the portal. This is achieved through the ClaimPortal API. The API is a web service designed using Python and the Flask [4] micro-framework. It provides end points for loading tweets on the GUI, search for hashtags, and search for users in applying from-user and user-mention filters. Based on the keyword search and filters requested by a user, the API queries the database to find the resulting list of tweet IDs and returns the list as a JSON response. A tweet ID is a unique number assigned to a tweet by Twitter. By using Twitter's card API [5] the system dynamically populates the latest activity of a tweet at the front-end, based on its ID.

The MySQL database has several normalized tables. For each tweet the database stores its text, when it was created, and who tweeted it. The database also stores information about re-tweets and quoted-tweets, hashtags and URLs mentioned in the tweets, and information about the accounts mentioned in the tweets.

ClaimPortal uses Elasticsearch to support keyword search over the stored tweets. Since Elasticsearch is equipped with incremental indexing, the system periodically feeds Elasticsearch the delta tweets since last update for indexing. For this the system uses a decoupled background batch process that takes care of incrementally inserting tweets and updating the Elasticsearch index.

2.3 Claim Spotter

In ClaimPortal, each tweet is given a check-worthiness score which denotes whether the tweet has a factual claim of which the truthfulness is important to the public. This score is obtained by probing the ClaimBuster API,[6] a well-known fact-checking tool, developed by our research group, that is being used by professional fact-checkers on a regular basis (Adair et al., 2019). Claim-Buster (Hassan et al., 2017a; Jimenez and Li, 2018) is a classification and ranking model trained on a human-labeled dataset of 8,000 sentences from past U.S. presidential debates. The Claim-Buster API returns a check-worthiness score for any given text. The score is on a scale from 0 to 1, ranging from least check-worthy to most check-worthy. The background task of probing Claim-Buster API for getting scores for tweets is another batch process, in parallel with the tweet collection and the Elasticsearch indexing processes.

2.4 Detecting Claim Types

ClaimPortal uses tweets to gain insights into factual claims that are being spread, by whom, how often, and whether they are true. To answer these questions we categorize tweets by the types of factual claims they promote. We employed a collection of FrameNet frames (Baker et al., 1998) and created several new frames specifically for factual claims. We then adopted the study of mapping frames to event types (Spiliopoulou et al., 2017).

2.4.1 Frame detection

FrameNet is a linguistic resource for English comprised of 1,224 manually established semantic *frames*. Each frame provides information about both the linguistic and the semantic structure of a type of event, situation, object, or relation along with its participants. The participants, called

---

[4] http://flask.pocoo.org

[5] https://developer.twitter.com/en/ docs/tweets/optimize-with-cards

[6] https://idir.uta.edu/claimbuster/

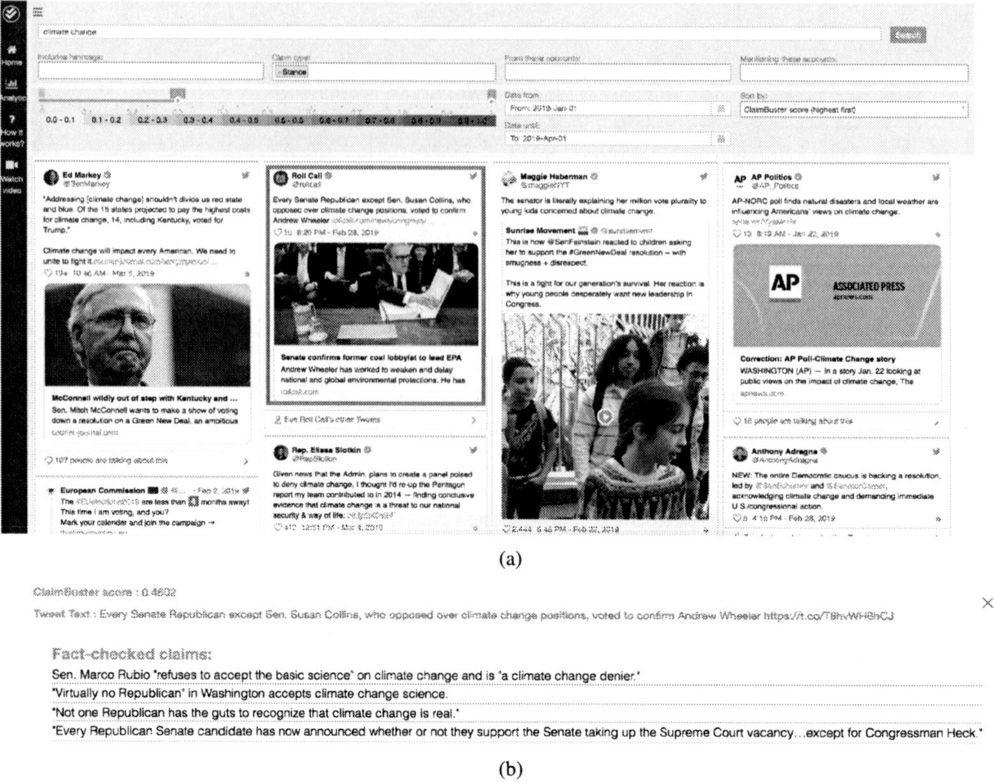

(a)

(b)

Figure 2: (a) ClaimPortal user interface. (b) Similar fact-checks for the highlighted tweet in Figure (a).

frame elements, are frame-specific semantic roles that provide additional information. Each frame is evoked by a set of lexical units, or words, which are a composition of the lemma and meaning of the word.

We created new frames after conducting a survey of existing fact-checks from PolitiFact [7] and followed it by grouping together semantically and syntactically similar factual claims from these fact-checks. If a group of claims did not share a common existing frame, we created a new frame for it. Details of these purposely created new frames can be found in (Arslan et al., 2019). The corpus of the newly-defined frames along with their annotated exemplary sentences is publicly available. [8]

We used open-sesame (Swayamdipta et al., 2017), a recurrent neural network based frame-semantic parser, to detect all possible frames a tweet can potentially hold. We retrained open-sesame on FrameNet 1.7 dataset after extending it with annotated sentences for the newly defined frames.

Open-sesame works as a pipeline of several tasks: target identification (detecting all lexical units), frame identification (detecting all frames in a sentence), and argument identification.

2.4.2 Claim type mapper

In (Spiliopoulou et al., 2017) eight ACE event types were listed along with their mapped frames: *Business, Conflict, Contact, Justice, Life, Movement, Personnel,* and *Transaction*. To accommodate the new frames explained in Section 2.4.1, we extended this list by introducing four new event types, namely *Comparison, Quantity, Stance,* and *Speech,* and their corresponding frames (Table 1). In ensuing discussion, we refer to these event types as *claim types,* for simplicity of terminology. More specifically, *Comparison* is for claims that show entities involved in some sort of comparisons based on some criteria, *Quantity* presents claims with quantities, *Stance* is for claims that have entities with viewpoints towards issues, events, etc., and *Speech* is for claims that communicate some messages in the written or spoken form. A script identifies the claim types of each tweet by mapping identified frames to their corresponding claim

---

[7]https://www.politifact.com

[8]https://github.com/idirlab/factframe

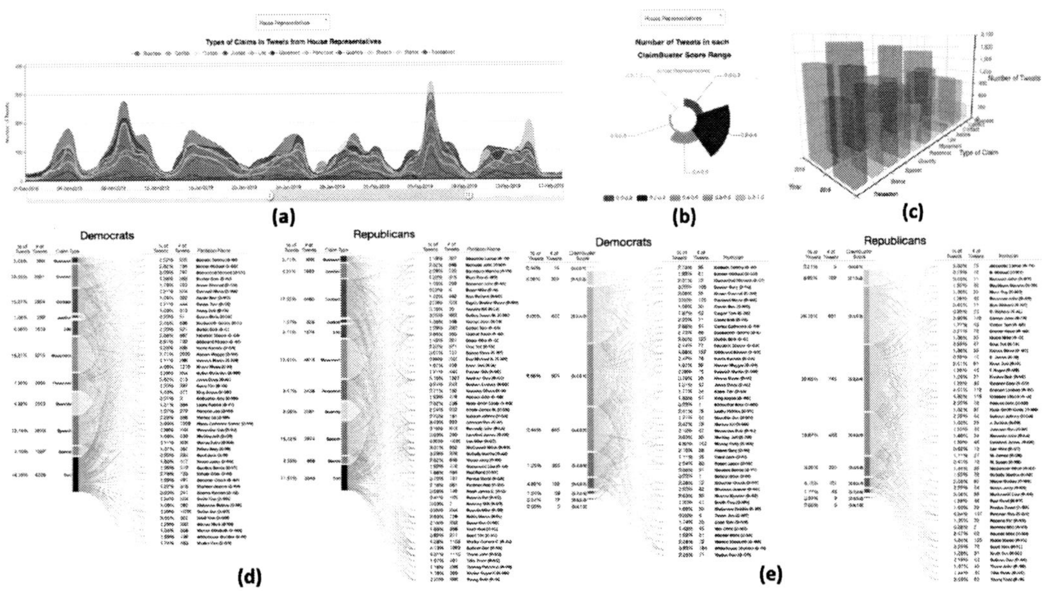

Figure 3: Examples of visualizations on ClaimPortal website.

types. A tweet can have multiple claim types.

2.5 Claim Matcher

Claim matching is an important step in the work-flow of fact-checking. Given a factual claim, it aims at finding identical or similar claims from a repository of existing fact-checks. The premise is that public figures keep making the same false claims. While politicians may refrain themselves from making outright false claims to avoid being fact-checked, oftentimes they even double down after their false claims are debunked. [9]

ClaimPortal leverages the claim matching function in the ClaimBuster API. The fact-check repository is composed of the Share-the-facts [10] fact checks as well as fact checks collected from several fact-checking organizations like PolitiFact, Snopes, factcheck.org, Washington Post, etc. The system measures the similarity between a claim and a fact-check based on the similarity of their tokens. An Elasticsearch server is deployed for searching the repository based on token similarity.

3 User Interface Features

ClaimPortal enables a user to sift through the tweets using multiple filters. The important filters are as follows. **(1) Keyword search:** It allows users to make a text-based search by key-words such as "climate change". **(2) Hashtags:** It allows users to further filter tweets by hashtags such as "#116thCongress" or "#2020". **(3) Claim type:** It enables users to search for tweets with a specific claim type, e.g., *Conflict* or *Stance*. **(4) From:** It looks for tweets posted by a particular user handle, e.g., "@realDonaldTrump". **(5) Mentions:** The search results can be filtered further by user mentions (i.e., using "@" to tag a user in a tweet, e.g., "@POTUS"). **(6) ClaimBuster score:** ClaimPortal also offers a slider to filter results based on a ClaimBuster score range. The result tweets are automatically updated as the slider is moved. **(7) Date range:** Additionally, the portal offers a date picker to filter tweets based on their creation dates. Figure 2a shows ClaimPortal user interface with the search results of a sample query. The sample query contains the following filtering conditions: a keyword "climate change", a claim type *Stance*, a range of ClaimBuster score from 0.3 to 1.0, and a date range from January 1, 2019 to April 1, 2019. Moreover, the ClaimPortal shares previously fact-checked claims with users by displaying matching fact-checks after a tweet's card view is clicked at. Figure 2b depicts the matching fact-checks of the highlighted tweet in Figure 2a.

4 Analytics and Visualizations

We work to make ClaimPortal the repository where one can find all factual claims made on

[9] https://wapo.st/2rucTq8
[10] http://www.sharethefacts.org/

Twitter. It can be a powerful tool for a diverse group of users. It enables web users to explore and analyze factual claims in tweets at scale. We use analytics and visualizations to shed more light on the importance of ClaimPortal and bring the hidden patterns in the data to light. For instance, a user can compare tweets from different political groups in detail based on check-worthiness of their claims and variety of their claims. Figures 3d and 3e compare Democratic Senators and Republican Senators based on the types of claims they made and check-worthiness of their claims. Figure 3a depicts the spread of all claim types made by different group of politicians in the past one year and Figure 3b shows the distribution of tweets over five ClaimBuster score ranges made by different group of U.S. politicians such as the 2020 presidential election candidates.

Acknowledgments

The work is partially supported by NSF grant IIS-1719054 and subawards from Duke University as part of a grant to the Duke Tech & Check Cooperative from the Knight Foundation and Facebook. Any opinions, findings, and conclusions or recommendations expressed in this publication are those of the authors and do not necessarily reflect the views of the funding agencies.

References

Bill Adair, Mark Stencel, Cathy Clabby, and Chengkai Li. 2019. The human touch in automated fact-checking: How people can help algorithms expand the production of accountability journalism. In *Computation+Journalism Symposium*.

Fatma Arslan, Damian Jimenez, Josue Caraballo, Gensheng Zhang, and Chengkai Li. 2019. Modeling factual claims by frames. In *Computation+Journalism Symposium*.

Mevan Babakar and Will Moy. 2016. The state of automated fact-checking. *Full Fact*.

Collin F. Baker, Charles J. Fillmore, and John B. Lowe. 1998. The berkeley framenet project. In *ACL*, pages 86–90.

Giovanni Luca Ciampaglia, Prashant Shiralkar, Luis M. Rocha, Johan Bollen, Filippo Menczer, and Alessandro Flammini. 2015. Computational fact checking from knowledge networks. *PLOS ONE*, 10:1–13.

Sarah Cohen, Chengkai Li, Jun Yang, and Cong Yu. 2011. Computational journalism: A call to arms to database researchers. In *CIDR*, pages 148–151.

Naeemul Hassan, Bill Adair, James T. Hamilton, Chengkai Li, Mark Tremayne, Jun Yang, and Cong Yu. 2015a. The quest to automate fact-checking. In *Computation+Journalism Symposium*.

Naeemul Hassan, Fatma Arslan, Chengkai Li, and Mark Tremayne. 2017a. Toward automated fact-checking: Detecting check-worthy factual claims by claimbuster. In *KDD*, pages 1803–1812.

Naeemul Hassan, Chengkai Li, and Mark Tremayne. 2015b. Detecting check-worthy factual claims in presidential debates. In *CIKM*, pages 1835–1838.

Naeemul Hassan, Gensheng Zhang, Fatma Arslan, Josue Caraballo, Damian Jimenez, Siddhant Gawsane, Shohedul Hasan, Minumol Joseph, Aaditya Kulkarni, Anil Kumar Nayak, Vikas Sable, Chengkai Li, and Mark Tremayne. 2017b. Claimbuster: The first-ever end-to-end fact-checking system. *PVLDB*, 10(12):1945–1948.

Damian Jimenez and Chengkai Li. 2018. An empirical study on identifying sentences with salient factual statements. In *IJCNN*.

Saehan Jo, Immanuel Trummer, Weicheng Yu, Xuezhi Wang, Cong Yu, Daniel Liu, and Niyati Mehta. 2019. Verifying text summaries of relational data sets. In *SIGMOD*.

Chengcheng Shao, Giovanni Luca Ciampaglia, Alessandro Flammini, and Filippo Menczer. 2016. Hoaxy: A platform for tracking online misinformation. In *WWW Companion*, pages 745–750.

Baoxu Shi and Tim Weninger. 2016. Discriminative predicate path mining for fact checking in knowledge graphs. *Knowledge-Based Systems*, 104(C):123–133.

Evangelia Spiliopoulou, Eduard Hovy, and Teruko Mitamura. 2017. Event detection using frame-semantic parser. In *Proceedings of the Events and Stories in the News Workshop*, pages 15–20.

Swabha Swayamdipta, Sam Thomson, Chris Dyer, and Noah A. Smith. 2017. Frame-semantic parsing with softmax-margin segmental rnns and a syntactic scaffold. *CoRR*, abs/1706.09528.

You Wu, Pankaj K. Agarwal, Chengkai Li, Jun Yang, and Cong Yu. 2017. Computational fact checking through query perturbations. *ACM Transactions on Database Systems (TODS)*, 42(1):4:1–4:41.

Texar: A Modularized, Versatile, and Extensible Toolkit for Text Generation

Zhiting Hu*, Haoran Shi, Bowen Tan, Wentao Wang, Zichao Yang,
Tiancheng Zhao, Junxian He, Lianhui Qin, Di Wang, Xuezhe Ma, Zhengzhong Liu,
Xiaodan Liang, Wangrong Zhu, Devendra Singh Sachan, Eric P. Xing

Carnegie Mellon University, Petuum Inc.

zhitinghu@gmail.com*

Abstract

We introduce Texar, an open-source toolkit aiming to support the broad set of *text generation* tasks that transform any inputs into natural language, such as machine translation, summarization, dialog, content manipulation, and so forth. With the design goals of modularity, versatility, and extensibility in mind, Texar extracts common patterns underlying the diverse tasks and methodologies, creates a library of highly reusable modules and functionalities, and allows arbitrary model architectures and algorithmic paradigms. In Texar, model architecture, inference, and learning processes are properly decomposed. Modules at a high concept level can be freely assembled or plugged in/swapped out. Texar is thus particularly suitable for researchers and practitioners to do fast prototyping and experimentation. The versatile toolkit also fosters technique sharing across different text generation tasks. Texar supports both TensorFlow and PyTorch, and is released under Apache License 2.0 at https://www.texar.io.[1]

1 Introduction

Text generation spans a broad set of natural language processing tasks that aim to generate natural language from input data or machine representations. Such tasks include machine translation (Brown et al., 1990; Bahdanau et al., 2014), dialog systems (Williams and Young, 2007; Serban et al., 2016; Tang et al., 2019), text summarization (Hovy and Lin, 1998), text paraphrasing and manipulation (Madnani and Dorr, 2010; Hu et al., 2017; Lin et al., 2019), and more. Recent years have seen rapid progress of this active area, in part due to the integration of modern deep learning approaches in many of the tasks. On the other hand, considerable research efforts are still needed

in order to improve techniques and enable real-world applications.

A few remarkable open-source toolkits have been developed (section 2) which largely focus on one or a few specific tasks or algorithms. Emerging new applications and approaches instead are often developed by individual teams in a more ad-hoc manner, which can easily result in hard-to-maintain custom code and duplicated efforts.

The variety of text generation tasks indeed have many common properties and share a set of key underlying techniques, such as neural encoder-decoders (Sutskever et al., 2014), attentions (Bahdanau et al., 2014; Luong et al., 2015; Vaswani et al., 2017), memory networks (Sukhbaatar et al., 2015), adversarial methods (Goodfellow et al., 2014; Lamb et al., 2016), reinforcement learning (Ranzato et al., 2015; Tan et al., 2018), structured supervision (Hu et al., 2018; Yang et al., 2018), as well as optimization techniques, data pre-processing and result post-processing, evaluations, etc. These techniques are often combined together in various ways to tackle different problems. Figure 1 summarizes examples of various model architectures.

It is therefore highly desirable to have an open-source platform that unifies the development of the diverse yet closely-related applications, backed with clean and consistent implementations of the core algorithms. Such a platform would enable reuse of common components; standardize design, implementation, and experimentation; foster reproducibility; and importantly, encourage technique sharing among tasks so that an algorithmic advance developed for a specific task can quickly be evaluated and generalized to many others.

We introduce *Texar*, a general-purpose text generation toolkit aiming to support popular and emerging applications in the field, by providing researchers and practitioners a unified and

---

[1]An expanded version of the tech report can be found at https://arxiv.org/abs/1809.00794

Proceedings of the 57th Annual Meeting of the Association for Computational Linguistics-System Demonstrations, pages 159–164
Florence, Italy, July 28 - August 2, 2019. ©2019 Association for Computational Linguistics

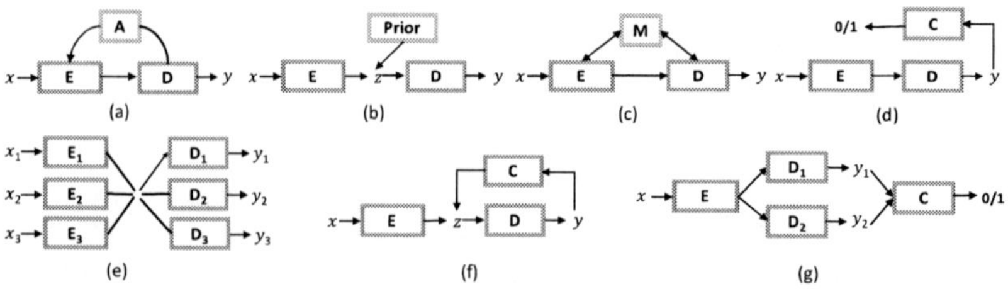

Figure 1: Examples of model architectures in recent text generation literatures (E: encoder, D: decoder, C: classifier). **(a):** The canonical encoder-decoder, sometimes with attentions A (Sutskever et al., 2014; Bahdanau et al., 2014; Vaswani et al., 2017) or copy mechanisms (Gu et al., 2016; Vinyals et al., 2015). **(b):** Variational encoder-decoder (Bowman et al., 2015). **(c):** Augmenting with external memory (Sukhbaatar et al., 2015). **(d):** Adversarial model using a binary discriminator C, w/ or w/o reinforcement learning (Zhang et al., 2017; Yu et al., 2017). **(e):** Multi-task learning with multiple encoders/decoders (Luong et al., 2016). **(f):** Augmenting with cyclic loss (Hu et al., 2017). **(g):** Adversarial alignment, either on samples y or hidden states (Lamb et al., 2016).

flexible framework for building their models. Texar has two versions, building upon TensorFlow (`tensorflow.org`) and PyTorch (`pytorch.org`), respectively, with the same uniform design.

Underlying the core of Texar's design is principled anatomy of extensive text generation models and learning algorithms, which subsumes the diverse cases in Figures 1 and beyond, enabling a unified formulation and consistent implementation. Texar emphasizes three key properties:

Versatility. Texar contains a wide range of features and functionalities for 1) arbitrary model architectures as a combination of encoders, decoders, embedders, discriminators, memories, and many other modules; and 2) different modeling and learning paradigms such as sequence-to-sequence, probabilistic models, adversarial methods, and reinforcement learning. Based on these, both workhorse and cutting-edge solutions to the broad spectrum of text generation tasks are either already included or can be easily constructed.

Modularity. Users can construct models at a high conceptual level just like assembling building blocks. It is convenient to plug in or swap out modules, configure rich module options, or even switch between distinct modeling paradigms. For example, switching from adversarial learning to reinforcement learning involves only minimal code changes (e.g., Figure 4). Modularity makes Texar particularly suitable for fast prototyping and experimentation.

Extensibility. The toolkit provides interfaces ranging from simple configuration files to full library APIs. Users of different needs and expertise are free to choose different interfaces for appropriate programmability and internal accessibility. The library APIs are fully compatible with the native TensorFlow/PyTorch interfaces, which allows seamless integration of user-customized modules, and enables the toolkit to take advantage of the vibrant open-source community by effortlessly importing any external components as needed.

Furthermore, Texar emphasizes on well-structured code, clean documentation, rich tutorial examples, and distributed GPU training.

2 Related Work

There exist several toolkits that focus on one or a few specific tasks. For neural machine translation and alike, there are Tensor2Tensor (Vaswani et al., 2018) on TensorFlow, OpenNMT (Klein et al., 2017) on PyTorch, Nematus (Sennrich et al., 2017) on Theano, MarianNMT (Junczys-Dowmunt et al., 2018) on C++, etc. ParlAI (Miller et al., 2017) is a specialized platform for dialogue. Differing from the task-focusing tools, Texar aims to cover as many text generation tasks as possible. The goal of versatility poses unique design challenges.

On the other end of the spectrum, there are libraries for more general NLP or ML applications: AllenNLP (`allennlp.org`), GluonNLP (`gluon-nlp.mxnet.io`) and others are designed for the broad NLP tasks in general, while Keras (`keras.io`) is for high conceptual-level programming without specific task focuses. In comparison, Texar has a proper focus on the text generation sub-area, and provide a comprehensive set of modules and functionalities that are well-tailored and readily-usable for relevant tasks. For example, Texar provides rich `text docoder` with optimized interfaces to support over ten decoding methods (see section 3.3 for an example).

160

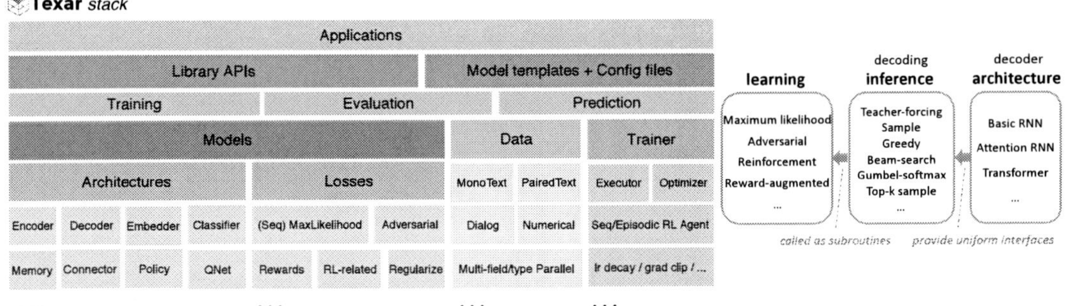

Figure 2: **Left:** The stack of main modules and functionalities in Texar. **Right:** The learning-inference-architecture anatomy, taking decoder for example. A sequence decoder can have an arbitrary architecture; all architectures expose uniform interfaces for specifying one of the tens of inference (decoding) strategies to generate samples or infer probabilities; a learning procedure repeated calls specified inference procedure during training.

3 Structure and Design

Figure 2, left panel, shows the stack of main modules and functionalities in Texar. In the following, we first present the design principles (sec 3.1) of the toolkit, and then describe the detailed structure of Texar with running examples to demonstrate the key properties (sec 3.2-3.4).

3.1 The Design of Texar

Designing a versatile toolkit is challenging due to the large variety of text generation tasks and fast-growing new models. We tackle the challenges by adopting principled anatomy of the modeling and experimentation pipeline. Specifically, we break down the complexity of rich tasks into three dimensions of variations, namely, varying data types/formats, arbitrary combinational model architectures and inference procedures, and diverse learning algorithms. Within the unified abstraction, all learning paradigms are each specifying one or multiple loss functions (e.g., cross-entropy loss, policy gradient loss), along with an optimization procedure that improves the losses:

$$\min_\theta \mathcal{L}(f_\theta, D) \tag{1}$$

where f_θ is the model that defines the model architecture and the inference procedure; D is the data; $\mathcal{L}$ is the learning objectives (losses); and **min** denotes the optimization procedure. Note that the above can have multiple losses imposed on different model parts (e.g., adversarial learning).

Further, as illustrated in Figure 2 right panel, we decouple learning, inference, and model architecture, forming abstraction layers of **learning – inference – architecture**. That is, different architectures implement the same set of inference procedures and provide the same interfaces, so that learning algorithms can call proper inference procedures as subroutines while staying agnostic to the underlying architecture and implementation details. For example, maximum likelihood learning uses teacher-forcing decoding (Mikolov et al., 2010); a policy gradient algorithm can invoke stochastic or greedy decoding (Ranzato et al., 2015); and adversarial learning can use either stochastic decoding for policy gradient-based updates (Yu et al., 2017) or Gumbel-softmax reparameterized decoding (Jang et al., 2016) for direct gradient back-propagation. Users can switch between different learning algorithms for the same model, by simply specifying the corresponding inference strategy and plugging into a new learning module, without adapting the model architecture (see section 3.3 for a running example).

3.2 Assemble Arbitrary Model Architectures

We develop an extensive set of frequently-used modules (e.g., various `encoders`, `decoders`, `embedders`, `classifiers`, etc). Crucially, Texar allows free concatenation between these modules in order to assemble arbitrary model architectures. Such concatenation can be done by directly interfacing two modules, or through an intermediate `connector` module that provides general functionalities of reshaping, reparameterization, sampling, and others.

Besides the flexibility of arbitrary assembling, it is critical for the toolkit to provide proper abstractions to relieve users from overly concerning low-level implementations. Texar provides two major types of user interfaces with different abstract levels, i.e., YAML configuration files and full Python library APIs. Figure 3 shows an exam-

```
1   source_embedder: WordEmbedder              1   # Read data
2   source_embedder_hparams:                   2   dataset = PairedTextData(data_hparams)
3     dim: 300                                 3   batch = DataIterator(dataset).get_next()
4   encoder: UnidirectionalRNNEncoder          4
5   encoder_hparams:                           5   # Encode
6     rnn_cell:                                6   embedder = WordEmbedder(dataset.vocab.size, hparams=embedder_hparams)
7       type: BasicLSTMCell                    7   encoder = TransformerEncoder(hparams=encoder_hparams)
8       kwargs:                                8   enc_outputs = encoder(embedder(batch['source_text_ids']),
9         num_units: 300                       9                         batch['source_length'])
10       num_layers: 1                         10
11      dropout:                               11  # Decode
12        output_dropout: 0.5                  12  decoder = AttentionRNNDecoder(memory=enc_outputs,
13        variational_recurrent: True          13                        hparams=decoder_hparams)
14  embedder_share: True                       14  outputs, length, _ = decoder(inputs=embedder(batch['target_text_ids']),
15  decoder: AttentionRNNDecoder               15                        seq_length=batch['target_length']-1)
16  decoder_hparams:                           16
17    attention:                               17  # Loss
18      type: LuongAttention                   18  loss = sequence_sparse_softmax_cross_entropy(
19  beam_search_width: 5                       19      labels=batch['target_text_ids'][:,1:], logits=outputs.logits, seq_length=length)
20  optimization: ...                          20
```

Figure 3: Two ways of specifying an attentional encoder-decoder model. **Left:** Part of an example YAML config file of the model template. Hyperparameters taking default values can be omitted in the file. **Right:** Python code assembling an encoder-decoder model using library APIs. Modules are created as Python objects, and called as functions to create computation operations and return output tensors. Other code such as optimization is omitted.

ple of specifying an attentional encoder-decoder model through the two interfaces, respectively.

Configuration file passes hyperparameters to a predefined model template, which instantiates the model for training and evaluation. Text highlighted in blue in the figure (left panel) specifies the names of modules to use. Most hyperparameters have sensible default values. Users only have to specify hyperparameter values that differ from the default. The interface is easily understandable for non-expert users, and has also been adopted in other tools (e.g., Klein et al., 2017).

Library APIs offer clean function calls. Users can efficiently build any desired pipelines at a high conceptual level. Power users have the option to access the full internal states for low-level manipulations. Texar modules support convenient *variable re-use*. That is, each module instance creates its own sets of variables, and automatically re-uses them on subsequent calls. Hence TensorFlow *variable scope* is transparent to users.

3.3 Plug-in and Swap-out Modules

It is convenient to change from one modeling paradigm to another by simply plugging in/swapping out a single or few modules, or even merely changing a configuration parameter. For example, given the base code of an encoder-decoder model in Figure 3 (right panel), Figure 4 illustrates how one can switch between different learning paradigms by changing only Lines.14–19 of the original code (maximum-likelihood learn-

ing). In particular, Figure 4 shows adversarial learning and reinforcement learning, which invokes Gumbel-softmax decoding and random-sample decoding, respectively.

3.4 Customize with Extensible Interfaces

Texar emphasizes on extensibility and allows easy addition of customized/external modules without editing the Texar codebase. Specifically, with the YAML configuration file, users can directly insert their own modules by providing the Python importing path to the module. For example, to use a customized RNN cell in the encoder, one can simply change Line.7 of Figure 3 (left panel) to `type: path.to.MyCell`, as long as `MyCell` has a compatible interface to other parts of the model. Using customized modules with the library APIs is even more flexible, since the APIs are designed to be fully compatible with native TensorFlow/PyTorch programming interfaces.

4 Case Study: Transformer on Different Tasks

We present a case study to show that Texar can greatly reduce implementation efforts and enable technique sharing among different tasks. Transformer, as first introduced in (Vaswani et al., 2017), has greatly improved the machine translation results and created other successful models such as BERT for text embedding (Devlin et al., 2019) and GPT-2 for language modeling (Radford et al., 2018). Texar supports easy construction of

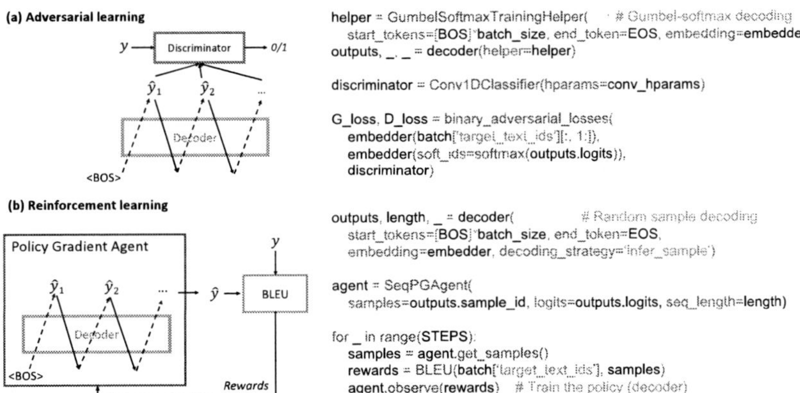


```
helper = GumbelSoftmaxTrainingHelper(     # Gumbel-softmax decoding
    start_tokens=[BOS]*batch_size, end_token=EOS, embedding=embedder)
outputs, _, _ = decoder(helper=helper)

discriminator = Conv1DClassifier(hparams=conv_hparams)

G_loss, D_loss = binary_adversarial_losses(
    embedder(batch['target_text_ids'][:, 1:]),
    embedder(soft_ids=softmax(outputs.logits)),
    discriminator)


outputs, length, _ = decoder(               # Random sample decoding
    start_tokens=[BOS]*batch_size, end_token=EOS,
    embedding=embedder, decoding_strategy='infer_sample')

agent = SeqPGAgent(
    samples=outputs.sample_id, logits=outputs.logits, seq_length=length)

for _ in range(STEPS):
    samples = agent.get_samples()
    rewards = BLEU(batch['target_text_ids'], samples)
    agent.observe(rewards)    # Train the policy (decoder)
```

Figure 4: Switching between different learning paradigms of a decoder involves only modification of Line.14-19 of Figure 3 (maximum-likelihood learning). The same decoder is called with different decoding modes, and discriminator or reinforcement learning agent is added as needed. **(Left):** Module structure of each paradigm; **(Right):** The respective code snippets. For adversarial learning in (b), continuous Gumbel-softmax approximation (Jang et al., 2016) to generated samples is used to enable gradient propagation from the discriminator to the decoder.

these models and fine-tuning pretrained weights. We can also deploy the Transformer components to various other tasks and get improved results.

The first task we explored is the variational autoencoder (VAE) language modeling (Bowman et al., 2015). We test two models, one with an LSTM RNN decoder which is traditionally used in the task, and the other with a Transformer decoder. All other model configurations including parameter size are the same across the two models. Table 1, top panel, shows the Transformer VAE consistently improves over the LSTM VAE. With Texar, changing the decoder from an LSTM to a Transformer is easily achieved by modifying only 3 lines of code. It is also worth noting that, building the VAE language model (including data reading, model construction, and optimization) on Texar uses only 70 lines of code (with the length of each line < 80 chars). As a (rough) reference, a popular public TensorFlow code (Li, 2017) of the same model has used around 400 lines of code for the same part (without line length limit).

The second task is conversation generation. The dialog history is encoded with the `HierarchicalRNNEncoder` module which is followed by a decoder to generate the response. We study the performance of a Transformer decoder v.s. a conventional GRU RNN decoder. Table 1, bottom panel, shows the Transformer outperforms GRU. Regarding the implementation effort, the Texar code has around 100 lines of code, while the reference TensorFlow code (Zhao et al., 2017) involves over 600 lines.

Dataset	Metrics	VAE-LSTM	VAE-Tran
Yahoo	PPL	68.31	**61.26**
(Yang et al.)	NLL	337.36	**328.67**
PTB	PPL	105.27	**102.46**
(Bowman et al.)	NLL	102.06	**101.46**

Dataset	Metrics	HERD-GRU	HERD-Tran
Switchboard	BLEU4-p	0.228	**0.232**
(Zhao et al.)	BLEU4-r	0.205	**0.214**

Table 1: **Top:** Transformer *vs* LSTM for VAE LM. Perplexity (PPL) and sentence negative log likelihood (NLL) are evaluated (The lower the better). **Bottom:** Transformer *vs* GRU decoders in HERD (Serban et al., 2016) for conversation response generation. BLEU4-p and -r are precision and recall (Zhao et al., 2017).

References

Dzmitry Bahdanau, Kyunghyun Cho, and Yoshua Bengio. 2014. Neural machine translation by jointly learning to align and translate. *arXiv:1409.0473*.

Samuel R Bowman, Luke Vilnis, Oriol Vinyals, Andrew M Dai, Rafal Jozefowicz, and Samy Bengio. 2015. Generating sentences from a continuous space. *arXiv:1511.06349*.

Peter F Brown, John Cocke, Stephen A Della Pietra, Vincent J Della Pietra, Fredrick Jelinek, John D Lafferty, Robert L Mercer, and Paul S Roossin. 1990. A statistical approach to machine translation. *CL*.

Jacob Devlin, Ming-Wei Chang, Kenton Lee, and Kristina Toutanova. 2019. BERT: Pre-training of deep bidirectional transformers for language understanding. *NAACL*.

Ian Goodfellow, Jean Pouget-Abadie, Mehdi Mirza, Bing Xu, David Warde-Farley, Sherjil Ozair, Aaron Courville, and Yoshua Bengio. 2014. Generative adversarial nets. *NeurIPS*.

Jiatao Gu, Zhengdong Lu, Hang Li, and Victor OK

Li. 2016. Incorporating copying mechanism in sequence-to-sequence learning. *arXiv:1603.06393*.

Eduard Hovy and Chin-Yew Lin. 1998. Automated text summarization and the SUMMARIST system. In *Advances in automatic text summarization*.

Zhiting Hu, Zichao Yang, Xiaodan Liang, Ruslan Salakhutdinov, and Eric P Xing. 2017. Toward controlled generation of text. In *ICML*.

Zhiting Hu, Zichao Yang, Ruslan Salakhutdinov, Xiaodan Liang, Lianhui Qin, Haoye Dong, and Eric Xing. 2018. Deep generative models with learnable knowledge constraints. In *NeurIPS*.

Eric Jang, Shixiang Gu, and Ben Poole. 2016. Categorical reparameterization with Gumbel-softmax. *arXiv:1611.01144*.

Marcin Junczys-Dowmunt, Roman Grundkiewicz, Tomasz Dwojak, Hieu Hoang, Kenneth Heafield, Tom Neckermann, Frank Seide, Ulrich Germann, Alham Fikri Aji, Nikolay Bogoychev, Andr F. T. Martins, and Alexandra Birch. 2018. Marian: Fast neural machine translation in C++. *arXiv:1804.00344*.

Guillaume Klein, Yoon Kim, Yuntian Deng, Jean Senellart, and Alexander M Rush. 2017. OpenNMT: Open-source toolkit for neural machine translation. *arXiv:1701.02810*.

Alex M Lamb, Anirudh Goyal Alias Parth Goyal, Ying Zhang, Saizheng Zhang, Aaron C Courville, and Yoshua Bengio. 2016. Professor forcing: A new algorithm for training recurrent networks. In *NeurIPS*.

Zhong-Yi Li. 2017. https://github.com/Chung-I/Variational-Recurrent-Autoencoder-Tensorflow.

Shuai Lin, Wentao Wang, Zichao Yang, Haoran Shi, Frank Xu, Xiaodan Liang, Eric Xing, and Zhiting Hu. 2019. Towards unsupervised text content manipulation. *arXiv preprint arXiv:1901.09501*.

Minh-Thang Luong, Quoc V Le, Ilya Sutskever, Oriol Vinyals, and Lukasz Kaiser. 2016. Multi-task sequence to sequence learning. In *ICLR*.

Minh-Thang Luong, Hieu Pham, and Christopher D Manning. 2015. Effective approaches to attention-based neural machine translation. *arXiv:1508.04025*.

Nitin Madnani and Bonnie J Dorr. 2010. Generating phrasal and sentential paraphrases: A survey of data-driven methods. *CL*.

Tomáš Mikolov, Martin Karafiát, Lukáš Burget, Jan Černocký, and Sanjeev Khudanpur. 2010. Recurrent neural network based language model. In *INTERSPEECH*.

Alexander H Miller, Will Feng, Adam Fisch, Jiasen Lu, Dhruv Batra, Antoine Bordes, Devi Parikh, and Jason Weston. 2017. ParlAI: A dialog research software platform. *arXiv:1705.06476*.

Alec Radford, Jeffrey Wu, Rewon Child, David Luan, Dario Amodei, and Ilya Sutskever. 2018. Language models are unsupervised multitask learners. Technical report, Technical report, OpenAI.

Marc'Aurelio Ranzato, Sumit Chopra, Michael Auli, and Wojciech Zaremba. 2015. Sequence level training with recurrent neural networks. *arXiv:1511.06732*.

Rico Sennrich, Orhan Firat, Kyunghyun Cho, Alexandra Birch, Barry Haddow, Julian Hitschler, Marcin Junczys-Dowmunt, Samuel Läubli, et al. 2017. Nematus: a toolkit for neural machine translation. *arXiv:1703.04357*.

Iulian Vlad Serban, Alessandro Sordoni, Yoshua Bengio, Aaron C Courville, and Joelle Pineau. 2016. Building end-to-end dialogue systems using generative hierarchical neural network models.

Sainbayar Sukhbaatar, Jason Weston, Rob Fergus, et al. 2015. End-to-end memory networks. In *NeurIPS*.

Ilya Sutskever, Oriol Vinyals, and Quoc Le. 2014. Sequence to sequence learning with neural networks. *NeurIPS*.

Bowen Tan, Zhiting Hu, Zichao Yang, Ruslan Salakhutdinov, and Eric Xing. 2018. Connecting the dots between MLE and RL for sequence generation. *arXiv:1811.09740*.

Jianheng Tang, Tiancheng Zhao, Chengyan Xiong, Xiaodan Liang, Eric P Xing, and Zhiting Hu. 2019. Target-guided open-domain conversation. In *ACL*.

Ashish Vaswani, Samy Bengio, Eugene Brevdo, Francois Chollet, Aidan N Gomez, Stephan Gouws, Llion Jones, Łukasz Kaiser, Nal Kalchbrenner, Niki Parmar, et al. 2018. Tensor2Tensor for neural machine translation. *arXiv:1803.07416*.

Ashish Vaswani, Noam Shazeer, Niki Parmar, Jakob Uszkoreit, Llion Jones, Aidan N Gomez, Łukasz Kaiser, and Illia Polosukhin. 2017. Attention is all you need. In *NeurIPS*.

Oriol Vinyals, Meire Fortunato, and Navdeep Jaitly. 2015. Pointer networks. In *NeurIPS*.

Jason D Williams and Steve Young. 2007. Partially observable Markov decision processes for spoken dialog systems. *CSL*.

Zichao Yang, Zhiting Hu, Chris Dyer, Eric P Xing, and Taylor Berg-Kirkpatrick. 2018. Unsupervised text style transfer using language models as discriminators. *arXiv:1805.11749*.

Zichao Yang, Zhiting Hu, Ruslan Salakhutdinov, and Taylor Berg-Kirkpatrick. 2017. Improved variational autoencoders for text modeling using dilated convolutions. *ICML*.

Lantao Yu, Weinan Zhang, Jun Wang, and Yong Yu. 2017. SeqGAN: Sequence generative adversarial nets with policy gradient. In *AAAI*.

Yizhe Zhang, Zhe Gan, Kai Fan, Zhi Chen, Ricardo Henao, Dinghan Shen, and Lawrence Carin. 2017. Adversarial feature matching for text generation. *arXiv:1706.03850*.

Tiancheng Zhao, Ran Zhao, and Maxine Eskenazi. 2017. Learning discourse-level diversity for neural dialog models using conditional variational autoencoders. In *ACL*.

Parallax: Visualizing and Understanding the Semantics of Embedding Spaces via Algebraic Formulae

Piero Molino
Uber AI Labs
San Francisco, CA, USA
piero@uber.com

Yang Wang
Uber Technologies Inc.
San Francisco, CA, USA
gnavvy@uber.com

Jiawei Zhang[*]
Facebook
Menlo Park, CA, USA
rivulet.zhang@gmail.com

Abstract

Embeddings are a fundamental component of many modern machine learning and natural language processing models. Understanding them and visualizing them is essential for gathering insights about the information they capture and the behavior of the models. In this paper, we introduce Parallax[1], a tool explicitly designed for this task. Parallax allows the user to use both state-of-the-art embedding analysis methods (PCA and t-SNE) and a simple yet effective task-oriented approach where users can explicitly define the axes of the projection through algebraic formulae. In this approach, embeddings are projected into a semantically meaningful subspace, which enhances interpretability and allows for more fine-grained analysis. We demonstrate[2] the power of the tool and the proposed methodology through a series of case studies and a user study.

1 Introduction

Learning representations is an important part of modern machine learning and natural language processing. These representations are often real-valued vectors also called embeddings and are obtained both as byproducts of supervised learning or as the direct goal of unsupervised methods. Independently of how the embeddings are learned, there is much value in understanding what information they capture, how they relate to each other and how the data they are learned from influences them. A better understanding of the embedded space may lead to a better understanding of the data, of the problem and the behavior of the model, and may lead to critical insights in improving such models. Because of their high-dimensional nature, they are hard to visualize effectively.

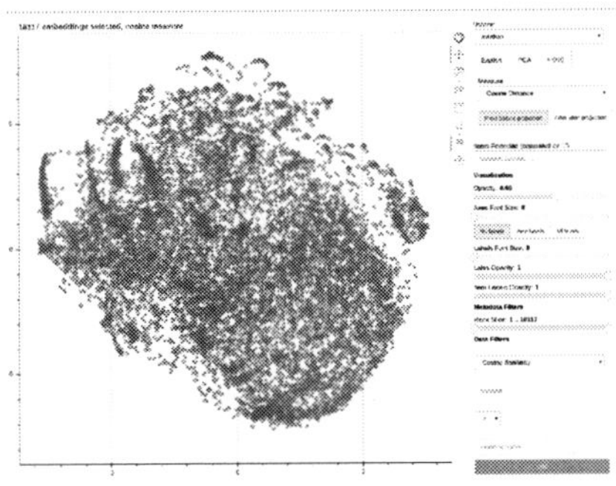

Figure 1: Screenshot of Parallax.

In this paper, we introduce Parallax, a tool for visualizing embedding spaces. The most widely adopted projection techniques (Principal Component Analysis (PCA) (Pearson, 1901) and t-Distributed Stochastic Neighbor Embedding (t-SNE) (van der Maaten and Hinton, 2008)) are available in Parallax. They are useful for obtaining an overall view of the embedding space, but they have a few shortcomings: 1) projections may not preserve distance in the original space, 2) they are not comparable across models and 3) do not provide interpretable axes, preventing more detailed analysis and understanding.

PCA projects embeddings on a lower dimensional space that has the directions of the highest variance in the dataset as axes. Those dimensions do not carry any interpretable meaning, so by visualizing the first two dimensions of a PCA projection, the only insight obtainable is semantic relatedness (Budanitsky and Hirst, 2006) between points by observing their relative closeness, and therefore, topical clusters can be identified. Moreover, as the directions of highest variance differ from embedding space to embedding space, the projections are incompatible among different embeddings spaces, and this makes them incomparable, a common issue among dimensionality reduction techniques.

---

[*]Work done while at Purdue University

[1]http://github.com/uber-research/parallax
[2]https://youtu.be/CSkJGVsFPIg

Proceedings of the 57th Annual Meeting of the Association for Computational Linguistics-System Demonstrations, pages 165–180
Florence, Italy, July 28 - August 2, 2019. ©2019 Association for Computational Linguistics

t-SNE, differently from PCA, optimizes a loss that encourages embeddings that are in their respective close neighborhoods in the original high-dimensional space to be close in the lower dimensional projection space. t-SNE projections visually approximate better the original embedding space and topical clusters are more clearly distinguishable, but do not solve the issue of comparability of two different sets of embeddings, nor do they solve the lack of interpretability of the axes or allow for fine-grained inspection.

For these reasons, there is value in mapping embeddings into a more specific, controllable and interpretable semantic space. In this paper, a new and simple method to inspect, explore and debug embedding spaces at a fine-grained level is proposed. This technique is made available in Parallax alongside PCA and t-SNE for goal-oriented analysis of the embedding spaces. It consists of explicitly defining the axes of projection through formulae in vector algebra that use embedding labels as atoms. Explicit axis definition assigns interpretable and fine-grained semantics to the axes of projection. This makes it possible to analyze in detail how embeddings relate to each other with respect to interpretable dimensions of variability, as carefully crafted formulas can map (to a certain extent) to semantically meaningful portions of the space. The explicit axes definition also allows for the comparison of embeddings obtained from different datasets, as long as they have common labels and are equally normalized.

We demonstrate three visualizations that Parallax provides for analyzing subspaces of interest of embedding spaces and a set of example case studies including bias detection, polysemy analysis and fine-grained embedding analysis, but additional ones, like diachronic analysis and the analysis of representations obtained through graph learning or any other means, may be performed as easily. Moreover, the proposed visualizations can be used for debugging purposes and, in general, for obtaining a better understanding of the embedding spaces learned by different models and representation learning approaches. We show how this methodology can be widely used through a series of case studies on well known models and data, and furthermore, we validate its usefulness for goal-oriented analysis through a user study.

Parallax interface, shown in Figure 1, presents a plot on the left side (scatter or polar) and controls on the right side that allow users to define parameters of the projection (what measure to use, values for the hyperparameters, the formuale for the axes in case of explicit axes projections are selected, etc.) and additional filtering and visualization parameters. Filtering parameters define logic rules applied to embeddings metadata to decide which of them should be visualized, e.g., the user can decide to visualize only the most frequent words or only verbs if metadata about part-of-speech tags is made available. Filters on the embeddings themselves can also be defined, e.g., the user can decide to visualize only the embeddings with cosine similarity above 0.5 to the embedding of "horse".

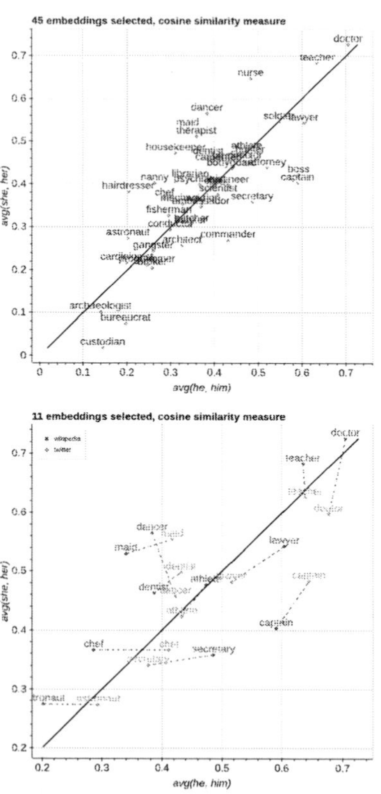

Figure 2: In the top we show professions plotted on "male" and "female" axes in $Wikipedia$ embeddings. In the bottom we show their comparison in $Wikipedia$ and $Twitter$ datasets.

In particular, Parallax's capability of explicitly defining axes is useful for goal-oriented analyses, e.g., when the user has a specific analysis goal in mind, like detecting bias in the embeddings space. Goals are defined in terms of dimensions of variability (axes of projection) and items to visualize (all the embeddings that are projected, after filtering). In the case of a few dimensions of variability (up to three) and potentially many items of interest, a Cartesian view is ideal. Each axis is the vector obtained by evaluating the algebraic formula it is associated with, and the coordinates displayed are similarities or distances of the items with respect to each axis. Figure 2 shows an example of a bi-dimensional Cartesian view. In the case where the goal is defined in terms of many dimensions of variability, a polar view is preferred. The polar view can visualize many more axes by showing them in a circle, but it is limited in the number of items it can display, as each item will be displayed as a polygon with each vertex lying on a different axis and too many overlapping polygons would make the visualization cluttered. Figure 5 shows an example of a five-dimensional polar view.

The use of explicit axes allows for interpretable comparison of different embedding spaces, trained on different corpora or on the same corpora but with different models, or even trained on two different time slices of the same corpora. The only requirement for embedding spaces to be comparable is that they contain embeddings for all labels present in the formulae defining the axes. Moreover, embeddings in the two spaces do not need to be of the same dimension, but they need to be normalized. Items will now have two sets of coordinates, one for each embedding space, and thus they will be displayed as lines. Short lines are interpreted as items being embedded similarly in the subspaces defined by the axes in both embedding spaces, while long lines are interpreted as really different locations in the subspaces, and their direction gives insight on how items shift in the two subspaces. The bottom side of Figure 2 shows an example of how to use the Cartesian comparison view to compare embeddings in two datasets.

2 Case Studies

In this section, a few goal-oriented use cases are presented, but Parallax's flexiblity allows for many others. We used 50-dimensional publicly available GloVe (Pennington et al., 2014) embeddings trained on Wikipedia and Gigaword 5 summing to 6 billion tokens (for short *Wikipedia*) and 2 billion tweets containing 27 billion tokens (*Twitter*).

Bias detection The task of bias detection is to identify, and in some cases correct for, bias in data that is reflected in the embeddings trained on such data. Studies have shown how embeddings incorporate gender and ethnic biases ((Garg et al., 2018;

Bolukbasi et al., 2016; Islam et al., 2017)), while other studies focused on warping spaces in order to de-bias the resulting embeddings ((Bolukbasi et al., 2016; Zhao et al., 2017)). We show how our proposed methodology can help visualize biases.

To visualize gender bias with respect to professions, the goal is defined with the formulae $avg(he, him)$ and $avg(she, her)$ as two dimensions of variability, in a similar vein to (Garg et al., 2018). A subset of the professions used by (Bolukbasi et al., 2016) is selected as items and cosine similarity is adopted as the measure for the projection. The Cartesian view visualizing *Wikipedia* embeddings is shown in the left of Figure 2. *Nurse*, *dancer*, and *maid* are the professions closer to the "female" axis, while *boss*, *captain*, and *commander* end up closer to the "male" axis.

The Cartesian comparison view comparing the embeddings trained on *Wikipedia* and *Twitter* is shown in the right side of Figure 2. Only the embeddings with a line length above 0.05 are displayed. The most interesting words in this visualization are the ones that shift the most in the direction of negative slope. In this case, *chef* and *doctor* are closer to the "male" axis in *Twitter* than in *Wikipedia*, while *dancer* and *secretary* are closer to the bisector in *Twitter* than in *Wikipedia*.

Polysemy analysis Methods for representing words with multiple vectors by clustering contexts have been proposed (Huang et al., 2012; Neelakantan et al., 2014), but widely used pre-trained vectors conflate meanings in the same embedding.

Widdows (2003) showed how using a binary orthonormalization operator that has ties with the quantum logic *not* operator it is possible to remove part of the conflated meaning from the embedding of a polysemous word. The authors define the operator $nqnot(a, b) = a - \frac{a \cdot b}{|b|^2} b$ and we show with a comparison plot how it can help distinguish the different meanings of a word.

For illustrative purposes, we choose the same polysemous word used by (Widdows, 2003), *suit*, and use the *nqnot* operator to orthonormalize with respect to *lawsuit* and *dress*, the two main meanings used as dimensions of variability. The items in our goal are the 20,000 most frequent words in the *Wikipedia* embedding space removing stopwords. In Figure 3, we show the overall plot and we zoom on the items that are closer to each axis. Words closer to the axis negating *lawsuit* are all related to dresses and the act of wearing something,

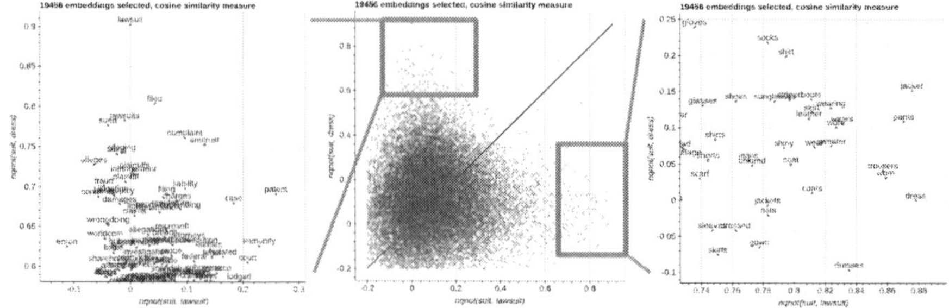

Figure 3: Plot of embeddings in *Wikipedia* with *suit* negated with respect to *lawsuit* and *dress* respectively as axes.

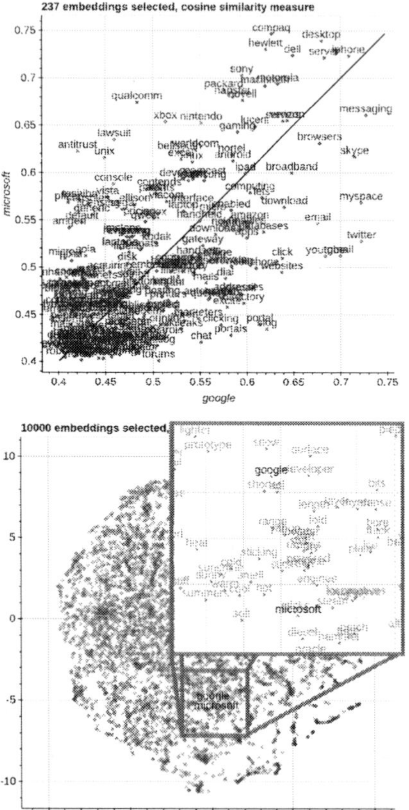

Figure 4: The top figure is a fine-grained comparison of the subspace on the axis *google* and *microsoft* in *Wikipedia*, the bottom one is the *t-SNE* counterpart.

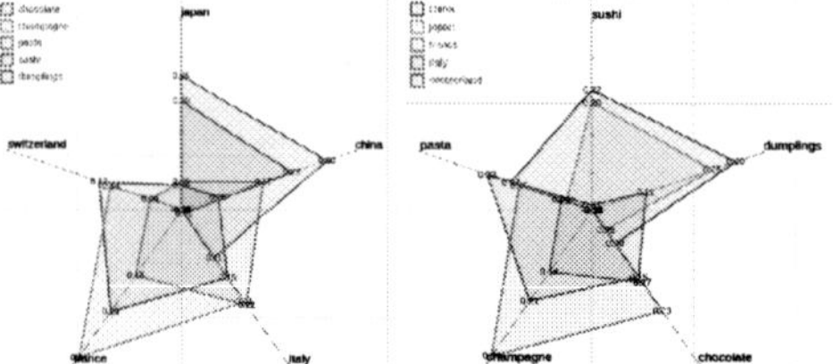

Figure 5: Two polar views of countries and foods.

ity to a bi-dimensional one, losing the fine-grained distinctions. The Cartesian view allows for a more fine-grained visualization that emphasizes nuances that could otherwise go unnoticed.

To demonstrate this capability, we select as dimensions of variability single words in close vicinity to each other in the *Wikipedia* embedding space: *google* and *microsoft*, as *google* is the closest word to *microsoft* and *microsoft* is the 3rd closest word to *google*. As items, we pick the 30,000 most frequent words removing stop-words and remove the 500 most frequent words (as they are too generic) and keeping only the words that have a cosine similarity of at least 0.4 with both *google* and *microsoft* and a cosine similarity below 0.75 with respect to $google + microsoft$, as we are interested in the most polarized words.

The left side of Figure 4 shows how even if those embeddings are close to each other, it is easy to identify peculiar words (highlighted with red dots). The ones that relate to web companies and services (*twitter, youtube, myspace*) are much closer to the *google* axis. Words related to both legal issues (*lawsuit, antitrust*) and videogames (*ps3, nintendo, xbox*) and traditional IT companies are closer to the *microsoft* axis.

For contrast, the t-SNE projection is shown in the right side of Figure 4: it is hard to appreciate the similarities and differences among those embeddings other than seeing them being close in the projected space. This confirms on one hand that the notion of similarity between terms in an em-

while words closer to the axis negating *dress* are related to law. This visualization clearly confirms the ability of the *nqnot* operator to disentangle multiple meanings from polysemous embeddings.

Fine-grained embedding analysis We consider embeddings that are close to be semantically related, but even close embeddings may have nuances that distinguish them. When projecting in two dimensions through PCA or t-SNE we are conflating a multidimensional notion of similar-

Accuracy	Factor	$F_{(1,91)}$	p-value
Projection	Projection	46.11	0.000***
×	Task	1.709	0.194
Task	Projection × Task	3.452	0.066
Projection	Projection	57.73	0.000***
×	Obfuscation	23.93	0.000***
Obfuscation	Projection × Obf	5.731	0.019*

Table 1: Two-way ANOVA analyses of Task (Commonality vs. Polarization) and Obfuscation (Obfuscated vs. Non-obfuscated) over Projection (Explicit Formulae vs. t-SNE).

bedding space hides many nuances that are captured in those representations, and on the other hand, that the proposed methodology enables for a more detailed inspection of the embedded space.

Multi-dimensional similarity nuances can be visualized using the polar view. In Figure 5, we show how to use Parallax to visualize a small number of items on more than two axes, specifically five food-related items compared over five countries' axes. The most typical food from a specific country is the closest to the country axis, with *sushi* being predominantly close to *Japan* and *China*, *dumplings* being close to both Asian countries and *Italy*, *pasta* being predominantly closer to *Italy*, *chocolate* being close to European countries and *champagne* being closer to *France* and *Italy*. This same approach could be also be used for bias detection among different ethnicities, for instance.

3 User Study

We conducted a user study to find out if and how visualizations using user-defined semantically meaningful algebraic formulae help users achieve their analysis goals. What we are not testing for is the projection quality itself, as in PCA and t-SNE it is obtained algorithmically, while in our case it is explicitly defined by the user. We formalized the research questions as: Q1) Does Explicit Formulae outperform t-SNE in goal-oriented tasks? Q2) Which visualization do users prefer?

To answer these questions we invited twelve subjects among data scientists and machine learning researchers, all acquainted with interpreting dimensionality reduction results. We defined two types of tasks, namely Commonality and Polarization, in which subjects were given a visualization together with a pair of words (used as axes in Explicit Formulae or highlighted with a big font and red dot in case of t-SNE). We asked the subjects to identify either common or polarized words w.r.t. the two provided ones. The provided pairs were:

banana & strawberry, google & microsoft, nerd & geek, book & magazine. The test subjects were given a list of eight questions, four per task type, and their proposed lists of five words are compared with a gold standard provided by a committee of two computational linguistics experts. The tasks are fully randomized within the subject to prevent from learning effects. In addition, we obfuscated half of our questions by replacing the words with a random numeric ID to prevent prior knowledge from affecting the judgment. We track the *accuracy* of the subjects by calculating the number of words provided that are present in the gold standard set, and we also collected an overall *preference* for either visualizations.

As reported in Table 1, two-way ANOVA tests revealed significant differences in accuracy for the factor of Projection and t-SNE against both Task and Obfuscation, which is a strong indicator that the proposed Explicit Formulae method outperforms t-SNE in terms of accuracy in both Commonality and Polarization tasks. We also observed significant differences in Obfuscation: subjects tend to have better accuracy when the words are not obfuscated. We run post-hoc t-tests that confirmed how the accuracy of Explicit Formulae on Non-obfuscated is significantly better than Obfuscated, which in turn is significantly better that t-SNE Non-obfuscated, which is significantly better than t-SNE Obfuscated. Concerning Preference, nine out of all twelve (75%) subjects chose Explicit Formulae over t-SNE. In conclusion, our answers to the research questions are that (Q1) Explicit Formulae leads to better accuracy in goal-oriented tasks, (Q2) users prefer Explicit Formulae over t-SNE.

4 Related Work

A consistent body of research went into researching distributional semantics and embedding methods ((Lenci, 2018) for a comprehensive overview), but we will focus om the embedding visualization literature. In their recent paper, (Heimerl and Gleicher, 2018) extracted a list of routinely conducted tasks where embeddings are employed in visual analytics for NLP, such as *compare concepts, finding analogies*, and *predict contexts*. iVisClustering (Lee et al., 2012) represents topic clusters as their most representative keywords and displays them as a 2D scatter plot and a set of linked visualization components supporting interactively constructing topic hierarchies. ConceptVector (Park et al., 2018) makes use of multiple keyword sets to encode the relevance scores of documents and topics: positive words, negative words, and irrelevant words. It allows users to select and build a concept iteratively. (Liu et al., 2018) display pairs of analogous words obtained through analogy by projecting them on a 2D plane obtained through a PCA and an SVM to find the plane that separates words on the two sides of the analogy. Besides word embeddings, visualization has been used to understand topic modeling (Chuang et al., 2012) and how topic models evolve over time (Havre et al., 2002). Compared to existing literature, our work allows for more fine-grained direct control over the conceptual axes and the filtering logic, allowing users to: 1) define concepts based on explicit algebraic formulae beyond single keywords, 2) filter depending on metadata, 3) perform multidimensional projections beyond the common 2D scatter plot view using the polar view, and 4) perform comparisons between embeddings from different data sources. Those features are absent in other proposed tools.

5   Conclusions

We presented Parallax, a tool for embedding visualization, and a simple methodology for projecting embeddings into lower-dimensional semantically-meaningful subspaces through explicit algebraic formulae. We showed how this approach allows goal-oriented analyses, more fine-grained and cross-dataset comparisons through a series of case studies and a user study.

References

Tolga Bolukbasi, Kai-Wei Chang, James Y. Zou, Venkatesh Saligrama, and Adam Tauman Kalai. 2016. Man is to computer programmer as woman is to homemaker? debiasing word embeddings. In *NIPS*, pages 4349–4357.

Alexander Budanitsky and Graeme Hirst. 2006. Evaluating wordnet-based measures of lexical semantic relatedness. *Comput. Ling.*, 32(1):13–47.

Jason Chuang, Christopher D. Manning, and Jeffrey Heer. 2012. Termite: visualization techniques for assessing textual topic models. In *AVI*, pages 74–77.

Nikhil Garg, Londa Schiebinger, Dan Jurafsky, and James Zou. 2018. Word embeddings quantify 100 years of gender and ethnic stereotypes. *Proceedings of the National Academy of Sciences*.

Susan Havre, Elizabeth G. Hetzler, Paul Whitney, and Lucy T. Nowell. 2002. Themeriver: Visualizing thematic changes in large document collections. *IEEE Trans. Vis. Comput. Graph.*, 8(1):9–20.

Florian Heimerl and Michael Gleicher. 2018. Interactive analysis of word vector embeddings. *Comput. Graph. Forum*, 37(3):253–265.

Eric H. Huang, Richard Socher, Christopher D. Manning, and Andrew Y. Ng. 2012. Improving word representations via global context and multiple word prototypes. In *ACL*.

Aylin Caliskan Islam, Joanna J. Bryson, and Arvind Narayanan. 2017. Semantics derived automatically from language corpora necessarily contain human biases. *Science*, 356:183–186.

Hanseung Lee, Jaeyeon Kihm, Jaegul Choo, John T. Stasko, and Haesun Park. 2012. ivisclustering: An interactive visual document clustering via topic modeling. *Comput. Graph. Forum*, 31(3):1155–1164.

Alessandro Lenci. 2018. Distributional models of word meaning. *Annual Review of Linguistics*, 4(1):151–171.

Shusen Liu, Peer-Timo Bremer, Jayaraman J. Thiagarajan, Vivek Srikumar, Bei Wang, Yarden Livnat, and Valerio Pascucci. 2018. Visual exploration of semantic relationships in neural word embeddings. *IEEE Trans. Vis. Comput. Graph.*, 24(1):553–562.

Laurens van der Maaten and Geoffrey Hinton. 2008. Visualizing data using t-SNE. *Journal of Machine Learning Research*, 9:2579–2605.

Arvind Neelakantan, Jeevan Shankar, Alexandre Passos, and Andrew McCallum. 2014. Efficient non-parametric estimation of multiple embeddings per word in vector space. In *EMNLP*, pages 1059–1069.

Deok Gun Park, Seungyeon Kim, Jurim Lee, Jaegul Choo, Nicholas Diakopoulos, and Niklas Elmqvist. 2018. Conceptvector: Text visual analytics via interactive lexicon building using word embedding. *IEEE Trans. Vis. Comput. Graph.*, 24(1):361–370.

K. Pearson. 1901. On lines and planes of closest fit to systems of points in space. *Philosophical Magazine*, 2:559–572.

Jeffrey Pennington, Richard Socher, and Christopher D. Manning. 2014. Glove: Global vectors for word representation. In *EMNLP*, pages 1532–1543.

Dominic Widdows. 2003. Orthogonal negation in vector spaces for modelling word-meanings and document retrieval. In *ACL*, pages 136–143.

Jieyu Zhao, Tianlu Wang, Mark Yatskar, Vicente Ordonez, and Kai-Wei Chang. 2017. Men also like shopping: Reducing gender bias amplification using corpus-level constraints. In *EMNLP*, pages 2979–2989.

A Appendix

In this appendix we show all the images presented in the main body of the paper in full size for making reading them easier.

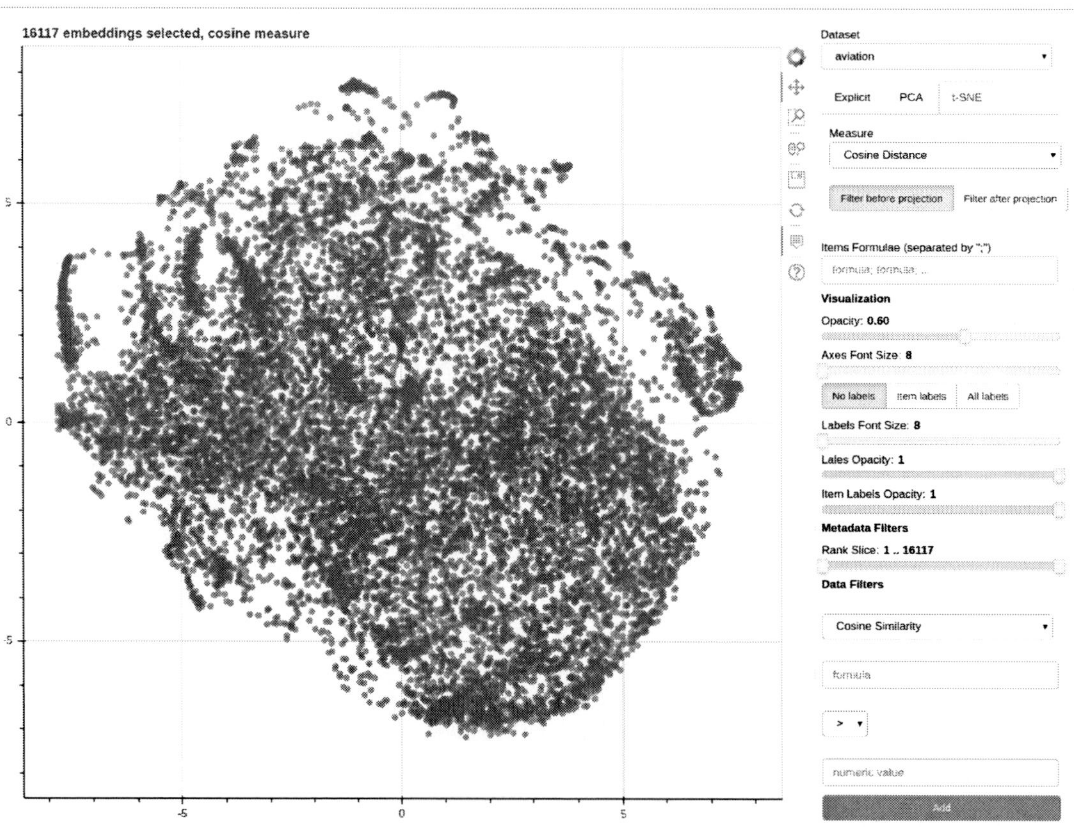

Figure 6: Screenshot of Parallax.

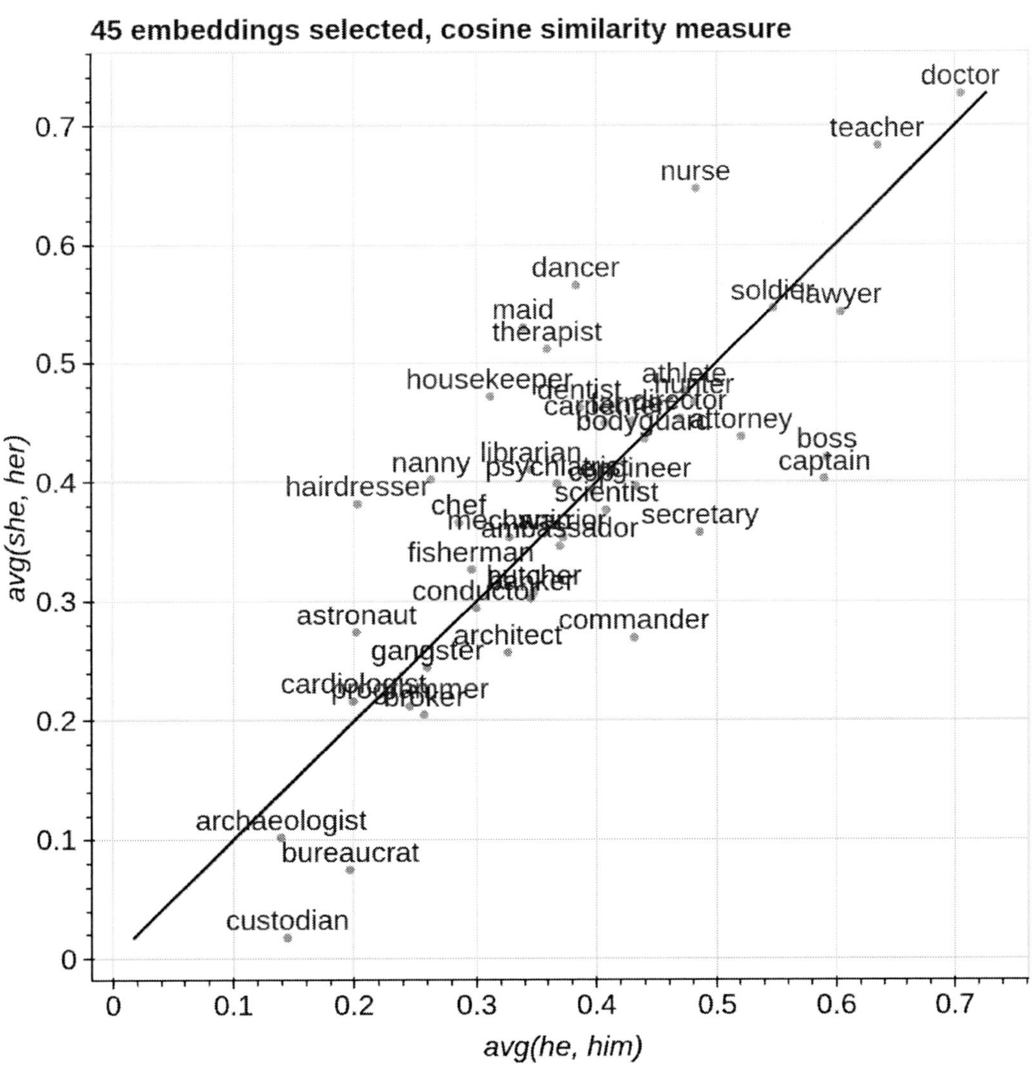

Figure 7: Professions plotted on "male" and "female" axes in *Wikipedia* embeddings.

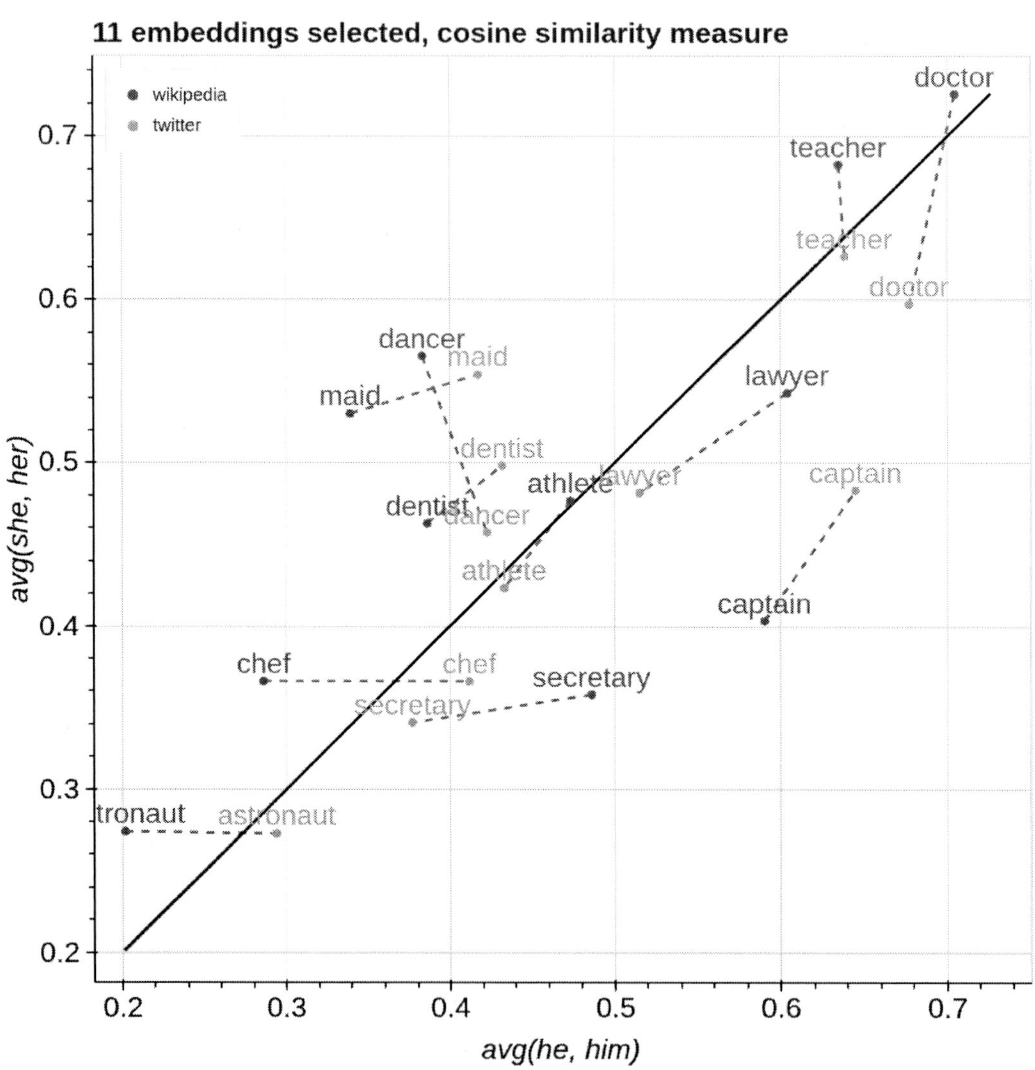

Figure 8: Professions plotted on "male" and "female" axes in $Wikipedia$ and $Twitter$ embeddings.

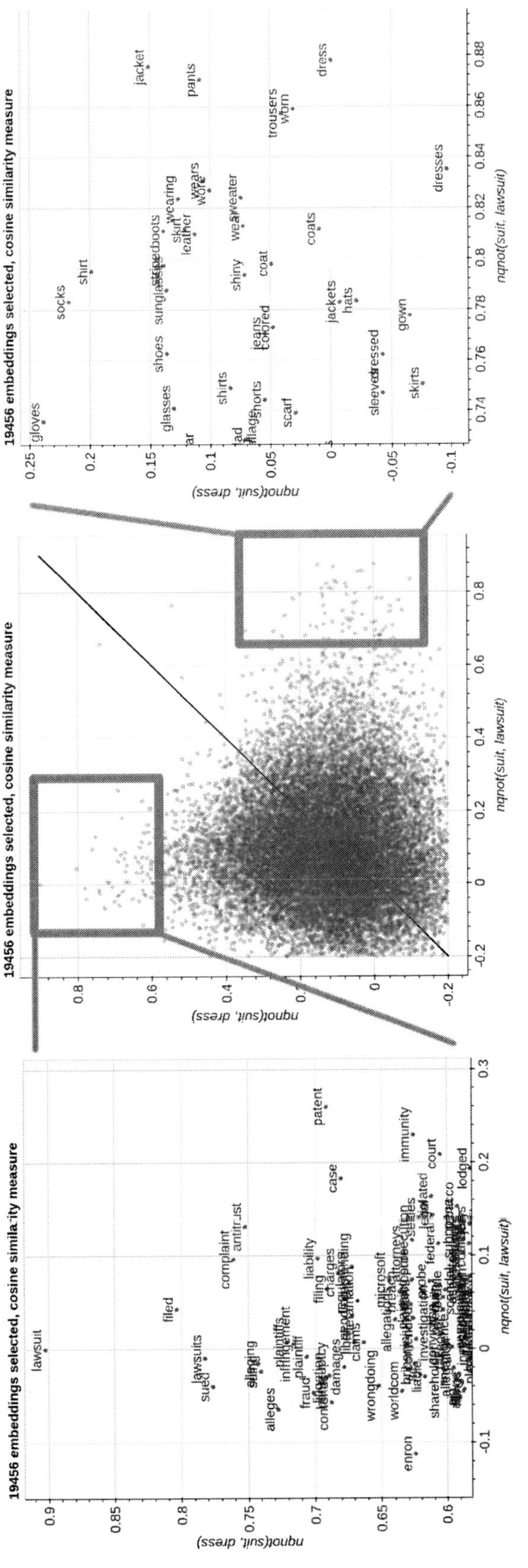

Figure 9: Plot of embeddings in *Wikipedia* with *suit* negated with respect to *lawsuit* and *dress* respectively as axes.

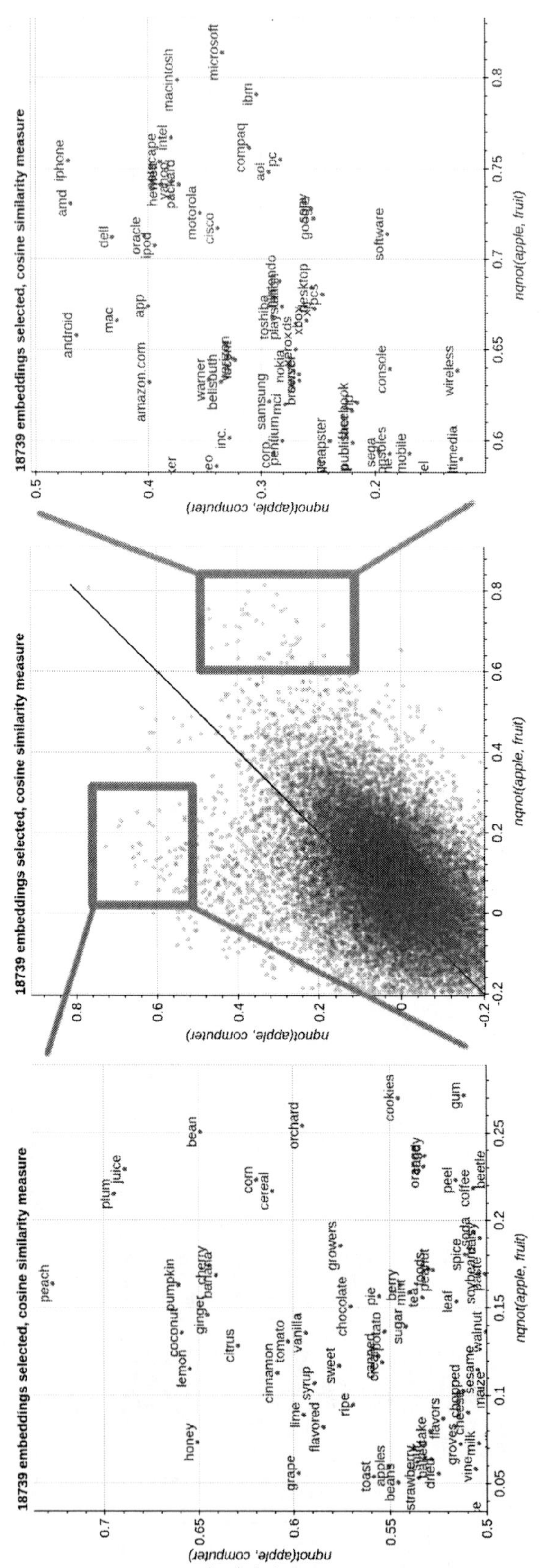

Figure 10: Plot of embeddings in *Wikipedia* with *apple* negated with respect to *fruit* and *computer* respectively as axes.

176

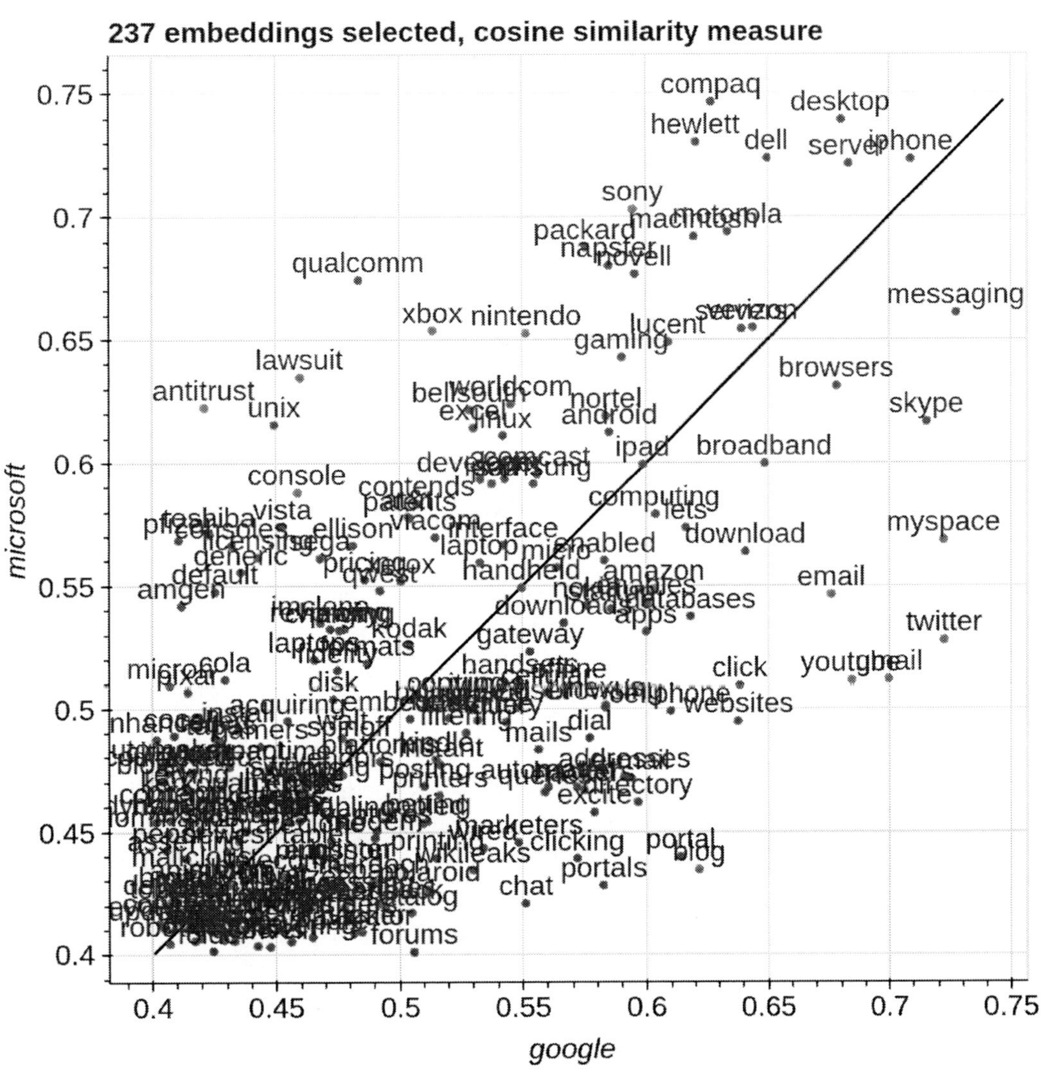

Figure 11: Fine-grained comparison of the subspace on the axis *google* and *microsoft* in *Wikipedia*.

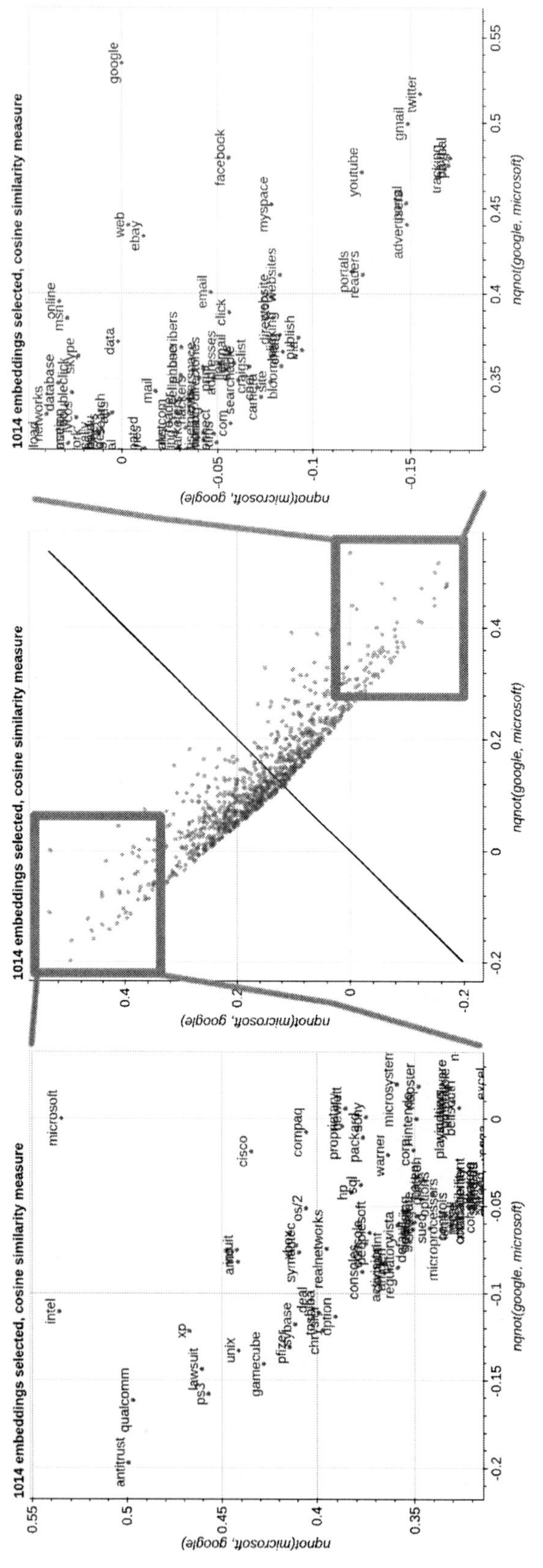

Figure 12: Fine-grained comparison of the subspace on the axis $nqnot(google, microsoft)$ and $nqnot(microsoft, google)$ in *Wikipedia*.

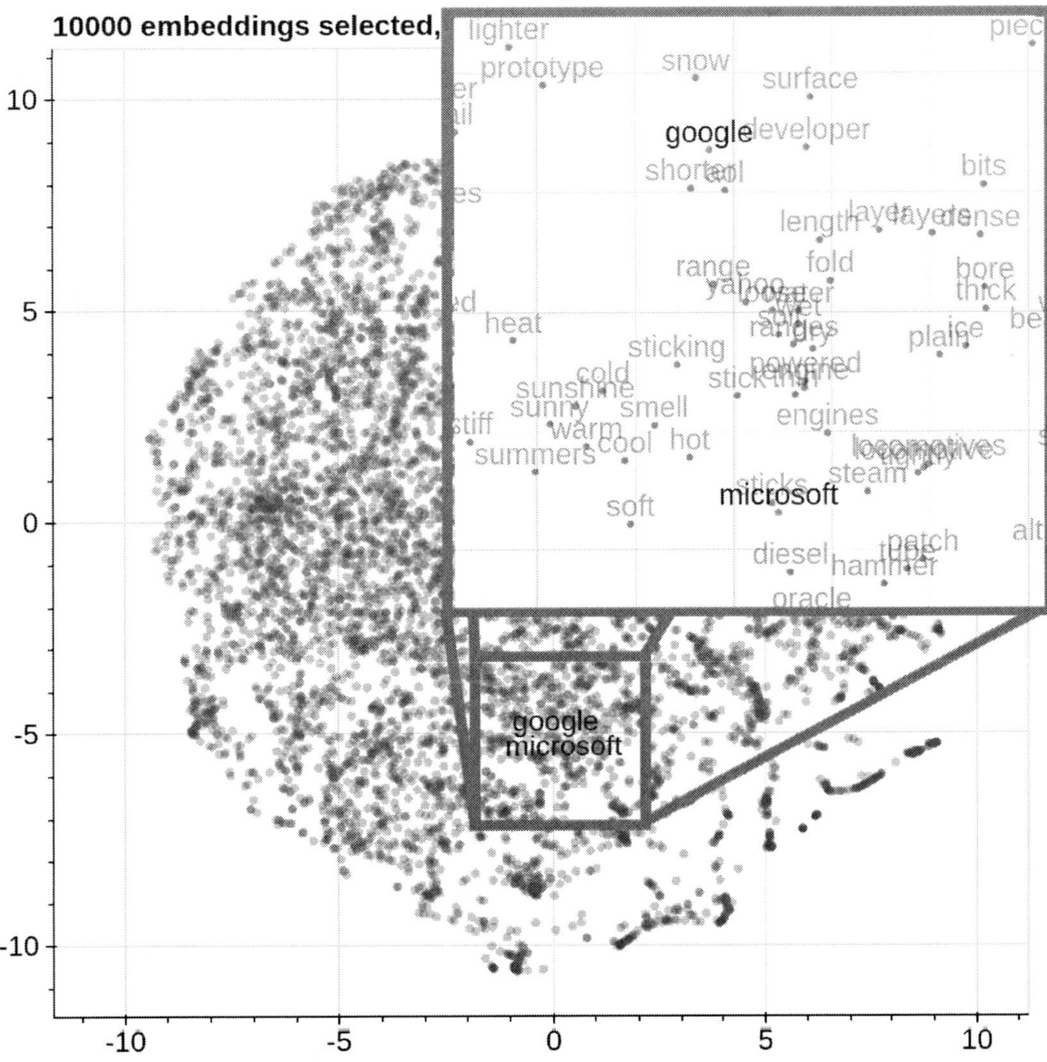

Figure 13: t-SNE visualization of *google* and *microsoft* in *Wikipedia*.

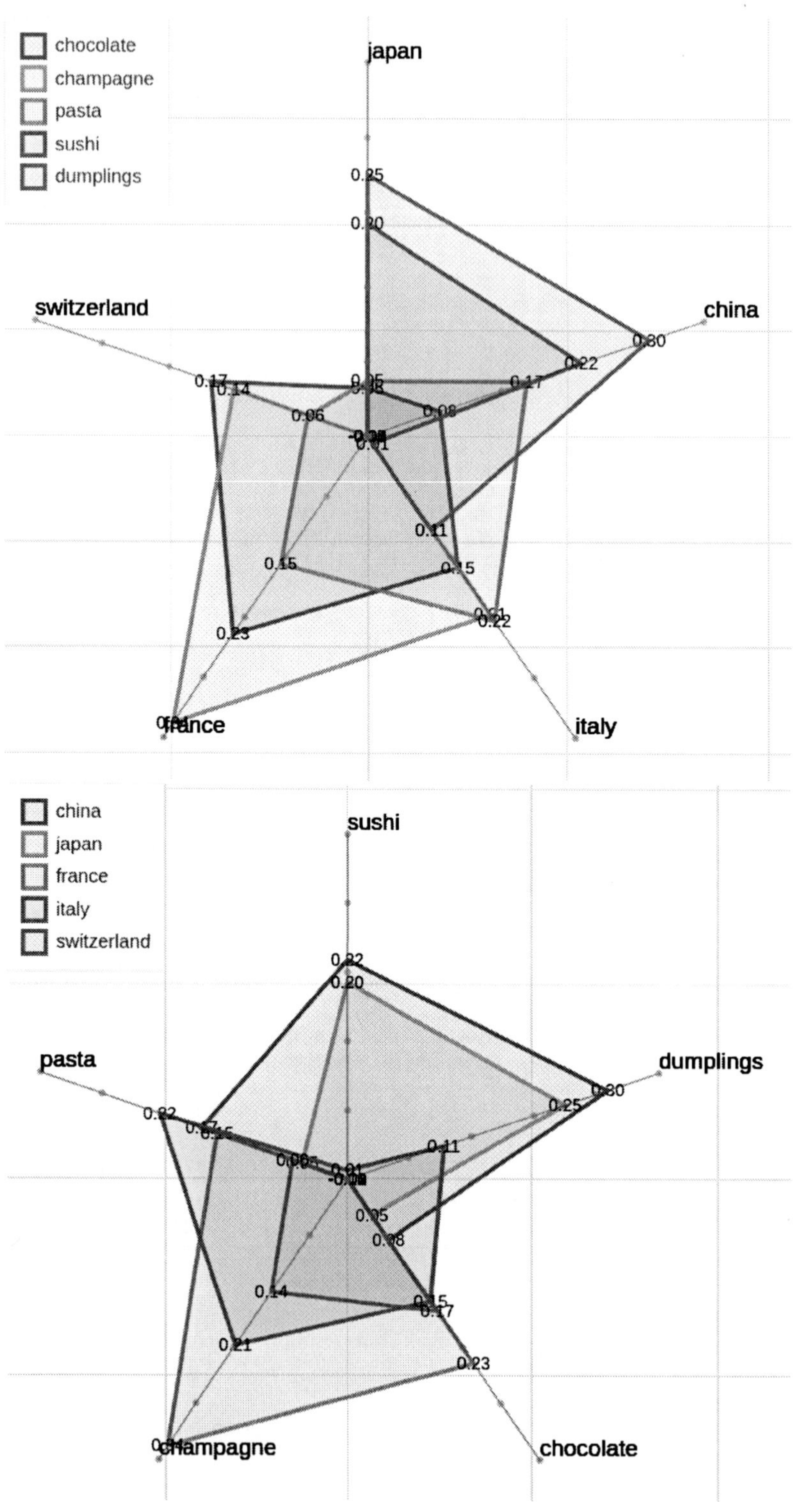

Figure 14: Two polar view of countries and foods in *Wikipedia*.

Flambé: A Customizable Framework for Machine Learning Experiments

Jeremy Wohlwend
ASAPP Inc.
jeremy@asapp.com

Nicholas Matthews
ASAPP Inc.
nick@asapp.com

Ivan Itzcovich
ASAPP Inc.
ivan@asapp.com

Abstract

Flambé is a machine learning experimentation framework built to accelerate the entire research life cycle. Flambé's main objective is to provide a unified interface for prototyping models, running experiments containing complex pipelines, monitoring those experiments in real-time, reporting results, and deploying a final model for inference. Flambé achieves both flexibility and simplicity by allowing users to write custom code but instantly include that code as a component in a larger system which is represented by a concise configuration file format. We demonstrate the application of the framework through a cutting-edge multistage use case: fine-tuning and distillation of a state of the art pretrained language model used for text classification. [1]

1 Introduction

Scientists and engineers in the machine learning community dedicate many hours and resouces towards preprocessing data, iterating on model architectures, tuning hyperparameters, aggregating results and ultimately deploying their most performant model. While frameworks like PyTorch (Paszke et al., 2017) and Tensorflow (et al., 2016) abstract away the details of operations like backprogpagation and make building models possible in a few lines of code, they do not explicitly aim to solve these other parts of the research cycle.

The explosion of available resources in the machine learning community (Dean et al., 2018) has included many tools that address one or more of these other phases of research, but these isolated tools do not always work harmoniously with one another, trading off customizability to provide high-level interfaces. Understanding that machine learning research particularly in the field of Natural Language Processing might require innovation at any level of abstraction and across any stage in the research process, we've built Flambé to include standardized implementations of modeling components, hyperparameter optimization and distributed execution that can all be effortlessly replaced with custom user-developed code.

By facilitating customization and iteration on a particular data pipeline and model architecture, we aim for Flambé users to spend the majority of their time doing research, not re-implementing tools for training, tuning, reporting and deploying.

Flambé's contributions are:

1. Modular machine learning components to develop replicable, state of the art research results. This includes: neural network components (pretrained or not), benchmark datasets, and standardized training and evaluation modules.

2. A configuration format that natively enables searching over hyperparameters and running remote multistage experiments at scale.

3. Smooth reporting and exporting, to facilitate sharing models and results with collaborators and the larger community.

4. An open source framework for both the academic community and teams in industry.

We demonstrate the application of our framework through a cutting-edge use case, namely knowledge distillation of a state of the art language model, the BERT model (Devlin et al., 2019), on a downstream text classification task.

2 Related work

Many different tools are attempting to tackle the various challenges of building machine learning

---

[1]The code and documentation can be found at https://flambe.ai

Proceedings of the 57th Annual Meeting of the Association for Computational Linguistics-System Demonstrations, pages 181–188
Florence, Italy, July 28 - August 2, 2019. ©2019 Association for Computational Linguistics

systems from different angles. Frameworks like
PyTorch and Tensorflow (et al., 2016) provide
the building blocks of models as simple modules
e.g. various linear and recurrent layers, losses,
optimizers etc. Many model implementations
have been built on top of these modules, with
some proposing new standardizations of specific
architectures like sequence-to-sequence modeling
(et al, 2019).

Libraries such as Keras (Chollet et al., 2015)
offer a high-level API for building and training
models. Others including AllenNLP (Gardner
et al., 2018), FastAI (Howard et al., 2018) and
Texar (et al, 2018) focus on some specific domains
or tasks like reading comprehension or text style
transfer. These types of frameworks tend to focus
on training a single model at a time, but many research experiments consist of complex multistage
pipelines, with hyperparameter tuning and distributed computation required at each stage. With
Flambé, users can write their custom code independent from these concerns, and then easily start
using algorithms like Hyperband (Li et al., 2016)
and Bayesian Optimization (Bergstra et al., 2013),
link components across stages, and run everything
on a cluster without any modifications.

MLFlow (Zaharia et al., 2018) focuses on experiment tracking, metric reporting, and contains
powerful features aimed at production deployment. However, it does not have a natural way to
run hyperparameter tuning, or advanced trial sampling and scheduling.

Ray (Moritz et al., 2017) implements infrastructure for distributing computational tasks on a cluster, and it also provides a higher level extension,
Tune (Liaw et al., 2018), that handles hyperparameter optimization.

Flambé leverages and builds upon existing
tools, connecting the dots between frameworks
like PyTorch and Ray, and providing a smooth integration between them with a powerful layer of
abstraction on top. By not trying to re-implement
solved problems like back-propagation and distributed task execution, we can focus our attention
on usability and efficiency.

3   The Flambé Framework

Flambé executes *experiments* which are composed of a pipeline of modeling and processing
stages (Subsection A), extensions that import user-
supplied code (Subsection B), links to existing

```
cl: github.com/.../classification   B
---

name: trec-text-classification

pipeline:   A

  stage0: !cl.TCProcessor
    dataset: !cl.TrecDataset

  stage1: !Trainer
    train_sampler: !BaseSampler
      data: !@ stage0.train   C
      batch_size: 32
    dev_sampler: !BaseSampler
      data: !@ stage0.dev
    model: !cl.TextClassifier
      embedding: !EmbeddingEncoder
        input_size: !@ stage0.vocab_size
        embedding_size: 300
      encoder: !RNNEncoder
        input_size: 300
        rnn_type: lstm
        n_layers: !g [2, 3, 4]   D
        hidden_size: 256
        pooling: last
      decoder: !SoftmaxDecoder
        input_size: 256
        output_size: !@ stage0.n_labels
    loss_fn: !NLLLoss
    metric_fn: !Accuracy
    optimizer: !torch.Adam
      params: !@ stage1.model.params
    max_steps: 100
    iter_per_step: 10

  stage2: !Evaluator
    model: !@ stage1.model
    metric_fn: !Accuracy
    eval_sampler: !BaseSampler
      data: !@ stage0.test
      batch_size: 512

schedulers:   E
  stage1: !tune.HyperBandScheduler

reduce:   F
  stage1: 1  # pick best
```

Figure 1: Example YAML config for text classification
on the TREC dataset. The highlighted and labeled sections refer to the subsections in 3.1. There are a number
of different objects that could be used in any place of
this config e.g. the optimizer could be `!torch.SGD`
and the scheduler `tune.HyperOpt` (Bayesian optimization). Note the pipeline stage names "stage0", etc.
are arbitrary.

components (Subsection C), and tunable hyperparameters (Subsections D, E, F). All of these
features are demonstrated in the `Experiment`
shown in Figure 1, which defines a simple text
classification task consisting of training an LSTM
(Hochreiter and Schmidhuber, 1997) on the TREC
dataset (Li and Roth, 2002).

Each tag in the YAML (Oren Ben-Kiki, 2009) config (anything beginning with '!') corresponds to a python object that will be initialized with the keyword arguments following the tag. These tags are not hardcoded into the system, and users can use their own classes in the config just as easily as the ones we've already built. After we explain all the aforementioned features, we introduce how Flambé saves object state, enables simple metric logging, and deploys models for production.

3.1 Walkthrough

In this section we present an example driven explanation of the core features as they're used in Figure 1.

A. Pipeline

The most important section of the YAML file is the `pipeline` section. This section contains a series of stages which each implement a `step` method. The example shown in Figure 1 contains 3 stages: (1) dataset loading and processing, (2) training of each model variant, and (3) evaluating the best model from `stage1`.

A stage in the pipeline can be any Python object. Users need only add a parent class to their class definition if they intend to use it in the YAML config. All objects will receive the keyword arguments given inline in the configuration file. For example, in Figure 1 the `TextClassifier` object receives an embedding, encoder and decoder, matching its definition in code:

```
from flambe.model import Model

class TextClassifier(Model):
  def __init__(self, embedding,
                 encoder, decoder):
    ...
```

All subclasses of Flambé classes like `Model` are automatically registered with YAML

B. Extending Flambé with Custom Code

Flambé is flexible because of its ability to use custom *Flambé objects* in the experiment configuration file. By default, only classes in the main Flambé library and PyTorch can be referenced, but by using the `extensions` feature users can include their own classes and functions, from either local or remote source code repositories.

To create an extension, users need only organize their code into one or more pip-installable packages. After declaring the extensions and including them at the top of the config file, they are useable anywhere in the YAML configuration file.

In the example, the `TRECDataset` object is defined in an external extension hosted in GitHub. By adding its URL at the top of the YAML configuration file, the `cl.TrecDataset` object and any other Flambé class can be used. If you cannot or do not want to inherit from one of our pipeline classes (Model, Trainer, etc.) you can inherit from `flambe.nn.Module` which will supply the minimum needed functionality to support use in the config file and automatic hierarchical serialization (See later sections).

C. Referencing Earlier Objects

A core feature of Flambé is the ability to connect (or "link") different components with the `!@` notation, a custom YAML tag we've implemented. Any value anywhere in the pipeline can be a reference to an earlier value that has already been defined. Each link consists of the identifier of a stage, e.g. "stage1" which in this case is the `Trainer` object, followed by the rest of the object attributes. In the highlighted example (C), the link `stage0.train` means that the data keyword argument for `BaseSampler` should point to the `train` attribute of the `TCProcessor`.

D. Hyperparameter Search

In addition to referencing other values via links, the value for any parameter in the config can be replaced with either a list of possible options to try (for grid search) or a distribution for sampling possible options. Grid search options are defined with the `!g` tag followed by the list of candidate values; Flambé will automatically duplicate the stage, choosing a single value for each variant of the stage. In the example we use this mechanism to search over different numbers of layers.

If distributions are used instead of lists of candidate values, Flambé performs a simple random search. Users can also specify a search field that maps stage names to the hyperparameter search algorithm, e.g. Bayesian optimization, which changes the distributions used to sample the tunable hyperparameters.

When `Links` reference stages with multiple variants, the stage containing the link is duplicated as many times as there are variants.

E. Trial Scheduling

Regardless of the strategy used to choose hyper-parameters, some variants will start to clearly out-perform others and scheduling algorithms like Hyperband (Li et al., 2016) use that information to intelligently allocate resources to the variants that are performing the best. Flambé surfaces an interface to these schedulers in the same way as the search algorithms: "schedulers" maps pipeline stage names to the desired scheduling algorithms, as shown in the example configuration.

F. Selecting the Best Variants

After trying many different combinations of hyperparameters, only the best will propagate to the next stages if the *reduce* operation is used. For example, with *reduce* mapping `stage1` to 1 in the example, only the single best configuration, with the optimal number of layers, will be evaluated in the final stage. In order to use this feature, the stages need to supply a *metric_fn* that can be used to rank the variants.

3.2 Hierarchical Serialization

While PyTorch already provides a clear and robust saving mechanism, we augment this functionality with a generic serialization protocol for all objects that includes opt-in versioning and a directory based file format that anyone can inspect. Rather than dumping all of the model weights and other state into a single file, the directory based structure mirrors the object hierarchy and enables the possibility of referencing a specific component. Rather than having to load the save file to inspect the contents, it can be navigated like any other directory. By default, only what PyTorch normally saves is included in the save file; users can add additional state by overriding `custom_state` and `load_custom_state`

3.3 Using a cluster

To run experiments on a cluster, an additional piece of YAML is needed to define the remote manager. As shown below in Figure 3 one can indicate the instance types and a timeout flag for both the orchestrator and the factories. We use this feature to keep our experiment tracking website running on the orchestrator once an experiment is over, but also to keep factories alive when rapidly experimenting or debugging. The orchestrator will communicate with workers in the cluster via Ray and Tune to execute and checkpoint

```
trec-text-classification/
  ...
  stage1/
    train_sampler/
      state.pt
    dev_sampler/
      state.pt
    model/
      embedding/
        state.pt
      encoder/
        state.pt
      decoder/
        state.pt
    optimizer/
      state.pt
  ...
```

Figure 2: Save file directory structure for the `Experiment` in Figure 1

progress at each step. If an experiment fails or is interrupted, it can be quickly resumed with an additional flag `resume:    True`. Crucially, this remote functionality allows to distribute the execution of the variants across a cluster of machines by only adding a few lines to the configuration.

```
manager: !AWSManager
  factories_num: 1
  factories_type: "p3.2xlarge"
  orchestrator_type: "t3.large"
  factory_timeout: 1   # in hours
  orchestrator_timeout: 1
```

Figure 3: Example remote config for AWS cluster.

3.4 Deploying

Typically after experimentation, machine learning projects require packaging a model together with some preprocessing and post-processing functions into a single inference-ready interface, e.g. a text classifier that actually takes raw string(s) as input. Flambé facilitates this use-case with the `Exporter` object, wherein users can define a new version of the model from the best variants tested, and with the right interface for later use.

3.5 Library usage

In addition to using the Flambé framework via YAML configuration files, users can also use the individual objects (e.g. the Trainer, or RNNEncoder classes) in any python script. This usage may be important for users that already have a production codebase (including training scripts) written purely in Python. In a future version of the software we plan to support creating full experiments and deploying models via code (instead of YAML) to enable dynamic experiment creation and model exporting.

3.6 Logging

Flambé provides full integration with Python's `logging` module and Tensorboard ((et al., 2016)). Users are able to visualize their results by simply including `log` statements in their code (See Figure 4).

```
from flambe import log
... # inside training step
log("loss", loss, step_num)
```

Figure 4: Example log statement. Logging can be done anywhere inside a custom object.

All variants will appear under the same plot for easy analysis (see Figure 5).

4 Case study: BERT Distillation

In this section we showcase Flambé's ability to transform a pre-existing codebase with no pre-existing support for hyperparameter optimization into a complex multi-stage pipeline with a YAML config less than 80 lines long. Furthermore, We were able to find the optimal set of parameters in roughly half the time otherwise needed by adding Hyperband scheduling (Li et al., 2016), and running the experiment over a large cluster.

BERT (Devlin et al., 2019) is a popular model which performs competitively across several NLP tasks by leveraging language model pre-training over a very large corpus. Two crucial issues with the BERT model are the size of the model, and its inference speed, which generally inhibits its use in production environments. To address this issue, recent efforts have shown that most of BERT's performance on a downstream task can be conserved, while dramatically reducing its memory footprint (Chia et al., 2018).

In this experiment, we fine-tune the BERT model on two standard text classification benchmarks: TREC (Li and Roth, 2002) and Sentiment Treebank (Socher et al., 2013). We then apply knowledge distillation to reduce the BERT model to a simple 4 layer, 256 units, SRU network (Lei et al., 2018). This is a typical multistage experiment with preprossessing, fine tuning, and distillation stages. All of this can be expressed in a sin-

Model	TREC	SST2	# Parameters
SRU	94.8	86.2	$\approx 5M$
BERT	96.8	91.0	$\approx 110M$
DISTILLED	95.5	87.8	$\approx 5M$

Table 1: Accuracy on benchmark text classification datasets: TREC and SST2 (Binary Sentiment Treebank). Distilling BERT improves the accuracy of the base SRU model, while reducing the number of parameters by more than 95%. All models were trained or fine-tuned using Flambé. The SRU and DISTILLED model have the same architecture, the SRU model being trained from scratch and the DISTILLED model benefiting from the BERT model's improved performance.

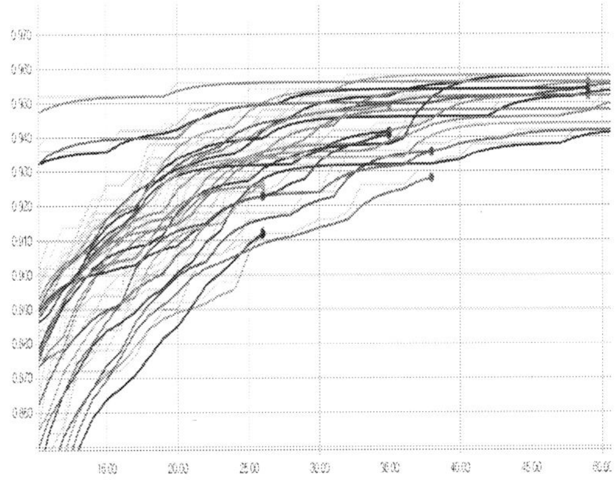

Figure 5: Some runs are pruned early by the Hyberband scheduling algorithm. The x-axis is training steps, and the y-axis is accuracy.

gle, concise configuration. Results are provided in Table 1. The full configuration, containing all three stages and their respective hyperparameters, is provided as supplementary material.

Not only can Flambé express the above experiment in a concise configuration, but using a state of the art trial scheduling algorithm such as Hyperband (Li et al., 2016) can be accomplished with a single additional line in the configuration. Figure 5 shows Hyperband allocating more training steps to the best-performing models. In this example, defining grid searches, running over a cluster, and using a scheduling algorithm on an existing codebase required little to no effort.

5 Future work

Flambé aims to integrate with research and engineering workflows through its focus on usability, modularity and reproducibility. We continue to pursue this goal by developing a large collection of machine learning components including state of the art models, benchmark datasets, and novel training strategies. Real, working, and reproducible experiment configurations will showcase these components alongside their performance in task-based leaderboards. In parallel, we will continue to develop user-friendly abstractions like the ability to auto-scale clusters based on the size of each stage in the pipeline, and to monitor or even alter experiment execution in real-time from a website.

References

Martin Abadi et al. 2016. Tensorflow: A system for large-scale machine learning. In *12th USENIX Symposium on Operating Systems Design and Implementation (OSDI 16)*, pages 265–283.

Myle Ott et al. 2019. fairseq: A fast, extensible toolkit for sequence modeling. In *Proceedings of the 2019 Conference of the North American Chapter of the Association for Computational Linguistics (Demonstrations)*, pages 48–53, Minneapolis, Minnesota. Association for Computational Linguistics.

Zhiting Hu et al. 2018. Texar: A modularized, versatile, and extensible toolbox for text generation. In *Proceedings of Workshop for NLP Open Source Software (NLP-OSS)*, pages 13–22, Melbourne, Australia. Association for Computational Linguistics.

James Bergstra, Dan Yamins, and David D Cox. 2013. Hyperopt: A python library for optimizing the hyperparameters of machine learning algorithms. In *Proceedings of the 12th Python in science conference*, pages 13–20. Citeseer.

Yew Ken Chia, Sam Witteveen, and Martin Andrews. 2018. Transformer to cnn: Label-scarce distillation for efficient text classification.

François Chollet et al. 2015. Keras. https://keras.io.

Jeff Dean, David Patterson, and Cliff Young. 2018. A new golden age in computer architecture: Empowering the machine-learning revolution. *IEEE Micro*, 38(2):21–29.

Jacob Devlin, Ming-Wei Chang, Kenton Lee, and Kristina Toutanova. 2019. BERT: Pre-training of deep bidirectional transformers for language understanding. In *Proceedings of the 2019 Conference of the North American Chapter of the Association for Computational Linguistics: Human Language Technologies, Volume 1 (Long and Short Papers)*, pages 4171–4186, Minneapolis, Minnesota. Association for Computational Linguistics.

Matt Gardner, Joel Grus, Mark Neumann, Oyvind Tafjord, Pradeep Dasigi, Nelson F. Liu, Matthew Peters, Michael Schmitz, and Luke Zettlemoyer. 2018. AllenNLP: A deep semantic natural language processing platform. In *Proceedings of Workshop for NLP Open Source Software (NLP-OSS)*, pages 1–6, Melbourne, Australia. Association for Computational Linguistics.

Sepp Hochreiter and Jürgen Schmidhuber. 1997. Long short-term memory. *Neural computation*, 9(8):1735–1780.

Jeremy Howard et al. 2018. fastai. https://github.com/fastai/fastai.

Tao Lei, Yu Zhang, Sida I Wang, Hui Dai, and Yoav Artzi. 2018. Simple recurrent units for highly parallelizable recurrence. In *Proceedings of the 2018 Conference on Empirical Methods in Natural Language Processing*, pages 4470–4481.

Lisha Li, Kevin Jamieson, Giulia DeSalvo, Afshin Rostamizadeh, and Ameet Talwalkar. 2016. Hyperband: A novel bandit-based approach to hyperparameter optimization. *arXiv preprint arXiv:1603.06560*.

Xin Li and Dan Roth. 2002. Learning question classifiers. In *COLING 2002: The 19th International Conference on Computational Linguistics*.

Richard Liaw, Eric Liang, Robert Nishihara, Philipp Moritz, Joseph E Gonzalez, and Ion Stoica. 2018. Tune: A research platform for distributed model selection and training. *arXiv preprint arXiv:1807.05118*.

Philipp Moritz, Robert Nishihara, Stephanie Wang, Alexey Tumanov, Richard Liaw, Eric Liang, William Paul, Michael I. Jordan, and Ion Stoica. 2017. Ray: A distributed framework for emerging AI applications. *CoRR*, abs/1712.05889.

Ingy döt Net Oren Ben-Kiki, Clark Evans. 2009. Yaml. https://yaml.org/spec/1.2/spec.html.

Adam Paszke, Sam Gross, Soumith Chintala, Gregory Chanan, Edward Yang, Zachary DeVito, Zeming Lin, Alban Desmaison, Luca Antiga, and Adam Lerer. 2017. Automatic differentiation in pytorch. In *NIPS-W*.

Richard Socher, Alex Perelygin, Jean Wu, Jason Chuang, Christopher D Manning, Andrew Ng, and Christopher Potts. 2013. Recursive deep models for semantic compositionality over a sentiment treebank. In *Proceedings of the 2013 conference on empirical methods in natural language processing*, pages 1631–1642.

Matei Zaharia, Andrew Chen, Aaron Davidson, Ali Ghodsi, Sue Ann Hong, Andy Konwinski, Siddharth Murching, Tomas Nykodym, Paul Ogilvie, Mani Parkhe, et al. 2018. Accelerating the machine learning lifecycle with mlflow. *Data Engineering*, page 39.

A Screenshots

Below is a screenshot of the reporting site that includes a progress bar, links to see the console output and Tensorboard, and a download link for the model weights:

When you launch an experiment from the console, you will see a series of status updates as shown below:

B BERT Configuration File

```
dist: https://github.com/.../flambe-extensions/tree/master/extensions/distillation
lm: https://github.com/.../flambe-extensions/tree/master/extensions/language_modeling
cl: https://github.com/..../flambe-extensions/tree/master/extensions/classification
---

!Experiment

name: flambe_distillation

pipeline:

  data: !cl.TRECDataset

  0_preprocess: !dist.DistillationProcessor
    student_processor: !cl.TCProcessor
      dataset: !@ data
      embeddings: !@ glove
      text_field: !TextField
    teacher_processor: !cl.TCProcessor
      dataset: !@ data
      text_field: !lm.BERTTextField.from_alias
        alias: 'bert-base-uncased'

  1_train_bert: !Trainer
    train_sampler: !BaseSampler
      data: !@ 0_preprocess.teacher_processor.train
      batch_size: 32
    dev_sampler: !BaseSampler
      data: !@ 0_preprocess.teacher_processor.dev
      batch_size: 32
    model: !cl.TextClassifier
      embedding: !lm.BERTEmbeddings.from_alias
        alias: 'bert-base-uncased'
      encoder: !lm.BERTEncoder.from_alias
        alias: 'bert-base-uncased'
      decoder: !SoftmaxDecoder
        input_size: !@ 1_train_bert.model.encoder.config.hidden_size
        output_size: !@ 0_preprocess.teacher_processor.num_labels
    loss_fn: !NLLLoss
    metric_fn: !Accuracy
    optimizer: !lm.BERTOptimizer
      params: !call 1_train_bert.model.named_parameters
      lr: 0.00005
      warmup: 0.1
    max_steps: 10
    iter_per_step: 100

  2_distillation: !dist.DistillationTrainer
    train_sampler: !BaseSampler
      data: !@ 0_preprocess.train
      batch_size: 64
    dev_sampler: !BaseSampler
      data: !@ 0_preprocess.dev
      batch_size: 64
    teacher_model: !@ 1_train_bert.model
    student_model: !cl.TextClassifier
      embedding: !EmbeddingEncoder
        input_size: !@ 0_preprocess.student_processor.vocab_size
        embedding_size: 300
        embedding_matrix: !@ 0_preprocess.student_processor.embeddings
      encoder: !RNNEncoder
        input_size: 300
        rnn_type: sru
        n_layers: 4
        hidden_size: 256
      decoder: !SoftmaxDecoder
        input_size: 256
        output_size: !@ 0_preprocess.student_processor.num_labels
    alpha_kl: !g [0.75, 0.9, 0.99]
    temperature: !g [10, 20, 30]
    loss_fn: !NLLLoss
    metric_fn: !Accuracy
    optimizer: !torch.Adam
      params: !@ 2_distillation.student_model.trainable_params
      lr: 0.001
    max_steps: 100
    iter_per_step: 100

schedulers:
  2_distillation: !tune.HyperBandScheduler
```

A Modular Tool for Automatic Summarization

Valentin Nyzam
LIASD - Universit Paris 8
`v.nyzam@iut.univ-paris8.fr`

Aurélien Bossard
LIASD - Universit Paris 8
`a.bossard@iut.univ-paris8.fr`

Abstract

This paper introduces the first fine-grained modular tool for automatic summarization. Open source and written in Java, it is designed to be as straightforward as possible for end-users. Its modular architecture is meant to ease its maintenance and the development and integration of new modules. We hope that it will ease the work of researchers in automatic summarization by providing a reliable baseline for future works as well as an easy way to evaluate methods on different corpora.

1 Introduction

Automatic summarization (AS) is studied since the late 1950s (Luhn, 1958). Automatic summarization methods were mostly extractive until recently, where abstractive methods have emerged thanks to the recent breakthrough in neural networks. Abstractive automatic summarization methods are for the most part supervized. However, because of the automatic summarization task complexity, huge corpora made of pairs of documents and their associated summary are needed. For example, the CNN and Dailymail news corpora on which are based the first neural-based news automatic summarizers are composed of more than 200,000 pairs of document and summary. Other summarization tasks can also be provided with large corpora, such as scientific articles summarization. However, most of real-life summarization tasks come without any learning corpus. The cost in human resources to build such corpora is such that unsupervized summarization methods cannot be excluded from the research field.

In the last decades, efforts have been made in different fields of computer science to release open source systems that encode several methods.

GATE[1](Dowman et al., 2005) platform is an example of such an open source system for NLP. Other research fields such as machine learning benefit from several open source modular systems, e.g., Weka (Hall et al., 2009), SPMF (Fournier-Viger et al., 2014), or Orange (Demšar et al., 2013). To our knowledge, no such tool exists for AS. A modular and open source tool for automatic summarization could allow to easily test different automatic summarization methods on different tasks / corpora. If such a tool is proven to be reliable, it can also be used as an acknowledged baseline for new systems – abstractive or extractive – to compare to. In fact, we found that some recent papers in neural abstractive summarization compare their results with naive extractive baselines or even no extractive baseline at all (e.g. (See et al., 2017) with a lead-based extractive baseline, (Chopra et al., 2016) with no extractive baseline at all). These works could have sorely benefited from a straightforward and easy-to-use summarization platform to establish fair comparisons to older extractive systems.

In this paper, we present an open source modular tool dedicated to automatic summarization. Written in Java, it is designed to first answer the lack of such a tool and so provide the community with an easy-to-use summarization tool, to allow a straightforward maintenance of existing modules and development of new modules, and to allow methods comparison in a unified framework. The tool is available on GitHub : `https://github.com/ToolAutomaticSum/MOTS`. We also present a study on DUC, TAC, CNN and Dailymail corpora.

---

[1]`http://gate.ac.uk`

Proceedings of the 57th Annual Meeting of the Association for Computational Linguistics-System Demonstrations, pages 189–194
Florence, Italy, July 28 - August 2, 2019. ©2019 Association for Computational Linguistics

2 Related Work

Open source summarizers can be classified into two categories: systems that only implement one or more methods defined by their authors as results of research and systems conceived as a way to implement existing methods. In the first category, one can cite MEAD (Radev et al., 2004a) that originally implemented centroid-based extraction method (Radev et al., 2004b) and later implemented LexRank (Erkan and Radev, 2004). However, this system does not seem to be available anymore. Among the other systems in that category, one can cite ICSISUMM (Gillick et al., 2009) that implements ILP-based summarization and MUSEEC (Litvak et al., 2016). However, systems in this first category cover only a few methods among existing methods, so there was a need for platforms with a better summarization methods coverage. SUMMA (Saggion, 2014) is a summarization toolkit implemented with GATE. It includes several sentence scorers, such as LexRank, Centroid and shallow features based. It benefits from GATE NLP methods. Sumy[2] is a more complete toolkit that implements eight different extraction methods, including baseline systems (random, first sentences only). As for PKUSum-Sum[3], (Zhang et al., 2016) implements ten different methods and handles three different summarization tasks: mono-document, multi-document and topic-based multi-document summarization. Modularity for these two system is however limited to tokenization/stemming and the choice of extraction method which is not decomposed itself in modules. This is the main asset of our tool: it is modular on a fine-grained level so automatic summarization methods are not defined globally but as a combination of small interchangeable modules. Table 1 shows details about the summarization methods implemented by SUMMA, Sumy and PKUSumSum.

3 Architecture

3.1 Modularity

Our tool is modular on a fine-grained level. Because of the modularity and the need of module compatibility definition, we made the choice of Java as programming language. Our tool can handle mono and multi-document summarization,

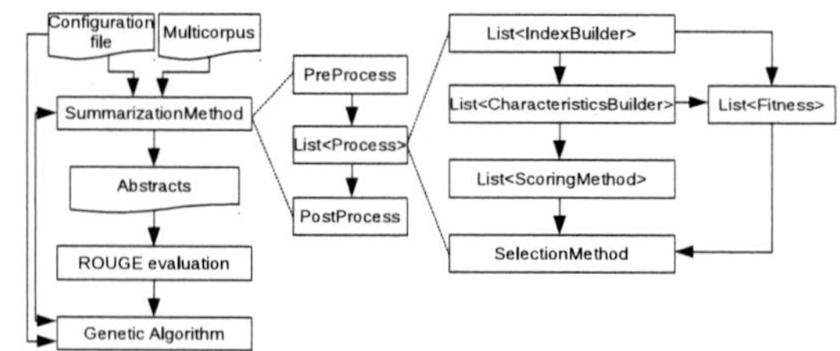

Figure 1: Architecture and workflow of our tool

topic-based or not. It embeds a genetic algorithm to tune hyperparameters. The summarization modules are all language-independent for multilingual summarization. Its architecture is conceived for both extractive, semi-extractive and abstractive paradigms. Also, using it as an end-user is straightforward.

It is divided in two branches: one for traditional greedy extractive methods, and one for global search algorithms such as genetic or knapsack algorithms (cf Figure 1). Our system can also handle fully abstractive methods.

The greedy branch is divided in four steps:
- IndexBuilder: an index is built using unigrams or n-grams for which a set of features is built;
- CharacteristicsBuilder: a set of features is computed for every text chunk[4] based on one or more indexes;
- SentenceScoring: score computation for every text chunk based on previous features;
- SelectionMethod: text chunks extraction with a method using previous scores.

The global search algorithms branch is divided in two steps:
- FitnessScore: a score computed for a candidate summary;
- SelectionMethod: the search algorithm itself guided by the fitness.

The four steps (or atomic processings) of a summarization method are independent, and they communicate via the Process class that controls their execution and compatibility. Input and output of the atomic processings are specified via inheritance of a specific method and the implementation of interfaces defined and documented in our tool. These interfaces make the Process class able to use Java methods to adapt input and output between each atomic processing. All atomic processings are independent and follow compatibility rules, so

---

[2]https://github.com/miso-belica/sumy
[3]https://github.com/PKULCWM/PKUSUMSUM

[4]e.g., sentences, phrases, defined during preprocessing

our system architecture is completely modular.

3.2 Embedded evaluation

If the gold standard summaries are provided with the corpus to summarize, our tool can perform a call to ROUGE (Lin, 2004) in order to instantly retrieve the results of a summarization method on a specific corpus.

3.3 Embedded genetic algorithm

All summarization methods have parameters that influence the quality of the summaries. Optimizing these parameters for a specific task is crucial. Litvak et al. (2010); Bossard and Rodrigues (2011) have shown that a genetic algorithm (GA) can be efficient for this kind of optimization. Our tool integrates a GA to optimize summarization methods hyperparameters. We specified a *dna* syntax for the definition of methods hyperparameters that can be used by any module implemented in our tool. The GA uses ROUGE-2 as objective function, but it can be overridden using the modular architecture of our tool. The GA is launched using a XML configuration file that sets the hyperparameters to be optimized.

4 Implemented modules

The IndexBuilder class defines what the tokens are and how they are represented. We can use unigrams or n-grams and each of them can be associated with a frequency, a tf.idf value, or a vector representation computed with LSA or word embeddings.

The CharacteristicsBuilder class defines the representation of a text chunk (most of the time, text chunks are sentences). We can use a bag-of-words representation, the mean vector (the mean vector of all the tokens in a text chunk), the matrix composed of all tokens vectors, the co-occurrence graph (Rousseau and Vazirgiannis, 2013), the k-core representation (Batagelj and Zaversnik, 2003), or a clustering based on any representation (Bossard and Rodrigues, 2011).

The SentenceScore class defines how to compute a score for a text chunk depending on the characteristics computed previously. We can choose the sum of tf.idf above a threshold, the similarity with a vector or a matrix (to emulate (Radev et al., 2004b)), the position of the text chunk in a document.

The SelectionMethod class defines how the sentences are selected. We can chose greedy algorithms such as MMR (Carbonell and Goldstein, 1998), CSIS (Radev et al., 2004a), an extraction method based on a previous clustering (Bossard, 2013) or a naive extraction of the best sentences, or global search algorithms such as Knapsack (Gillick et al., 2008), a genetic algorithm (Bossard and Rodrigues, 2017), ILP (Gillick et al., 2009) or a reinforcement algorithm (Ryang and Abekawa, 2012).

Our tool can also call an abstractive external summarization method, retrieve the results and use them for postprocessing or evaluation purposes. This is not trivial as the index has to be updated in order to take into account out of vocabulary words.

Combining these modules, we can emulate most of the most known summarization methods. Table 1 shows a comparison between our tool and other summarization tools introduced in Section 2. It shows that, to our knowledge and at the moment we write this paper, our tool covers the most of the summarization methods covered by other known summarizers. Moreover, two of the three methods not yet implemented: Manifold rank (Wan et al., 2007) and Submodular functions (Lin and Bilmes, 2011) are currently under development and should be released soon.

5 Using our tool

Using our tool as an end user is straightforward. It only requires a configuration file that describes the summarization method to use by defining every module used and their parameters, and a descriptor file for the multicorpus to summarize. Even if a configuration file can be written from scratch, we supply standard configuration files that encode the most known and used summarization methods.

6 Study

We evaluated some summarization methods from our tool on different corpora: DUC 2006 and 2007 and TAC 2008, 2009 and 2010 corpora (multidocument news summarization) and CNN/Dailymail corpus.

We used 264.999 documents of the merged corpus of CNN and Dailymail to train the pointer-generator abstractive method. It was then validated on 11.659 documents and tested on 12.143 documents. We used the same evaluation set for all methods. We evaluated all methods with a limit

	Luhn	Edmundson	Lead	Centroid	LexRank	TextRank	KL incr.	Manifold Rank	Clust.	ILP	LDA	Submodular	Knapsack	Genetic	Pointer Generator
SUMMA	✓	✓	✓	✓	✗	✗	✗	✗	✗	✗	✗	✗	✗	✗	✗
Sumy	✓	✓	✗	✗	✓	✓	✓	✗	✗	✗	✓	✗	✗	✗	✗
PKUSumSum	✗	✗	✓	✓	✓	✓	✗	✓	✓	✓	✗	✓	✗	✗	✗
Our tool	✓	✗	✓	✓	✓	✓	✓	✗	✓	✓	✓	✗	✓	✓	✓

Table 1: Comparison of systems summarization methods handling capabilities

of 100 and 50 words, because we found out that Pointer-Generator often produces only 50 words long summaries.

As DUC and TAC corpora do not provide enough data to train a neural network, we used the model learned on CNN/Dailymail to generate a summary for DUC and TAC and applied it on the most recent newswire article of each set of documents.

Table 2 shows the results of a small sample of methods from our tool on DUC, TAC and CNN/DailyMail corpora. We made the choice of selecting methods that show the modularity of our tool:

- lead: the first n words of a document (for DUC and TAC the first n words of the most recent document);

- tf.idf MMR: sentences are scored with the sum of tf.idf scores and selected with MMR;

- Centroid MMR: sentences are scored with the Centroid method and selected with MMR;

- 2G Centroid MMR: sentences are scored with the Centroid method on bigrams and selected with MMR;

- 3G Centroid MMR: sentences are scored with the Centroid method on trigrams and selected with MMR;

- LexRank MMR: sentences are scored with the LexRank method on unigrams and selected with MMR;

- 2G LexRank MMR: sentences are scored with the LexRank method on bigrams and selected with MMR;

- 2G Centroid KS: sentences are scored with the LexRank method on bigrams and selected with a knapsack algorithm;

- 2G JS KS: sentences are extracted with a knapsack algorithm that uses the Jensen-Shannon divergence as fitness and bigrams as tokens;

- ILP: sentences are extracted with an ILP based solver under the constraints of (Gillick et al., 2009);

- Genetic: sentences are extracted with a genetic algorithm that uses the Jensen-Shannon divergence as fitness and bigrams as tokens;

- Pointer Generator: our tool calls the Pointer Generator (See et al., 2017) and retrieves its results.

DUC and TAC were evaluated using the best ROUGE parameters for these corpora in Graham (2015)'s study. CNN/Dailymail tasks were evaluated using a standard configuration of ROUGE: recall as score, bigrams as tokens, no stemming, removal of stop words.

As one can see in Table 2, 2G JS KS, ILP and Genetic methods perform badly on the CNN/DailyMail task. This is due to the fact that ILP method is designed for multidocument summarization. 2G JS KS and Genetic use the same fitness: a Jensen-Shannon divergence. We hypothesize that the CNN/DailyMail documents are too small for such a fitness based on the bigrams probability distribution. Without any suprise, Pointer Generator performs badly on DUC and TAC corpora. Even if the corpora are close (newswire articles for both DUC/TAC and CNN/DailyMail), the task is not exactly the same. This confirms that sometimes, unsupervised extractive methods are the only solution available, and that such methods shall not yet be laid aside by the research community.

7 Conclusion

This paper introduces a new tool for automatic summarization. Written in Java, it is completely modular and can emulate most of the most known extractive summarization methods. The tool is open source, and modules can be added easily. Compared to other existing tools, ours is modular on a fine-grained level, so a summarization method can be defined as a combination of different modules: token representation, text chunk representation, text chunk scoring, and text chunk se-

	DUC2006	DUC2007	TAC2008	TAC2009	TAC2010	CNN/DM(100)	CNN/DM(50)
lead	6.69	8.76	8.81	7.44	6.58	19.62	9.51
tf.idf MMR	8.08	9.48	7.72	7.1	7.72	19.71	10.69
Centroid MMR	8.73	9.34	8.39	7.63	7.93	21.15	12.55
2G Centroid MMR	9.88	11.21	10.84	9.29	10.15	21.58	11.85
3G Centroid MMR	9.10	10.94	10.84	9.29	10.40	21.14	11.50
LexRank MMR	8.83	10.44	8.98	9.36	9.24	21.17	10.96
2G LexRank MMR	8.37	9.82	8.62	8.9	8.94	17.62	10.78
2G Centroid KS	8.85	9.34	8.4	9.03	9.65	18.47	10.69
2G JS KS	10.18	12.61	11.28	11.35	10.01	14.92	8.55
ILP	9.63	11.35	10.96	9.88	10.43	14.89	5.44
Genetic	10.55	12.17	11.01	10.62	10.79	15.35	10.51
Pointer Generator	3.07	7.47	3.33	5.75	4.26	10.24	10.24

Table 2: Results on DUC, TAC and CNN/Dailymail corpora

lection. As we write this paper, and to our knowledge, our tool covers more automatic summarization methods than the three other existing summarizers.

As an end-user, using our tool, available on GitHub (`https://github.com/ToolAutomaticSum/MOTS`), is straightforward. It only needs a description of the corpus to summarize and a configuration file that describes the modules to use. We provide configuration files for the most known summarization methods.

For this paper, we evaluated a small sample of the methods that can be ran with our tool. Except for three methods that are really specific to multidocument summarization, the evaluated summarization methods beat the naive baseline that extracts the n first words from a document. This is still a competitive baseline when summarizing newswire articles.

Due to its ease of use and to its results on different summarization tasks, our tool can be used as a baseline for forthcoming research on automatic summarization.

Acknowledgement

This work is supported by a public grant overseen by the French National Research Agency (ANR) as part of the "Young researchers program" (reference : ANR-16-CE38-0008 ASADERA).

References

Vladimir Batagelj and Matjaz Zaversnik. 2003. An o(m) algorithm for cores decomposition of networks. *CoRR*, cs.DS/0310049.

Aurélien Bossard. 2013. Generating update summaries: Using an unsupervized clustering algorithm to cluster sentences. In *Multi-source, Multilingual Information Extraction and Summarization*, Theory and Applications of Natural Language Processing, pages 205–227. Springer.

Aurélien Bossard and Christophe Rodrigues. 2011. Combining a multi-document update summarization system–cbseas–with a genetic algorithm. In *Combinations of intelligent methods and applications*, pages 71–87. Springer.

Aurélien Bossard and Christophe Rodrigues. 2017. An evolutionary algorithm for automatic summarization. In *Proceedings of the International Conference Recent Advances in Natural Language Processing, RANLP 2017*, pages 111–120, Varna, Bulgaria. INCOMA Ltd.

Jaime Carbonell and Jade Goldstein. 1998. The use of mmr, diversity-based reranking for reordering documents and producing summaries. In *Proceedings of the 21st annual international ACM SIGIR conference on Research and development in information retrieval*, pages 335–336. ACM.

Sumit Chopra, Michael Auli, and Alexander M. Rush. 2016. Abstractive sentence summarization with attentive recurrent neural networks. In *Proceedings of the 2016 Conference of the North American Chapter of the Association for Computational Linguistics: Human Language Technologies*, pages 93–98, San Diego, California. Association for Computational Linguistics.

Janez Demšar, Tomaž Curk, Aleš Erjavec, Črt Gorup, Tomaž Hočevar, Mitar Milutinovič, Martin Možina, Matija Polajnar, Marko Toplak, Anže Starič, Miha Štajdohar, Lan Umek, Lan Žagar, Jure Žbontar, Marinka Žitnik, and Blaž Zupan. 2013. Orange: Data mining toolbox in python. *Journal of Machine Learning Research*, 14:2349–2353.

Mike Dowman, Valentin Tablan, Hamish Cunningham, and Borislav Popov. 2005. Web-assisted annotation, semantic indexing and search of television and radio news. In *Proceedings of the 14th International World Wide Web Conference*, Chiba, Japan.

Günes Erkan and Dragomir R Radev. 2004. Lexrank: Graph-based lexical centrality as salience in text summarization. *Journal of AIR*, 22:457–479.

P. Fournier-Viger, A. Gomariz, T. Gueniche, A. Soltani, C. Wu., and V. S. Tseng. 2014. SPMF: a Java Open-Source Pattern Mining Library. *Journal of Machine Learning Research (JMLR)*, 15:3389–3393.

Daniel Gillick, Benoit Favre, and Hakkani-Tür. 2008. The icsi summarization system at tac 2008. In *Proc. of the Text Analysis Conference workshop*.

Daniel Gillick, Benoit Favre, Dilek Hakkani-Tür, Berndt Bohnet, Yang Liu, and Shasha Xie. 2009. The icsi/utd summarization system at tac 2009. In *Proc. of the Text Analysis Conference workshop, Gaithersburg, MD (USA)*.

Yvette Graham. 2015. Re-evaluating automatic summarization with bleu and 192 shades of rouge. In *Proceedings of the 2015 Conference on Empirical Methods in Natural Language Processing*, pages 128–137, Lisbon, Portugal. Association for Computational Linguistics.

Mark Hall, Eibe Frank, Geoffrey Holmes, Bernhard Pfahringer, Peter Reutemann, and Ian H. Witten. 2009. The weka data mining software: An update. *SIGKDD Explor. Newsl.*, 11(1):10–18.

Chin-Yew Lin. 2004. Rouge: A package for automatic evaluation of summaries. In *Text summarization branches out: Proceedings of the ACL-04 workshop*, volume 8. Barcelona, Spain.

Hui Lin and Jeff Bilmes. 2011. A class of submodular functions for document summarization. In *Proceedings of the 49th Annual Meeting of the Association for Computational Linguistics: Human Language Technologies-Volume 1*, pages 510–520. Association for Computational Linguistics.

Marina Litvak, Mark Last, and Menahem Friedman. 2010. A new approach to improving multilingual summarization using a genetic algorithm. In *Proceedings of the 48th annual meeting of the association for computational linguistics*, pages 927–936. Association for Computational Linguistics.

Marina Litvak, Natalia Vanetik, Mark Last, and Elena Churkin. 2016. Museec: A multilingual text summarization tool. In *Proceedings of ACL-2016 System Demonstrations*, pages 73–78. Association for Computational Linguistics.

H. P. Luhn. 1958. The automatic creation of literature abstracts. *IBM J. Res. Dev.*, 2(2):159–165.

Dragomir R Radev, Timothy Allison, Sasha Blair-Goldensohn, John Blitzer, Arda Celebi, Stanko Dimitrov, Elliott Drabek, Ali Hakim, Wai Lam, Danyu Liu, et al. 2004a. Mead-a platform for multidocument multilingual text summarization. In *LREC*.

Dragomir R Radev, Hongyan Jing, Małgorzata Styś, and Daniel Tam. 2004b. Centroid-based summarization of multiple documents. *Information Processing & Management*, 40:919–938.

François Rousseau and Michalis Vazirgiannis. 2013. Graph-of-word and tw-idf: new approach to ad hoc ir. In *Proceedings of the 22nd ACM international conference on Information & Knowledge Management*, pages 59–68. ACM.

Seonggi Ryang and Takeshi Abekawa. 2012. Framework of automatic text summarization using reinforcement learning. In *Proceedings of the 2012 Joint Conference on Empirical Methods in Natural Language Processing and Computational Natural Language Learning*, pages 256–265. Association for Computational Linguistics.

Horacio Saggion. 2014. Creating summarization systems with summa. In *Proceedings of the Ninth International Conference on Language Resources and Evaluation (LREC'14)*, Reykjavik, Iceland. European Language Resources Association (ELRA).

Abigail See, Peter J. Liu, and Christopher D. Manning. 2017. Get to the point: Summarization with pointer-generator networks. In *Proceedings of the 55th Annual Meeting of the Association for Computational Linguistics, ACL 2017, Vancouver, Canada, July 30 - August 4, Volume 1: Long Papers*, pages 1073–1083.

Xiaojun Wan, Jianwu Yang, and Jianguo Xiao. 2007. Manifold-ranking based topic-focused multi-document summarization. In *Proceedings of the 20th International Joint Conference on Artifical Intelligence*, IJCAI'07, pages 2903–2908, San Francisco, CA, USA. Morgan Kaufmann Publishers Inc.

Jianmin Zhang, Tianming Wang, and Xiaojun Wan. 2016. PKUSUMSUM : A java platform for multilingual document summarization. In *COLING (Demos)*, pages 287–291. ACL.

TARGER: Neural Argument Mining at Your Fingertips

Artem Chernodub[1,2], Oleksiy Oliynyk[3], Philipp Heidenreich[3], Alexander Bondarenko[4],
Matthias Hagen[4], Chris Biemann[3], and Alexander Panchenko[5,3]

[1]Grammarly
[2]Faculty of Applied Sciences, Ukrainian Catholic University, Lviv, Ukraine
[3]Language Technology Group, Universität Hamburg, Hamburg, Germany
[4]Big Data Analytics Group, Martin-Luther Universität Halle-Wittenberg, Halle, Germany
[5]Skolkovo Institute of Science and Technology, Moscow, Russia

Abstract

We present TARGER, an open source neural argument mining framework for tagging arguments in free input texts and for keyword-based retrieval of arguments from an argument-tagged web-scale corpus. The currently available models are pre-trained on three recent argument mining datasets and enable the use of neural argument mining without any reproducibility effort on the user's side. The open source code ensures portability to other domains and use cases, such as an application to search engine ranking that we also describe shortly.

1 Introduction

Argumentation is a multi-disciplinary field that extends from philosophy and psychology to linguistics as well as to artificial intelligence. Recent developments in argument mining apply natural language processing (NLP) methods to argumentation (Palau and Moens, 2011; Lippi and Torroni, 2016a) and are mostly focused on training classifiers on annotated text fragments to identify argumentative text units, such as claims and premises (Biran and Rambow, 2011; Habernal et al., 2014; Rinott et al., 2015). More specifically, current approaches mainly focus on three tasks: (1) detection of sentences containing argumentative units, (2) detection of the argumentative units' boundaries inside sentences, and (3) identifying relations between argumentative units.

Despite vital research in argument mining, there is a lack of freely available tools that enable users, especially non-experts, to make use of the field's recent advances. In this paper, we close this gap by introducing TARGER: a system with a user-friendly web interface[1] that can extract argumentative units in free input texts in real-time using

models trained on recent argument mining corpora with a highly configurable and efficient neural sequence tagger. TARGER's web interface and API also allow for very fast keyword-based argument retrieval from a pre-tagged version of the Common Crawl-based DepCC (Panchenko et al., 2018).

The native PyTorch implementation underlying TARGER has no external depencies and is available as open source software:[2] it can easily be incorporated into any existing NLP pipeline.

2 Related Work

There are three publicly available systems offering some functionality similar to TARGER. ArgumenText (Stab et al., 2018) is an argument search engine that retrieves argumentative sentences from the Common Crawl and labels them as *pro* or *con* given a keyword-based user query. Similarly, args.me (Wachsmuth et al., 2017) retrieves pro and con arguments from 300,000 arguments crawled from debating portals. Finally, MARGOT (Lippi and Torroni, 2016b) provides argument tagging for free-text inputs. However, answer times of MARGOT are rather slow for single input sentences (>5 seconds) and the F1 scores of 17.5 for claim detection and 16.7 for evidence detection are slightly worse compared to our approach (see Section 4.1).

TARGER offers a real-time retrieval functionality similar to ArgumenText and fast real-time free-text argument tagging with the option of switching between different pre-trained state-of-the-art models (MARGOT offers only a single one).

3 Architecture of TARGER

The independent components of the modular and flexible TARGER framework are shown in Figure 1. In an offline training step, a neural

---

[1]ltdemos.informatik.uni-hamburg.de/targer

[2]github.com/achernodub/targer

Proceedings of the 57th Annual Meeting of the Association for Computational Linguistics-System Demonstrations, pages 195–200
Florence, Italy, July 28 - August 2, 2019. ©2019 Association for Computational·Linguistics

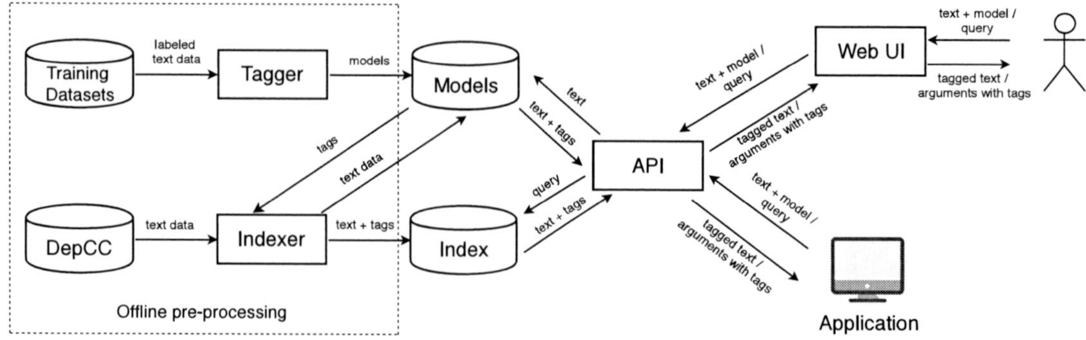

Figure 1: Modular architecture of TARGER. The central API is accessed through the Web UI or directly from any application; it routes requests either to the tagging models or to the retrieval component. TARGER's components communicate via HTTP requests and can be deployed on different servers—in Docker containers or natively.

BiLSTM-CNN-CRF sequence tagger is trained on different datasets yielding a variety of argument mining models (details in Section 3.1). As part of the preprocessing, the trained models are run on the 14 billion sentences of the DepCC corpus to tag and store argument unit information as additional fields in an Elasticsearch BM25F-index of the DepCC (details in Section 3.2).

The online usage is handled via a Flask-based web app whose API accepts AJAX requests from the Web UI component or via API calls (details in Sections 3.3 and 3.4). The API routes free text inputs to the respective selected model to be tagged with argument information or it routes keyword-based queries to the index to retrieve sentences in which the query terms match argument units.

3.1 Neural Sequence Tagger

We implement a BiLSTM-CNN-CRF neural tagger (Ma and Hovy, 2016) for identifying argumentative units and for classifying them as claims or premises. The BiLSTM-CNN-CRF method is a popular sequence tagging approach and achieves (near) state-of-the-art performance for tasks like named entity recognition and part-of-speech tagging (Ma and Hovy, 2016; Lample et al., 2016); it has also been used for argument mining before (Eger et al., 2017). The general method relies on pre-computed word embeddings, a single bidirectional-LSTM/GRU recurrent layer, convolutional character-level embeddings to capture out-of-vocabulary words, and a first-order Conditional Random Field (Lafferty et al., 2001) to capture dependencies between adjacent tags.

Besides the existing BiLSTM-CNN-CRF implementation of Reimers and Gurevych (2017), we

	Essays	WebD	IBM
Claims	22,443	3,670	8,073,589
Premises	67,157	20,906	35,349,501
Major Claims	10,966	-	-
Backing	-	10,775	-
Refutations	-	867	-
Rebuttals	-	2,247	-
None	47,619	46,352	3,710,839
Combined	**148,185**	**84,817**	**47,133,929**

Table 1: Number of tokens per category in the training datasets. Note that the IBM data contains many duplicate claims; it was originally published as a dataset to identify relevant premises for 150 claims.

also use an own Python 3.6 / PyTorch 1.0 implementation that does not contain any third-party dependencies, has native vectorized code for efficient training and evaluation, and supports several input data formats as well as evaluation functions.

The different argument tagging models currently usable through TARGER's API are trained on the persuasive essays (Essays) (Eger et al., 2017), the web discourse (WebD) (Habernal and Gurevych, 2017), and the IBM Debater (IBM) (Levy et al., 2018) datasets (characteristics in Table 1). The models use GloVe (Pennington et al., 2014), fastText (Mikolov et al., 2018), or dependency-based embeddings (Levy and Goldberg, 2014) (overview in Table 2).

For training, the following variations were used for hyperparameter tuning: optimizer [SGD, Adam], learning rate [0.001, 0.05, 0.01], dropout [0.1, 0.5], number of hidden units in recurrent layer [100, 150, 200, 250]. On all datasets, GloVe embeddings, Adam with learning rate of 0.001 and dropout rate of 0.5 performed

Data	Embeddings	Tagger
Essays	fastText	(Reimers and Gurevych, 2017)
Essays	Dependency	(Reimers and Gurevych, 2017)
Essays	GloVe	Ours
WebD	fastText	(Reimers and Gurevych, 2017)
WebD	Dependency	(Reimers and Gurevych, 2017)
WebD	GloVe	Ours
IBM	fastText	(Reimers and Gurevych, 2017)
IBM	GloVe	Ours

Table 2: Models currently deployed in TARGER.

Essays		Web Discourse	
Approach	F1	Approach	F1
STag_{BLCC}	64.74	SVM^{hmm}	22.90
TARGER (GloVe)	64.54	TARGER (GloVe)	24.20

Table 3: Comparison of TARGER's performance on the essays (Eger et al., 2017) and web discourse data (Habernal and Gurevych, 2017) to the best approaches from the original publications.

best (hidden units: 200 on the persuasive essays, 250 on web discourse and IBM data).

3.2 Retrieval Functionality

Our background collection for the retrieval of argumentative sentences is formed by the DepCC corpus (Panchenko et al., 2018), a linguistically pre-processed subset of the Common Crawl containing 14.3 billion unique English sentences from 365 million web documents.

The trained WebD-GloVe model was run on all the sentences in the DepCC corpus since it performed best on the web data in a pilot experiment. The respective argumentative unit spans and labels were added as additional fields to an Elasticsearch BM25F-index of the DepCC.

3.3 TARGER API

To keep the TARGER framework modular and scalable while still allowing access to the models from external clients, online interaction is handled via a restful API. Each trained model is associated with a separate API endpoint accepting raw text as input. The output is provided as a list of word-level tokens with IOB-formatted labels for argument units (premises and claims) and the tagger's confidence scores for each label.

3.4 TARGER Web UI

The web interface of TARGER offers two functionalities: *Analyze Text* and *Search Arguments*. On the analysis tab (cf. Figure 2), the user can choose one of the deployed models to identify arguments in a user-provided free text. The result is shown with colored labels for different types of argumentative units (premises and claims) as well as detected named entities (nested tags for entities in argumentative units are supported). Once a result is shown, it is possible to customize the display by enabling/disabling different labels without performing additional tagging runs.

On the retrieval tab (cf. Figure 3), the user can enter a keyword query and choose whether it should be matched in claims, premises, etc. Every retrieved result is rendered as a text fragment colorized with argument and entity information just as on the analysis tab. To enable provenance, the URL of the source document is also provided.

4 Evaluation

To demonstrate that our neural tagger is able to reproduce the originally published argument mining performances, we compare the best performing of our pre-trained models (parameter settings at the end of Section 3.1) to the best performances from the original dataset publications. We also report on a pilot study using TARGER as a subroutine in runs for the TREC 2018 Common Core track.

4.1 Experimental Results

Table 3 shows a comparison of TARGER's best performing models (parameter settings at the end of Section 3.1) on the Persuasive Essays and the Web Discourse datasets to the best performance in the original publications. We apply the experimental settings of the original papers: a fixed 70/20/10 train/dev/test split on the Essays data, and a 10-fold cross-validation for Web Discourse (in our case allocating 7 folds for training and 2 for development in each iteration).

On the Persuasive Essays dataset (paragraph level), the best TARGER model achieves a span-based micro-F1 of 64.54 for extracted argument components matching the best performance of 64.74±1.97 reported by Eger et al. (2017) for their STag_{BLCC} approach (BiLSTM-CRF-CNN approach (BLCC) similar to ours).

On the Web Discourse dataset, TARGER's best model's token-based macro-F1 of 24.20 slightly improves upon the originally reported best macro-F1 of 22.90 (Habernal and Gurevych, 2017)

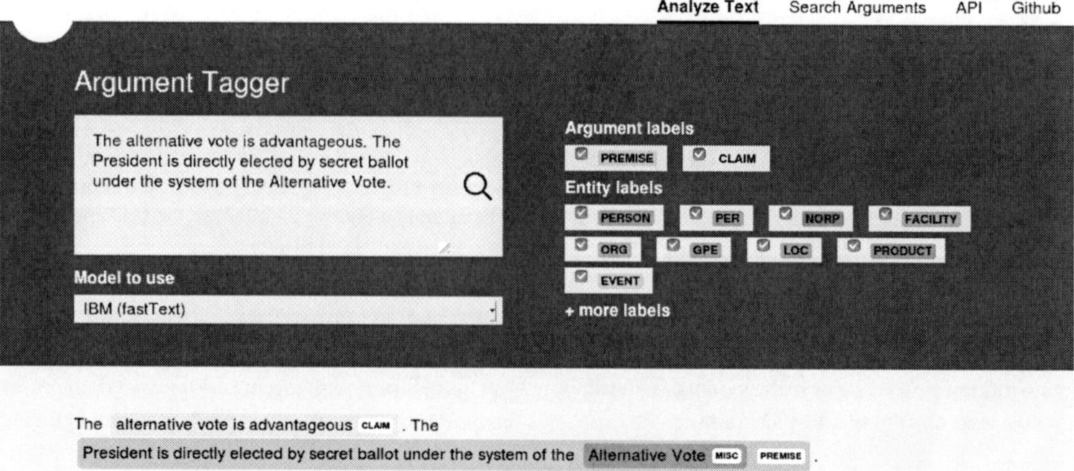

Figure 2: **Analyze Text**: input field, drop-down model selection, colorized labels, and tagged result.

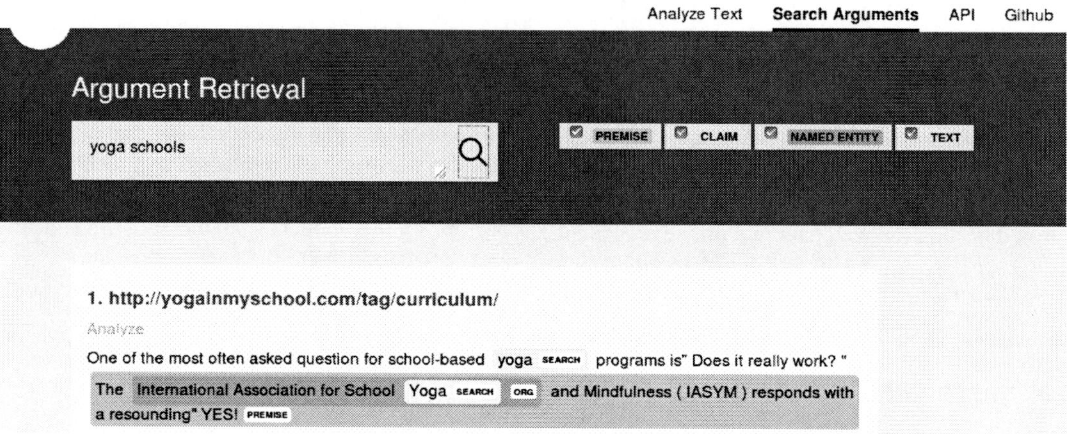

Figure 3: **Search Arguments**: query box, field selectors, and result with link to the original document.

achieved by a structural support vector machine model SVM^{hmm} for sequence labeling (Joachims et al., 2009). The SVM^{hmm} model uses lexical, structural, and other handcrafted feature types. In contrast, TARGER just uses word embeddings since especially for cross-domain scenarios, handcrafted features show a strong tendency to overfit on the topics of the training texts (Habernal and Gurevych, 2017). Thus, we chose "word embeddings only" as a more robust feature type for our domain-agnostic general-purpose argument mining system (free input text and web data).

We cannot compare TARGER's performance on the IBM dataset to originally published performances since the tasks are different. Instead of TARGER's identification of claims and premises, Levy et al. (2018) focus on the identification of relevant premises for a given claim (called "topic" in the original publication). Still, a large number of potential general domain premises for the overall 150 topics (i.e., claims) are contained in the dataset, such that we transformed the original entries to a token-level claim and premise annotation. This way, only some 2500 distinct tokens were labeled as not argumentative (e.g., punctuation) while the vast majority are tokens in claims and premises (but the only 150 different claims are heavily duplicated).

Not surprisingly—given the class imbalance and duplication—, the resulting trained TARGER models "optimistically" identify some argumentative units in almost every input text. We still provide the models as a starting point with the intention to de-duplicate the data and to add more non-

Title / Query	BM25F	Axiomatic Re-Ranking
declining middle class in u.s.	0.91	0.98 (+0.07)
euro opposition	0.81	1.00 (+0.19)
airport security	0.52	0.72 (+0.20)
law enforcement, dogs	0.43	0.63 (+0.20)

Table 4: The TREC 2018 Common Core track topics with argument axiom re-ranked nDCG@10 improvements > 0.05 over a BM25F baseline.

argumentative text passages for a more balanced / realistic training scenario.

4.2 TARGER @ TREC Common Core Track

As a proof of concept, we used TARGER's model pre-trained on essays with dependency-based embeddings in a TREC 2018 Common Core track submission (Bondarenko et al., 2018). The TARGER API served as a subroutine in a pipeline axiomatically re-ranking (Hagen et al., 2016) BM25F retrieval results with respect to their argumentativeness (presence/absence of arguments). For the Washington Post corpus used in the track, the dependency-based essays model best tagged argumentative units in a small pilot study.

Out of 25 topics manually labeled as argumentative from the 50 Common Core track topics, the TARGER-based argumentativeness re-ranking improved the retrieval quality by > 0.05 nDCG@10 for 4 topics (see Table 4). Argumentativeness-based re-ranking might thus be a viable way to integrate neural argument mining into the retrieval process—for instance, using TARGER.

5 Conclusion

We have presented TARGER: an open source system for tagging arguments in free text and for retrieving arguments from a web-scale corpus. With the available RESTful API and the web interface, we make the recent argument mining technologies more accessible and usable to researchers and developers as well as the general public. The different argument mining models can easily be used to perform manual text analyses or can seamlessly be integrated into automatic NLP pipelines. New taggers can be deployed to TARGER at any time, so that users can have the state of the art in argument mining at their fingertips. For future work, we plan to integrate contextualized embeddings with ELMo- and BERT-based models (Peters et al., 2018; Devlin et al., 2018).

Finally, by looking at our experimental results as well as tagging examples for free input texts or the DepCC web data, we noticed that despite the recent advances in argument mining, there is still considerable headroom to improve in-domain, but especially out-of-domain argument tagging performance. Free input texts of different styles or genres taken from the web are tagged very inconsistently by the different models. More research on domain adaptation and transfer learning (Ruder, 2019) in the scenario of argument mining needs to address this issue—and could then ideally directly be deployed to TARGER as new models.

Acknowledgments

This work was partially supported by the German Academic Exchange Service (DAAD) through the short-term research grant 57314022 "Argument Mining in Web Documents using Orthogonal Simple Recurrent Networks" and by the Deutsche Forschungsgemeinschaft (DFG) through the project "ACQuA: Answering Comparative Questions with Arguments" (grants BI 1544/7-1 and HA 5851/2-1) as part of the priority program "RATIO: Robust Argumentation Machines" (SPP 1999).

References

Or Biran and Owen Rambow. 2011. Identifying Justifications in Written Dialogs. In *Proceedings of the 5th IEEE International Conference on Semantic Computing (ICSC 2011)*, pages 162–168.

Alexander Bondarenko, Michael Völske, Alexander Panchenko, Chris Biemann, Benno Stein, and Matthias Hagen. 2018. Webis at TREC 2018: Common Core Track. In *27th International Text Retrieval Conference (TREC 2018)*.

Jacob Devlin, Ming-Wei Chang, Kenton Lee, and Kristina Toutanova. 2018. BERT: Pre-training of Deep Bidirectional Transformers for Language Understanding. *CoRR*, abs/1810.04805.

Steffen Eger, Johannes Daxenberger, and Iryna Gurevych. 2017. Neural end-to-end learning for computational argumentation mining. In *Proceedings of the 55th Annual Meeting of the Association for Computational Linguistics (Volume 1: Long Papers)*, pages 11–22.

Ivan Habernal, Judith Eckle-Kohler, and Iryna Gurevych. 2014. Argumentation Mining on the Web from Information Seeking Perspective. In *Proceedings of the Workshop on Frontiers and Connections between Argumentation Theory and Natural Language Processing*, pages 26–39.

Ivan Habernal and Iryna Gurevych. 2017. Argumentation Mining in User-Generated Web Discourse. *Computational Linguistics*, 43(1):125–179.

Matthias Hagen, Michael Völske, Steve Göring, and Benno Stein. 2016. Axiomatic Result Re-Ranking. In *25th ACM International Conference on Information and Knowledge Management (CIKM 2016)*, pages 721–730.

Thorsten Joachims, Thomas Finley, and Chun-Nam J. Yu. 2009. Cutting-plane training of structural svms. *Machine Learning*, 77(1):27–59.

John D. Lafferty, Andrew McCallum, and Fernando C. N. Pereira. 2001. Conditional Random Fields: Probabilistic Models for Segmenting and Labeling Sequence Data. In *Proceedings of the Eighteenth International Conference on Machine Learning (ICML 2001)*, pages 282–289.

Guillaume Lample, Miguel Ballesteros, Sandeep Subramanian, Kazuya Kawakami, and Chris Dyer. 2016. Neural architectures for named entity recognition. In *Proceedings of the 2016 Conference of the North American Chapter of the Association for Computational Linguistics: Human Language Technologies*, pages 260–270.

Omer Levy and Yoav Goldberg. 2014. Dependency-based word embeddings. In *Proceedings of the 52nd Annual Meeting of the Association for Computational Linguistics (Volume 2: Short Papers)*, pages 302–308.

Ran Levy, Ben Bogin, Shai Gretz, Ranit Aharonov, and Noam Slonim. 2018. Towards an Argumentative Content Search Engine Using Weak Supervision. In *Proceedings of the 27th International Conference on Computational Linguistics, COLING*, pages 2066–2081.

Marco Lippi and Paolo Torroni. 2016a. Argumentation Mining: State of the Art and Emerging Trends. *ACM Trans. Internet Techn.*, 16(2):10:1–10:25.

Marco Lippi and Paolo Torroni. 2016b. MARGOT: A Web Server for Argumentation Mining. *Expert Syst. Appl.*, 65:292–303.

Xuezhe Ma and Eduard Hovy. 2016. End-to-end sequence labeling via bi-directional LSTM-CNNs-CRF. In *Proceedings of the 54th Annual Meeting of the Association for Computational Linguistics (Volume 1: Long Papers)*, pages 1064–1074.

Tomas Mikolov, Edouard Grave, Piotr Bojanowski, Christian Puhrsch, and Armand Joulin. 2018. Advances in Pre-Training Distributed Word Representations. In *Proceedings of the Eleventh International Conference on Language Resources and Evaluation, LREC 2018*, pages 52–55.

Raquel M. Palau and Marie-Francine Moens. 2011. Argumentation Mining. *Artif. Intell. Law*, 19(1):1–22.

Alexander Panchenko, Eugen Ruppert, Stefano Faralli, Simone P. Ponzetto, and Chris Biemann. 2018. Building a Web-Scale Dependency-Parsed Corpus from CommonCrawl. In *Proceedings of the Eleventh International Conference on Language Resources and Evaluation, LREC 2018*, pages 1816–1823.

Jeffrey Pennington, Richard Socher, and Christopher D. Manning. 2014. Glove: Global vectors for word representation. In *Proceedings of the 2014 Conference on Empirical Methods in Natural Language Processing (EMNLP)*, pages 1532–1543.

Matthew Peters, Mark Neumann, Mohit Iyyer, Matt Gardner, Christopher Clark, Kenton Lee, and Luke Zettlemoyer. 2018. Deep contextualized word representations. In *Proceedings of the 2018 Conference of the North American Chapter of the Association for Computational Linguistics: Human Language Technologies, Volume 1 (Long Papers)*, pages 2227–2237.

Nils Reimers and Iryna Gurevych. 2017. Reporting score distributions makes a difference: Performance study of LSTM-networks for sequence tagging. In *Proceedings of the 2017 Conference on Empirical Methods in Natural Language Processing*, pages 338–348.

Ruty Rinott, Lena Dankin, Carlos Alzate Perez, Mitesh M. Khapra, Ehud Aharoni, and Noam Slonim. 2015. Show me your evidence - an automatic method for context dependent evidence detection. In *Proceedings of the 2015 Conference on Empirical Methods in Natural Language Processing*, pages 440–450.

Sebastian Ruder. 2019. *Neural Transfer Learning for Natural Language Processing*. Ph.D. thesis, National University of Ireland, Galway.

Christian Stab, Johannes Daxenberger, Chris Stahlhut, Tristan Miller, Benjamin Schiller, Christopher Tauchmann, Steffen Eger, and Iryna Gurevych. 2018. ArgumenText: Searching for arguments in heterogeneous sources. In *Proceedings of the 2018 Conference of the North American Chapter of the Association for Computational Linguistics: Demonstrations*, pages 21–25.

Henning Wachsmuth, Martin Potthast, Khalid Al-Khatib, Yamen Ajjour, Jana Puschmann, Jiani Qu, Jonas Dorsch, Viorel Morari, Janek Bevendorff, and Benno Stein. 2017. Building an argument search engine for the web. In *Proceedings of the 4th Workshop on Argument Mining*, pages 49–59.

MoNoise: A Multi-lingual and Easy-to-use Lexical Normalization Tool

Rob van der Goot
Center for Language and Cognition
University of Groningen
`r.van.der.goot@rug.nl`

Abstract

In this paper, we introduce and demonstrate the online demo as well as the command line interface of a lexical normalization system (MoNoise) for a variety of languages. We further improve this model by using features from the original word for every normalization candidate. For comparison with future work, we propose the bundling of seven datasets in six languages to form a new benchmark, together with a novel evaluation metric which is particularly suitable for cross-dataset comparisons. MoNoise reaches a new state-of-art performance for six out of seven of these datasets. Furthermore, we allow the user to tune the 'aggressiveness' of the normalization, and show how the model can be made more efficient with only a small loss in performance. The online demo can be found on: `http://www.robvandergoot.com/monoise` and the corresponding code on: `https://bitbucket.org/robvanderg/monoise/`

1 Lexical Normalization

Because many natural language processing (NLP) systems are designed with standard texts in mind, they suffer performance drops when applied to texts from other domains. In recent years, social media has become a major source of information. Due to their hasty and spontaneous nature, texts on social media are particularly non-standard.

One solution to adapt NLP systems, is to 'translate' these non-standard texts to their standard equivalent. This task is also called *lexical normalization*, see Figure 1 for the normalization of "most social pple r troublesome". Previous work on normalization is fragmented; a variety of approaches is evaluated on a variety of benchmarks, using a variety of evaluation metrics and assumptions. Furthermore, most normalization systems are not opensource or publicly available.

| most | social | pple | r | troublesome |
| most | social | people | are | troublesome |

Figure 1: Example normalization of "most social pple r troublesome"

In this paper, we present MoNoise, an easy-to-use normalization system, consisting of an online demo as well a more elaborate command line interface. We include benchmarks, results and pre-trained models for a variety of languages.

2 Multi-lingual Normalization Benchmark

The manually annotated datasets on which we will evaluate MoNoise are summarized in Table 1. In all datasets, gold tokenization was assumed. When 1-N is indicated in the table, this means that splitting of words was included in the annotation, and in some rare cases also merging. Since capitalization is usually not corrected (merely kept) in almost all of these datasets, we will lowercase everything in our evaluation. For datasets with existing splits, those are used, in other cases the data is split 80%-10%-10% (train-dev-test). For LexNorm1.2 we use LiLiu as training and development data, in line with previous work (Li and Liu, 2014, 2015).[1]

3 MoNoise

In this section, we will give a summary of the normalization model MoNoise (van der Goot and van Noord, 2017). Additionally, we added one group of features which improves the performance of this model.

---

[1]This benchmark can be obtained by running `./scripts/0.getNormData.sh` from the repository

Proceedings of the 57th Annual Meeting of the Association for Computational Linguistics-System Demonstrations, pages 201–206
Florence, Italy, July 28 - August 2, 2019. ©2019 Association for Computational Linguistics

Corpus Source	Words	Lang.	%normed	1-N	Caps
GhentNorm De Clercq et al. (2014)	12,901	NL	4.8	+	+-
TweetNorm Alegria et al. (2013)	13,542	ES	6.3	+	+-
LexNorm1.2 Yang and Eisenstein (2013)	10,576	EN	11.6	-	-
LiLiu Li and Liu (2014)	40,560	EN	10.5	-	+-
LexNorm2015 Baldwin et al. (2015)	73,806	EN	9.1	+	-
IWT Eryiǧit and Torunoǧ-Selamet (2017)	38,918	TR	8.5	+	+
Janes-Norm Erjavec et al. (2017)	75,276	SL	15.0	-	+-
ReLDI-hr Ljubešić et al. (2017a)	89,052	HR	9.0	-	+-
ReLDI-sr Ljubešić et al. (2017b)	91,738	SR	8.0	-	+-

Table 1: Comparison of the normalization corpora used in this work. %normed indicates the percentage of words which is normalized. The '1-N' column indicates whether words are split/merged in the annotation, the 'caps' column indicates whether everything was lowercased (-), capitalization was transferred to the normalization (+-), or corrected (+).

3.1 The Architecture

MoNoise splits the normalization task in two sub-tasks; candidate generation and candidate ranking. In contrast to most other systems, no error detection is performed beforehand, the decision whether to normalize is made during ranking. Because the normalization task consists of a variety of replacement types (van der Goot et al., 2018), MoNoise is developed in a modular way. Some of the modules are based on raw, external data. This dependency allows the model to be transferred to new domains and timespans more easily. For both sub-tasks a variety of modules is designed, which are described in the following two paragraphs.

Important modules for candidate generation are Aspell[2], a dictionary learned from the training data and word embeddings (Mikolov et al., 2013) trained on non-standard data (where the 40 closest words using cosine distance are used). Because no normalization detection is done, the original word is also included as a candidate.

For the ranking of candidates, features from the

generation are complemented with additional features. The additional features are: N-gram probabilities over non-standard text as well as standard texts, a feature which indicates whether a word contains alphanumeric characters or is a domain-specific token (hashtags, usernames and URLs) and the length of the original word and the candidate. All these features are combined in a random forest classifier, and the probability that a candidate belongs to the 'correct' class is used to rank the candidates.

3.2 Re-use Features of Original Word

A word should only be normalized when a substantially better candidate is found, this was not taken into account in the original model. To incorporate this intuition, we copy the features from the orginal word to all the other normalization candidates as additional features.

3.3 Models

For reproducability and reusability of the system, we provide pre-trained models for all the languages available in our multi-lingual benchmark (Section 2). These models are all trained using the default settings of MoNoise. These models exploit raw data from the source (non-standard) as well as the target (standard) domain, as n-gram probabilities and word embeddings are derived from these. As target domain data we use Wikipedia dumps from 01-01-2019[3]. For the non-standard data, we use raw data based on an in-house twitter collection[4]. In contrast to van der Goot and van Noord (2017), we do not not use language specific collections, but collect random tweets provided by the Twitter API during 2012 and 2018, and filter these by language based on the FastText language identifier (Joulin et al., 2016). Furthermore, we train embeddings with only 100 dimensions as opposed to van der Goot and van Noord (2017), who used 400. Because of these new embeddings, MoNoise uses 2-3 times less RAM, while experiencing only a very minor performance loss.

The pre-trained models can be found on: `http://www.robvandergoot.com/data/monoise`

---

[2]`http://aspell.net/`

[3]cleaned with `https://github.com/attardi/wikiextractor`

[4]`https://developer.twitter.com/`

Corpus	Lang	ERR	Precision	Recall	Prev. SOTA	Metric	Prev.	MoNoise
GhentNorm	NL	44.62	89.19	50.77	Schulz et al. (2016)	WER	3.2	1.36[5]
TweetNorm	ES	38.73	94.37	41.19	Porta and Sancho (2013)	OOV-Precision	63.4	70.40
LexNorm1.2	EN	59.21	80.87	77.56	Li and Liu (2015)	OOV Accuracy	87.58	87.63
LexNorm2015	EN	77.09	95.49	80.91	Jin (2015)	F1	84.21	86.58
IWT	TR	28.94	96.24	30.12	Eryiğit et al. (2017)	OOV Accuracy	67.37	48.99
Janes-Norm	SL	31.67	85.19	0.3833	Ljubešic et al. (2016) L1	CER	0.38	0.53
Janes-Norm	SL	63.90	95.66	0.6694	Ljubešic et al. (2016) L3	CER	1.58	2.24
ReLDI-hr	HR	51.65	95.66	0.541				
ReLDI-sr	SR	64.61	94.70	68.43				

Table 2: Results of MoNoise on the test data and a comparison with previous benchmarks. For WER and CER lower scores are better. Words normalized to the wrong candidate are classified as false positive (recall).

4 Evaluation

In this section, we first discuss existing evaluation metrics and their shortcomings and then introduce our novel metric. Secondly, we evaluate MoNoise on the test-splits of the multi-lingual benchmark, this is done twofold: using our preferred metric as well as a comparison to previous work.

4.1 Evaluation Metrics

Evaluation beyond word-level Some previous work used evaluation metrics which allow for evaluation beyond the word level. However, most of the normalization corpora do not include annotation beyond the word-level, except for the work of Zhang et al. (2013). Sometimes, BLEU score is used, whereas others use word error rate (WER) or character error rate (CER). We consider these metrics to be overly complex, since the word-order is not altered during annotation.

F1 In the shared task on normalization hosted at WNUT (Baldwin et al., 2015), F1 score was used as main evaluation. During development of MoNoise, we found multiple reasons why this might not be the preferable metric:

- Hard to interpret (how much of the problem is solved with an F1 score of 0.35?)

- It is unclear what to do with a word which should be normalized, but is normalized incorrectly, does this harm recall (false positive), precision (false negative) or both? [6]

- Because of the previous point, reproducibility and comparison with previous work can be difficult.

---

[5] Results are not directly comparable as different splits and tokenization is used

[6] For a more extensive discussion on this, we refer to van der Goot (2019). In the WNUT share task, they are FP and FN, in this paper they are considered only FP (recall).

Accuracy Early work on normalization often used accuracy over the words in need of normalization as main evaluation (Han and Baldwin, 2011; Liu et al., 2012) (OOV accuracy in Table 2). However, in this setting, the detection of which words need to be normalized is not taken into account. To include the full task of normalization, accuracy over all the words could be used. Accuracy is much easier interpretable compared to F1 score. However, accuracy does not allow for easy comparison across corpora, as different percentages of words might be in need of normalization. This is the main motivation for a novel evaluation metric, discussed in the next paragraph.

Error Reduction Rate Because previous metrics are overly complicated, hard to interpret or do not allow for an easy comparison between different datasets, we introduce the Error Reduction Rate (ERR). Error reduction rate can be interpreted as accuracy normalized for the number of words that are normalized in the gold standard. This allows for a direct comparison with a baseline which always copies the original word, the accuracy of such a baseline is equal to the percentage of words which need to be normalized. The formula for ERR is:

$$ERR = \frac{Accuracy_{system} - Accuracy_{baseline}}{1.0 - Accuracy_{baseline}} \tag{1}$$

The ERR will usually have a value between 0.0 and 1.0. A negative ERR indicates that the system normalizes makes more erroneous than correct normalizations. A baseline which always keeps the original word scores exactly 0.0, and a perfect system will score 1.0. We will use ERR as main evaluation metric and additionally report precision and recall, to gain more insights into the strengths and weaknesses of the system. A more

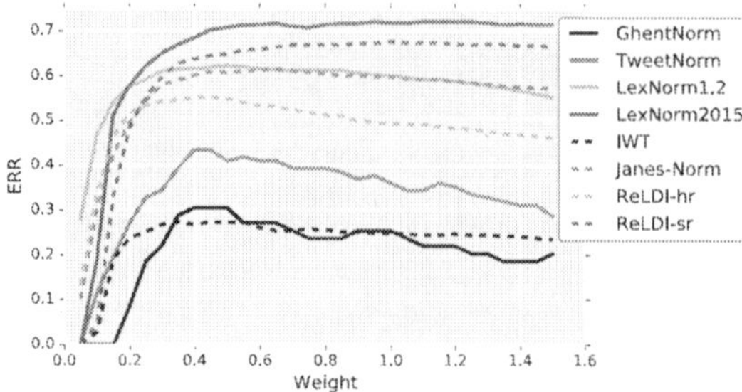

Figure 2: The effect of tuning the weight of the original candidate. A low weight indicates a more aggressive system.

detailed discussion on the motivation behind ERR can be found in (van der Goot, 2019).

4.2 Results

We present the results on all corpora of the multilingual benchmark in Table 2. We report the ERR, precision, recall, as well as the standard metric for each dataset. During development, no tuning was done on the test data, as described in more detail in (van der Goot and van Noord, 2017).

As mentioned in Section 4.1, it is disputable whether words which are normalized to the wrong normalization candidate should be counted as false positive or false negative. We choose to categorize these as false negatives, and thus be accounted for in the recall.

The ERR differs quite substantially across the datasets, this is due to different sizes of training data as well as differences in annotation. In the LexNorm2015 dataset, for example, phrasal abbreviations are expanded ('lol'↦'laughing out loud'), leading to a lot of very common replacements, which can easily be learned from the training data. On all datasets, the precision is higher than the recall. In other words, the model is conservative. This is arguably a desirable result, as it is important to avoid over-normalization.

When we look at the comparison to the previous state-of-the-art systems, we see that MoNoise performs highly competitive. Only on the Slovenian and Turkish datasets, the previous state-of-the-art is not surpassed.

5 Aggressiveness

To gain more control over the output normalization, we introduce a parameter which controls for the aggressiveness of the model. This is done by weighing the confidence score estimated for the original word (see also Section 3.1). If this is given a high weight, the original word is more likely to rank high.

The effect of tuning this parameter is plotted in Figure 2. It becomes apparent that the default weight of 1.0 leads to rather stable performance. For some datasets, minor gains can be achieved by a more aggressive setting. Furthermore, we can see that the parameter only becomes effective with extreme values, which is because the classifier is relatively certain about its predictions, and often gives very high scores to a certain candidate ($>$0.99). Although this parameter only leads to minor gains, it can still be useful to adapt the model to other domains, or to inspect whether the model was close to the correct normalization.

6 Efficiency

The main bottleneck for efficiency in the model is the searching of the 40 closest words in the word-embeddings. In the original word2vec (Mikolov et al., 2013) code, this is done by a for-loop which iterates through the whole vocabulary, and calculates the cosine distance for every word. There are more efficient techniques to calculate these distance, like the one used by Gensim (Řehůřek and Sojka, 2010). However, this still takes half a second per word on a modern pc for our English embeddings with a vocabulary size of 4,500,000. Therefore, we cache the 40 closest candidates in the embeddings for each word. We included the cached embeddings with each of our models. [7]

The next bottleneck of the model is the random forest classifier. So, further gains in efficiency can be gained by limiting the number of allowed candidates, as previously done by (Jin, 2015). This can be done by only considering words which occur in the corrected data, or a larger list by also including the Aspell dictionary.

The effect of filtering the candidates on the LiLiu dataset is shown in Table 3. Results on the other datasets showed similar trends. Filtering candidates based on only the training data results in a huge speedup, however also substantially harms performance. However, if we add the Aspell dictionary to the list of allowed candidates, performance remains relatively close, and a speedup of factor 2 is achieved.

---

[7]The code to cache embeddings (including a python wrapper) is available at: `https://bitbucket.org/robvanderg/cacheembeds`.

Restrictions	ERR	avg. cands	words/ sec	trainTime (seconds)
None	61.83	84	29	2,171
Train	51.64	12	137	280
Train + Aspell	61.12	43	62	1,104

Table 3: ERR when filtering candidates before ranking, and speed of the model when predicting and training. All reported results are the average of five runs on the LiLiu development set.

7 Interface

We provide two interfaces to use MoNoise; a command line application and a demo website.

7.1 Command Line

The only requirement to install MoNoise is a somewhat recent c++ compiler (c++11 or newer). In this section, we will highlight the most useful commands, for the full list of options we refer to the repository.

`--cands N`   Outputs at most N candidates for each word and their probability. These probabilities are obtained by normalizing the confidence scores of the classifier so that they sum to 1.0.

`--caps`   Do not lowercase everything, can be used during training as well as testing/running. This parameter is enabled for the online demo.

`--feats`   Lets you provide a bytestring with which specific modules can be disabled, the modules are explained in van der Goot and van Noord (2017) and listed in `utils/feats.txt`.

`--known N`   Only allow normalization candidates which occur in the normalized version of the training data(N=1), or allow candidates which occur in the training data or the Aspell dictionary(N=2).

`--tokenize`   Employ a conservative tokenizer, which splits sequences of punctuation (*."?!(){} :;/, \˜&) from the beginning and end of a word. Here, we assume that the normalization model will take care of other irregularities.

`--weight N`   Weigh the confidence of the original word with N, thereby tuning the aggressiveness (Section 5).

7.2 Online

In the online interface (Figure 3), the user can type a sentence and get the predicted normalization. The dropdown menu includes all languages for which a pre-trained model is available. The aggressiveness (Section 5) can be tuned with a

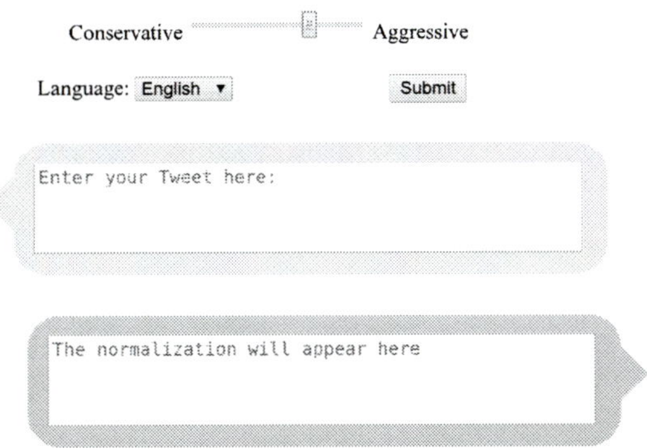

Figure 3: The layout of the online demo on a low resolution screen.

slider which converts this agressiveness factor to a weight for the original word. This allows the user to inspect beyond the top-1 predicted normalization sequence. Additionally, some example social media posts are displayed for the user, which are not shown in Figure 3 due to privacy issues. The online demo can be used on: `http://www.robvandergoot.com/monoise`

8 Conclusion

In this paper, we have demonstrated the online interface and command line interface of MoNoise. For this system, we release models for 6 different languages, of which a new state-of-the-art is reached for multiple datasets. The system is easy to install and use on Unix-based systems and has many useful extra options. For even easier usage, the online demo can be used from any device with internet access and a browser. We discussed multiple practical issues, like evaluation, efficiency, and extra tuning parameters.

Acknowledgements

I would like to thank Kevin Humphreys for his help with integrating Aspell into MoNoise, Ian Matroos for providing the python wrapper for the cached embeddings, Gertjan van Noord for his suggestions during the development of MoNoise, and Hessel Haagsma for the suggesting the name 'error reduction rate'. This system is developed in the 'Parsing Algorithms for Uncertain Input' project, funded by the Nuance foundation.

References

Inaki Alegria, Nora Aranberri, Víctor Fresno, Pablo Gamallo, Lluis Padró, Inaki San Vicente, Jordi Turmo, and Arkaitz Zubiaga. 2013. Introducción a la tarea compartida Tweet-Norm 2013: Normalización léxica de tuits en español. In *Tweet-Norm@ SEPLN*, pages 1–9.

Timothy Baldwin, Marie-Catherine de Marneffe, Bo Han, Young-Bum Kim, Alan Ritter, and Wei Xu. 2015. Shared tasks of the 2015 workshop on noisy user-generated text: Twitter lexical normalization and named entity recognition. In *Proceedings of the Workshop on Noisy User-generated Text*, pages 126–135, Beijing, China.

Orphée De Clercq, Sarah Schulz, Bart Desmet, and Véronique Hoste. 2014. Towards shared datasets for normalization research. In *Proceedings of the Ninth International Conference on Language Resources and Evaluation (LREC'14)*, Reykjavik, Iceland. European Language Resources Association (ELRA).

Tomaž Erjavec, Darja Fišer, Jaka Čibej, Špela Arhar Holdt, Nikola Ljubešić, and Katja Zupan. 2017. CMC training corpus janes-tag 2.0.

Gülşen Eryiğit and Dilara Torunoğ-Selamet. 2017. Social media text normalization for turkish. *Natural Language Engineering*, 23(6):835–875.

Rob van der Goot. 2019. *Normalization and Parsing Algorithms for Uncertain Input*. Ph.D. thesis, University of Groningen.

Rob van der Goot and Gertjan van Noord. 2017. MoNoise: Modeling noise using a modular normalization system. *Computational Linguistics in the Netherlands Journal*, 7:129–144.

Rob van der Goot, Rik van Noord, and Gertjan van Noord. 2018. A taxonomy for in-depth evaluation of normalization for user generated content. In *Proceedings of the Eleventh International Conference on Language Resources and Evaluation (LREC 2018)*, Miyazaki, Japan. European Language Resources Association (ELRA).

Bo Han and Timothy Baldwin. 2011. Lexical normalisation of short text messages: Makn sens a #twitter. In *Proceedings of the 49th Annual Meeting of the Association for Computational Linguistics: Human Language Technologies*, pages 368–378, Portland, Oregon, USA.

Ning Jin. 2015. NCSU-SAS-Ning: Candidate generation and feature engineering for supervised lexical normalization. In *Proceedings of the Workshop on Noisy User-generated Text*, pages 87–92, Beijing, China.

Armand Joulin, Edouard Grave, Piotr Bojanowski, and Tomas Mikolov. 2016. Bag of tricks for efficient text classification. *arXiv preprint arXiv:1607.01759*.

Chen Li and Yang Liu. 2014. Improving text normalization via unsupervised model and discriminative reranking. In *Proceedings of the ACL 2014 Student Research Workshop*, pages 86–93, Baltimore, Maryland, USA.

Chen Li and Yang Liu. 2015. Joint POS tagging and text normalization for informal text. In *Proceedings of IJCAI 2015, Buenos Aires, Argentina, July 25-31, 2015*, pages 1263–1269.

Fei Liu, Fuliang Weng, and Xiao Jiang. 2012. A broad-coverage normalization system for social media language. In *Proceedings of the 50th Annual Meeting of the Association for Computational Linguistics (Volume 1: Long Papers)*, pages 1035–1044, Jeju Island, Korea.

Nikola Ljubešić, Tomaž Erjavec, Maja Miličević, and Tanja Samardžić. 2017a. Croatian Twitter training corpus ReLDI-NormTagNER-hr 2.0.

Nikola Ljubešić, Tomaž Erjavec, Maja Miličević, and Tanja Samardžić. 2017b. Serbian Twitter training corpus ReLDI-NormTagNER-sr 2.0.

Nikola Ljubešic, Katja Zupan, Darja Fišer, and Tomaz Erjavec. 2016. Normalising slovene data: historical texts vs. user-generated content. *Bochumer Linguistische Arbeitsberichte*.

Tomas Mikolov, Kai Chen, Greg Corrado, and Jeffrey Dean. 2013. Efficient estimation of word representations in vector space. *Proceedings of Workshop at ICLR*.

Jordi Porta and José-Luis Sancho. 2013. Word normalization in Twitter using finite-state transducers. *Tweet-Norm@ SEPLN*, 1086:49–53.

Radim Řehůřek and Petr Sojka. 2010. Software Framework for Topic Modelling with Large Corpora. In *Proceedings of the LREC 2010 Workshop on New Challenges for NLP Frameworks*, pages 45–50, Valletta, Malta. ELRA.

Sarah Schulz, Guy De Pauw, Orphée De Clercq, Bart Desmet, Véronique Hoste, Walter Daelemans, and Lieve Macken. 2016. Multimodular text normalization of Dutch user-generated content. *ACM Transactions on Intelligent Systems Technology*, 7(4):1–22.

Yi Yang and Jacob Eisenstein. 2013. A log-linear model for unsupervised text normalization. In *Proceedings of the 2013 Conference on Empirical Methods in Natural Language Processing*, pages 61–72, Seattle, Washington, USA.

Congle Zhang, Tyler Baldwin, Howard Ho, Benny Kimelfeld, and Yunyao Li. 2013. Adaptive parser-centric text normalization. In *Proceedings of the 51st Annual Meeting of the Association for Computational Linguistics (Volume 1: Long Papers)*, pages 1159–1168, Sofia, Bulgaria.

Level-Up: Learning to Improve Proficiency Level of Essays

Wen-Bin Han, Jhih-Jie Chen, Ching-Yu Yang, Jason S. Chang
Department of Computer Science
National Tsing Hua University
{vincent.han, jjc, chingyu, jason}@nlplab.cc

Abstract

We introduce a method for generating suggestions on a given sentence for improving the proficiency level. In our approach, the sentence is transformed into a sequence of grammatical elements aimed at providing suggestions of more advanced grammar elements based on originals. The method involves parsing the sentence, identifying grammatical elements, and ranking related elements to recommend a higher level of grammatical element. We present a prototype coaching system, *Level-Up*, that applies the method to English learners' essays in order to assist them in writing and reading. Evaluation on a set of essays shows that our method does assist user in writing.

1 Introduction

Many essays (e.g., *"Amazingly, the child is so fashionable and creative that he makes the ugly house modern."*) are submitted to tutoring services by English learners on the Web every day, and an increasing number of services on the Web specifically target learners' essays. For example, *LanguageToolPlus* (languagetoolplus.com) uses rule-based model with n-grams extracted from the numerous data to inspect essays for grammatical errors, while *Grammarly* (grammarly.com), *1checker* (1checker.com) and *Ginger* (gingersoftware.com) use proprietary neural network approaches to proofread texts, check grammar, review style, and enrich vocabulary.

Tutoring services such as *Write&Improve* (writeandimprove.com) and *WhiteSmoke* (whitesmoke.com) typically correct and grade essays as a whole. However, very few systems provide focused suggestions on how to raise the level of proficiency. Learners could raise their level of grammatical proficiency, if a system can identify grammatical elements and suggest the learner to use related elements with a higher level.

Consider the essay *"Amazingly, the child is so fashionable and creative that he makes the ugly house modern."*. The useful suggestion for this sentence is definitely not just a level for the whole essay, which is pointless for learners, but the levels of grammatical elements with explanation and level-up grammatical elements. A helpful suggestion for an essay should not only contain the pairs of level and explanation such as: *"B1 - make the ugly house modern - Can use adjectives as object complement after 'make'."* but also suggest improvement: *"B2 - Can use a limited range of degree adjectives ('real', 'absolute', 'complete') before a noun to express intensity."*. These grammatical elements can be retrieved from English Grammar Profile (EGP) with more than a thousand grammatical elements with levels stipulated by Common European Framework of Reference (CEFR). Intuitively, by categorizing grammatical elements, we can provide more informative instruction for learners to improve their essays.

We present a new system, *Level-Up*, that parses essays into trees expected to recommend related advanced grammatical elements. An example *Level-Up* recommending for the essay *"Amazingly, the child is so fashionable and creative that he made the ugly house modern."* is shown in Figure 1. *Level-Up* has identified several grammatical elements (e.g., {*make NOUN ADJ*}) for the given essay. *Level-Up* detects these grammatical elements by matching patterns against the parse trees. We describe the *Level-Up* model in more detail in Section 3.

At run-time, *Level-Up* starts with a given essay submitted by the learner (e.g., *"Amazingly, the child is so fashionable and creative that he made the ugly house modern."*), which is first converted into a set of grammatical elements. Then,

Proceedings of the 57th Annual Meeting of the Association for Computational Linguistics-System Demonstrations, pages 207–212
Florence, Italy, July 28 - August 2, 2019. ©2019 Association for Computational Linguistics

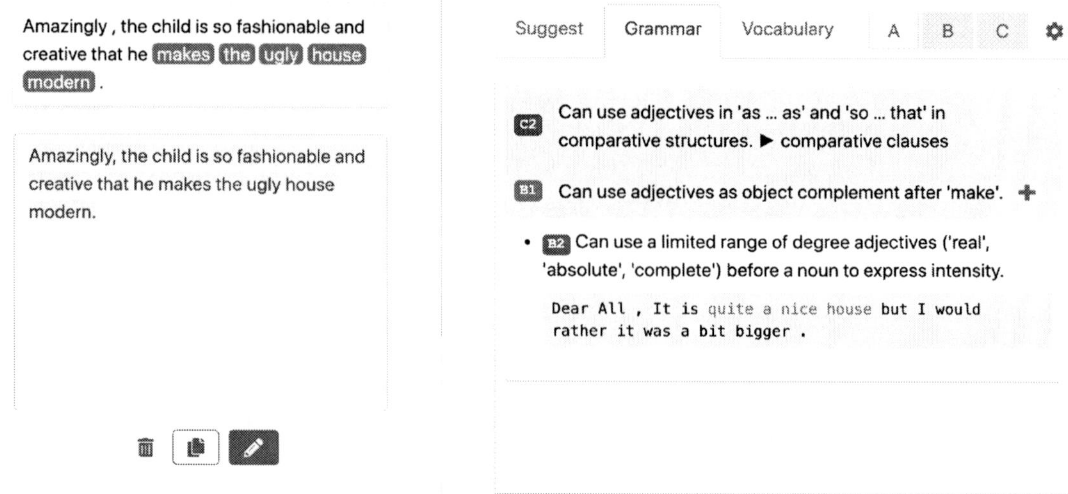

Figure 1: The screenshot of *Level-Up*

Level-Up ranks categorized elements and retrieves the related elements with a higher level as suggestions. In our prototype, *Level-Up* returns detected grammatical elements and recommendations of higher level elements to English learners directly (see Figure 1); alternatively, the elements and levels returned by *Level-Up* can be used as input to an essay scoring system.

The rest of the paper is organized as follows. We review the related work in the next section. Then we present our method for detecting grammatical elements in learners' essays expected to suggest more advanced elements. In our evaluation, *Level-Up* can provide useful collocations with levels for learners during writing.

2   Related work

English Language Teaching (ELT) has been an area of active research in Applied Linguistics and Computational Linguistics. Recently, the state-of-the-art research in ELT has been represented in the 13th Workshop on Innovative Use of NLP for Building Educational Applications (Tetreault et al., 2018) in the Association for Computational Linguistics (ACL) community. The workshop involves developing applications based on NLP approaches for teachers and learners of English as a Second Language (ESL) in educational settings. For example, Bryant and Briscoe (2018) build a competitive system only requiring minimal annotated data by using a simple Language Model approach. In our work, we address an aspect of English Language Teaching which is not the focus of correcting errors. Instead, we concentrate on how to analyze grammatical elements and suggest more advanced elements for learners to level up their essays.

More specifically, we focus on grammatical analysis for assisting learners in writing English, namely, suggesting grammatical elements at higher proficiency level based on identified grammatical elements in learner's writing. Grammaticality improvement for learners has been the focus of ELT research with much works concentrating on Grammar Error Correction (GEC). In general, GEC systems are aimed at correcting errors in learners' essays without considering the levels of grammatical elements used in the essays. In contrast, we will analyze the levels of grammatical elements in a given essay and provide more grammatically and lexically advanced elements to inform learners of how to refine and level up their essays.

The most commonly used criteria for measuring the proficiency levels is the Common European Framework of Reference for Languages (CEFR) (Council of Europe, 2001) with six proficiency levels: the basic level (A1 and A2), independent level (B1 and B2) and proficient level (C1 and C2). As an aid to defining levels for learning, teaching and assessment, CEFR describes what language learners can do ("can-do" statement) at different learning stages. (e.g., level A1 - Can use

Regex	Level	Statement
JJR and JJR	B1	Can use 'and' to join a limited range of comparative adjectives.
too JJ TO VB	B1	Can use 'too' before adjectives followed by 'to'-infinitive.
very JJ	A1	Can use 'very' to modify common gradable adjectives.

Table 1: Example regular expressions

commas and "and" to join more than two adjectives, after "be".) Moreover, Cambridge University Press organizes a wealth of information related to CEFR, including English Grammar Profile (EGP) and English Vocabulary Profile (EVP). EGP grades learners' ability in terms of grammatical form and CEFR levels, while EVP defines words and phrases of different CEFR levels.

Previous works targeting CEFR level detection of learners' essays include Hancke and Meurers (2013) for German and Vajjala (2014) for Estonian based on annotated learner data. To cope with high cost of collecting learners' data, Pilán et al. (2016) investigated the benefits of using texts from language learning coursebooks to train classifiers for predicting proficiency levels of learners' texts. Vajjala (2017) and Tack et al. (2017) present methods for identifying the linguistic variables that are indicative of writing quality to evaluate a learner's proficiency. Their researches and Bartning et al. (2019) all use CEFR to assess proficiency levels. We also utilize CEFR criteria in our research to evaluate essays, but focusing more on grammatical elements laid out in Cambridge EGP.

In a study more closely related to our work, *Write&Improve*[1] (Andersen et al., 2013; Yannakoudakis et al., 2018) supports self-assessment and learning by correcting common errors and returning an overall score for an essay. Furthermore, it also indicates potentially worst sentences. In contrast, we focus on providing specific information on raising the proficiency level as the learner writes.

Researches have pointed out that supplying suggestions while writing is more helpful than suggesting after the fact (Hearst, 2015). *Grammarly* tries to correct grammatical errors and provides the explanation while the user is writing. *WriteAhead*[2] (Yen et al., 2015) provides real-time writing suggestions on what to write next in the form of grammar patterns and example sentences. Similarly, *ColloCaid*[3] (Lew et al., 2018) checks if the

collocation is used correctly and provides frequent collocates so that writers can choose words that go well together.

In contrast to the previous research in English Language Teaching and Grammatical Error Correction, we present a tutoring system, *Level-Up*, that provides writing assistance, focusing on analyzing grammatical elements and suggesting higher level elements during writing.

3   The *Level-Up* System

To improve learners' essays, grammatical error correction (GEC) is not sufficient. Unfortunately, very few Language tools go beyond GEC and provide suggestions on proficiency level improvement for learners. In this section, we address such a problem. *Level-Up* displays a set of suggestions based on leveled grammatical elements for improving an unfinished sentence or complete sentences in essays. We transform criteria (e.g., EGP) into a pattern-matching program to identify grammatical elements and example n-grams from the corpus. We describe the process of our solution to this problem in the subsections that follow.

3.1   Extracting Grammatical Elements

Due to the lack of annotated data on grammatical elements, we attempt to extract grammatical elements using rules representing grammatical elements. The method involves using regular expressions, a lexical dictionary, and a parser, since regular expression is straightforward for matching patterns. Table 1 shows the examples of regular expression corresponding to EGP elements.

After converting these elements into regular expressions, we first parse the given corpus, and then retrieve grammatical elements and example n-grams for recommendation later at run-time. Since regular expressions have some limitations on flexibility, we solve this problem by using a dependency parser. Therefore, we take advantage of dependency tree to generate all phrasal elements from the parse tree layer by layer, and then match all the rules with these element candidates. We

---

[1] www.writeandimprove.com
[2] www.writeahead.nlpweb.org
[3] www.collocaid.uk

(1) Parse the sentence into POS tags and keywords.

    S: Actually, the child is very nice and friendly.

       "ADV , DET NOUN be ADV ADJ and ADJ ."

(2) Generate all element candidates layer by layer.

    S: Actually, the child is very nice and friendly.

       "is", "Actually , child is nice", "Actually , the child is very nice and friendly ."

       "be", *"ADV , NOUN be ADJ"*, *"ADV , DET NOUN be ADV ADJ and ADJ ."*

(3) Match candidates against all regular expressions.

    (a) *"ADV"*

    (b) *"be ADJ"*

    (c) *"ADJ and ADJ"*

(4) Extract these matches with the corresponding n-grams.

    (a) Actually, *"ADV"*

    (b) is nice, *"be ADJ"*

    (c) nice and friendly, *"ADJ and ADJ"*

Figure 2: Outline of the process used to identify elements in an example sentence

(1) Obtain n-grams belonging to the given element.
(2) Remove the n-grams not containing the last word in the unfinished sentence.
(3) Calculate Language Model of the unfinished sentence with each n-gram.
(4) Retain top 10 highest n-grams of Language Model.
(5) Calculate the n-grams of the average word level.
(6) Select the highest n-gram and its corresponding grammatical elements.

Figure 3: Outline of the process used to select top 1 n-gram to exemplify a given suggested grammatical element.

(1) Obtain grammatical elements in the same subcategory.
(2) Retain elements with higher level than the identified element.
(3) Select the first one element for recommendation

Figure 4: Outline of the process of recommending level-up elements for identified grammatical elements.

then record every matching phrase and sentence for generating suggestions at run-time. Figure 2 shows the process of identifying grammatical elements in an example sentence.

3.2 Automated Writing Suggestion for Leveling up

Once the grammatical elements and n-grams are automatically extracted and counted from the given corpus, they are stored as suggestion candidates. *Level-Up* constantly returns suggestions based on the last word the user types in the writing area. With the last word as a query, *Level-Up* retrieves and displays n-grams, ranked by Language Model and the level of words. Furthermore, each n-gram exemplifies different grammatical elements and is accompanied with three example sentences. The process of selecting n-grams is shown in Figure 3.

3.3 Analyzing Elements and Ranking Suggestions

Level-Up also analyzes essays after users finish writing. The process of analyzing is the same as described in Subsection 3.1. However, we do not display all the matches to the user. Instead, if the grammatical element is completely overlapped by the other element, we only retain the one with higher level.

Our system not only identifies grammatical elements but also suggests level-up elements. EGP contains the broad categories of the grammatical elements, including adjectives and adverbs. Furthermore, every category includes several subcategories (e.g., adjectives - comparatives and superlatives). We group those elements by the categories and then select the most related level-up element in the same group. The process of selecting level-up elements is shown in Figure 4.

4   Experiments and Results

In this section, we describe the details of our experiments and the results. First, we introduce how we preprocess the corpus and extracted grammatical elements. Then, we explain the analysis of vocabularies in *Level-Up*. Finally, we describe the program architecture and the toolkits used, and show the evaluation results of our system.

4.1   English Grammar Profile

CEFR lists total 1,222 grammatical elements in EGP. In our prototype, we experimented with two categories, adjectives and adverbs, as a pilot study to prove that our approach is effective. Some specific types of words, such as degree adverbs, are enumerated from Sinclair (2005). For preprocessing, we used British National Corpus (BNC) (Corpus, 2001), containing over four million sentences, to collect example n-grams for grammatical elements. To be more specific, we parsed all the sentences and generated grammatical element candidates by using SpaCy parser (Honnibal and Montani, 2017). Then, we matched all the candidates against all the rules. Every detected match of grammar pattern is stored with its n-gram and sentence.

4.2   English Vocabulary Profile

In addition to EGP, we also utilize EVP in our system. *Level-Up* not only analyzes the levels of vocabularies defined by EVP in learner's essays but also provides similar vocabularies at higher level. For example, *Level-Up* can suggest "strive" (C2 level) for the verb "try" (A2 level). However, analyzing vocabulary in our study is not described in Section 3 due to our focus of EGP. First of all, we obtained the full six-level vocabularies from EVP[4], which covers levels A1-C2 of CEFR. However, disambiguating the meanings of polysemy is still an open problem. Therefore, we use the lowest level of a word directly. In other words, after tokenizing sentences with SpaCy, we match these tokens against the lookup table, EVP, to obtain the lower level.

For word suggestions, we use the pre-trained 300 dimension Word2Vec (Mikolov et al., 2013) trained on Google News to generate top 100 similar words as candidates using Gensim (Řehůřek and Sojka, 2010). Then, we filter out those candidates that are not in EVP, at a lower level, or

Suggestion	Count	Percent	Precision
1st suggestions	22	0.53	0.44
2nd suggestions	13	0.32	0.26
3rd suggestions	6	0.15	0.12
Top 3 suggestions	**41**	-	**0.82**
Not in Top 3	9	-	0.18

Table 2: Human evaluation of *Level-Up*

different POS tags. Finally, we choose the top 10 candidates to show to learners.

4.3   Technical Architecture

Leve-Up was implemented in Python with the Flask Web framework. We stored the suggestions in JSON format and read the content into memory for fast access. *Level-Up* server obtains client input from a popular browser (Safari, Chrome, or Firefox) dynamically with AJAX techniques.

4.4   Evaluating *Level-Up*

To evaluate the performance of *Level-Up*, we randomly sampled sentences from learner's corpus. For simplicity, we tested if learners can acquire suitable n-grams with advanced grammatical structures from using *Level-Up* and evaluate the performance. We randomly selected 50 sentences with adjectives or adverbs from EF-Cambridge Open Language Database (EFCAM-DAT) as test data and segmented each sentence from start to adjective or adverb word for recommended n-grams. After typing it in *Level-Up*, we considered n-grams from first one to third one, and counted the position of good suggestions. We assumed that learners can fit the n-grams to the input with less tolerance of edit. Finally, we manually determined the appropriateness of suggestions based on the precision of the Top-3 suggestions. Table 2 shows the performance of *Level-Up*.

5   Future Work and Conclusion

Many avenues exist for future research and improvement of our system, *Level-Up*. For example, other categories in EGP could be handled. The method of ranking n-grams could be improved by considering the relevancy of n-gram to learner's sentence more precisely. NLP and Machine Learning techniques could be applied to identify and rank grammatical elements. Additionally, an interesting direction to explore is recommending well-spoken words and phrases to level up learner's essays lexically. For example,

---

[4]vocabulary.englishprofile.org/staticfiles/about.html

we could suggest "the better part of a week" to level up "almost a week". Similarly, we could suggest "in the making" for "happening." Yet another direction of research is evaluating an essay as a whole based on the detected grammatical elements. In other words, teachers can assess students' essays more efficiently using *Level-Up*.

In summary, we have proposed a method for analyzing grammatical elements and suggesting level-up elements while a user is writing. The approach involves extracting, retrieving, and ranking grammatical elements and examples. We have implemented and evaluated the proposed approach as applied to a large corpus with promising results.

References

Øistein E. Andersen, Helen Yannakoudakis, Fiona Barker, and Tim Parish. 2013. Developing and testing a self-assessment and tutoring system. In *BEA@NAACL-HLT*.

Inge Bartning, M Martin, and Ineke Vedder. 2019. Communicative proficiency and linguistic development: intersections between sla and language testing research.

Christopher Bryant and Ted Briscoe. 2018. Language model based grammatical error correction without annotated training data. In *BEA@NAACL-HLT*.

British National Corpus. 2001.

Council of Europe. 2001. *Common European Framework of Reference for Languages: Learning, Teaching, Assessment*. Common European Framework of Reference for Languages: Learning, Teaching, Assessment. Cambridge University Press.

Julia Hancke and Detmar Meurers. 2013. Exploring cefr classification for german based on rich linguistic modeling. pages 54–56.

Marti A. Hearst. 2015. Can natural language processing become natural language coaching? In *ACL*.

Matthew Honnibal and Ines Montani. 2017. spacy 2: Natural language understanding with bloom embeddings, convolutional neural networks and incremental parsing. *To appear*.

Robert Lew, Ana Frankenberg-Garcia, Geraint Paul Rees, Jonathan C Roberts, and Nirwan Sharma. 2018. Collocaid: A real-time tool to help academic writers with english collocations. In *The XVIII EURALEX International Congress*, page 165.

Tomas Mikolov, Ilya Sutskever, Kai Chen, Greg Corrado, and Jeffrey Dean. 2013. Distributed representations of words and phrases and their compositionality. In *Proceedings of the 26th International Conference on Neural Information Processing Systems -* *Volume 2*, NIPS'13, pages 3111–3119, USA. Curran Associates Inc.

Ildikó Pilán, Elena Volodina, and Torsten Zesch. 2016. Predicting proficiency levels in learner writings by transferring a linguistic complexity model from expert-written coursebooks. In *COLING*.

Radim Řehůřek and Petr Sojka. 2010. Software Framework for Topic Modelling with Large Corpora. In *Proceedings of the LREC 2010 Workshop on New Challenges for NLP Frameworks*, pages 45–50, Valletta, Malta. ELRA. http://is.muni.cz/publication/884893/en.

J. Sinclair. 2005. *Collins Cobuild English grammar*. Collins Cobuild. HarperCollins.

Anaïs Tack, Thomas Franois, Sophie Roekhaut, and Cédrick Fairon. 2017. Human and automated cefr-based grading of short answers. In *BEA@EMNLP*.

Joel Tetreault, Jill Burstein, Ekaterina Kochmar, Claudia Leacock, and Helen Yannakoudakis. 2018. Proceedings of the thirteenth workshop on innovative use of nlp for building educational applications. In *Proceedings of the Thirteenth Workshop on Innovative Use of NLP for Building Educational Applications*. Association for Computational Linguistics.

Sowmya Vajjala. 2014. Automatic cefr level prediction for estonian learner text.

Sowmya Vajjala. 2017. Automated assessment of non-native learner essays: Investigating the role of linguistic features. *International Journal of Artificial Intelligence in Education*, 28:79–105.

Helen Yannakoudakis, Øistein E. Andersen, Ardeshir Geranpayeh, Ted Briscoe, and Diane Nicholls. 2018. Developing an automated writing placement system for esl learners.

Tzu-Hsi Yen, Jian-Cheng Wu, Jim Chang, Joanne Boisson, and Jason Chang. 2015. Writeahead: Mining grammar patterns in corpora for assisted writing. *Proceedings of ACL-IJCNLP 2015 System Demonstrations*, pages 139–144.

Learning to Link Grammar and Encyclopedic Information to Assist ESL Learners

Jhih-Jie Chen[1], Ching-Yu Yang[1], Pei-Chen Ho[2], Ming Chiao Tsai[1],
Chia-Fang Ho[2], Kai-Wen Tuan[2], Chung-Ting Tsai[2], Wen-Bin Han[1], Jason S. Chang[1]
[1]Department of Computer Science
National Tsing Hua University
[2]Institute of Information Systems and Applications
National Tsing Hua University
{jjc, chingyu, patina, jason}@nlplab.cc

Abstract

We introduce a method for learning to extract vocabulary and encyclopedic information to assist second language (L2) learners acquiring deep knowledge of target vocabulary. In our approach, grammar patterns, collocations, representative examples are extracted, aimed at providing rich lexical information for any target words. The method involves word sense disambiguation on target words, automatically parsing the sentences in a large-scale corpus, automatically generating grammar patterns, collocations, examples, and quizzes for every target word, and automatically linking named entities to corresponding Wikipedia information. We present a prototype vocabulary learning system, *Linggle Booster*, that applies the method to corpora and web pages. Evaluation on a set of target words shows that the method has reasonably good performance in terms of generating useful and correct information for vocabulary learning.

1 Introduction

Many English learners read articles and watch videos on the Web everyday to improve their language skills, and an increasing number of services uses Web-based content to assist learning languages. For example, *VOA Learning English*[1] provides level-appropriate articles with a vocabulary list. Websites, such as *VoiceTube*[2], allow learners to watch English videos and read English subtitles with on-demand Chinese translations of vocabulary. *WordBooster*[3], highlights target words in user submitted articles, and provides vocabulary quizzes for users to learn and self-assess vocabulary and reading comprehension skills. These web services, however, do not support easy customization for different users' English proficiency level,

nor do they provide other lexical information than definitions and examples. The lack of grammar patterns and collocations makes it inefficient for learners to acquire rich vocabulary knowledge.

To facilitate a more efficient learning process, we develop a prototype interactive system, *Linggle Booster*[4]. At run-time, *Linggle Booster* starts with an URL or text submitted by user, and then generates a reformatted, reader-friendly content in the left column of our system. In the column, vocabulary that fit user's English proficiency level is underlined and words linkable to Wikipedia information are shown in blue (see Figure 1). By clicking on an underlined word, the system will provide the Chinese definition of the target word. The most appropriate definition (e.g., 決賽 in Figure 1) is presented in the first line under the target word, along with other senses appended under the definition (e.g., 期中考試 in Figure 1). Additionally, we offer grammar patterns, collocations and examples of the target word with native language support (i.e., translation in learners' native language). Additionally, *Linggle Booster* also identifies and displays relevant Encyclopedic information (e.g., Wikipedia) to provide another level of information to users. Furthermore, a quiz is generated based on vocabulary in input text for self-assessment (see Figure 2).

2 Related Work

Learning English as a Second Language (ESL) has been an area of active research. For example, many researches have done on autonomous language learning (e.g., Kormos and Csizer (2014)) and on ESL learning strategy on the part of teachers (e.g., Richards and Renandya (2002)). In the field closely related to our work, the Common European Framework of Reference (CEFR)

---

[1]learningenglish.voanews.com
[2]tw.voicetube.com
[3]wordbooster.com
[4]https://read.linggle.com/

Proceedings of the 57th Annual Meeting of the Association for Computational Linguistics-System Demonstrations, pages 213–218
Florence, Italy, July 28 - August 2, 2019. ©2019 Association for Computational Linguistics

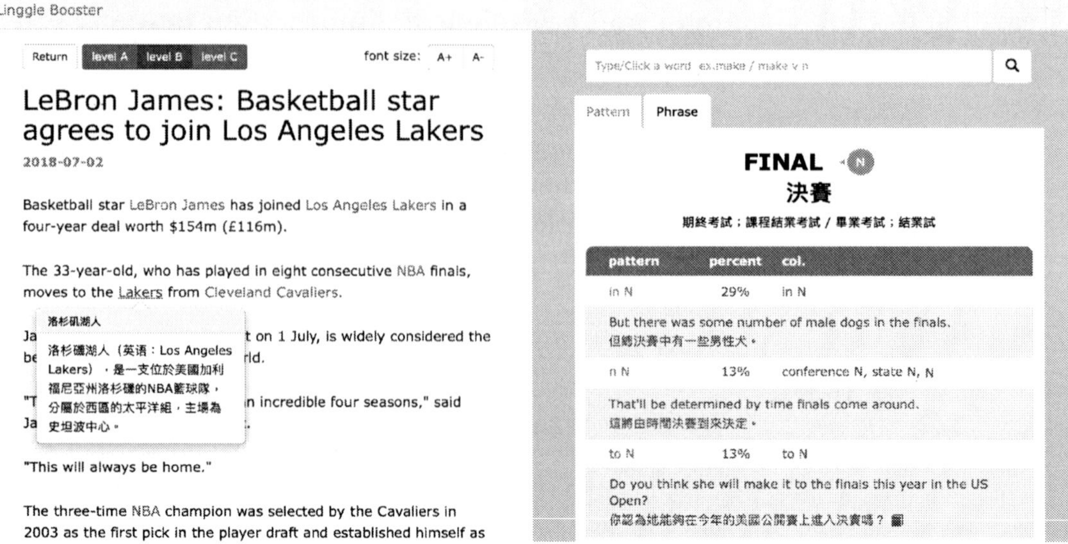

Figure 1: An example *Linggle Booster* session for the user-selected web page [5], presenting the reformatted article in the left column, where Wikipedia information shown in a pop-up, and we provide the following vocabulary information for the highlighted word, *finals*: Chinese translations of the word sense, grammar patterns, collocations, and examples in the right column.

describes what language learners can do at six language stages (i.e., A1, A2, B1, B2, C1, and C2), which has a major effect on language exams and course material design. Stemmed from CERF, Cambridge University Press compiles the English Vocabulary Profile which classifies words and phrases by CERF levels. In our system, we perform word sense disambiguation on user-submitted content and label words with simplified CERF level (i.e., A, B, C) offered by Cambridge online Dictionary and English Vocabulary Profile.

In the field of computer-assisted English learning, there have been an increasing interest in helping second language learners acquire the grammatical usage of a target word. Hunston et al. (1996) and Francis et al. (1998) manually mapped out lexical grammar patterns for common verbs, nouns, and adjectives, using the Collins COBUILD corpus. To explore the feasibility of identifying grammar patterns computationally, Mason (2004) conducted a limited experiment of automatic parsing based on COBUILD grammar patterns with reasonable success. More recently, Yen et al. (2015) introduced a method for inducing grammar patterns to use in an interactive writing environment aimed at assisting language learners in writing.

Identifying the intended word sense relevant to the context has long been an active topic of word sense disambiguation (WSD) research. In general, WSD systems typically use supervised learning approach with a sense inventory such as WordNet WSD systems based on dictionary-based sense inventory (e.g., WordNet) and a sense-annotated corpus (e.g., Semcor Miller et al. (1994)). In our work, we adopt BERT introduced by Devlin et al. (2018) to disambiguate words in user-submitted contents to provide correct word definition and appropriate quizzes.

Wikification of educational materials has been touted as a novel approach to facilitate reading and learning. In this work, we use the existing method proposed by Kolitsas et al. (2018), to identify potentially ambiguous mentions of key phrases in a document and link them to relevant Wikipedia articles.

Much of previous work shows that one of the most efficient way to learn a second language is through extensive reading, using engaging extracurricular articles, news or books (e.g., Coady (1997), Pigada and Schmitt (2006)). Inspired by their insights, we present *Linggle Booster*, an interactive environment which provides helpful information related to input article, to help learners acquiring deeper knowledge while reading.

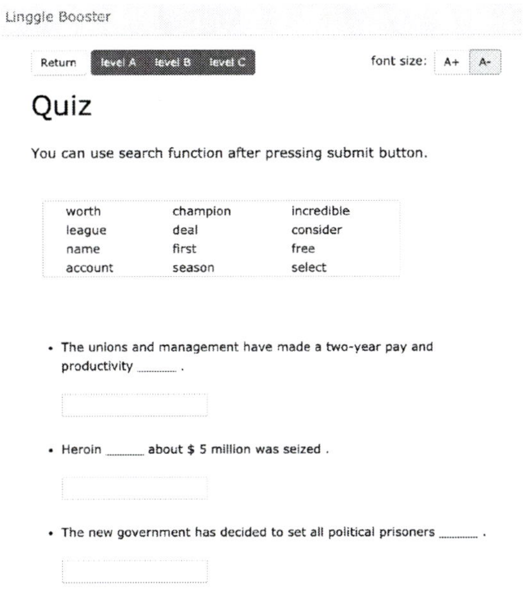

Figure 2: An example of auto-generated test items for the user-selected web page [6]

3 Method

Our system is composed of four main components: (i) extracting grammar patterns, collocations, and example sentences; (ii) generating words or phrases linked to Wikipedia information; (iii) training language representations for WSD; (iv) generating vocabulary quizzes.

3.1 Extracting grammar patterns, collocations and example sentences

We extract grammar patterns, collocations and example sentences from Corpus of Contemporary American English (COCA) and data from Cambridge online dictionary (CAM)[7]. We first parse sentences in the two datasets using spaCy toolkit. From the result of dependency parsing, we extract grammar patterns of content words (i.e., verbs, nouns and adjectives) based on handcrafted templates. For each target content word, we only keep words which are its children and labeled by specific dependency relations. For example, the extracted grammar pattern of the verb *chew* in the sentence *"She is chewing at her nail"* is **V at n**.

Then, to cope with noise caused by parser errors, we discard extracted grammar patterns not listed in extended Collins COBUILD Grammar Patterns (COBUILD) (Hunston et al., 1996). We

---

[7]https://dictionary.cambridge.org/

also extract collocations to accompany grammar patterns. For example, the grammar pattern of **role** is extended from **N in n** to **v N in n** by adding the verb collocation **play** (school **play** an important **role in** society).

After that, for each target word, we calculate patterns and collocations and filter out those less frequent than the mean by 1.0 standard deviation.

Finally, we select examples of each pattern from COCA and Cambridge online dictionary (with Chinese translations) using the GDEX method (Kilgarriff et al., 2008).

3.2 Link Words or Phrases to Wikipedia Information

To link words and phrases in user-submitted contents to correct Wikipedia entries, we perform Mention Detection and Entity Disambiguation on user-submitted contents, using the End-to-End Neural Entity Linking method (Kolitsas et al., 2018). We generate possible spans from unigram to trigram, and each span selects some Wikipedia entry candidates with an empirical probabilistic entity map (Ganea and Hofmann, 2017) from Wikipedia hyperlinks, Crosswikis and YAGO dictionaries. Each mention candidate produces a local contextual similarity scores. Accordingly, we provide correct Wikipedia knowledge for words to assist ESL better understanding the contents and world knowledge.

3.3 Word Sense Disambiguation

We disambiguate polysemous words in user-submitted contents using a pre-trained language representation model, BERT (Devlin et al., 2018). We use word definitions in CAM as word sense labels. For a given word, CAM offers all possible word definitions, CERF levels and example sentences. We view example sentence as the feature of a word sense. Then, we use the last four hidden layers of BERT hidden state to compute the vector representations of each example sentence. Next, we use BERT again to compute word vector for words in user-submitted contents. Finally, we disambiguate the word sense by calculating the cosine similarity of the representations and each representation of word definition in CAM, and return the word definition of which examples contains the most similar representation. After word sense disambiguation, we provide appropriate word definitions and correspondent word level to learners.

215

3.4 Generating Quizzes

Fill in the blank questions (FBQ) are automatically generated after the reading session. We randomly select vocabulary from user-submitted content that matches the user-declared proficiency level. To form questions, we select representative examples containing the target word with the word sense in the user-submitted content from CAM. Then, the target word is replaced with a blank to help learners self-assess the acquisition of vocabulary. After users complete a test, *Linggle Booster* presents the scores and corrections to the users.

4 Run-Time Interactive Environment

Linggle Booster is implemented in Python based on Django Web framework. For faster retrieval, we save the added reference information (cf. Section 3.1) in JSON format using PostgreSQL and hash table. We choose to host *Linggle Booster* on Heroku, a cloud-platform-as-a-service site for uninterrupted service and scalability. The server of *Linggle Booster* with AJAX techniques receives users-submitted content (e.g., Web page URLs, URL of YouTube video with closed caption, or essay draft) from any popular browser (e.g., Chrome, Safari, or Firefox).

If users submit an URL, we use an existing tool [8] to parse the html of give URL and extract article content. We detect possible Named Entity and link to correct Wikipedia entries using the method in Section 3.2. At the same time, we parse the article content using spaCy toolkit and compute representations using BERT. After disambiguating the word sense of each word using the method in Section 3.3, we can access the Word Level of the word sense in CAM.

Then, we reformat the article content in a reader-friendly layout presented in the left column of *Linggle Booster*. Words with the level matched to the user-selected level are underlined, and keywords and phrases linked to Wikipedia information are presented in blue. For each word in the content, we retrieve five pieces of information, the definition of the word sense in Chinese, the grammar patterns of the word, the frequency, collocations, and example for each grammar pattern, and commonly used phrases if they exist. If a key word lacks grammar patterns, we present the vocabulary definitions and synonyms based on

	WSD	Pattern	Col.	Example
Level A	70 %	92 %	82 %	85 %
Level B	90 %	91 %	89 %	89 %
Level C	75 %	92 %	87 %	91 %

Table 1: Accuracy of human evaluations of *Linggle Booster* for CNN news article.

WordNet (Miller, 1998). We process rare words not in vocabulary by decomposing them into affixes and stems, and retrieving linguistic information accordingly. In the self-assessment session, users can access a vocabulary quiz with one click, along with scores and corrections after answering the quizzes.

5 Evaluation

In this section, we report the results of preliminary evaluations on automated extraction of grammar patterns, collocations, and examples. The quality evaluation of Wikification and word sense disambiguation is also included in this section.

Vocabulary knowledge extraction is a king of information extraction (IE) tasks, which are traditionally evaluated based on the quality of accuracy or appropriateness of generated result. We selected a CNN news article[9] to assess *Linggle Booster's* performance. We examined the Chinese word sense, grammar patterns, collocations, and examples for first 20 unique vocabulary in each word level. We checked if *Linggle Booster* returns the correct word sense used in the article. For each vocabulary, we check if grammar patterns more frequent than 5% frequency are valid. We also examined the accuracy of collocations. Finally, we evaluated whether the example for each grammar pattern is actually a good representation of it's usage.

Across all three Word Levels, the results (shown in Table 1) indicates *Linggle Booster* provides good definition at least 70% of time and grammar patterns, collocations and examples are all close to 90% correct.

To evaluate the quality of linking words to Wikipedia information, we conduct experiments on public Entity Linking dataset AIDA Hoffart et al. (2011) using the Gerbil platform Usbeck et al. (2015). Micro and macro F1 scores are 0.83

---

[8]`https://github.com/buriy/`
`python-readability`

[9]`https://edition.cnn.com/2019/04/10/`
`australia/australia-china-election-intl/`
`index.html`

Dataset	F1 Score
senseval2	66.8
senseval3	66.1
SemEval 2007	55.1
SemEval 2013	62.8
SemEval 2015	67.8

Table 2: WSD evaluation

and 0.84 respectively.

We also performed an experiment on word sense disambiguation based on method proposed in ELMO using SemCor 3.0 Miller et al. (1994) and OMSTI Taghipour and Ng (2015) as training data. After training, we take the average representations for each Wordnet sense. To test our WSD method using (Raganato et al., 2017), we use BERT again to compute word vectors for every target word and take the most similar sense from the training set. If lemma is not in training set, we use the first sense from Wordnet as our word sense. The result of this test is shown in Table 2.

6 Conclusion and Future Work

We have presented *Linggle Booster*, an interactive and customizable environment for reading to improve language skills, where ESL learners can submit self-selected engaging content and set an appropriate proficiency level of vocabulary. With *Linggle Booster*, second language learners should have a much better chance of acquiring deeper vocabulary knowledge (e.g. grammar patterns, collocations, examples and encyclopedic information). In addition, users can self-assess how well they have acquired the vocabulary. Our methodology supports adaptive, self-paced vocabulary learning, resulting in an effective and engaging system that combines the advantages of freedom in the selection of learning content and rich and rewarding learning experiences enhanced by technology.

Many avenues exist for improving *Linggle Booster*. We could improve the ability to download an URL and parse the content. Our system cannot extract part of or all of the content for some web pages due to the limit of the adopted tool Readability. One solution is to use different parsing tools (e.g., Mercury[10]). Linggle Booster attempts to disambiguate words in user-submitted

content and provide users with correspondent Chinese definitions. We will take one step further to offer users with grammar patterns and collocations specific to a word sense. Besides, we could improve our results by expanding training corpus for WSD. Additionally, an interesting direction to explore is ranking grammar patterns to match the proficiency level of readers. Yet another direction of research would be using the same design to assist writing in English. Instead of providing supports for reading a user-selected article, the system could take the user's own writing as input and use grammar patterns and collocations to improve writing quality and correct grammatical errors.

References

James Coady. 1997. 1 1 l2 vocabulary acquisition through extensive reading. *Second language vocabulary acquisition: A rationale for pedagogy*, page 225.

Jacob Devlin, Ming-Wei Chang, Kenton Lee, and Kristina Toutanova. 2018. Bert: Pre-training of deep bidirectional transformers for language understanding. *arXiv preprint arXiv:1810.04805*.

G Francis, S Hunston, and E Manning. 1998. Cobuild grammar patterns 2: Nouns.

Octavian-Eugen Ganea and Thomas Hofmann. 2017. Deep joint entity disambiguation with local neural attention. *arXiv preprint arXiv:1704.04920*.

Johannes Hoffart, Mohamed Amir Yosef, Ilaria Bordino, Hagen Fürstenau, Manfred Pinkal, Marc Spaniol, Bilyana Taneva, Stefan Thater, and Gerhard Weikum. 2011. Robust disambiguation of named entities in text. In *Proceedings of the Conference on Empirical Methods in Natural Language Processing*, pages 782–792. Association for Computational Linguistics.

Susan Hunston, Gill Francis, and E Manning. 1996. Collins cobuild grammar patterns 1: verbs.

Adam Kilgarriff, Milos Husák, Katy McAdam, Michael Rundell, and Pavel Rychlỳ. 2008. Gdex: Automatically finding good dictionary examples in a corpus. In *Proc. Euralex*.

Nikolaos Kolitsas, Octavian-Eugen Ganea, and Thomas Hofmann. 2018. End-to-end neural entity linking. *arXiv preprint arXiv:1808.07699*.

Judit Kormos and Kata Csizer. 2014. The interaction of motivation, self-regulatory strategies, and autonomous learning behavior in different learner groups. *Tesol Quarterly*, 48(2):275–299.

---

[10]`https://mercury.postlight.com/web-parser/`

Oliver Mason. 2004. Automatic processing of local grammar patterns. In *Proceedings of the 7th Annual Colloquium for the UK Special Interest Group for Computational Linguistics, University of Birmingham*, pages 166–171. Citeseer.

George Miller. 1998. *WordNet: An electronic lexical database*. MIT press.

George A Miller, Martin Chodorow, Shari Landes, Claudia Leacock, and Robert G Thomas. 1994. Using a semantic concordance for sense identification. In *Proceedings of the workshop on Human Language Technology*, pages 240–243. Association for Computational Linguistics.

Maria Pigada and Norbert Schmitt. 2006. Vocabulary acquisition from extensive reading: A case study. *Reading in a foreign language*, 18(1):1–28.

Alessandro Raganato, Jose Camacho-Collados, and Roberto Navigli. 2017. Word sense disambiguation: A unified evaluation framework and empirical comparison. In *Proceedings of the 15th Conference of the European Chapter of the Association for Computational Linguistics: Volume 1, Long Papers*, pages 99–110.

Jack C Richards and Willy A Renandya. 2002. *Methodology in language teaching: An anthology of current practice*. Cambridge university press.

Kaveh Taghipour and Hwee Tou Ng. 2015. One million sense-tagged instances for word sense disambiguation and induction. In *Proceedings of the nineteenth conference on computational natural language learning*, pages 338–344.

Ricardo Usbeck, Michael Röder, Axel-Cyrille Ngonga Ngomo, Ciro Baron, Andreas Both, Martin Brümmer, Diego Ceccarelli, Marco Cornolti, Didier Cherix, Bernd Eickmann, et al. 2015. Gerbil: general entity annotator benchmarking framework. In *Proceedings of the 24th International Conference on World Wide Web*, pages 1133–1143. International World Wide Web Conferences Steering Committee.

Tzu-Hsi Yen, Jian-Cheng Wu, Jim Chang, Joanne Boisson, and Jason Chang. 2015. Writeahead: Mining grammar patterns in corpora for assisted writing. *Proceedings of ACL-IJCNLP 2015 System Demonstrations*, pages 139–144.

Author Index

Preface

Welcome to the 1st Workshop on Sense, Concept and Entity Representations and their Applications (SENSE 2017). The aim of SENSE 2017 is to focus on addressing one of the most important limitations of word-based techniques in that they conflate different meanings of a word into a single representation. SENSE 2017 brings together researchers in lexical semantics, and NLP in general, to investigate and propose sense-based techniques as well as to discuss effective ways of integrating sense, concept and entity representations into downstream applications.

The workshop is targeted at covering the following topics:

- Utilizing sense/concept/entity representations in applications such as Machine Translation, Information Extraction or Retrieval, Word Sense Disambiguation, Entity Linking, Text Classification, Semantic Parsing, Knowledge Base Construction or Completion, etc.

- Exploration of the advantages/disadvantages of using sense representations over word representations.

- Proposing new evaluation benchmarks or comparison studies for sense vector representations.

- Development of new sense representation techniques (unsupervised, knowledge-based or hybrid).

- Compositionality of senses: learning representations for phrases and sentences.

- Construction and use of sense representations for languages other than English as well as multilingual representations.

We received 21 submissions, accepting 15 of them (acceptance rate: 71%).

We would like to thank the Program Committee members who reviewed the papers and helped to improve the overall quality of the workshop. We also thank Aylien for their support in funding the best paper award. Last, a word of thanks also goes to our invited speakers, Roberto Navigli (Sapienza University of Rome) and Hinrich Schütze (University of Munich).

Jose Camacho-Collados and Mohammad Taher Pilehvar
Co-Organizers of SENSE 2017